ART

AT THE

CROSS

ROADS

ART AT THE CROSS ROADS

THE SURPRISING AESTHETICS OF THE TEXAS PANHANDLE

AMY VON LINTEL

TEXAS TECH UNIVERSITY PRESS

This book is typeset in EB Garamond. The paper used in this book meets the minimum requirements of ANSI/NISO Z39.48-1992 (R1997). ⊗

Designed by Hannah Gaskamp
Cover design by Hannah Gaskamp

Library of Congress Cataloging-in-Publication Data

Names: Von Lintel, Amy, author. Title: Art at the Crossroads: The Surprising Aesthetics of the Texas Panhandle / Amy Von Lintel. Description: Lubbock, Texas: Texas Tech University Press, [2025] | Includes bibliographical references and index. | Summary: "Rich and varied art stories about the Texas Panhandle, a region that should be known for more than just wide-open spaces"—Provided by publisher.
Identifiers: LCCN 2024039519 (print) | LCCN 2024039520 (ebook) |
ISBN 978-1-68283-235-6 (cloth) | ISBN 978-1-68283-236-3 (ebook)
Subjects: LCSH: Art—Texas—Amarillo Region. | Architecture—Texas—Amarillo Region. | Influence (Literary, artistic, etc.) | Amarillo Region (Tex.)—In art. | Amarillo Region (Tex.)—Social life and customs.
Classification: LCC N8214.5.U6 V66 2024 (print) | LCC N8214.5.U6 (ebook) |
DDC 700.976482—dc23/eng/20240910
LC record available at https://lccn.loc.gov/2024039519
LC ebook record available at https://lccn.loc.gov/2024039520

Printed in the United States of America
25 26 27 28 29 30 31 32 33 / 9 8 7 6 5 4 3 2 1

Texas Tech University Press
Box 41037
Lubbock, Texas 79409-1037 USA
800.832.4042
ttup@ttu.edu
www.ttupress.org

This book is dedicated to all those who have found a love for the places where they land.

CONTENTS

ILLUSTRATIONS

ACKNOWLEDGMENTS

This volume could not have been completed without the ongoing commitment of Texas Tech University Press, especially Editor in Chief Travis Snyder, across the years of a pandemic and the resulting delays. But thankfully, we persevered. I am also indebted to the anonymous peer-review readers of my manuscript, whose feedback made my writing and argumentation measurably stronger.

I am very grateful to the many art collectors and enthusiasts who have made the Panhandle an art center, including the Bivins family, especially Claire and Paul Burney and Mark Bivins; Robin Gilliland, for her commitment to architectural preservation and her willingness to share this commitment with me, my family, and my students, as well as the community; and the Dord Fitz Family, especially Brewster Fitz and Carol Moder for hosting me in their home and sharing their collection with me. I want to express my great gratitude to the family of Ted Reid and Emilio Caballero—especially Jan and Chelsea Minton—for preserving the papers of their family members and donating them to the Cornette Library Special Collections at West Texas A&M University (WT) so that they can be explored by scholars like me.

I am also very appreciative of the artists who have shared their work and ideas through interviews with me and artist talks presented at WT, including Chip Lord, Matthew Williams, Bob Lile, David Rindlisbacher, Nancy Holt (d. 2014), Ed Ruscha, Michael Raburn (d. 2021), and Larry Bob Phillips.

I also must thank the librarians, archivists, and curators at WT and the Panhandle-Plains Historical Museum (PPHM): Sidnye Johnson for her invaluable assistance on my research into Emilio Caballero and his connections to Georgia O'Keeffe; Warren Stricker and Renea Dauntes for their incredible ability to mine archives for not only relevant but also fascinating sources, especially for my chapter on aviation; Patrick Diepen for his help finding sources and images on WT's aviation history; and Deana Craighead and Jenni Opalinski for assisting with information and expertise on art objects in the PPHM collection.

My work writing the book was significantly enhanced by presentations I gave on related topics. For instance, I thank Alex Hunt and the Western Literature Association for allowing me to present my chapter on the art of decay in Estes Park, Colorado, in September 2019; the College Art Association, and specifically Sophia Maxine Farmer and Giovanni Casini, for inviting me to deliver a paper on fakes and forgeries for the panel "The Modernist Myth of the Original Object" in February 2020; the Friends of the Amarillo Public Library and the Friends of the Cornette Library for inviting me to speak alongside Nick Gerlich and the late Melissa Griswold at a program on the history of Amarillo and Route 66 in October and November 2019, which was moderated brilliantly by Cindy Wallace; and the West Texas Historical Association for inviting me to present in April 2019 on the art frauds in the area, and then again in April 2023 to present on the aesthetics of aviation in the Panhandle. Both talks then turned into articles in the *Lubbock Avalanche-Journal*'s Caprock Chronicles series edited by Jack Becker of Texas Tech University. I specifically thank Jack for his continued support of my work. I am also grateful for all those who came together to preserve the Ted Reid–Emilio Caballero Family Papers donated to Cornette Library at WT and then to present them to the regional public in 2023 in a beautiful and informative exhibition *Georgia O'Keeffe's Letters at WTAMU*, on the date of O'Keeffe's birthday (November 15), for which I was invited to be a speaker. These people include Sidnye Johnson, Jeffrey Farris, Shawna Witthar, Renea Dauntes, Joanna Kimbell, Chip Chandler, Rebecca Reid Wheeler, and Warren Reid.

I am also indebted to curators and staff at museums and art collections, including Erin Dodson, curator of the Hallmark Art Collection; Shelley Smith at the Chinati Foundation; Caitlin Murray, director of archives and programs at the Judd Foundation; Kelly Alison at the Contemporary Art Museum Plainview, for working with me on my essay for the catalogue of the exhibition *Yellow City Art* in 2018; and the current and past managers of the *Cadillac Ranch* site. I want to thank the organizers of Aviation Day at Rick Husband International Airport and the Texas Air and Space Museum in Amarillo in October 2022, and scholar Anna Boydstun for sharing all the informative resources with the public, me included, regarding the aviation history of the region.

And I owe so very much to my colleagues—scholars, writers, historians, educators, and artists—who have guided me through my research process and inspired my thoughts and writing, especially Barbara Buhler Lynes and Judy Walsh for carefully editing my work and mentoring me through the process of drafting my chapter on the Canyon Suite; Hikmet Sydney Loe, for sharing her expertise on land art in the West; Mark Forgy, for his profound knowledge on Elmyr de Hory and the topic of art fraud and for introducing me to the work of Colette Loll; Wes Reeves, for his unquenchable thirst for researching and writing local history; Walt Henson for sharing area aviation stories; Luke Seaber for reading and offering feedback on my aviation chapter; the folks at the Space Between Conference in June 2023—especially Rebecca VanDiver, Rossitza Jekova-Goza, Matthew Madison Rowe, Parks Lowe, Rachael Barron-Duncan, and Sarah Cornish—for listening to descriptions of my work and offering their insight; Jason Boyett, Michele McAffrey, Mason Rogers, Mike Ritter, and Angelina Marie for including me in their *Brick & Elm* project featuring the Frank Lloyd Wright–designed Kinney House; and the folks at the Oklahoma State University Doel Reed Center for the Arts in Taos, New Mexico—especially Ryan Slesinger, Jennifer Lynch, Carol Moder, Brewster Fitz, Carolyn Fitz, and Dale Fitz—for offering feedback on my work and emotional support in the final stages of editing.

I also thank my many WT colleagues—present and past—for their helpful support and patience with me talking about this research for years, and often reading sections or drafts for me, including Eric Meljac, whose expertise on Jacques Derrida was so valuable for my chapter on decay; Brian Ingrassia, whose interest in transportation history inspired much of my thought on the automotive and aviation histories of the region; Royal Brantley and Scott Frish for taking a chance by hiring me back in 2010; Rebecca Weir, who shared stories about spending time in the Kinney House; Ixchel Houseal for sharing stories of their father flying his plane to make medical house calls; Deana Craighead, for sharing her amazing tales of growing up in the Panhandle in an aviation family, as well as for being a constant source of positivity and intellectual (and emotional) feedback; and my various administrators, including Jessica Mallard, Stephen Crandall, Anne Medlock, and Kristina Drumheller, for allowing me to teach courses related to my research and to have both travel money and release time to attend conferences so that I could share this research with others. And perhaps above all, I could not be nearly as productive without my writing and teaching partners at WT, especially my dear friends Bonnie Roos and Jon Revett, whose support and collegiality has enriched, complicated, and assuredly bettered my ideas and writing over our many years together. I would not love this place nearly as much without you.

Additionally, I owe so very much to my students—too many to name but you know who you are—for helping me work through concepts as I taught courses relevant to this research, including students in Fakes and Forgeries (Spring 2020); Art of the New West (Spring 2012 and 2022); History of Design (Fall 2022); Ways of Seeing (Spring 2011 and 2019); Modern Architecture (Spring 2018); Art at the Crossroads: Panhandle Perspectives (Fall 2014 and Spring 2021); Art within Reach: Art Treasures of the WT Area (Spring 2011 and 2017); my honors students in the Global Art History of the Texas Panhandle (Fall 2022); and my graduate students in Art and Abstraction (Fall 2023). I especially thank Patrick Diepen for his research labor in preparation for our exhibition *Architecture, Nature, and Abstraction: Emilio Caballero at WTAMU* held in 2017; Chelsea Minton and Michaela Wegman for their work organizing and cataloging the Emilio Caballero papers; and KassiAnne Fondow and Dare "Samson" Akinwole for their research on the sculpture *Ozymandias*. I also thank my students Taryin Tovar and Chelsea Minton for their careful reading and interpretation of the unpublished memoir of Caballero.

And finally, I could not have forged forward in this trying time of a global pandemic, coupled with personal challenges, without the love and support of my amazing family. They know that I am a workaholic, but they love me still. They know that it helps me to focus on research and writing when the world seems to be falling apart. And they often give me the space to find this focus. I owe them my sanity.

ART

AT THE

CROSS

ROADS

INTRODUCTION

I first laid eyes on the Texas Panhandle in March 2010 and found myself over-whelmed by the color brown. It was still winter when I visited; the ground cover remained dormant and the few trees that grew here and there were barren, leafless. Everything looked depressed, even dead. For a few years prior to this visit, I had been living in Pasadena, California, where color abounds year-round with the mild climate, trees are always verdant, and flowers continuously bloom. This brown landscape of West Texas, a typical seasonal occurrence, was indeed a shock to my system.

I had flown to the Panhandle to interview for a faculty job at West Texas A&M University (hereafter WT). I remember how I loved that flight, leaving from LAX and watching the vast urban jungle of the greater Los Angeles area fall away behind me as the plane traveled eastward. I felt my blood pressure and stress drop when the space opened up to canyons and farmland below. I had grown up in Kansas, so wide-open spaces felt like home. My flight stopped over in Denver, as there was no direct route from L.A. to Amarillo—a legacy of Amarillo's aviation history, which I discuss in chapter 4 of this volume. My plane left Denver and flew south, reaching that northernmost square portion of Texas called "the Panhandle," but which hardly resembles the actual handle of any pan I've ever seen. And I remember thinking how the patchwork quilt of flat agricultural and ranching land sprawling below the plane was quite beautiful in its structured order, even mesmerizing in the way it represented an abstract modernist painting.[1]

But once my plane landed, the brown color took over. The runway and tarmac of Rick Husband International Airport were barren and dusty, as was the land surrounding the airport, with only a few grain elevators to break up the predomi-nant horizontality. And my car ride on Interstate 40 from the airport to my hotel presented only open fields, truck stops, low-budget motels, and a giant wooden cowboy on a sign luring me in to "enjoy a 72-oz. steak for free"—if I could eat it all, that is. That day, I wondered if I could actually live in a place that seemed this desolate, this flat, this uncolorful. I called my husband and said, "Honey, I don't think I can do it here."

What happened the next day, however, changed my mind, and I have lived in the region now for a decade and a half. The chair of the WT Art, Theatre, and Dance Department at the time, Royal Brantley, picked me up at my hotel and drove me to the campus for morning interviews. We drove down Interstate 27 from Amarillo to Canyon, where the university is located, at about 7:45 a.m. Royal was probably just trying to get us to campus on time for the interviews, but his timing coincided with the exact moment of sunrise. The Texas Panhandle lies at the western edge of the Central Time Zone, so the sun there seems to take its sweet time making an appearance in the morning, waiting just for the moment of the workday commute. And when it does, the brown landscape suddenly shimmers with color—lavenders, light greens, navy blues, and salmons. The dust-ridden atmosphere glistened as the horizontal sunlight streamed across the immense flatness of the terrain. On that drive, as if Royal Brantley planned this light and color spectacle just for me, I witnessed firsthand the beauty that inspired Georgia O'Keeffe to paint it, again and again, in the 1910s when she worked at WT in the very department where I was soon to be hired (see, for example, fig. 2.7).[2] I saw the diaphanous veils of light and color that she captured with her watercolor pigments on paper, those fleeting but powerful moments when the sky and land glow like gems.

During my visit, Royal also drove me around to see works of public art in the area. And unlike bigger cities, where pristine sculptures might grace the city streets, the art in Amarillo was dilapidated and strange, but it was fascinating for this quality. For instance, he took me to an exit on I-27 north of Canyon at Sundown Lane where we looped around and saw a set of ruined faux-stone legs "wearing" painted tube socks at the time (fig. 1.16). We motored down the main drag of Old Route 66 in Amarillo, where as many buildings stood vacant as were in use, but the glory of the "good old days" of the Mother Road—with its vintage signs, its low-lying store fronts, and its gas stations that inspired artist Ed Ruscha to photograph them, print them, and paint them (figs. 1.22–25)—still strikes the viewer looking out the window of a slow moving car.[3] Royal took me a bit farther west on I-40 for a "drive by" of *Cadillac Ranch*, Amarillo's most visited roadside attraction (figs 1.1–3), where the buried cars broke up the flat fields with their diagonal verticality and structural repetition, and where the view is enlivened by the countless layers of colored spray paint on the cars and the dirt that buries them.

Car culture has inspired some of the most exciting art connected to Amarillo, something I explore in chapter 1.

In large part because of this discovered beauty and art, and the surprise finds of color that counterbalanced all that brown, I accepted the job offer at WT and moved to the Panhandle. I realized that what at first appeared a flat, drab place was in fact highly contoured and had an unexpected richness of art stories I could explore. Little did I know just how many I would find, and little did I know it would be enough to sustain a whole career as an art historian.

Not only is the landscape unique enough to inspire artists from the modernist O'Keeffe to the earth artist Robert Smithson, but the residents of the region have also demonstrated an impressive and sustained commitment to patronage of the visual arts. In addition to Stanley and Wendy Marsh, Sterling and Dorothy Ann Kinney, and the descendants of Lee Bivins—all of whom I discuss in the following pages of this volume—there have been dozens upon dozens of art collectors in the area whose stories are worth telling. I have traced a number of these stories in other research projects, including my coauthored book *Three Women Artists: Expanding Abstract Expressionism in the American West* and my co-curated exhibition *Southwest Abstractions of Emil Bisttram* with its companion published catalogue.[4]

This current volume continues a recognition of such art patrons in the Texas Panhandle. But it is also a place for me to tell some new art stories that have yet to be fully or widely appreciated, such as that of the Frank Lloyd Wright house in Amarillo (chapter 3). It is a place to revisit some forgotten narratives that are well known among area residents but have yet to be catalogued and preserved by historians—such as the aviation aesthetics of the region discussed in chapter 4, the way area architecture and design has been deeply impacted by the common experiences of flight. This book is a place to reinvestigate the famous art scandal that began in the area—the unauthenticated O'Keeffe watercolors that surfaced in the late 1980s after the artist's death (chapter 2)—and how this case reflects the deep desire to connect to artistic celebrity, especially in regions outside the arts mainstream. And it is a place to explore the conceptual relationship to decay in the area's art—that relationship I saw in my first full day in the region, driving around with Royal Brantley, seeing fake ruined monuments and buried Cadillacs (chapter 1). Decay predominates in a region like the Panhandle, where the closure of the Amarillo Air Force Base in 1968 stunted the population and economic growth in dramatic ways.[5] But the art of decay also underscores the hardiness of the region, the paradoxical cycle of always decaying but never being fully decayed, an identity that defines both the people and the places of West Texas, like its scraggly trees—scrappy, not verdant, but still hanging on, full of grit and survival, season after season.

The geographic scope of this book is somewhat narrow. It does not cover the entire Texas Panhandle, which would include places as far north as Perryton, Spearman, and Canadian—all of which have rich art histories in and of themselves, and some of them I have addressed in other publications.[6] It also does not cover the southernmost part of the Panhandle, especially the city of Lubbock (if one chooses to include Lubbock in the Panhandle)which likewise has a strong art scene and art history, especially given that Texas Tech University, with its student population of more than 36,000, is located there, and Lubbock's art stories deserve their own volume, something I am not the person to provide. My book focuses on the Amarillo "greater area," if we can call it that, and includes smaller towns within a fifty-mile radius, such as Canyon to the south, where West Texas A&M University is located, Pampa to the northeast, and Bushland to the west.

The chronological scope of this book deals with the modern and contemporary eras of history and art history. I argue that what readers might conceive of as modernist subjects—including automobility and aviation, aesthetic abstraction, artistic celebrity and its valuation, and avant-garde architecture—gain new and significant meaning when we take the time to study them in the context of a specific region, such as the Texas Panhandle. The incidents and stories featured in this book are important both for how they link an understudied place to larger currents of cultural practice and how they interrupt those currents with a new kind of specificity that takes form when out-of-the-way places are included. This book focuses on the Panhandle's constitutive art-cultural episodes, which take their shape from but also shape the region in a meaningful reciprocity. These episodes are just as instructive of our understanding of twentieth-century art and visuality as those that have been popularly studied in more conventional contexts.

This book is not an orthodox scholarly study that focuses on building either an objective history or theorizing an overarching conceptual thesis. In contrast, it adopts a mode of scholarship in which the essence of "region" itself is a central component and the subjectivity of my own authorship as a resident of the region in question is of tantamount importance.[7] The pages that follow take on a declaratively self-reflective stance, whereby my own experiences become a kind of evidence in and of themselves. While such experiential knowledge might not be held in the same regard as other academic methodologies, I argue that this approach fits my topic in the most effective way. I also aim to write for an audience as much outside of academia as within it. The Panhandle is rife with folks who love the kinds of art stories I am telling here, whose passion for area art is based less on academic study than on lived experience. I am writing for their eyes as much as for those of my art history and academic colleagues.

My goal with this book is for readers to learn more about art stories they may have already heard and discover some new ones. Above all, I hope they can join me in my assertion that the art of the Texas Panhandle is worthy of our attention. Regional art has long been sidelined in the narratives of art history, and the designation of "regional" presumes that the subject is localized outside of a center, that it is provincial and peripheral to mainstream developments.[8] Long-standing biases have formed the assumption that what is important happens in cosmopolitan places first and only later elsewhere, invariably in some dissipated and watered-down form. But even the largest art centers are themselves "regions" of art, places with localized contexts that need to be defined specifically rather than allowing them to masquerade as synecdoche for the national or global—a part that stands in for the whole. The entirety of US art history is vastly complex, with places like the plains and the prairies producing different aesthetic traditions than the coasts and different ones from each other. As I argue in chapter 3, Frank Lloyd Wright's Prairie Style did not directly translate to the canyon country of the West Texas High Plains. Wright was aware of this fact and designed his Dorothy Ann and Sterling Kinney House with a novel aesthetic vocabulary keyed uniquely to the region. Not only do we discover that the Panhandle boasts a treasured Wright residential design, but the Kinney House can also teach us to appreciate the distinct aesthetics of this area, just as viewing O'Keeffe's watercolors from her time in Canyon can give us the unique eyes to appreciate those spectacular sunrises and sunsets, the immensely vast night skies full of stars, and the infinitely flat horizon seen in every direction.

The horizon, O'Keeffe reminds us, is an idea, a perception, and not a literal or physical line. It is a representation of the edge of what is known, which always shifts as we move in space. O'Keeffe's watercolors, such as her *Light Coming on the Plains* series (fig. 2.7), captured this quality by leaving a thin horizontal gap of open paper not colored by pigment. That open gap is utterly pregnant with meaning for me: it is the promise of ever-new discoveries of beauty, knowledge, and artistic inspiration. That is how I have come to feel about the art of the Texas Panhandle. I continue to find more and more subjects to investigate and stories to tell. This book is about four of my favorite art stories from the region, but it is also a statement about the potential of new research and new perspectives, the promise of a continuous horizon-like narrative of surprising color and interest, creativity and historical value.

CHAPTER 1

ART AND
DECAY IN
AMARILLO

In September 2019, a still unidentified arsonist set fire to the oldest of the vehicles in the art installation just west of Amarillo, called *Cadillac Ranch* (fig. 1.1).[1] At first glance, this seems an egregious crime. Why would someone set alight this quirky monument? *Cadillac Ranch* is arguably one of the best-known and most popular tourist destinations in the region, with more than a million visitors per year and even more who see it from I-40 as they drive by on that major cross-country artery.[2] But beyond a simple roadside attraction, *Cadillac Ranch* is an important work of land art, constructed by the San Francisco and Houston-based artist collective Ant Farm in June 1974.[3] And unlike most famous works of art that are in museums and therefore generally removed from physical interaction by guards, ropes, and security cameras, *Cadillac Ranch* has always been a completely open-access work of art. It has facilitated public interaction in many forms, including climbing on the cars, spray-painting them, and taking pieces of them as souvenirs, activities enjoyed by children and adults alike. So, this artwork in West Texas has been subject to much decay—and indeed it has been an embodiment of the concept of decay—since its very inception. It was created not from pristine Cadillacs but from old, junked cars purchased on the cheap from used car lots like Uncle Buddie's in Dalhart, Texas.[4] And the first installation photos show that already the cars had begun to rust from exposure to the West Texas elements even before they were buried in a cow pasture (fig. 1.2).

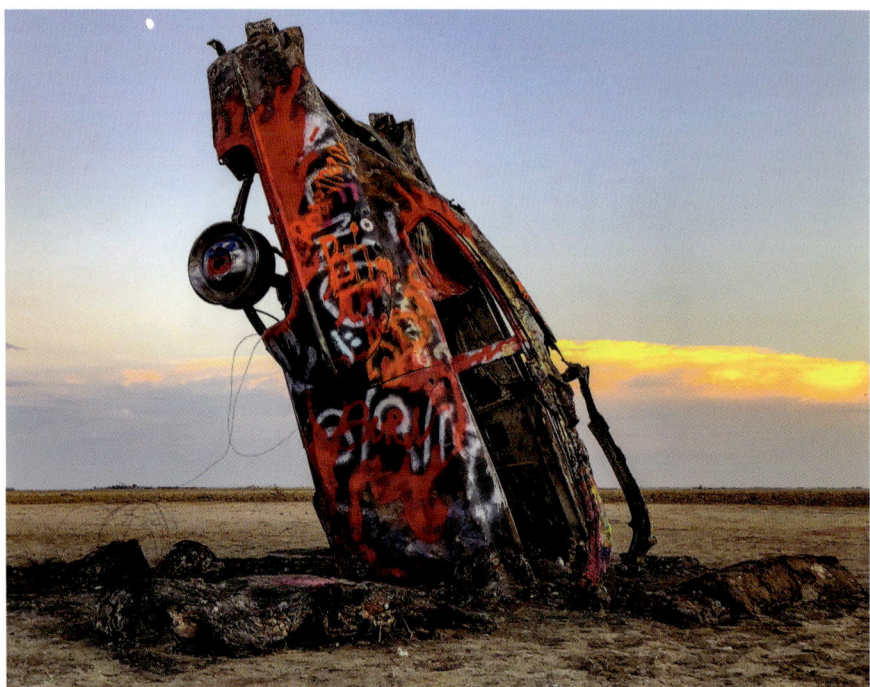

Figure 1.1. Car from Ant Farm's *Cadillac Ranch* after an arsonist burned it on September 9, 2019. (Photo by Nick Gerlich. With permission of Chip Lord.)

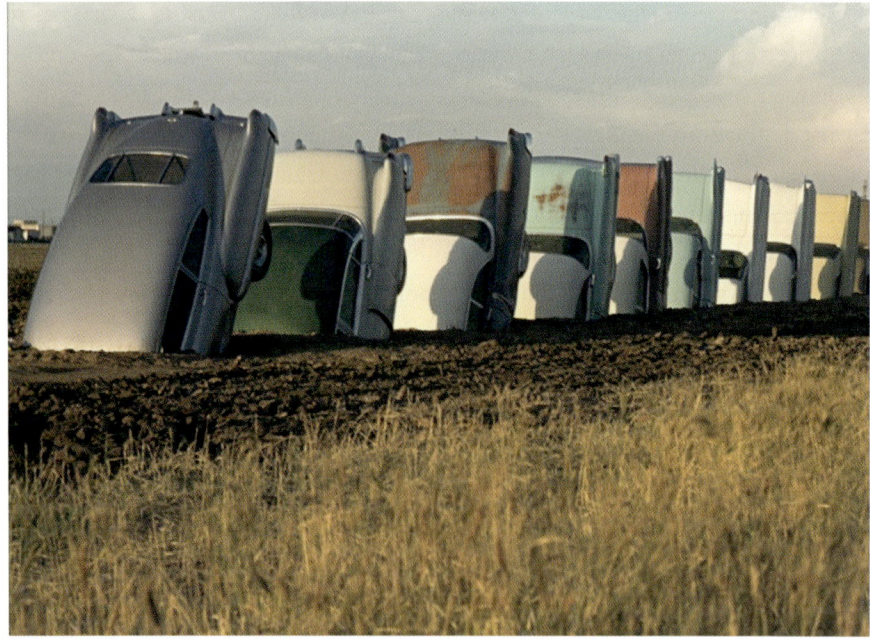

Figure 1.2. Ant Farm, *Cadillac Ranch*. (Photo taken by Ant Farm on June 22, 1974. Courtesy of Chip Lord.)

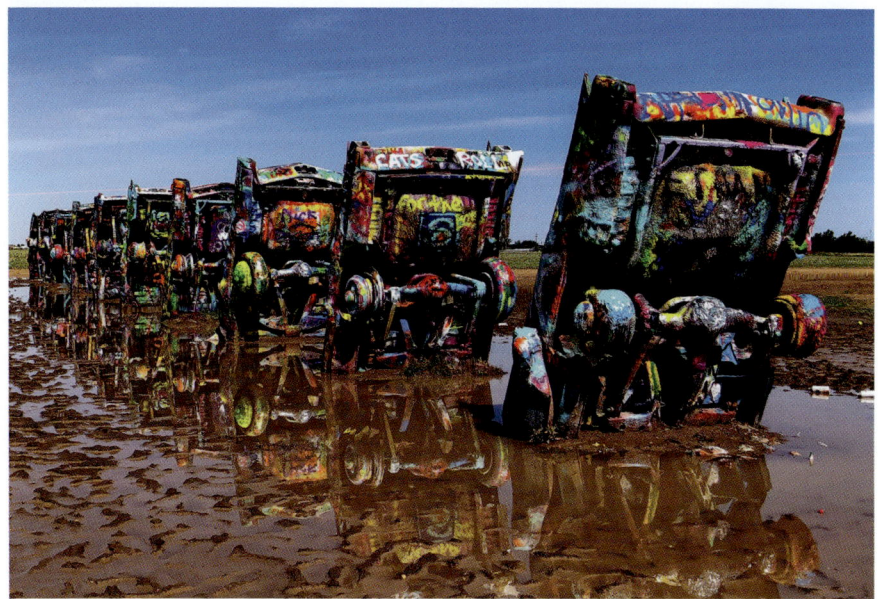

Figure 1.3. Ant Farm, *Cadillac Ranch*, 1974. (Photo by Nick Gerlich, July 2018. With permission of Chip Lord.)

More decay continued with a now-almost-forgotten move westward of *Cadillac Ranch* due to the urban expansion of Amarillo in 1997. Construction workers hired by the patron and landowner Stanley Marsh 3 dug up the cars and reburied them a few miles outside the new city limits, all without involving the Ant Farmers.[5] And now, lately, the cars often float in a quagmire of mud, surrounded by a new playa lake created by the feet of all the visitors that trek out there every day. There is also the constant sea of trash around them as a result of the unmonitored public access (fig. 1.3)—a kind of "tragedy of the commons"[6]—reminding everyone that the work was essentially about the obsolescence of American consumer products from its conception. The used cars were buried in the ground, creating a kind of graveyard to the American automobile industry, presaging the financial failures and bank buyouts of the early 2000s.[7] The Cadillacs were entombed and enshrined, forging a monument to the "American dream" with which the Ant Farm members were raised—the promise that anyone can own a Caddy if they work hard enough—but a dream based more in nostalgia and myth than reality.[8]

And yet, the Ant Farm and Marsh also believed in another American dream: the future of public art, an art for the people rather than for private patrons and exclusive museums. Works like *Cadillac Ranch* were monuments made for and by the public, based in performance and collaboration that has involved audience

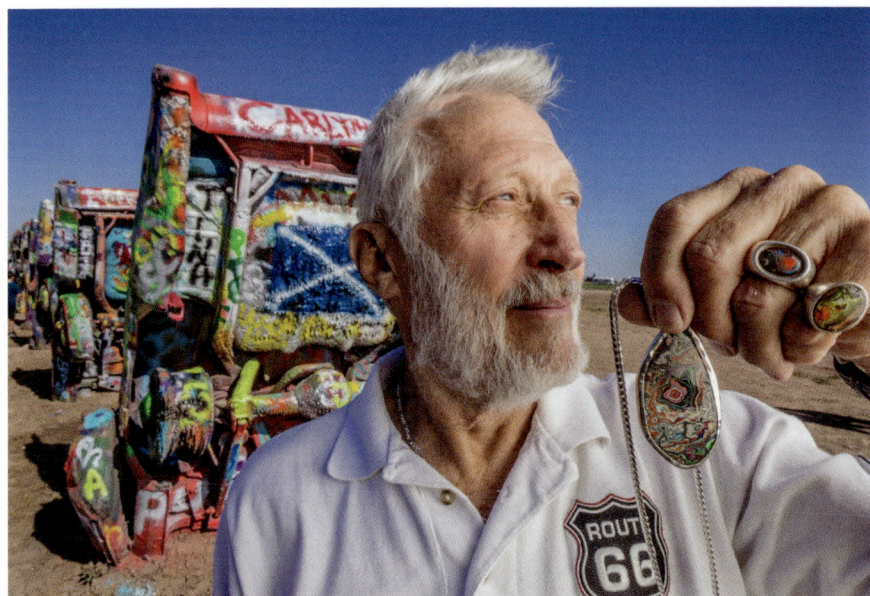

Figure 1.4. Bob Lile at *Cadillac Ranch* displaying his "Cadilite" jewelry, 2018. (Photo courtesy of Will van Overbeek / *Texas Highways*.)

adaptation and interaction over decades. Never new, always old, but also being constantly reworked and reinvented, *Cadillac Ranch* continuously regenerates even while it is perpetually in decline. This paradox is at the heart of much art that has emerged and germinated in the city of Amarillo—a trend that this chapter explores.[9]

CADILLAC RANCH, THE SIGN PROJECT, AND THE ART OF DECAY

When considering the actions of the *Cadillac Ranch* arsonist in 2019, we must also consider the element of criminality, or the intentional destruction of a work of art. But criminality is a very gray area with a work like this, where tourists, taggers, and even vandals have never been prohibited from and are even invited to deface the cars and rip off souvenir paint chips. The metal of the cars—which again was already decaying when the cars were purchased in the early 1970s—is now almost entirely gone and impossible to find in all those layers of added paint. So, when Amarillo artist and gallery owner Bob "Crocodile" Lile uses discarded pieces of the *Cadillac Ranch* to make his line of "Cadilite" jewelry (fig. 1.4) that he sells in his Route 66 Gallery in Amarillo, he may be seen as plagiarizing Ant Farm's art for his own financial gain, stealing from someone else's "original" work of art to make something he calls uniquely his own.[10] But in fact the paint chips Lile uses were never part of the "original" or initial installation completed in 1974; they were added much later by anonymous members of the public. Lile instead seems to be continuing the chain of collaborative, cyclical creation and decay that brought about *Cadillac Ranch* in the first place.

"Decay" in the context of Amarillo art involves various layers of meaning. First, decay refers to processes of physical and material dilapidation, to the rust, ruination, and decline of objects or forms. In the Texas Panhandle, the exposure of places and things to the harsh climate exacerbates and catalyzes the processes of decay—the region's aridity, its extreme fluctuations of temperature, its windiness and dustiness, its searing light undiminished by the shade of trees or tall buildings.[11] Artists working in the area have responded to this physical and material reality, this constant presence and threat of decay. But "decay" also refers to a semiotic and philosophical play of ideas, including the ongoing state of entropy in the existence of all matter, which Amarillo-area artists have also tuned into for their work, as well as the fascinating overlaps of "old" and "new" in the regional identity.[12] In West Texas, the past and present merge, nostalgia drives the desire for an Old West "good ol' days," one that may never have actually happened. The mythos of the Old West—from cowboys to the open road, to the American dream—has already always been decay*ing* but will never be fully dead or consumed, for it lives on so powerfully in the popular cultures that shape Texas, the West, and the United States.[13]

This collapse of new and old, now and then, also points to the philosophies of Jacques Derrida, who most famously defined the theoretical practice of "deconstruction."[14] According to Derrida, everything we experience happening "right now" is no different from every other "now" that we have experienced; our past always influences our perception of the present. But at the same time, our experience of the present is also always shaped by our anticipation of the future. So, the unique event of the "now" is never pure, always inflected by both the past and the future.[15] Temporality—the experience of time—is perpetually plural, never singular, just as the origin of anything and anyone is always heterogeneous, always multiple. Derrida's concepts can help us understand the art of Amarillo, including works such as the *Cadillac Ranch*. The "origins" of *Cadillac Ranch* were never singular or pure but have always been a rich combination of old and new, of reuse and invention, of borrowing and creativity. Not only does this combination comment on our contemporary world that is so rapidly changing, with the built-in obsolescence of consumer and now digital culture, when things are made to break down so that we must buy new things, which break down again, in an endless cycle of economic and material renewal and decay. But decay-based art in Amarillo likewise points to key mythologies of so-called America and the West, of the presumption by colonizing forces that the land was "virgin," untouched, and open for the taking, but which in fact required an act of criminality, of theft, to possess and reconstruct the land into new uses defined as "better" only by the takers.[16]

Amarillo artists—including artists such as Ant Farm, who worked in the area only briefly but often returned to the region for visits and guest lectures, as well as local artists[17]—have been deeply aware of these paradoxical resonances of time and history. They have been willing to play through both materials and meaning, embracing the inevitable decomposition and reconstruction by forces beyond their own personal and artistic control—including the weather, the public, and even other artists. They have explored the very ellipses of creativity, experience, and existence in their work, highlighting how both art and life in this region have been continuously forged and broken down, made and destroyed. In other words, the layers of decay in Amarillo's art are both literal and conceptual, producing powerful statements about the conditions of existence and the purpose of art.

Cadillac Ranch represents only one of the many projects of West Texas art founded upon and exploring decay. Numerous works paid for by Marsh between the 1970s and his death in 2014 all take decay as their subject and their reason for being. Most extensively, after collaborating with Ant Farm, Marsh founded his own art collective called the Dynamite Museum. This name typifies Marsh's goal to shatter the status of protected and precious art in museums, in metaphorically "dynamiting" those museums until art took over the city of Amarillo. In notable ways, Marsh responded to the sentiment made most famous in the artistic manifestos of the Italian Futurists and British Vorticists, penned just prior to World War I. In 1909, F. T. Marinetti suggested that artists "destroy the museums," comparing these hallowed institutions to cemeteries and "absurd abattoirs of painters and sculptors ferociously slaughtering each other with color-blows and line-blows, the length of the fought-over walls!" Marinetti continued, calling for "the gay incendiaries with charred fingers" to "take up your pickaxes, your axes and hammers" and complete the destruction.[18] Likewise, in 1914 when Wyndham Lewis founded the British magazine *BLAST!*, with its searing pink cover, he had the goal to "blast" art into a new radicality.[19] Marsh heeded the calls of Marinetti and Lewis nearly a century later with his foundation and financial support of the Dynamite Museum collective.

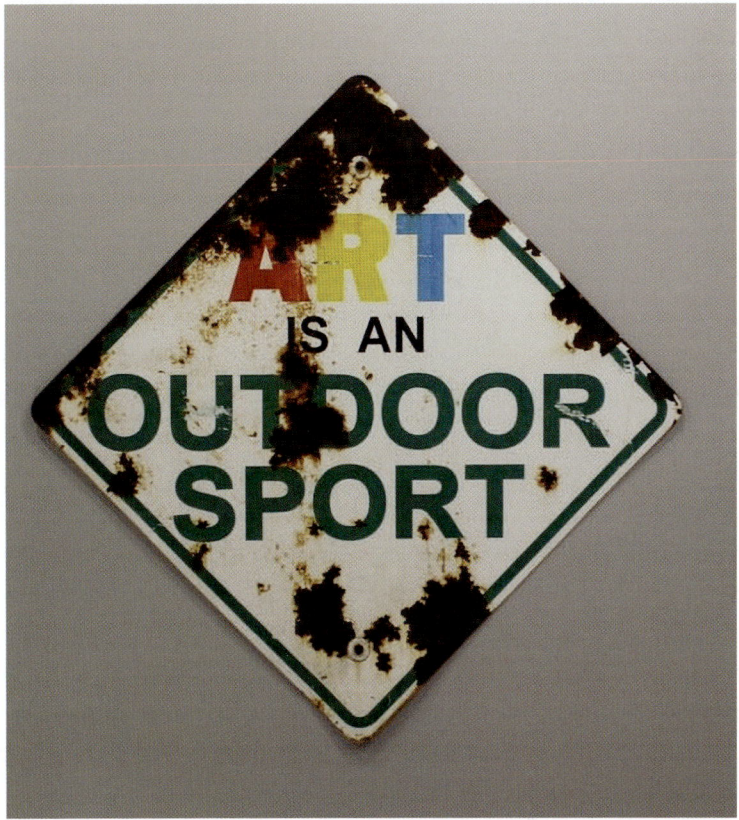

Figure 1.5. Dynamite Museum, *Art is an Outdoor Sport*. (Photo courtesy of Jon Revett.)

Starting in the 1990s, the collective began its major endeavor, the Sign Project, for which Marsh purchased around one thousand industrial blank road signs, and then employed dozens of young, emerging area artists to design fake and ironic road signs with strange phrases and pictures.[20] These artist-employees also drove Polaroids of the signs around Amarillo in cars and trucks, recognizable as "art cars" because they were painted garish colors and ironically bedecked with longhorns, in a campy performance of the cowboy lifestyle of the region. The team of artists knocked on residential doors around Amarillo and offered to install the signs with concrete—for free—in the yards of homeowners who wanted an "art sign" chosen from the Polaroid photos to fit their unique taste in some way. In other words, the signs were both everywhere and nowhere in the city. They could be seen by any driver or pedestrian who moved through the urban spaces, but none were actually on city-owned property. They were therefore private enough to be public legally, and public enough to serve the purpose of making the city into its own "exploded" museum. "Art is an outdoor sport," they claimed—a literal example of the text on one of the signs (fig. 1.5).[21]

But like those art cars exposed to the elements of the harsh and arid western climate at *Cadillac Ranch*, the signs began rapidly to rust and deteriorate. They were never meant to last, or at least Marsh and his collective never initially planned for their preservation. Longevity and sustainability were not the point of these artistic interventions into the city. The art installation was more about a revolutionary blitz that had vast ripple effects, including various public controversies, but the legacy of the signs as art would only be determined by a future public.[22] For instance, a young artist in 2013 named Jacob Aaron Morin began to paint over some of the remaining signs around Amarillo, erasing the designs and placing his own new artistic works on top.[23]

Like Lile with his Cadilite jewelry, Morin claimed to be participating in the chain of creation and decay that founded the project, but he was quickly shamed and scorned on social media platforms. People who cared about the signs as part of Amarillo's art legacy balked, arguing that Morin's actions did not constitute art themselves but instead an egregious erasure and destruction of "original" works of art—an egotistical and distasteful claim of control over other artists' works and a criminal colonizing of the signs to gain media attention. And yet, when in 1953 the up-and-coming artist Robert Rauschenberg erased a drawing by the abstract expressionist master Willem de Kooning, the art world celebrated the work as a new and original Rauschenberg creation.[24] To this day, the San Francisco Museum of Modern Art titles the work "*Erased de Kooning Drawing* by Robert Rauschenberg." Why was this artistic gesture by Rauschenberg any different from Morin painting over those Dynamite Museum signs? One key difference is that de Kooning was in on the anti-art ruse and had given the drawing to Rauschenberg willingly, if begrudgingly. In contrast, Morin did not ask permission from the Dynamite Museum members, and their agency had been forcibly erased along with the erasure of their painted creations.

Given this case, it appears there is a functional difference between artistic creation and destruction, even in Amarillo, a likely candidate for the decay capital of the art world. According to Paula Newton, writing for *Glasstire*, Morin had asked the homeowners' permission to paint over "their" signs. But again, ownership of these art signs is contested. Did the current homeowners have legal permission to grant the right to repaint a sign located on their property?[25] Or did the artists of the Dynamite Museum collective have to be consulted before the art sign was changed? If the signs are seen by the public and by the law as "art," then they would fall under artist copyright legislation, and any destruction of them would constitute a crime. The control over a work of art in the United States doesn't follow the owner or patron of a physical piece, but rather follows the maker.[26]

In 1990, Congress passed the Visual Artists Rights Act (VARA) to protect a visual artist's work from being destroyed or altered by the owner of the work without the consent of the artist.[27] The definition of "visual art" under this law is, however, limited, and one might argue that the art signs are not covered by this law. Paintings, drawings, prints, fine-art photographs, and sculptures in single copies or limited editions fall under the definition of art under VARA, but motion pictures, technical drawings, books, architecture, and applied arts—that is, anything "used"—does not. So where do the Dynamite Museum's signs fall? Are they "technical drawings?" Maybe. Are they architectural? No, because they are not habitable; one cannot physically enter them.[28] Are they "used" as anything other than art? They are functional, but only functional as art; they are not working road signs. So, if their only function is decorative or artistic, they fall best under the category of sculpture. But as Susan Bielstein explains in her highly useful book *Permissions, a Survival Guide*, VARA's definition of art is "extremely narrow and does not begin to address the variety of production that now dominates the art scene and current discourses of visual culture," including public art installations like the Sign Project.[29] In order for this legislation to be enacted, we may also have to know exactly which of the many Dynamite Museum artists painted which particular sign and track down each of these artists and trust their claims of being the creators. The whole thing is complicated and full of chaos and decay, both literal and legal.

Over the years, Marsh Enterprises did play a role in managing the legacy of the art signs. While many homeowners cherished their signs even as they deteriorated—their surfaces rusting and their colors fading from sun exposure—others called the Marsh headquarters requesting to have their signs removed, which Marsh paid more artists to do at no cost to the homeowners.[30] Marsh began collecting the discarded signs in what became known as "the sign graveyard" on his property (fig. 1.6)—a graveyard of course being a space designated for decay and death, but also for the preservation of memory.[31] The signs went from art monuments to ruins, entombed in a special space but not thrown away as trash. After Marsh's death in 2014, and after plans to sell the Marsh homestead had been made, some of the Dynamite Museum artists got involved again to move the signs out of the "graveyard" and to new homes.[32] Jon Revett, my colleague who teaches painting and drawing at WT, helped reinstall some of the signs at the Mariposa Eco-Village

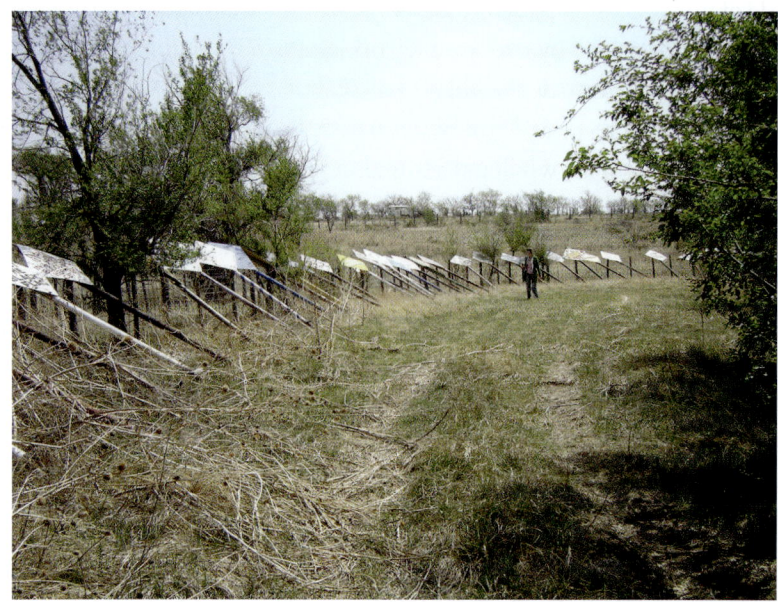

Figure 1.6. The Sign Graveyard, Toad Hall, Amarillo, 2011. (Photo by author.)

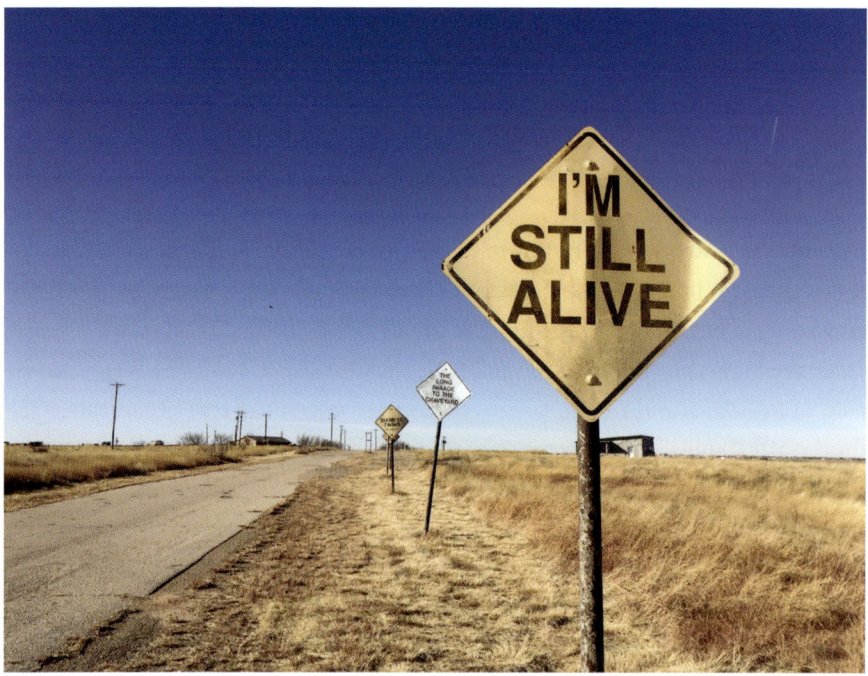

Figure 1.7. Dynamite Museum signs. Temporary reinstallation at Mariposa Eco-Village, 2017–18. (Photo by Jon Revett.)

outside of Amarillo—another project connected to the Marsh-Bush family (fig. 1.7)[33]—though he kept my favorite one for his own living room (fig. 1.5). Revett also founded the "BIG ART" initiative at WT that involves art students in the management and preservation of works like those of the Sign Project, creating important avenues of art-world professionalization for students and contributing to the university's campus-to-community endeavors.[34] So, when Revett was out at Mariposa reinstalling the signs in their new location, our students were out there with him, playing a role in the collective and collaborative legacy of the work. Much like the *Cadillac Ranch* cars moved in 1997 to make way for the city's development, the signs were relocated but not destroyed. Marsh, the Ant Farm members, and the Dynamite Museum artists all recognized that cities develop organically and that public art projects would require creative adaptation in response to their unavoidable decay.

The Dynamite Museum Sign Project, much like *Cadillac Ranch* that gets fresh paint from the public daily, continues to live on today. In 2013, Revett along with his friend and fellow Dynamite Museum member Matthew Williams, helped curate an art show precisely about this creation-decay theme in Amarillo. *Amarillo Entropy* ran at the Power Station Gallery in Dallas and included a dozen of the original Dynamite Museum signs.[35] Again, creative problem-solving in the display of these signs was necessary, as they could not be installed into cement in the gallery like they were when erected around Amarillo. Instead, the curators laid the signs down in neat rows in the center of the gallery, almost reminiscent of the rows of royal tombs in Westminster Abbey with their eerie sculpted effigies (fig. 1.8). Viewers looked down on the "bodies" of these signs in reverence, recognizing their removal from functionality, their metaphorical "death" and entombment, but also their worthiness of memorialization. Around this time, Dynamite Museum artists including Revett, Williams, and the now New Mexico–based Larry Bob Phillips, began producing some new signs (fig. 1.9) that mimicked the earlier versions but with a clear sense of the time that had passed and the artistic maturity that the members had achieved since the 1990s.[36] Williams has founded an Instagram page that documents the art signs still standing around Amarillo and records valuable history about the project, which he hopes to turn into a book publication in the future.[37] At the same time, Williams, who trained as a printmaker, continues to produce new signs, photographing the originals as source material and printing them, thereby preserving the decaying signs but in reproductive form utilizing digital technologies.[38]

Still, decay runs even to the level of human death in this ongoing Sign Project. Some of the signs were designed by Brian Denecke, the young punk artist who was

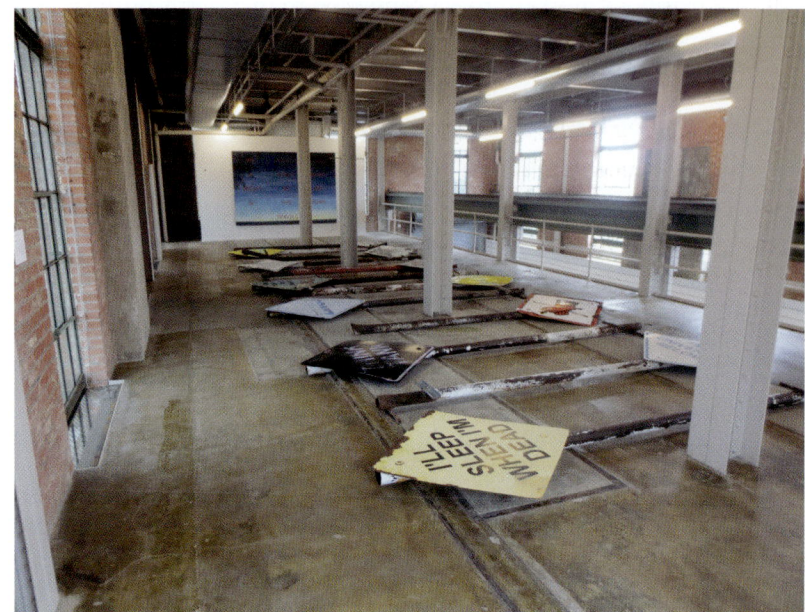

Figure 1.8. Installation view of *Amarillo Entropy*, Power Station Gallery, Dallas, 2013. (Photo by Jon Revett.)

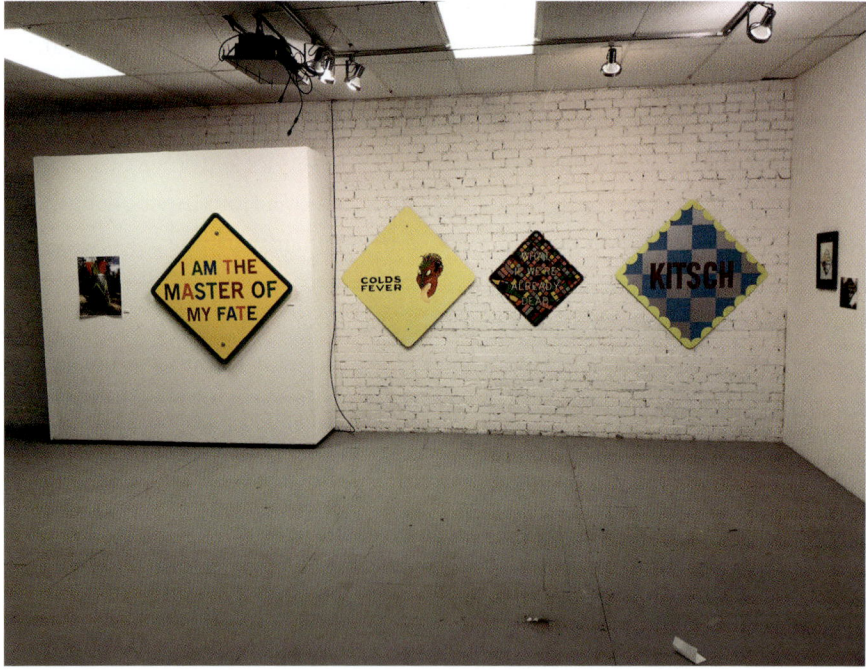

Figure 1.9. Installation view of *My Art at the Dynamite Museum*, Contemporary Art Museum Plainview, 2019. (Photo by Matthew Williams.)

brutally killed in 1997 when a fight between punks and jocks in Amarillo went terribly wrong, a story revisited in the film *Bomb City* (2017). This tragic event was clearly on the minds of the artists and allies who protested when Morin controversially painted over the Dynamite Museum signs in 2013. Many saw Denecke's memory being eradicated in the gesture of repainting the signs, and for them the signs stand for the precious legacy of an artist taken by death in the prime of his youth, among other things.

DECAY BEYOND CADILLACS AND SIGNS

Although the Dynamite Museum signs were Marsh's most extensive project, and the *Cadillac Ranch* his most famous, Marsh also sponsored other decay-based art in the Amarillo area. He hosted the sculptor John Chamberlain at his ranch, which Marsh called Toad Hall, in 1972, enabling Chamberlain to produce his series of crushed car sculptures, Texas Pieces, the titles of which played upon the spaces, places, and people of Texas, especially the Amarillo area.[39] Chamberlain had turned away from car metal as his material for seven years in protest of art critics misreading his work as "car crashes."[40] But he returned to the crushed car works while in Amarillo, a place steeped in automotive history, and his engagement with recycled cars in 1972 presages Ant Farm's *Cadillac Ranch*, constructed two years later. With Amarillo being located on the "Mother Road," Route 66, and at the crossroads of Highways 60, 87, and 287 and the intersection of Interstates 27 and 40, the city has inspired many creators to explore cars and car culture in their works.[41] But Chamberlain's Texas Pieces in particular need to be connected back to their Amarillo context, which has been nearly forgotten after their installation at the Chinati Foundation in Marfa, Texas, where they seem so at home, as if they were born there.

Just after Chamberlain's time at Toad Hall, the artist published a catalogue titled *In Amarillo, Texas*, which features his work produced there and a telling dedication: "This catalogue is dedicated to Stanley Marsh 3 by his friend, John Chamberlain." The cover juxtaposes an image of one of Chamberlain's sculptures in the foreground with a horse grazing in a pasture in the background (fig. 1.10), a clever play on how the "new West" and "old West" confront one another in West Texas, and how "horsepower" has evolved over time—from animal to automobile and then to the ironically inoperable abstractions of Chamberlain, but which were made with motorized machines measured in horsepower that crushed, molded, lifted, and deposited the metal. We still have the rental agreement that was signed by Chamberlain in 1975 for the construction equipment to move and install

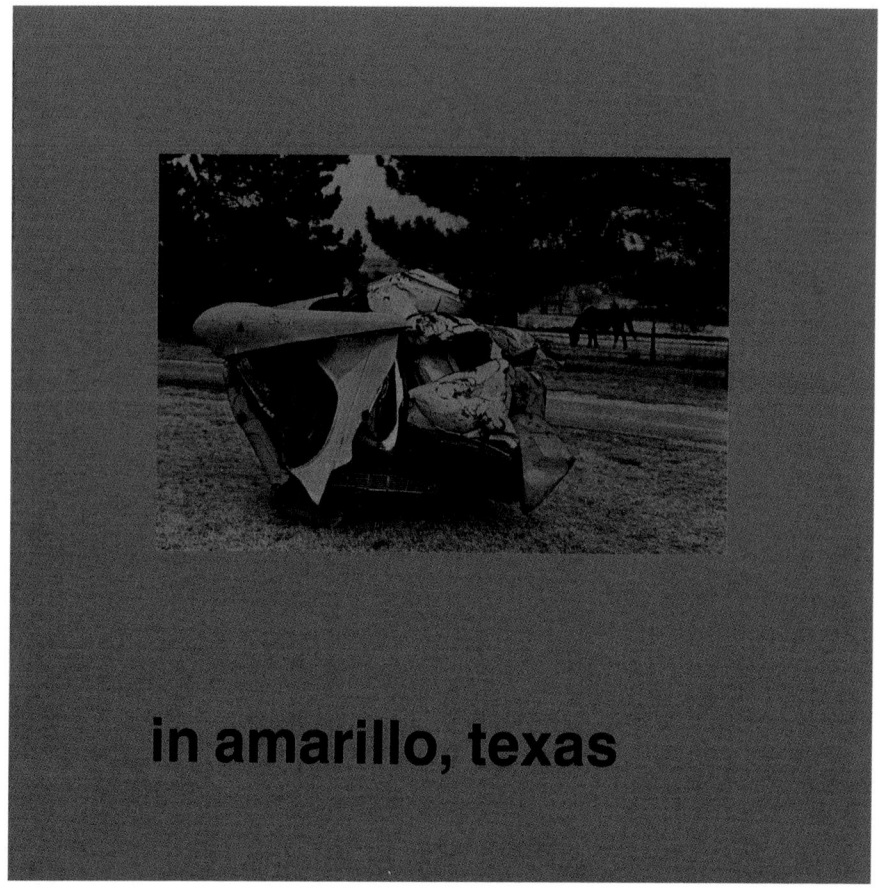

in amarillo, texas

Figure 1.10. Cover, *In Amarillo, Texas*, published 1972. (Courtesy of the Marsh family. ©2025 Fairweather & Fairweather LTD / Artists Rights Society (ARS), New York. Courtesy the John Chamberlain Estate and Hauser & Wirth.)

the Texas Pieces around Toad Hall property, the outcome of which we also see in the pages of *In Amarillo, Texas*, which shows photographs of the works in their location at Marsh's ranch and lists both their dimensions and their titles given at the time.[42] But the contrast on this catalogue cover between horse and car sculpture, between supposed tradition and innovation, needs to be deconstructed a bit. The horse appears native to its Panhandle pasture, and a perfect symbol of the so-called Old West. Despite the common assumption that horses were introduced to the region during the European Age of Exploration and not indigenous to North America, horses have grazed on the land for millions of years.[43] But their use by ranchers and cowboys was a "new" stage compared to the previous Comanche use of the horse to dominate the Southwest between 1750 and 1850, which itself was a new and revolutionary moment in the Indigenous history of the North American Plains.[44] Again, the notions of old and new here are relative and fluid.

The titles of Chamberlain's sculptures were never simplistic references to a single fixed concept. As Chamberlain said in an interview, "I wasn't sure what [my titles] meant either, except that [they were] agreeable to me. . . . I thought, why should I tell [someone] what it means? Even if I knew, I could only know what I thought it meant, and if he couldn't figure it out 'what it meant' then it didn't mean anything to him."[45] In this notion, Chamberlain leaves meaning open to both interpretation and decay. However, a bit of discussion of the title choices for the Texas Pieces can specifically illuminate their Amarillo context, especially Chamberlain's friendship with Marsh. For example, the second part of the title for the work *Glasscock-Notrees* likely recalls the barren, alien, wide-open High Plains devoid of trees except for around creek draws, much like the contrast between flat, open spaces and treelined sections as we can see in photographs in *In Amarillo, Texas* (fig. 1.11). In turn, the first part, "glasscock," evokes the fragility of masculinity and machismo, especially in the cowboy patriarchal culture of the West. Marsh's own complicated personality and sexuality, and his camp performances of the cowboy identity—including the exaggerated twang with which he spoke, the way he wore rodeo formal wear with fringe and a cowboy hat on a daily basis, the way he drove a car with longhorns affixed to the hood—are notorious and even infamous.[46] One film short that Marsh produced with Ant Farm in 1974 shows him in a fringed leather jacket and cowboy hat, identified by his nickname "Leo Wyoming," shooting the letters A, N, T, F, A, R, and M into the side of a Cadillac (fig. 1.12). In this film, Marsh states:

> Out here in the West, men are men. And we like to pull our wagons in the circle, and sometimes those wagons are Cadillacs. And we like to see those fins lined up goin' round and round the circle. May remind us of the ocean, those whales going round and round. Those fins, they are somethin' else. Make you feel comfy? The Ant Farm makes you feel comfy? Cause they are underground. You gotta admit that they go down underneath the ground. And do whatever they're doin.' But they are okay on top of the ground, I can swear to that. And besides that, they have built this halfway on top, halfway on the bottom.[47]

Here we see Marsh connecting the "wagon train days" to the days of the American Cadillac, the old West and the new, not unlike Chamberlain's catalogue opening with the car sculpture juxtaposed with the horse. Marsh also mentions in

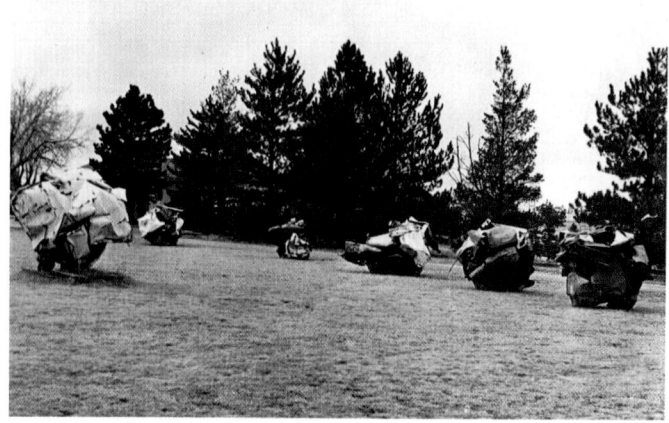

Figure 1.11. Photograph of John Chamberlain sculptures on Toad Hall property, as reproduced for the catalogue *In Amarillo, Texas*. (Courtesy of the Marsh family. ©2025 Fairweather & Fairweather LTD / Artists Rights Society (ARS), New York. Courtesy the John Chamberlain Estate and Hauser & Wirth.)

his soliloquy the stereotyped cowboy patriarchy with clear irony in his tone: "where men are men." His comment about driving wagons and cars into "the circle" references tactics of protection against "outsiders" in the region—whether against Indians threatening the pioneers who desired to control the West, like Marsh's own ancestors, or the feeling of being queer outsiders to the conservative majority in the area. Marsh's maintenance of his "circle" of creatives with alternative lifestyles harkens back to those circled-up Conestoga wagons, a protective shield against the threats and imposed norms, where unique people can "feel comfy."

But this comment also shows the futility of "going around in circles" and getting nowhere, the kind of inertia of small-town traditionalists that Marsh was always bucking, in large part through his support of avant-garde artists such as Chamberlain, Ant Farm, and the Dynamite Museum. The endless circle of wagons or cars with tailfins, which Marsh also compares to whales, further suggests a conceptual cyclicality and the deconstructivist notion that things are both the same and not the same: wagons are cars are whales. In his speech, Marsh celebrates the underground or alternative art methods of the Ant Farm, the half above–half below identity that the *Cadillac Ranch* reveals, an identity that the ever-extroverted but ever-elusive Marsh also shared. And of course, the *Cadillac Ranch* cars are not in a circle but in a straight line—one that seems to tell a linear story of the history of the Cadillac's tailfin from the 1940s to the 1960s when read left to right. But viewers of the monument traveling on I-40 come from both directions, day in and day out, undermining any strict linear, progressive, "from then until now" meaning

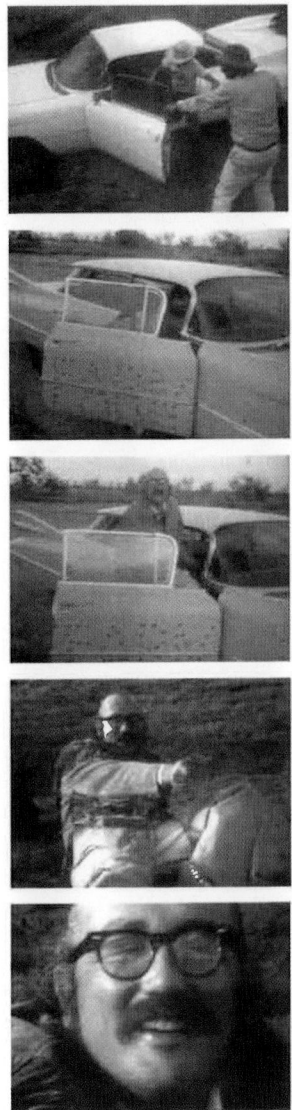

Figure 1.12. Ant Farm and Stanley Marsh 3, film stills, 1974. (Courtesy of Chip Lord.)

of the monument. It threatens to shift at any moment from a line back into the circle that Marsh references, from linear time into cyclical, repeated temporalities. All these layers of personal, historical, and geographical identity likewise became embedded in the crushed car sculptures Chamberlain produced at Toad Hall.

Two more titles in Chamberlain's Texas Pieces refer directly to Marsh. *Falfurrias (Marshmellow)*, a predominantly white piece that indeed resembles

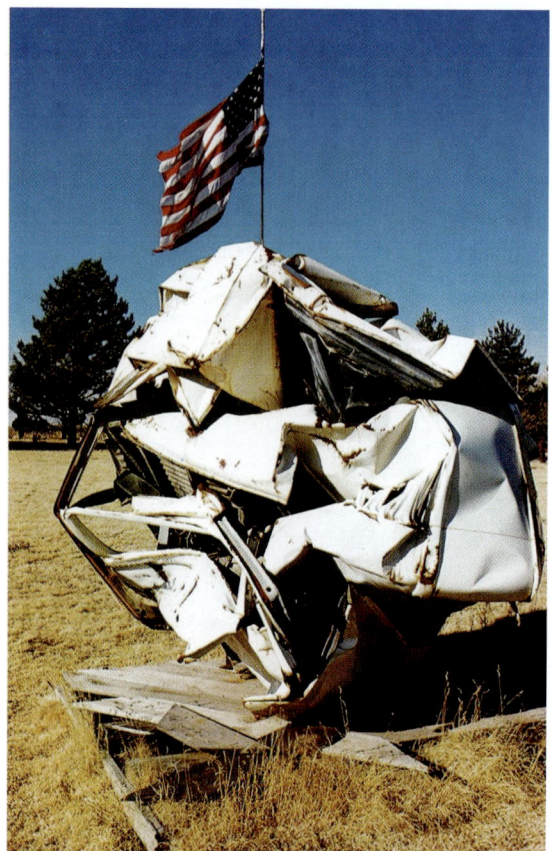

Figure 1.13. John Chamberlain, *Falfurrias (Marshmellow)*, 1972, 84 x 98 x 100 inches, as reproduced in the catalogue *In Amarillo, Texas*. (Courtesy of the Marsh family. ©2025 Fairweather & Fairweather LTD / Artists Rights Society (ARS), New York. Courtesy the John Chamberlain Estate and Hauser & Wirth.)

the sugary air-puffed treat by that name, but with a slight misspelling—"mellow" versus "mallow"—also points to yet another of Marsh's nicknames (fig. 1.13). On his company letterhead, Marsh's "cable address" is listed as "Marshmellow."[48] And on letters written from Ant Farm to Marsh in the context of the planning for *Cadillac Ranch*, the mailing address reads "c/o Stanley Marshmellow. Box 12077. Amarillo Nat. Bank Bldg. Amarillo, Texas."[49] The first part of the title *Falfurrias* likely refers to the town in South Texas by that name, which in the 1890s was one of the largest ranches in Texas, comparable to the Marsh family's own historic Frying Pan Ranch.[50]

Perhaps the most colorfully vibrant and beautifully designed sculpture of all the Texas Pieces again references Marsh by name: *Bushland-Marsh III* (fig. 1.14).[51] The work is a kaleidoscopic combination of bright French blue, orange, light seafoam green, pumpkin orange, yellow, and a wide range of reds. Its overall shape is rounded and contained rather than emphasizing any protruding edges or sharp points. The textures of the metal, with its grooves, layers, folds, and gouges, are immensely expressive. And the piece is a lively and balanced abstraction, with decay as a central component, both in its form and content. As Marianne Stockebrand and Rob Weiner write, "The car parts are visibly aged; rather than the garish, gleaming hues of fresh paint jobs, the color has dulled through use, covered with scratches and abrasions; only the pure chrome parts still gleam."[52] The description of Chamberlain's Texas Pieces by Stockebrand and Weiner is worth quoting at length:

> One realizes that these sculptures are not conceived from bottom to top, but rather expand from the center outwards. They are voluminous, but not massive. A peculiar polarization arises between these hulking forms and their light-footedness, between the force with which their materials were shaped and the vulnerability of their forms. These metal parts, processed using scrap presses and other heavy-duty tools, form arcs and diagonal turns with fragile, frayed edges and reveal arches and folds that seal off or open up volumes, all combined to create sculptures out of dance-like lightness and rounded massivity.[53]

The authors describe the way Chamberlain investigates the very formation of mass and matter, the transition from chaos to order and back to chaos again that shapes everything from the smallest particles of matter to the greatest aspects of the universe. In each car sculpture, we can find atoms and galaxies, individual cells, bodies, and the entire human population. But we can also find the residue of Amarillo. The first part of the title of *Bushland-Marsh* refers to things specific to the Texas Panhandle: the town of Bushland just west of Amarillo that included land once on the Frying Pan Ranch. This land was purchased in 1881 with profits from a barbed-wire manufacturing company begun in DeKalb, Illinois, by Joseph F. Glidden and William Henry Bush, both of whom were ancestors of Stanley's wife Wendy, whose given name was Gwendolyn Bush O'Brien.[54] The town itself was named after this family.

Still other works by Chamberlain also reference places in and around Amarillo. For instance, *Iraan Crockett* recalls not only a famous fighter of the Battle of the Alamo in 1836, Davy Crockett, but also the street in Amarillo named after this Texas hero, a street that became one of the few that maintained its north–south path despite the construction of I-40 through the city in the 1960s. The "Iraan"

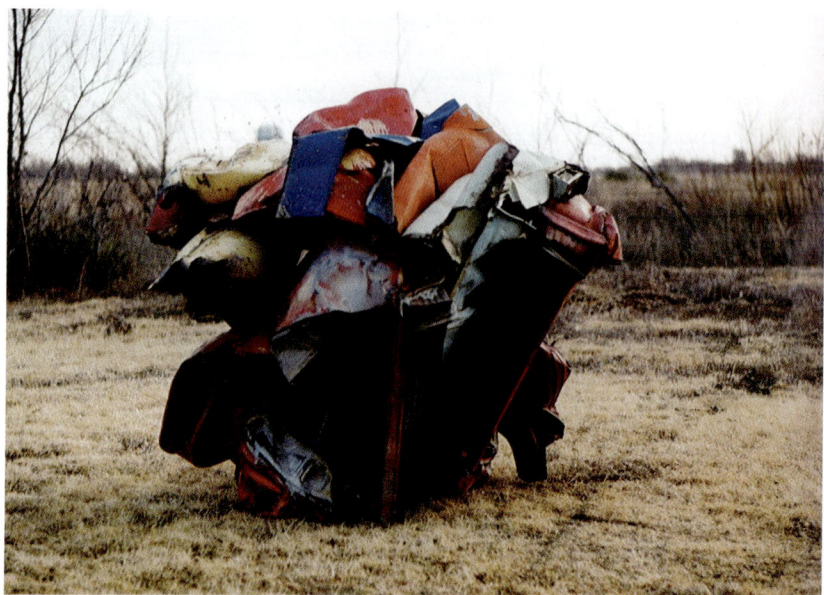

Figure 1.14. John Chamberlain, *Bushland-Marsh III*, 1972, 68.5 x 90 x 83.5 inches, as reproduced in the catalogue *In Amarillo, Texas*. (Courtesy of the Marsh family. ©2025 Fairweather & Fairweather LTD / Artists Rights Society (ARS), New York. Courtesy the John Chamberlain Estate and Hauser & Wirth.)

part could point to the town by that name in West Texas but also to Marsh's connections with the country of Iran, a place he and Wendy had visited several times, and where he met the Iranian American artist Tony Shafrazi, who returned to Marsh's Toad Hall in 1973 with Robert Smithson and Nancy Holt, as discussed below. Then *Papalote Goliad* references the Spanish word for "kite" or "hang glider" along with yet another street in Amarillo, Goliad, which references a major battle site in the Texas Revolution; perhaps the use of "papalote" points to the whipping winds of the region that would threaten the flight of any kite or glider, in an ironic nod to futility, or even to the aviation history of the region, which I discuss in chapter 4. *Capote Peak*, in turn, is likely an unofficial title for one of the many mesas on Marsh's land, which was named after a favorite author of Marsh: Truman Capote. *Canyon Road Shell* may have been a reference to the nearby town of Canyon, Texas, as much as the famous art corridor of Canyon Road in Santa Fe, or even to a Shell Oil Station on the road to Canyon, something Ed Ruscha equally responded to in his work on gas stations.

But why did these Texas Pieces not wind up staying long in Amarillo? The works were all relocated to Marfa and Donald Judd's Chinati Foundation, excepting only the two destroyed works, *Capote Peak* and *Canyon Road Shell*, which

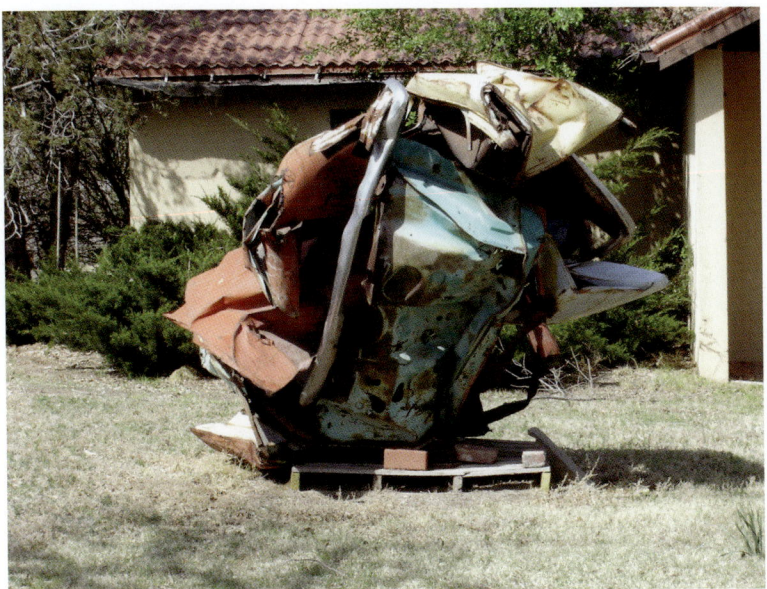

Figure 1.15. John Chamberlain, *Harvey*, 1972–74, 7 x 6 x 10 feet. (Photo by author in 2011 at Toad Hall in Amarillo. Courtesy of the Marsh family. ©2025 Fairweather & Fairweather LTD / Artists Rights Society (ARS), New York. Courtesy the John Chamberlain Estate and Hauser & Wirth.)

were ruined in transit between Minnesota and New York in 1977, and *Old Anson Impact*, which is in the Museum of Fine Arts, Houston.[55] In 1975, apparently Marsh and Chamberlain had a falling out after Marsh, as a prank, inserted extra objects into the sculptures, including stuffed animals, when Chamberlain shipped his Texas Pieces from Amarillo to Houston for a solo exhibition of his work.[56] Chamberlain then connected with Judd in the later 1970s on plans to install his crushed car sculptures, including nine of the Texas Pieces works, in the south artillery shed at Chinati.[57] Ultimately, the Chamberlain sculptures were installed in another building on the compound, one with sand-colored walls, smooth floors, and plenty of space for the works to be seen from all sides to appreciate their intricate complexity.

However, one crushed car work titled *Harvey* remained on the Toad Hall property in Amarillo after this falling out, and though it did not appear in the Chamberlain catalogue raisonné, we have extant documents that seem to authenticate the work as part of the Texas Pieces series (fig. 1.15).[58] For years, *Harvey* was installed outside the main family home on the Toad Hall property. The colors are not as bright as with some of the other Texas Pieces, likely from the same environmental exposure that faded the Dynamite Museum signs. But the overall aesthetic of the piece—recycled car metal in a variety of colors manipulated into an abstract

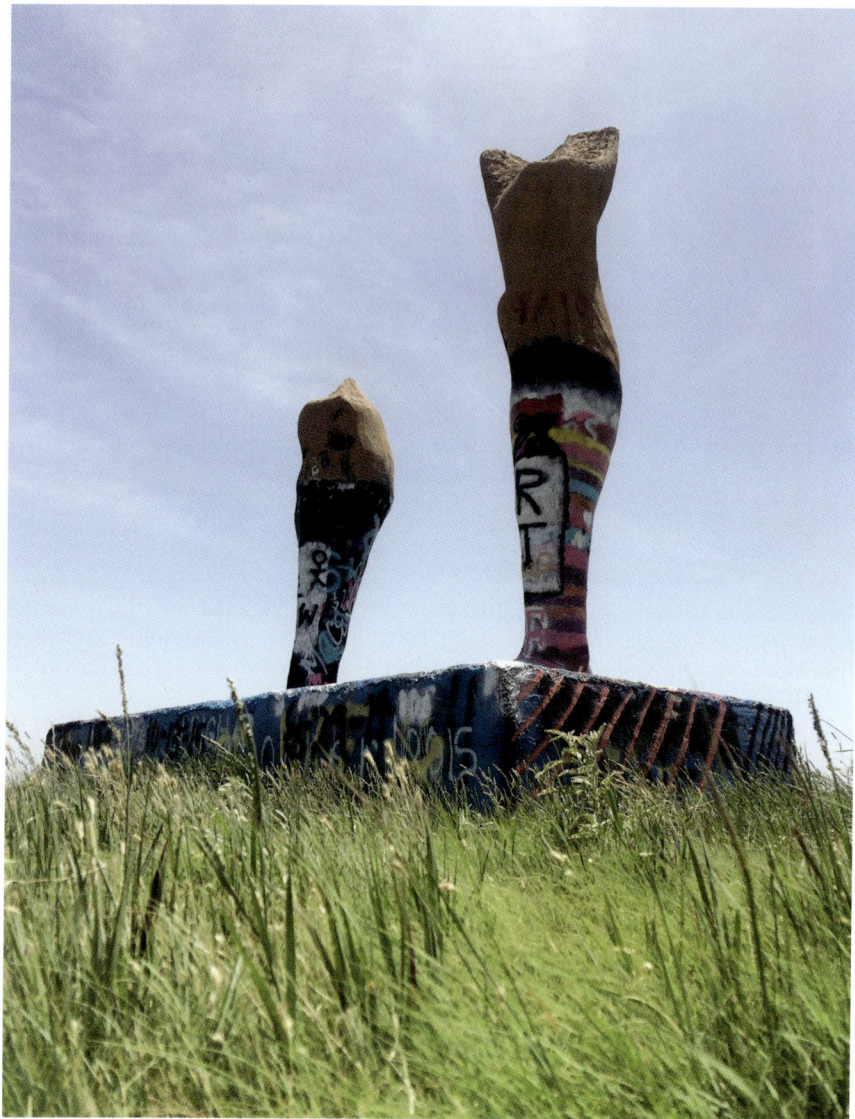

Figure 1.16. Lightnin' McDuff, *Ozymandias*, 1994–96. (Photo by Nick Gerlich.)

form that is almost organic and floral—fits well with Chamberlain's Amarillo Texas Pieces. And though the friendship between Marsh and Chamberlain ultimately decayed, the context of the production of Chamberlain's works in Amarillo must not be forgotten.

Jumping back to the 1990s, during the decade when the majority of the Dynamite Museum signs were produced, Marsh also paid for the creation of the strange fake monument *Ozymandias*, a work executed by Amarillo artist Lightnin'

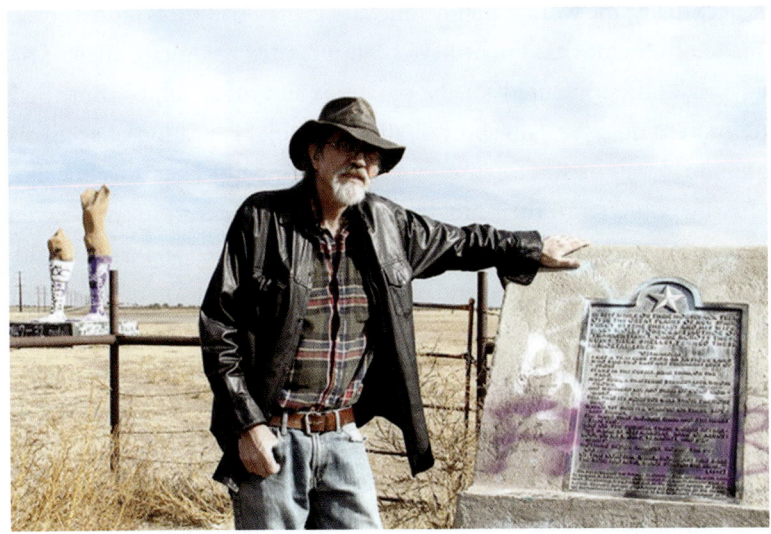

Figure 1.17. Lightnin' McDuff next to the *Ozymandias* plaque. (Photo by Elizabeth Beckham. Courtesy of *Reporting Texas*.)

McDuff between 1994 and 1996. This work was installed at the intersection of I-27 and Sundown Lane between Amarillo and Canyon, the town where WT is located (fig. 1.16).[59] The I-27 corridor between those two cities is not a desolate country road but a heavily traveled "expressway."[60] This work was designed specifically as a conceptual commentary on ruin and decay. It plays upon a poem by Percy Bysshe Shelley about "two vast and trunkless legs" that are found by an explorer, who learns that they are the remains of a colossal statue of the great Egyptian pharaoh Ozymandias. But in Marsh and McDuff's ironic appropriation of this idea, we learn that Shelley found these legs not in Egypt but in the Texas Panhandle when he was on a journey there—where of course the British poet never was. The joke plaque—as every good monument has to have a commemorative plaque—says that the statue was damaged in a Lubbock-Amarillo student rivalry, but reassures the reader that the preserved original is in a museum—one that doesn't even exist.[61] The design of the plaque strategically mimics the historic plaques seen around Texas, with its star at the top (fig. 1.17), as it was ordered by Marsh from the same company that makes the Texas Historical Commission signs, a purposeful move on the part of Marsh.[62] And like *Cadillac Ranch*, these legs have invited graffiti from the surrounding community, including the high schoolers who attend school down the road, and they have been given tube socks, pantyhose, and a variety of other adornments in an enduring commentary on the ephemerality of art and life, especially in the West.[63]

31

Conceptually, the work is highly innovative; materially, it is crudely executed. It is made of cement that might have been intended to imitate ancient rock or the Egyptian limestone used for the pyramids and other tombs. But the work, when observed up close, falls short of any believable replication of aged, durable sculpting material. Its surfaces are rough, appearing not like ruins but like they were hastily poured into their molds. According to McDuff in an interview, he and Marsh "wanted [the work] to look like it was weathered and old and had been through prairie fires and storms and one thing or another."[64] In other words, they wanted a manufactured sense of decay. Though they failed to create the effect fully, the fact that they sought it out puts this work squarely within our story. Anatomically, the legs and feet are awkward, being too far apart to allow the viewer to imagine they were once the base of a larger human statue. The feet are flattened and cartoonish. And, finally, the scale is only effective when viewers are up close, where its monumentality can be experienced. As seen from the highway, the legs almost disappear into the wide-open spaces of the High Plains and the big Texas sky. McDuff was not unaware of these shortcomings in the work: "It's supposed to be the ruins of an ancient statue. If I had understood how much the scale shrinks out there, I probably would have made it three times as big."[65]

According to KassiAnne Fondow, a former art history student at WT, her visit to the monument initially resonated with disillusionment: "My first impression upon seeing the giant stone legs was that of disappointment, both in the scale of the sculpture and in the atmosphere created by the surrounding landscape. First, the area was littered with debris. The sculpture's placement also lacked emphasis, as it was tucked behind and almost hidden by the Sundown overpass." That debris included "beer cans and bottles, plastic sacks, wrinkled papers, and a few unusual items that might not have been there by chance"—large novels, a blue sleeveless coat and a green and gold letterman's jacket "neatly hung on hangers and strategically placed on the fence." This collection of random and eclectic junk, not unlike the piles of things always found around *Cadillac Ranch*, perfectly describes West Texas decay in material form, things carried in on the wind and things left behind from human interactions. But then Fondow summarizes the success of the work: "it was meant to remind people that the great and powerful, whether people or things, cannot last forever, despite how hard one tries to immortalize them." It is the "satirical nature" of the work that defines its artistic value, Fondow explains. "The true value in *Ozymandias* was conceptual. While many people might see this sculpture as merely a passing curiosity or the commission of a wealthy eccentric, the playful concept at the heart of the work is the true power of the piece."[66] The concept at the heart of this piece ties back to Derrida and deconstruction theory. The "now" and "then" of the sculpture are fake and artistically fabricated, but their presentation of "time" is all the more real and honest for this fabrication.

McDuff also created some decay-themed sculptures around the campus at WT. McDuff kept a studio that he referred to as the "scrap yard" in downtown Amarillo at 508 Bowie Street, where he produced the sculptures, which were installed on the WT campus modeled on the university's mascot, the buffalo.

The history of the American bison (commonly, buffalo) is a rich part of the legacy of the Panhandle. Until after the US Civil War, herds of tens of millions of bison roamed the Great Plains, including the High Plains region of the Panhandle. An artistic witness to this presence of the bison was George Catlin, who visited the Great Plains in the 1830s and painted many images of the animals. However, "eastern hide hunters who moved into buffalo country in the second half of the century coupled with advancing incursion in the form of railroads and settlements . . . spelled the buffalo's near demise."[67] When the cattleman Charles Goodnight settled in the area of the Panhandle that is now Palo Duro Canyon and (with John Adair) founded the JA Ranch there, he hunted the remaining buffalo to make way for his cattle herds—that is, until his wife Molly Goodnight began rescuing and raising orphaned buffalo calves. And with Charles, she established the Goodnight herd. Together, the Goodnights have become the so-called saviors of the Texas buffalo herd, and their statues stand prominently on the WT campus.[68]

The first buffalo sculpture that McDuff made for WT was a larger version composed of scrap metal, including propane tanks, completed in 1995 and placed across the street from the Panhandle-Plains Historical Museum on Fourth Avenue (fig. 1.18). The second was a reworking of this piece in bronze in 1997, displayed as part of a sculptural herd of buffalo outside Old Main, the oldest building on campus. But McDuff's sculpted buffaloes stand out from the many other versions of the animal seen around campus. Far from the naturalistic rendering of so many others, McDuff's abstracted 1995 buffalo looks to be made from the animal's hide alone, a thin layer of rust-colored metal stretched and arched upward with empty holes where the eyes and nostrils would be. The jagged edges of the thin metal "skin" look threatening rather than soft, rotten rather than healthy or polished, as if they could slice the skin of the viewer, just as the bison's hide would have been sliced from its carcass by Plains Indian women before making it into clothing, shelter, and other functional items.

This hide-like appearance of McDuff's buffalo also points to the colonizing forces of the American West in the later 1800s, which included the extermination

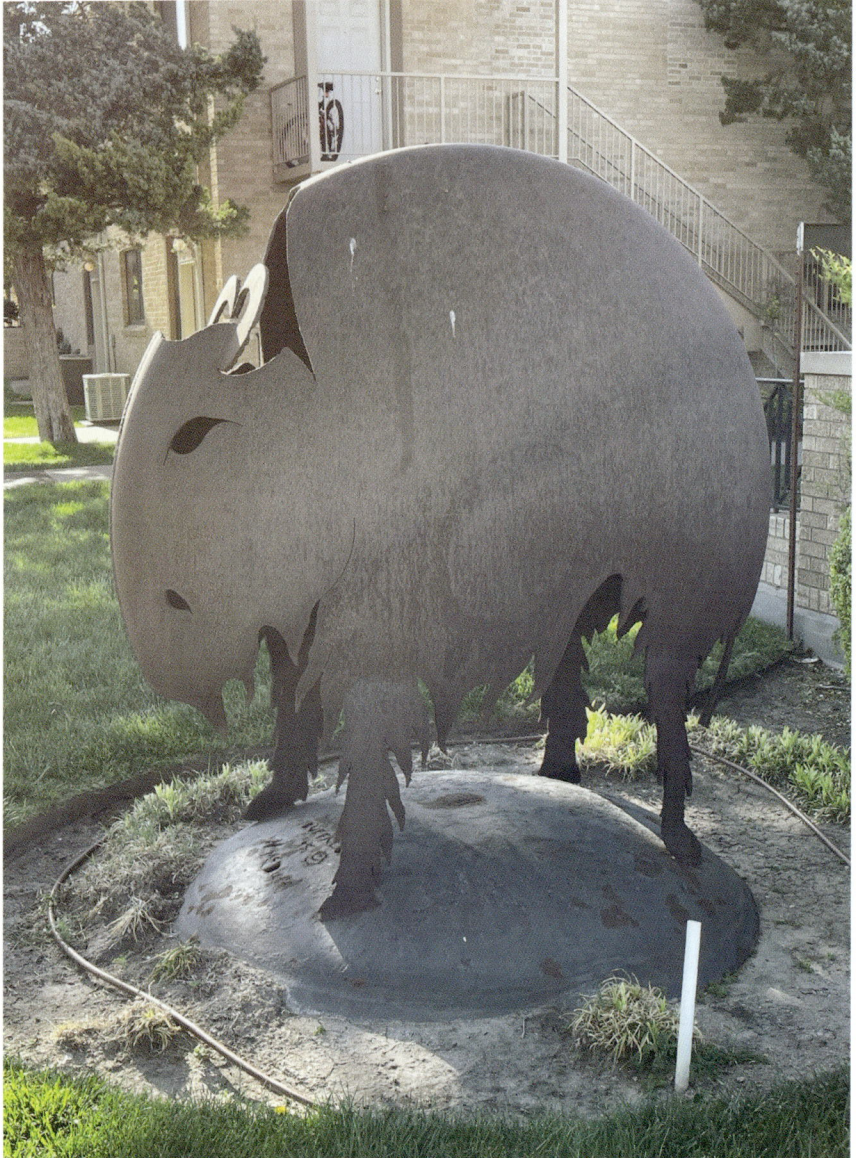

Figure 1.18. Lightnin' McDuff, *Buffalo*, 1995, scrap metal. West Texas A&M University campus. (Photo by Renea Dauntes.)

of the bison mainly for their hides. The hide trade directly supported industrial development by supplying material for machine belts used in factories (fig. 1.19), as well as agricultural development by removing the free-range bison to make way for property enclosures and a takeover of the cattle industry.[69] The very barbed wire that made the money to buy the Bush-Marsh family's Frying Pan Ranch,

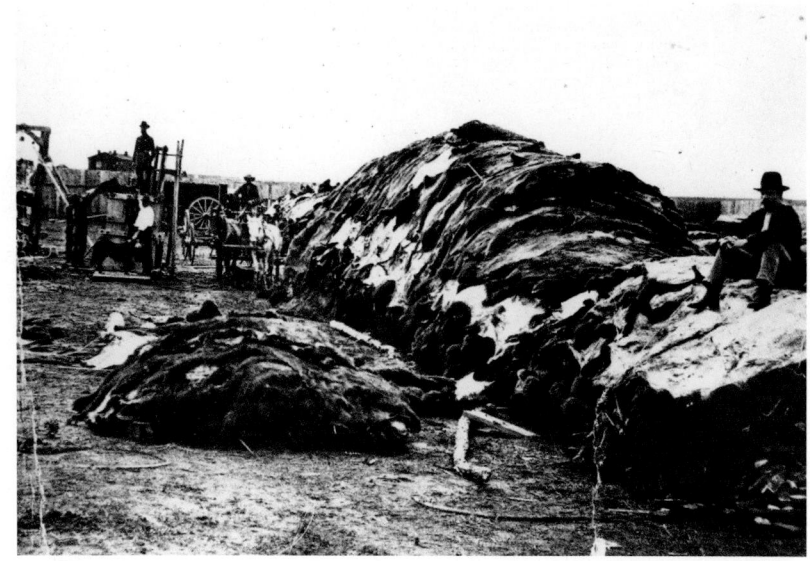

Figure 1.19. Buffalo hide yard in Dodge City, Kansas, in 1878. Panhandle-Plains Historical Museum, Canyon, Texas.

and which enclosed the land to raise massive herds of beef cattle, is symbolic of the Manifest Destiny narrative—that moral imperative to conquer the West for modernity and industry, but one that clearly has had its victims. This fall of the buffalo and the rise of ranching in the West is a point that McDuff's sculpture subtly but nonetheless pointedly makes.[70]

Of all the buffalo pieces on campus, McDuff's are by far my favorite. They do not celebrate the mythology of "how the West was won," but they ask instead, for whom was it won? For Anglos? For cattle? Certainly not for the buffalo, at least beyond becoming a university mascot in later centuries. McDuff's works critique the very mistreatment of the environment and ecology of the West and the ongoing erasure of the bison herds as unwanted trash forced into decay. They recall those rotting carcasses left in the "notrees"—the shadeless High Plains—by Anglo buffalo hunters, even in those areas designated by signed treaties as protected Indian hunting grounds, a practice that catalyzed the Second Battle of Adobe Walls in the northern Panhandle, where the last remaining free-ranging Southern tribes of Comanche, Cheyenne, Apache, and Arapaho Indians unified around 700 warriors to attack a camp of buffalo hunters in 1874.[71] The attack followed a ritual sun dance where Comanche medicine man Isa-tai had promised victory and immunity from bullets to those warriors who took up the fight against the encroaching enemy. Though the

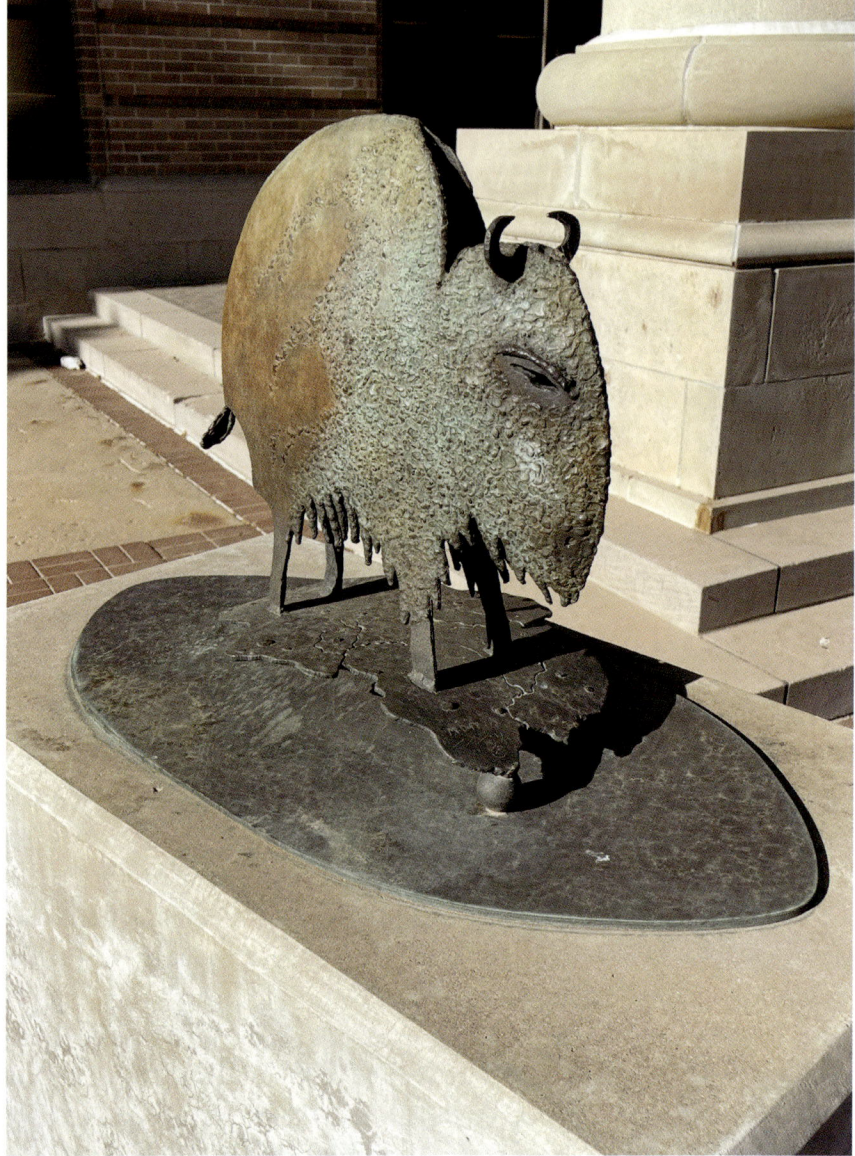

Figure 1.20. Lightnin' McDuff, *Mo*, 1997, bronze. West Texas A&M University campus. Gift of PlainsCapital Bank. (Photo by Renea Dauntes.)

hunting camp only held twenty-eight men and one woman, the camp residents were able to defend their location with guns, until the Indian warriors retreated, having suffered significant losses; over seventy Indians were killed and many more were wounded. The battle was "a crushing spiritual defeat" for the Plains tribes and led

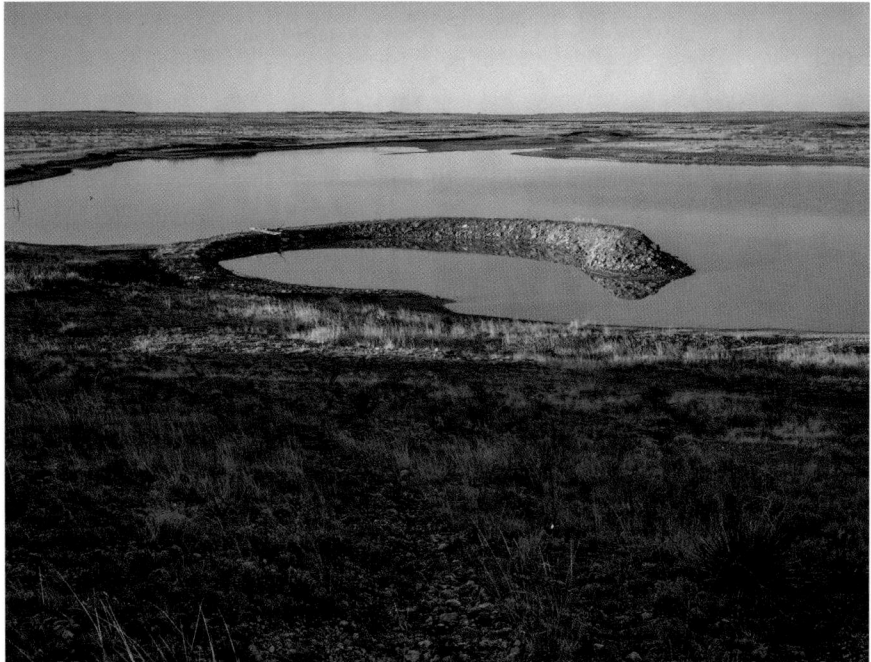

Figure 1.21. Robert Smithson, *Amarillo Ramp*, 1973. (©2025 Holt/Smithson Foundation / Licensed by Artists Rights Society (ARS), New York. Photo ©Wyatt McSpadden.)

to a new wave of the US military action against them, leading to their ultimate loss of freedom and forced relocation to Oklahoma Territory (statehood was declared in 1907).[72] McDuff's smaller bronze version (fig. 1.20), with its shaggy mane-like fur around the animal's head, eerily resembles rotting skin or cancerous cells consuming the creature with a green patina that recalls the threatening growth of gangrene or mold. To be sure, McDuff's more monstrous, more hollow, more skinned-alive, more decomposing buffalo sculptures are strikingly realistic and honest depictions of this region's deep history of decay.

Still another Marsh-paid work dealing with both decay and death, created by the most famous artist to work in Amarillo excepting only Georgia O'Keeffe (see chapter 2), is Robert Smithson's *Amarillo Ramp* completed in 1973 (fig. 1.21).[73] Born in New Jersey, Smithson discovered the lure of the US West for his land art projects starting in 1968 when he traveled with his wife, artist Nancy Holt, to desert locations in Nevada and California. Smithson's best-known and most visited work is *Spiral Jetty*, completed in 1970 on the Great Salt Lake of Utah.[74] Smithson's art was profoundly engaged in theories of entropy and the processes of natural decline and exchanges of energy.[75] And nowhere could he explore this better than in the vast open spaces of the West. Smithson used construction equipment to create sculptures employing the land itself as his materials, and he was fully aware that his works would change over time. He also specifically chose sites scarred by industry and human interaction. For example, *Spiral Jetty* was located near an abandoned mine, and soon after it was built, the water level rose and the artwork was submerged. Then, when it was re-exposed in the 2000s, it was entirely covered in white salt crystals.[76] Smithson foresaw that such changes were inevitable and felt they were an important part of his work.

However, Smithson never saw these specific changes to *Spiral Jetty* himself, as he died tragically while constructing *Amarillo Ramp* in 1973.[77] Marsh was the patron for this work and supplied the land with the man-made lake where it was staked out by Smithson. Marsh even furnished the plane that Smithson was surveying from when it crashed, killing the artist as well as the pilot and a photographer, a crash I discuss further in chapter 4. The work was built from Smithson's specs by Holt and two of his friends, artists Richard Serra and Tony Shafrazi, a month after Smithson's death. Today, *Amarillo Ramp* has seen both dry and wet weather, snowstorms and tornadoes, and has been traversed by many a cow as it still exists on a working ranch. Hardy and hard-to-remove mesquite trees—a native species of tree that has grown unchecked in the region because of fire prevention practices[78]—must be continuously cut back. And my colleague Revett and our art students have been variously tasked with "curating" the work to keep this overgrowth at bay and to keep the dirt structure from entirely eroding and disappearing from existence. Whether this curation is what Smithson would have wanted is another question altogether. How much West Texas entropy is too much?

RUSCHA AND DECAY

Beyond the many Marsh-funded projects, we must also address the work of Ed Ruscha, an artist whose pieces engage extensively with decay in the US West, and whose connection with Amarillo is well known on a surface level, but not sufficiently examined in the depth it deserves. Driving back and forth from Oklahoma to L.A. along Route 66 in the 1950s and '60s, Ruscha began to photograph the ordinary Americana of gas stations.[79] As Kerry Brougher writes, "The cookie-cutter road signs, widescreen billboards, and ramshackle filling stations that Ruscha saw as he traveled down Route 66 were a surreal presence; their attention to commonplace matters of life—the interstate highway designation, speed limit, brand of gas, type of aftershave—were juxtaposed with the limitless sky and setting sun. Ruscha's experience on the desert highway was one of words floating in emptiness,

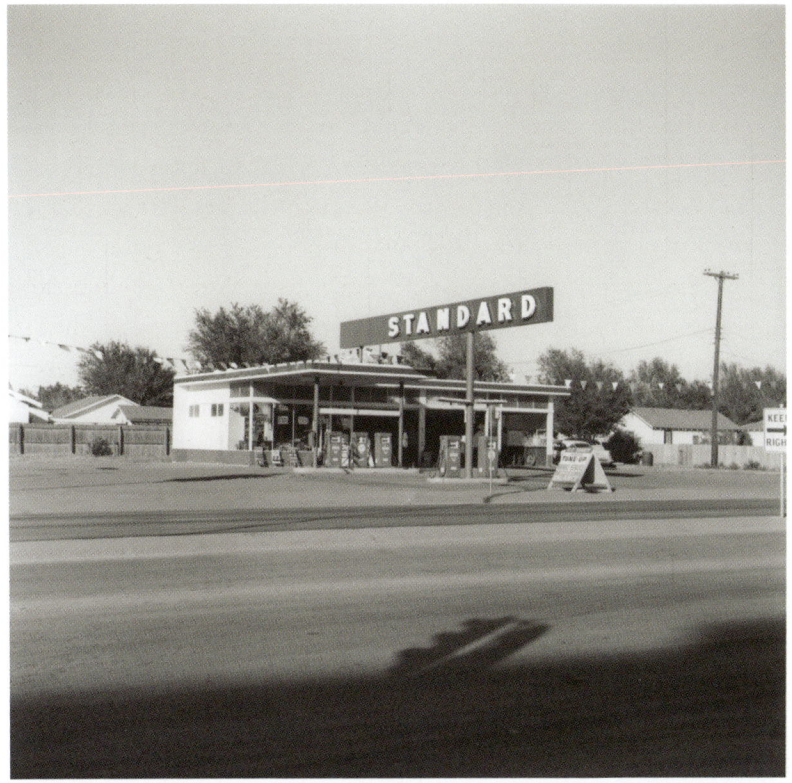

Figure 1.22. Ed Ruscha, *Standard Station, Amarillo, Texas*, 1962, gelatin silver print, 3.94 x 4.88 inches (10 x 12.4 centimeters). (©Ed Ruscha. Courtesy of the artist and Gagosian.)

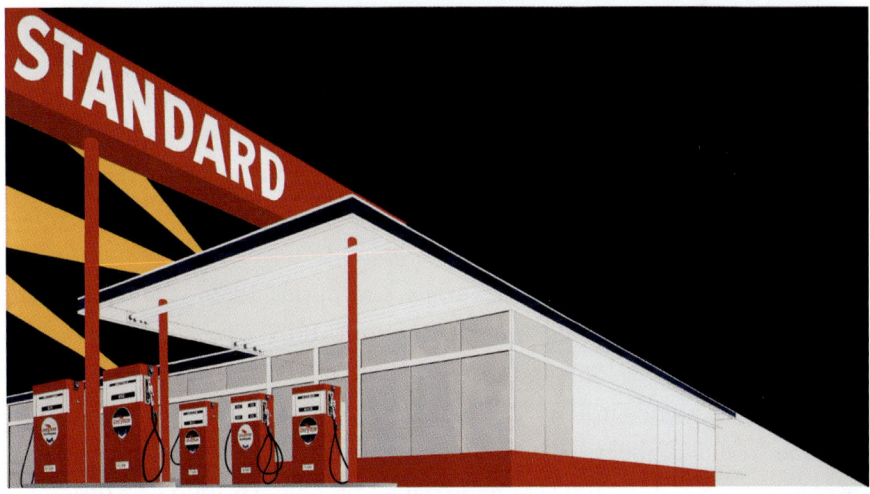

Figure 1.23. Ed Ruscha, *Standard Station, Amarillo, Texas*, 1963, oil on canvas, 65 x 124 inches (165.1 x 314.96 centimeters). Hood Museum of Art, Dartmouth College. Gift of James J. Meeker, in memory of Lee English, class of 1958. (©Ed Ruscha. Courtesy of the artist and Gagosian.)

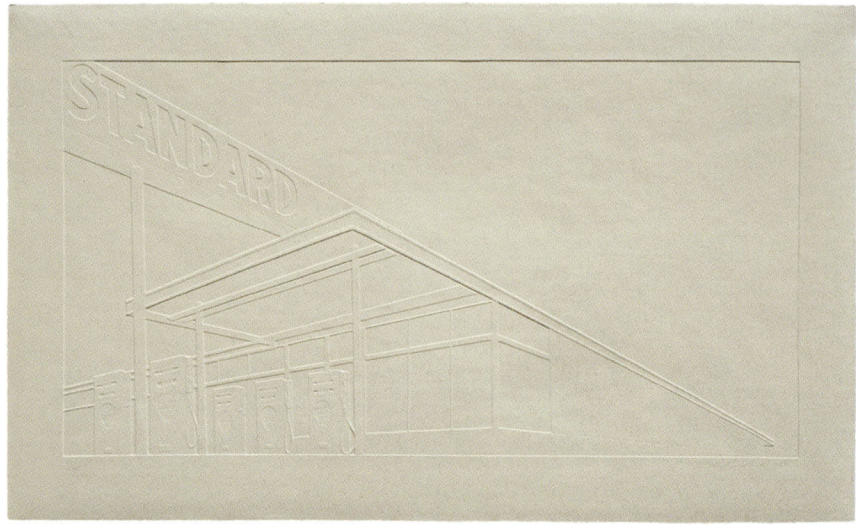

Figure 1.24. Ed Ruscha, *Ghost Station*, 2011. Mixografía® print on handmade paper, 27.25 x 46 inches (69.2 x 116.8 centimeters). (©Ed Ruscha. Courtesy of the artist and Gagosian.)

their messages of comfort attempting to mask the landscape of awe, signs and advertisements trying to fill up the uneasy void of the desert."[80]

This description does not refer directly to Ruscha's experience of Amarillo, but it could. Amarillo is a city full of signs that suddenly break up the endless open plains and huge sky of the long stretch of highway between Oklahoma and New Mexico. Some folks call Amarillo "the longest truck stop in America," an oasis of roadside commerce in a vast sea of wide-open space. So, it should come as no surprise that Ruscha was especially drawn to Amarillo's forms of pop culture and Americana on his cross-country journeys. He first featured Amarillo's Standard Oil Station within his book *Twentysix Gasoline Stations*, published in 1963 (fig. 1.22). And then he reworked this image into an extensive series of prints and paintings over decades.[81] These included *Standard Station: Amarillo, Texas*, oil on canvas, 1963 (fig. 1.23); *Standard Station, 10-Cent Western Being Torn in Half*, oil on canvas, 1964; *Standard Station*, screenprint, 1966; *Double Standard*, screenprint, 1969; *Mocha Standard*, screenprint, 1969; *Cheese Mold Standard with Olive*, screenprint, 1969; and *Ghost Station*, metal relief print, 2011 (fig. 1.24). Eleanor Antin, writing in 1973, called Ruscha's work a confrontation of high art with the "reality of the trivial and casual" in a way that was "very systematic" in its presentation.[82] What needs to be recognized is how Amarillo is at the center of Ruscha's "system" in ways that perhaps even the artist did not realize. Not only was that city a kind of geographic center point of his journeys from Middle

America to the West Coast, it also marks an undeniable centerpiece in his body of artistic production, as so many works were built upon the Amarillo Standard Station as an icon.

Ruscha recognized from the outset of his engagement with gas stations that these structures would not stay pristine or untouched by time and decline. He soon began to explore the decay of American monuments and myths, not unlike Ant Farm's *Cadillac Ranch* or McDuff's *Ozymandias*. For instance, Ruscha reworked the Amarillo station again with a pulp western magazine torn in half, as if lamenting how the days of the Old West cowboy had passed—both the working cowboys of the western frontier and the Hollywood and Spaghetti Western cowboys of the 1950s and '60s. Ruscha also painted the Hollywood sign, another American pop culture icon along with the gas station and the cowboy. First, in 1968, he featured the sign as a silkscreen rendered in its supposed original perfection, and then in 2006, he showed it in a dystopic and dilapidated future state. But we should also recall that the sign initially read "Hollywoodland" and was an advertisement for a new residential subdivision in L.A. constructed in 1923. So even the famous sign Ruscha painted in 1968 was already the victim of decay. Ruscha called his later Hollywood sign painting *Landmark Decay*, in a nod, as with those Ozymandias legs, to the inevitable decline of all monuments over time. As Ruscha wrote, "Vital art is made out of things that the general population has overlooked. The things that are forgotten and thrown away are the things that eventually come back around and cry for attention. The artist sees possibilities in things that are overlooked. Seeing the electric vibrancy in something that's so dead. The forgotten things are a source of food."[83] Ruscha notes that decay produces a nutritional substance for further creation, something that Amarillo's artists, both visiting and local, have distinctly embraced.

One of Ruscha's eeriest works that again connects to Amarillo reflects the ghost towns that so many Western communities have become—his *Ghost Station*, a metal relief print from 2011, takes the Amarillo Standard Station design and embosses it on white paper, like a specter of its former existence (fig. 1.24). Finally in 2014, Ruscha's *That Was Then This Is Now* print was produced in a print shop run by master printer Michael Raburn (d. 2021) at his studio on Route 66 in Amarillo, a few miles from the original Standard Oil Station that started Ruscha on his long-lasting engagement with that Amarillo icon—then and now, paradoxical and endless cycles of renewal and decay with Amarillo as a center.

Still another work commissioned by Marsh and installed on the Toad Hall property likely responds to Ruscha's art as well. On a mesa at some distance from the main house, Marsh had installed metal letters reading the words "actual size," in a clear homage to the Hollywood sign above L.A. But the phrase "actual size" likely also corresponds to an oil on canvas work by Ruscha completed in 1962 with that same title—*Actual Size*—depicting a container of the meat product Spam rendered in its actual, material size, shown with a trail of flames like a comet or rocket ship zooming diagonally downward from upper left to lower right. Above the container in giant yellow letters on a dark blue ground is the word "SPAM."[84] What does all this mean? What is the "actual size" of Spam? Nineteen sixty-two was also the year that Andy Warhol produced his Campbell's Soup silkscreens on canvas and exhibited them at the Ferus Gallery in L.A., a show that Ruscha would surely have seen. Perhaps Ruscha was responding to Warhol in depicting yet another consumer product seen on American shelves.[85] Ruscha explored the "actual size" of other consumer products in the 1960s, including his flattened box of Sun Maid raisins in *Box Smashed Flat (Vicksburg),* 1960–61.[86]

Such works seem to question the purpose of art itself, of representation and illusion. Ruscha explained, "I had the idea of doing small objects that were rendered actual size, to not try to attempt to do anything that was not actual size, with the exception of words because words could be any size."[87] In other instances, Ruscha repeated this notion: "Words . . . live in a world of no size. You can make them any size, and what's the real size. Nobody knows."[88] Marsh's version of the words "actual size" made into an art sign picks up this challenge and renders those very words as the content of his sculpture, playing on the anti-materiality of words as opposed to objects, but also giving them a literal materiality. As Ruscha observed, "words are horizontal objects. You're almost making a landscape" when working with words.[89] Marsh's *Actual Size* monument embedded words into the landscape, against a horizontal mesa on the distant High Plains horizon, highlighting the relationship of words to the land, especially in Amarillo art. The *Actual Size* monument at Toad Hall also prompts us to question the real size of the land out west, particularly in Texas, where "everything" is supposed to be "bigger," but where we humans might feel small and forgotten. It also explores the tensions between the real and the virtual, the actual and the illusionary, tensions which lay at the heart of contemporary life today.

But Ruscha and his flaming-tailed Spam also bring us back, full circle, to the question of arson, fire, and art in the American West. Like our unknown arsonist of *Cadillac Ranch* in 2019 (fig. 1.1), Ruscha investigated the idea of fire as something we must contend with. He made an artist's book called *Various Small Fires and Milk* (1964) that showed fifteen photographs of cigarettes, lighters, candles,

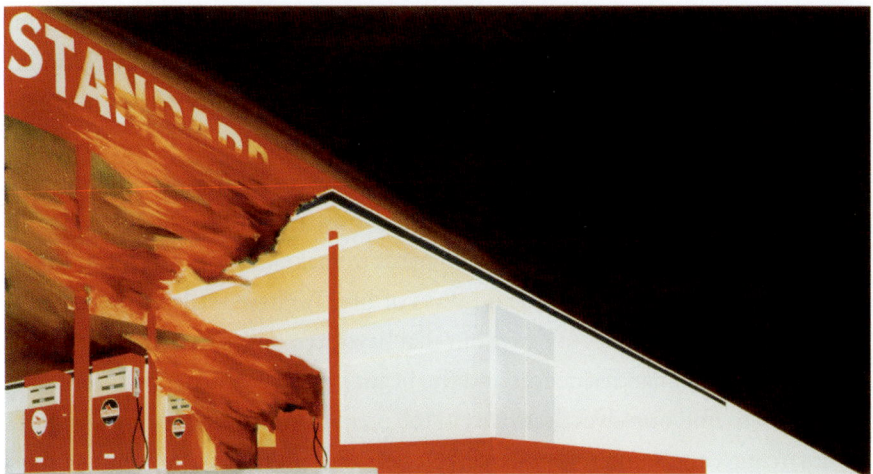

Figure 1.25. Ed Ruscha, *Burning Gas Station*, 1965–66, oil on canvas, 20.5 x 39 inches (52.1 x 99.1 centimeters). (©Ed Ruscha. Courtesy of the artist and Gagosian.)

pipes, and stovetops, followed by a glass of milk at an elegant table setting.[90] He also painted the Amarillo Standard Station again in 1965–66 but now set ablaze (fig. 1.25), as he did with other Western American landmarks, like Norm's restaurant in L.A. (1964). He even painted the Los Angeles County Museum of Art on fire in a mural-sized work in 1965–68.

Why did he suddenly become obsessed with fire in his art? Was this another layer of his ongoing commentary on landmark decay? Or was it a hope to destroy the museum as a place where art dies rather than lives, along the same lines as the works of the Dynamite Museum collective supported by Marsh? As Ruscha said about art in 1982, "I've always felt like the number one rule is that there are no rules."[91] Maybe those fires are burning down the expectations of the rules of art. But there might be more layers to Ruscha's fire-based works, too. When we view them today, they seem to point to that major threat of decay in the arid American West: wildfire. Over-plentiful water is usually not the problem in the West. More often, drought is. Fire is. With the 2018 devastation by fire in Paradise, California, for example, where no fewer than eighty-nine people perished, the whole community was burned, and a refugee situation ensued for Central California, or the devastating Panhandle fires of early 2024, when 15,000 head of cattle were killed and more than one million acres of land were burned, Ruscha's burning Western structures seem all the more poignant and potent today, as wildfires continue to rage throughout the West.

So, we know that art in the West will always be subject to decay, but perhaps that arsonist at *Cadillac Ranch*—consciously or not—is reminding us, through the burning of art, to be more mindful of the environmental realities we are facing right now and have long faced in our region. Maybe the Cadillac fire is forcing us to contend with these realities in an uncomfortable but brutally honest way, not unlike McDuff's buffalo sculptures. For decades, even centuries, Americans have insisted upon building homes and communities to the detriment of the land they are built upon. We have dug up the grasslands, leaving the Dust Bowl in our wake. We have exterminated the buffalo herds to make way for the beef industry, which feeds our expected tastes and ways of life. We have settled in places that require healthy burn cycles to thrive but that have been protected from such cycles to preserve the human residences and the beauty as we define it, not as it defines itself, only to find ourselves destroyed in the process. According to one journalist summarizing this destructive practice, "Recent conditions have boosted the risks. Years of drought exacerbated by global warming have left its forests achingly dry and littered with dead trees. And because there has been a policy of suppressing wildfires to protect homes and businesses in the state [of California] since the early 1900s, the landscape is now unusually dense with shrubs and young trees that would otherwise have been burned off by naturally occurring blazes. Fire experts, who have long spoken out about the danger, don't see this as vegetation – they see it as fuel."[92]

So, there is something worth noticing in the arson of that Amarillo Cadillac. Something not so different from the joy we can find in climbing on the art cars, in spraying our names on them in paint, in removing pieces of them to adorn our homes and bodies—something about the human hubris of it all. There is a powerful message in that burned-out Caddy. A message that art in the West can continue to share with us. Something about the pace of decay and decline that is both inevitable and dramatically exacerbated by humans living and visiting here. When humans take for our own gain without recognition of any consequences, when we live blindly human-centric lives without seeing the broader ecology of our behaviors, we are all arsonists. We are all destroyers. I only wish it were clearer today how to be a creator and preserver rather than a destroyer. How can we best preserve what is here—both in art and the natural landscape? As with the *Cadillac Ranch*, we can't go back to a perfectly restored original, because the "original" was always already embedded in cycles of decay. We can't turn back time, erase entropy, or pretend that it doesn't exist. The art in Amarillo, however, can remind us that we can only go forward, but we must do so with creative adaptation and with a deep awareness of the complex meanings of decay.

CHAPTER 2

A FAMOUS ART SCANDAL REVISITED

In 1988, an Amarillo resident named Terry Lee Caballero sold a collection of twenty-nine watercolors on paper thought to be original Georgia O'Keeffe works to Santa Fe dealer Gerald Peters for $1.25 million. Peters then resold them in 1994 for $5 million, according to press accounts, to Kansas City banker and philanthropist Crosby Kemper.[1] This set of watercolors was soon dubbed the Canyon Suite because of its connection to O'Keeffe's time spent in Canyon, Texas, from 1916 to 1918, when she was head of the Art Department at West Texas State Normal College (now West Texas A&M University).[2] In the years between the alleged discovery of the objects in a Panhandle garage and the completion of the sale to Kemper, the art world was utterly abuzz with the news of uncovered treasures from O'Keeffe's early career. The pieces were shown in seven different museums,[3] they were featured in at least three monographs,[4] and their discovery story was slated to be featured in a PBS documentary, which never actually aired.[5] But by 1999, when the catalogue raisonné on O'Keeffe's entire body of work hit shelves after six and a half years of scholarly research[6]—and when none of the watercolors from the Canyon Suite were included—one of the biggest art discoveries turned into one of the biggest art disappointments.[7]

The complete story of what took place with the Canyon Suite case may never be known. Though the national press covered the scandal in depth beginning in

45

1999, when the catalogue raisonné was published, the details of the research that led to the exclusion of the Canyon Suite from the catalogue raisonné were not made public because they could be shared only with its owner, Crosby Kemper. Thus, this chapter cannot present the definitive history of the case—perhaps this history will be provided by those whose research led to the decision not to put the watercolors in the catalogue raisonné: its author, art historian, curator, and professor, Barbara Buhler Lynes, now the authority on the artist's work, and paper conservator and professor Judith C. Walsh, then the paper conservator at the National Gallery of Art, and now the authority on the technical components of O'Keeffe's works on paper.

With this chapter I aim to set forth the part of the story that connects most directly to the Texas Panhandle, for which new evidence has recently appeared in documents donated to WT in 2016. These included half a dozen letters penned by O'Keeffe to members of the Ted Reid family between 1946 and 1978 (Reid was Terry Lee Caballero's grandfather), documentation about the sale of the Canyon Suite to Peters, and ephemera related to O'Keeffe's career, all carefully collected and stored over the years. These materials have facilitated my theory about who might have painted the Canyon Suite pieces and, perhaps more importantly, why or to what end. This chapter relates how West Texas was involved in one of the most world-renowned art scandals in history—surely an "art story of the Panhandle" for posterity, but it also examines how we value and evaluate art and artistic fame. Our appraisal of the worth of artworks is based on expert testimonies, of course, but also on our deep psychological desire to believe and to share in an artist's fame.

A summary of the so-called facts that were presented in the press is worth reviewing here, if only to lay some groundwork on what still needs to be researched. When Kemper purchased the Canyon Suite from Peters in 1994, he had been asked to donate it to the National Gallery in Washington, DC.[8] But instead, he opened his new Kemper Contemporary Art Museum in Kansas City with the works as an inaugural exhibit. The Kemper Museum also loaned the works out to high-profile O'Keeffe exhibitions such as *O'Keeffe and Texas* at the McNay Art Museum in San Antonio.[9] Kemper, as buyer, collector, and museum founder, clearly trusted Peters, a dealer with the long-standing reputation of buying and selling works by O'Keeffe.[10] In the art world, a dealer's expertise is vital to the sale of a work of art, especially a high-dollar one; the burden of proof of authenticity lies above all with the dealer. And when the Canyon Suite did not appear in the catalogue raisonné, and when Lynes and Walsh presented Kemper with their research, Peters returned Kemper's money and took back the watercolors. Peters also gave Kemper a large-scale O'Keeffe painting from his personal collection so that there would still be an authenticated O'Keeffe in Kemper's new museum.[11]

Peters, however, did not declare the Canyon Suite to be O'Keeffe paintings before turning to Juan Hamilton, O'Keeffe's colleague since 1972 and the executor of her estate at the time.[12] The contract for the sale of the Canyon Suite had a clause stating that Hamilton's authentication of the works was required.[13] It specified that if any of the works were declared inauthentic by Hamilton, the sales price would be reduced by $20,000 per questionable work. It also noted that if Hamilton authenticated fewer than twelve of the works, the contract was null and void.[14] This contract shows how an art sale is often negotiated: expert opinions are sought and protections for both buyer and seller are established. According to the press, Hamilton did give his approval of the collection, but only verbally and never in writing, and Peters paid him $10,000 for this verbal approval.[15]

In conversations with Lynes, I learned the criteria for authenticating a work of art. It has to display components of the artist's style and handling of materials in the years that the work was supposedly produced (connoisseurship); its physical characteristics had to be determined, if possible (technical components); and the history of its ownership had to be established and confirmed through documents (provenance). The Canyon Suite did not meet any of these criteria.

FAILING THE TEST

One wonders why so many people were fooled into thinking the watercolors were by O'Keeffe.[16] One reason is obvious: the Canyon Suite series is close in subject matter, composition, and style to authenticated O'Keeffes. Even Peters, after the works were rejected from the catalogue raisonné, said to one reporter that he was "speechless" by their rejection, and that he "refused to believe that they were not by O'Keeffe. They were so consistent with her way of thinking."[17] In another interview, Peters repeats, "They seemed so intimate to Georgia's thinking."[18] Although research completed on the technical components of the Canyon Suite is not yet available to scholars, additional comments on connoisseurship and provenance can be offered here. There are views in the Canyon Suite of the Palo Duro Canyon, some with crows, some without, with similarities to *Canyon with Crows* (fig. 2.1). There is a nude, with general correspondence to her series of nudes.[19] There is yet another Portrait of "W," who we now know was a boyfriend of O'Keeffe's from Amarillo, Kindred Marion Watkins (figs. 2.2 and 2.3).[20] There are also views of trees similar to her *Tree and Picket Fence* from 1918, painted when she was in San Antonio. And there are very strange celestial compositions that don't seem much

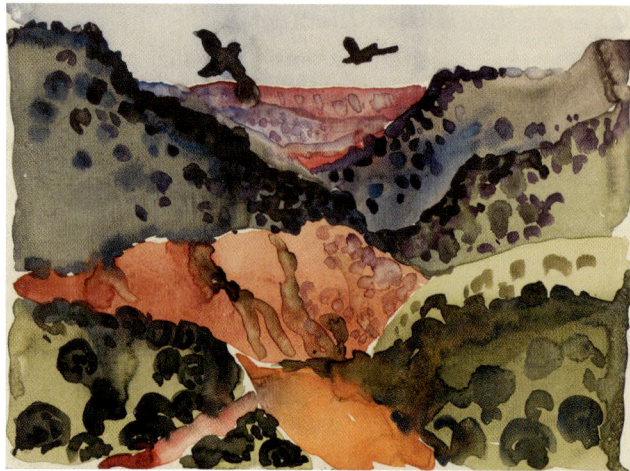

Figure 2.1. Georgia O'Keeffe, *Canyon with Crows*, 1917, watercolor and graphite on paper, 8.875 x 12 inches. Georgia O'Keeffe Museum. Gift of The Burnett Foundation. (©Private Collection*. [2007.1.5])

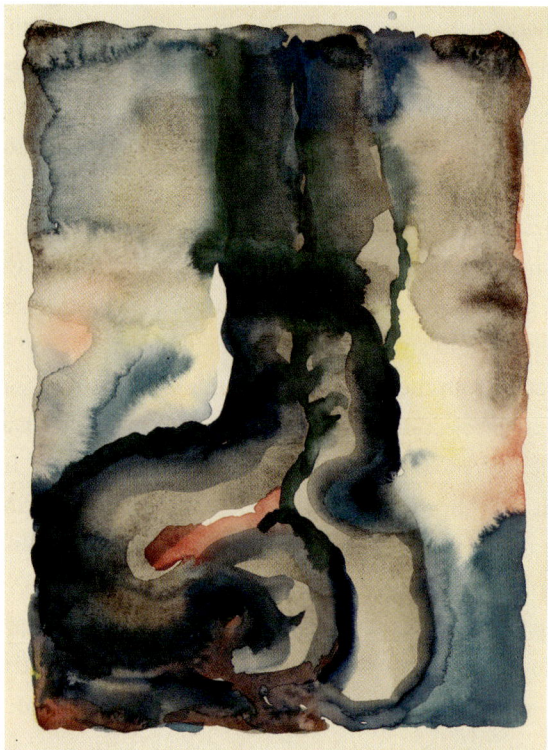

Figure 2.2. Georgia O'Keeffe, *Portrait-W - No. III*, 1917, watercolor on paper, 12 x 8.875 inches. Georgia O'Keeffe Museum. Gift of The Burnett Foundation and The Georgia O'Keeffe Foundation. (© 2025 Georgia O'Keeffe Museum [1997.4.16] / Artists Rights Society (ARS), New York. Photo: Tim Nighswander/IMAGING4ART.)

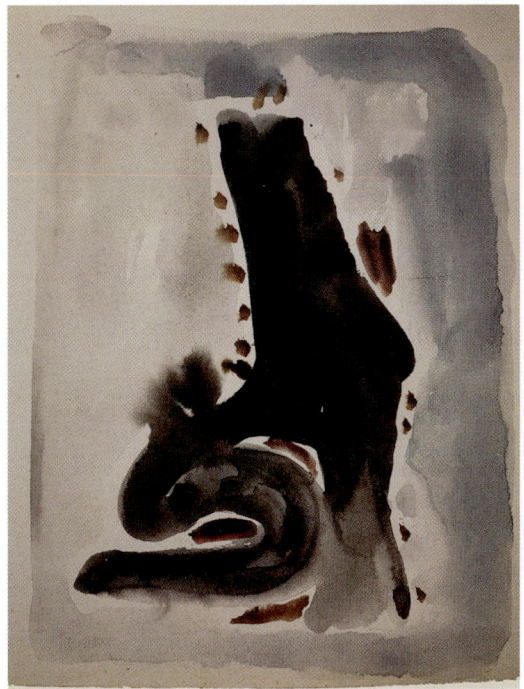

Figure 2.3. *Portrait-W*, from the Canyon Suite.

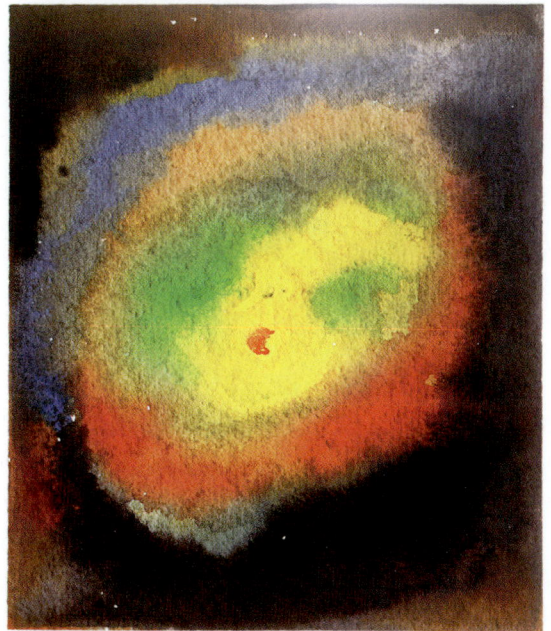

Figure 2.4. *Abstraction, Sunset*, from the Canyon Suite.

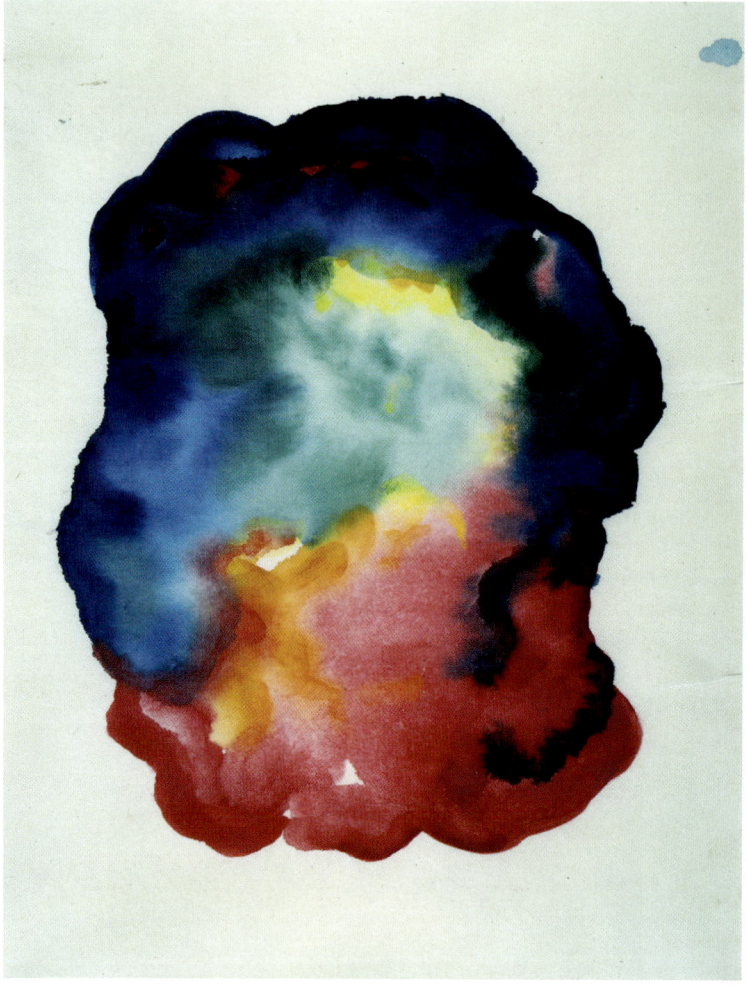

Figure 2.5. Georgia O'Keeffe, *Untitled (Red, Blue and Green)*, 1916, watercolor on paper, 17.5 x 13.375 inches. Private Collection. (© 2025 Georgia O'Keeffe Museum / Artists Rights Society (ARS), New York.)

like O'Keeffe at all (fig. 2.4). They appear to be planetary, closer to the works of the Transcendental Painting Group based in Taos, New Mexico, in the late 1930s, as if rendering the solar system seen from a distance, or the Milky Way in rainbow tones.[21] But, upon closer inspection, these celestial forms do converse quite closely with O'Keeffe's abstraction *Untitled (Red, Blue and Green)* (fig. 2.5).

Though the Canyon Suite works corresponded to aspects of O'Keeffe's style, and to some of the subjects and compositions that O'Keeffe painted in Texas, how the paint was applied to some of the pieces diverged greatly from that of O'Keeffe's authenticated watercolors. Above all, these works lack the control of

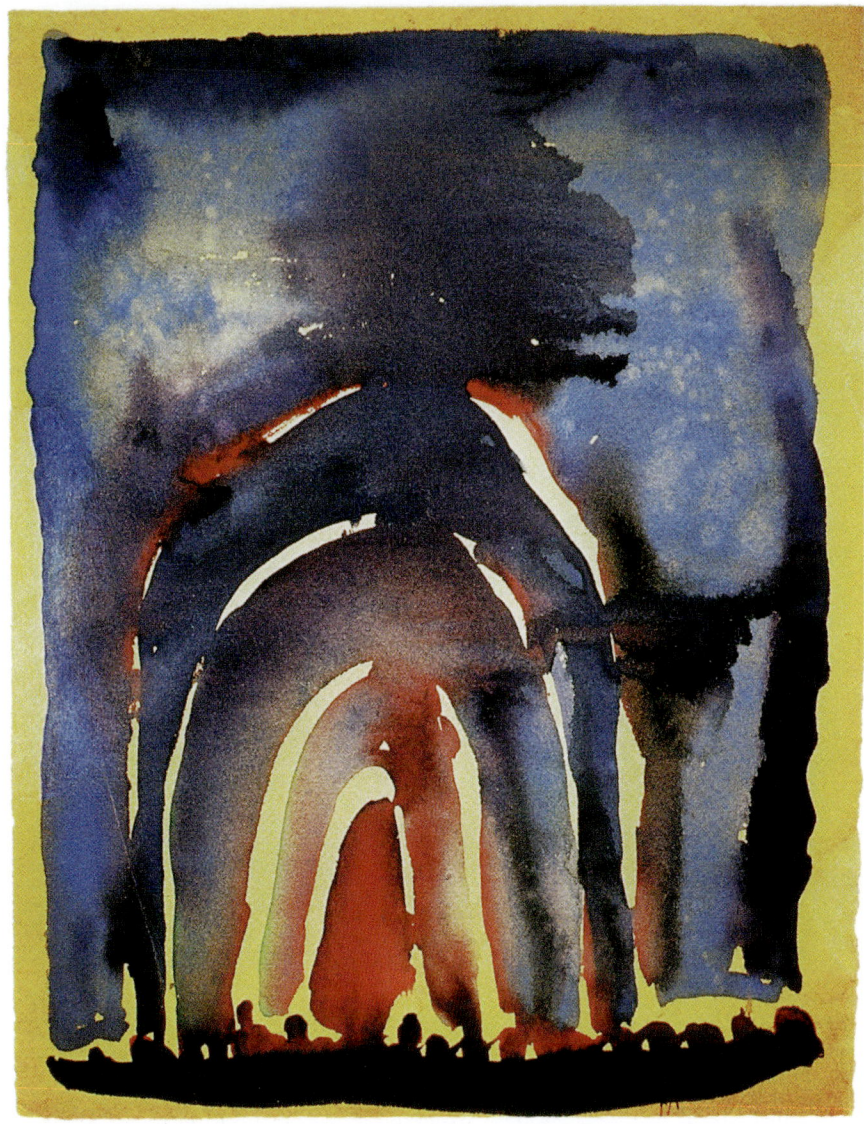

Figure 2.6. *First Light Coming on the Plains*, from the Canyon Suite.

materials present in authentic O'Keeffe watercolors. The Canyon Suite work *First Light Coming on the Plains* (fig. 2.6) bears a strikingly similar composition to O'Keeffe's *Light Coming on the Plains No. 1* (fig. 2.7) with its rainbow-shaped striations of watercolor pigment divided by thin curved gaps of uncolored paper.[22] In the authenticated O'Keeffe painting, now at the Amon Carter Museum of American Art in Fort Worth, the colorless divisions are carefully rendered. O'Keeffe pushes the gem-like blue and green pigments just up against those curving

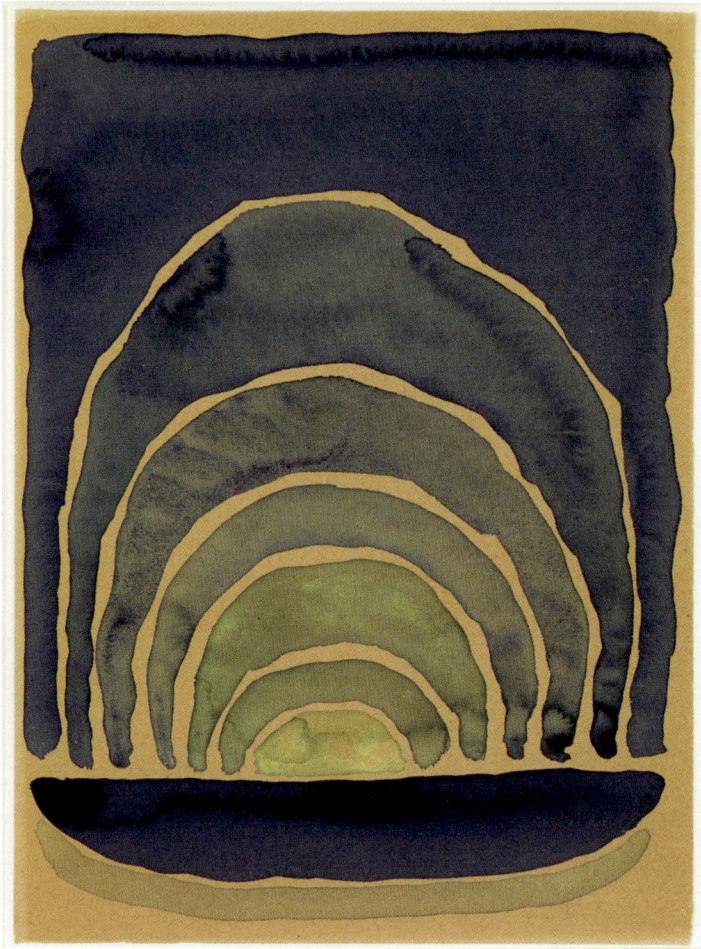

Figure 2.7. Georgia O'Keeffe, *Light Coming on the Plains No. 1*, 1917, watercolor on newsprint paper, 11.875 x 8.875 inches. Amon Carter Museum of American Art, Fort Worth, 1966.30. (©Amon Carter Museum of American Art.)

spaces, but skillfully never across them. The edgework of this piece is phenomenal; the edgework throughout O'Keeffe's career is one of her most recognizable qualities. This control was made especially clear in the recent exhibition *Georgia O'Keeffe: To See Takes Time* at the Museum of Modern Art (MoMA), where her careful working methods from sketches to paintings, and across series of similar subject matter, reveal the skill in rendering as well as her innovation in precise design.[23] The catalogue raisonné substantiates that O'Keeffe had been making watercolors since 1902, so her works from this period were not made by someone groping for ways to use the medium. She was exploring form and

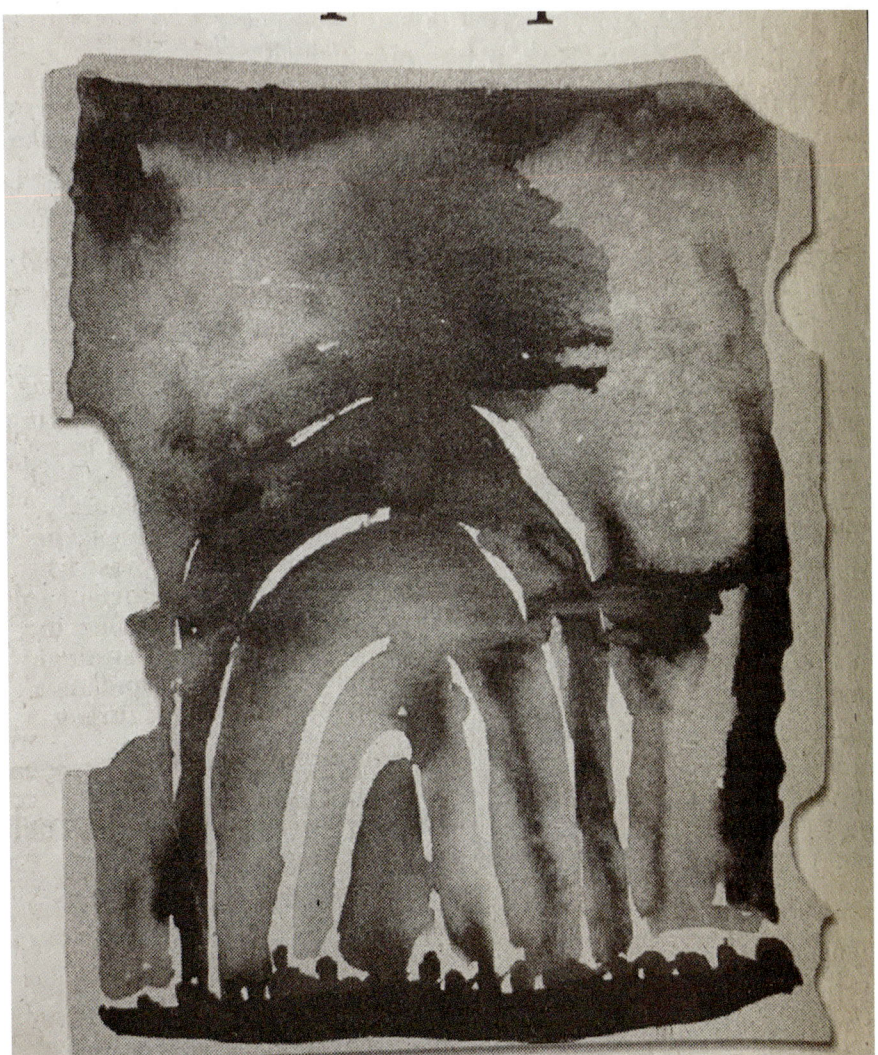

Figure 2.8. *First Light Coming on the Plains*, from the Canyon Suite, prior to conservation, as published in the *Kansas City Star*, January 14, 2001.

subject matter, but as the same publication demonstrates, she'd already mastered the medium by 1916.[24]

The catalogue raisonné included an essay about O'Keeffe's use of papers, written by Walsh, the "Paper Survey" that she and Lynes had established. It demonstrated that the artist stayed highly consistent with her choice of paper throughout her career.[25] She used either cream-colored cartridge paper with very little surface texture while in Canyon, or, in the case of a few watercolors made there, she used artist's newsprint.[26] This latter choice was true for works like the three *Light*

Coming on the Plains from the Amon Carter, as well as *Starlight Night* now in the collection of the Georgia O'Keeffe Museum in Santa Fe—all of which are fragile and highly light sensitive. For instance, when her Texas watercolors were featured in an exhibition at the O'Keeffe Museum in 2016, none of the Amon Carter pieces could travel because their pigments are so susceptible to light exposure.[27] According to reporters for the *Kansas City Star*, some of the paper used in the Canyon Suite works appeared salvaged. This newspaper published one work from the collection that had large chunks of paper missing (fig. 2.8). However, by the time the Canyon Suite was featured in numerous monographs, the work had been repaired so that it would better resemble *Light Coming on the Plains No. 1* (figs. 2.6 and 2.7).[28]

One possible explanation for O'Keeffe having painted the Canyon Suite was that she made them after leaving Canyon in 1918, possibly during one of her journeys between New Mexico and New York, which took her through the Texas Panhandle. But this explanation seems unlikely for several reasons. First, O'Keeffe rarely painted with watercolor after she left Texas for New York in 1918, when she left behind her teaching career and focused full-time on her professional art career. At that point, she was being supported by the famous photographer, gallerist, and America's first promoter of modern art, Alfred Stieglitz, in New York City. As her dealer and lover (they married in 1924), Stieglitz convinced her to focus on oil on canvas as her primary medium.[29] Second, it seems far-fetched that she would have returned to Panhandle subjects with such commitment, making twenty-nine new works at a later point in her career, when she was living in and focusing on Lake George (in the Adirondacks of Upstate New York), New Mexico, or New York City.[30] Indeed, she did return to Texas subjects in a few works—namely *From the Plains* (1919, Georgia O'Keeffe Museum), *From the Plains I* (1953, McNay Art Museum), and *From the Plains II* (1954, Museo Nacional Thyssen-Bornemisza, Madrid)—but they were all large-scale oil paintings on canvas, not small-scale watercolors in the style and format she employed in the 1910s.[31] Again, the Canyon Suite watercolors did not correspond to the material, ground, or medium O'Keeffe used when working on Texas subjects later in life.

The provenance established for the Canyon Suite was based on a story about O'Keeffe's friendship with Ted Reid that seemed plausible. It derived from the ongoing relationship of O'Keeffe and the Reid family documented by its recent gift to WT. Ted Reid, a "tall and lean and good-looking" cowboy studying education, was also involved in the Theater Department and served as drama club president (figs. 2.9 and 4.3).[32] O'Keeffe was asked to paint sets for the college theater, and it was while performing this academic service that she met Reid.[33] The two became close: Reid would walk O'Keeffe from the post office after she got her mail, and

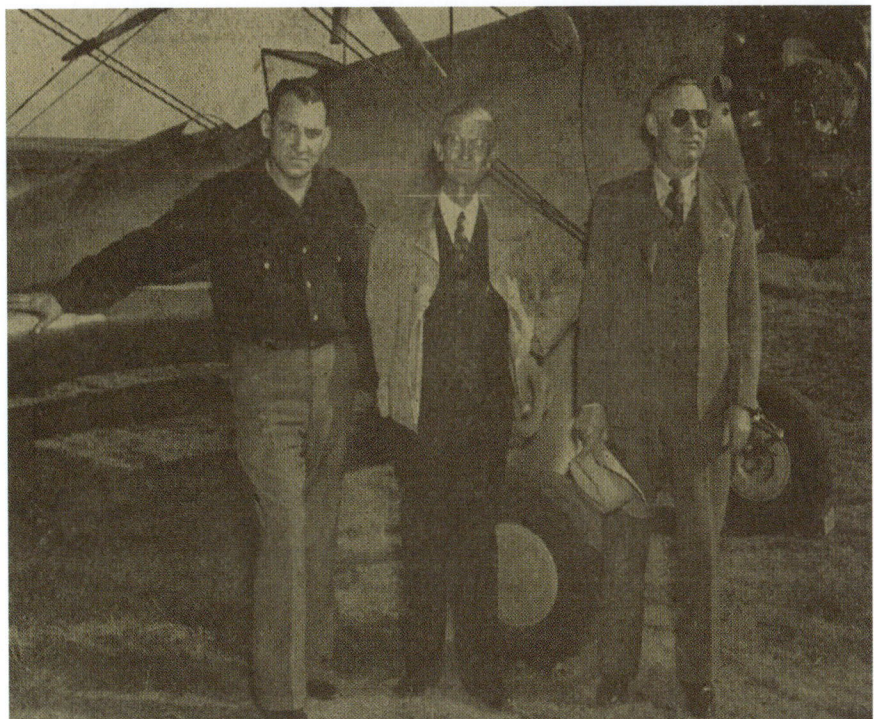

Figure 2.9. Photograph of Ted Reid (on the right) published in the *Prairie*, March 4, 1949, with the article "Wild Blue Yonder Calls WT Aviation Enthusiasts." Panhandle-Plains Historical Museum, Canyon, Texas.

he helped her fix a broken shoe and tie up a package like you "tie up a calf."[34] At a college function, he "grabbed [her] hand right tight" and danced with her.[35] At one point, O'Keeffe even tried to paint a portrait of Reid but couldn't find lines "fine enough." She wrote: "No—I've never made Ted—I wonder why—Some folks make me see shapes that I have to make—other folks don't. . . . It seems with him—there is something so fine—so beautiful—just a very slender streak of it—sometimes wider sometimes very thin—almost to breaking—so delicate. And it terrifies me when I feel that I may unwittingly break it.—I don't know any lines fine enough to make it."[36] As Reid stated in a 1978 interview, he got "quite well acquainted with Georgia."[37]

What we know about the earliest moments of their relationship comes especially from letters penned by O'Keeffe that she sent to her future husband Stieglitz, taunting him with her flirtations with other men.[38] In these letters, O'Keeffe even admitted that if Reid had asked her to marry him, she wouldn't even need time to "get [her] hat."[39] In another letter, also from 1917, she wrote, attempting to put her complex feelings for Reid into words: "Ted . . . has a ranch and cattle down there [by the Rio Grande]—I want to go along—I want to get right out and go

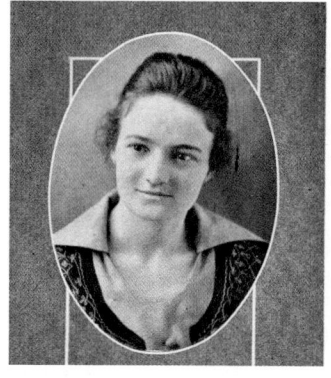

RUBY FOWLER
Lockney, Texas.

Home Economics. Secretary of Ellen H.
Richards Club, second quarter.

"She did her seaming and other work well,
And, as a cook, she could always excel."

Figure 2.10. Page from the *Mirage*, the annual from West Texas State Normal College, 1918.
Cornette Library, West Texas A&M University.

somewhere now—I was laughing at the way he walks today and he said—Why that's because I've always lived in boots—Queer the way I like him. . . . I ought not to even let Ted look at me—It's something tingling to my very fingertips that I feel almost burns folks. . . . I feel like a fire-cracker."[40] She continued, in June of that year: "There is something great about him—really fine—We talked a long time and have a lot more to talk—He makes me afraid of myself again. . . . My honesty makes it hard for most twenties to understand and believe—and I so much want him to."[41]

But things quickly got in the way of their relationship. The United States declared war on Germany in April 1917, and Reid began seriously considering signing up for the army. WT was offering degree completion for male students who signed up. Several times O'Keeffe and Reid discussed their choices—marriage or war, escaping to Reid's cattle ranch or separating from each other, with Reid going off to fight and O'Keeffe, being a woman, staying behind.[42] Then things got even more complicated, as Reid's hometown girlfriend, Ruby Fowler—ironically one of O'Keeffe's own students at WT—entered the picture again (fig. 2.10).[43] At this point, O'Keeffe told Reid that he should go ahead and settle down with Fowler. But "there is something in you that she hasn't got," Reid said to O'Keeffe. "She just hasn't *got* it—nobody else has."[44]

In the end, Reid went off to war, and by December 28, 1917, O'Keeffe had learned that Reid was engaged to Fowler.[45] By February 1918, O'Keeffe had fallen sick with an influenza-like virus, and she left Canyon to recover in the warmer climate of San Antonio.[46] But the Ted Reid–Georgia O'Keeffe relationship did not end there. Rather, O'Keeffe and Reid kept in touch for the rest of their lives; Reid passed away in 1983 and O'Keeffe in 1986. One letter shows that when O'Keeffe's first retrospective was held at the MoMA in 1946, Reid was stationed at a military base in Valley Forge, Pennsylvania. Reid traveled to New York to attend the show and saw her there. O'Keeffe penned the powerful but terse words to signify how much this reunion with Reid meant to her: "Seeing you was very good—I must see you again to tell you how good."[47] A few days later, she sent him an invitation to her exhibition reception, writing, "I will only have one friend there that I knew before you," demonstrating Reid's status as a close friend from her past. She ended the letter with a repetition of her feelings: "Seeing you has been very good for me at this time."[48] According to some sources, Reid showed up at the exhibition in full military dress, and O'Keeffe walked him around showing off her works.[49]

In another letter from 1951, O'Keeffe asked Reid to come to Abiquiu, New Mexico, to be interviewed for a book that a friend of hers was writing: "She [the author] would like to ask you what I was like in the Texas days."[50] It seems that Reid was unable to come for this interview, but the fact that O'Keeffe would trust him to talk about her on the record says a lot. At that time, she carefully chose who got to speak on her behalf, received permission to interview her and write about her, and was able to photograph her. She actively curated her reputation, biography, and identity.[51] And Reid was apparently one of the people she trusted to share her truth in a way she could abide. In 1978, an elderly O'Keeffe sent Reid a typewritten letter signed in shaky handwriting, giving Reid her private unlisted phone number. She also had an assistant write in all capital letters: "PLEASE DO NOT GIVE THIS PHONE [NUMBER] TO ANYONE."[52] In other words, Reid remained one of the people with whom she wanted to be in touch despite becoming more private after moving to New Mexico in 1949, especially when her fame led to paparazzi plaguing her at the home in Abiquiu.[53] In addition to the correspondence between Ted Reid and O'Keeffe, there are letters from O'Keeffe to other family members, such as Marcelete Reid Dana, who was Ted Reid's daughter and Terry Lee Caballero's mother. In 1969, for example, Dana wrote to O'Keeffe in 1969 inviting her to the opera in Santa Fe, to which O'Keeffe responded with characteristic bluntness that she did not prefer the opera.[54]

Still other evidence of the continued connection between O'Keeffe and the Reids can be found in the short notes and postcards that O'Keeffe sent to Ted and Ruby Reid in Canyon when she drove through the Texas Panhandle on her way to New Mexico, a journey she made almost annually after 1929 until she moved to New Mexico permanently.[55] The greetings said things like "Came into Amarillo late last night—called you this A.M. You were not at home."[56]

Likewise, Reid's granddaughter (Terry Lee Caballero's sister), Jan Minton, related in interviews how her "Pa" even made a late-in-life visit to O'Keeffe's Abiquiu home and drank whiskey with her, a story he shared with his children and grandchildren.[57] About Reid, O'Keeffe wrote lovingly in 1917, "Our acquaintance began with a laugh—We have always laughed."[58] And we can imagine them laughing together over that whiskey in their old age. This visit occurred in 1977 and involved Reid traveling with WT's university president Max Sherman to Abiquiu to see if O'Keeffe would donate a work to the university, a request the artist denied.[59] As Sherman relates, "Three weeks ago, Gene, Alice, and I joined Ted and Ruby on a trip to New Mexico for a visit with Georgia O'Keeffe. It was almost a birthday celebration: on November 8, Ted Reid was to be 82, and on November 15, Miss O'Keeffe was to be 90. For over 60 years, this teacher and student have maintained a lasting friendship. I can still see these two friends walking side by side out of that adobe home in the bright November sun. Their relationship reflects the lasting pleasure of an educational experience."[60] Here, Sherman avoids any mention of the romantic relationship between Reid and O'Keeffe, pointing instead to a teacher-student bond, probably to maintain propriety given that Reid was a married man and Sherman was trying to promote the high quality of teaching at WT. However, O'Keeffe was never actually Reid's teacher, and their relationship was not simply about educational mentoring.

The many connections between O'Keeffe, Ted Reid, and his family seem to provide a believable origin story for the Canyon Suite: O'Keeffe had a crush on a young cowboy in Canyon, to whom she may have gifted a set of her watercolors. But this story begins to unravel quickly when we take a closer look. In 1917, when Reid and O'Keeffe parted ways because of the war and Ruby Fowler, O'Keeffe was in the habit of sending her artworks back to Stieglitz in New York. In April of that year, she had her first solo show at Stieglitz's 291 Gallery, the leading gallery for modernist art at the time. In the context of that show, O'Keeffe had sold her first work to a friend of Stieglitz.[61] And although 291 closed with the start of US involvement in the war, O'Keeffe was beginning in 1917 to define herself as a professional artist with a following in the New York art center. So why would she choose to hold back such a significant collection of the few works she was able to produce while working full-time as an educator?[62] Would she have given Reid her "mess-ups," things that were sloppy sketches not good enough for New York? Did she love him enough to give him some draft versions but not enough to share any of her best work?[63] Such a gift would be uncharacteristic of O'Keeffe, who rarely held onto anything she felt was not of high quality, let alone so many of them.

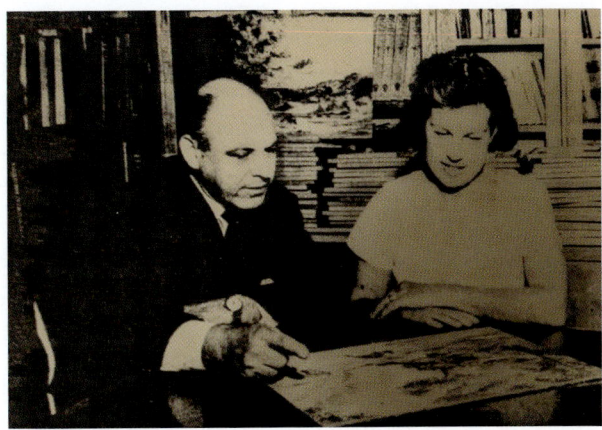

Figure 2.11. Emilio Caballero and Olive Vandruff Bugbee looking at Vandruff Bugbee's paintings at the Panhandle-Plains Historical Museum, *Amarillo Citizen*, July 30, 1963. Panhandle-Plains Historical Museum, Canyon, Texas.

And why would she gift them to Reid then, just when he was off to war? Where would he have kept them? With his fiancée, Ruby? The timing and circumstances of this gift seem terribly unlikely.

Moreover, the Canyon Suite watercolors did not come to their seller Terry Lee Caballero directly as part of a Reid family inheritance. There was a middleman involved: Emilio Caballero, the art professor who took the position of head of the WT Art Department more than thirty years after O'Keeffe (fig. 2.11). People who knew Caballero indicate that he became utterly fascinated with how his own life seemed closely to parallel O'Keeffe's.[64] Both studied at Columbia Teachers College in New York City and both became head of the Art Department at WT. Caballero celebrated the fact that he sat in the same chairs as O'Keeffe and washed his brushes in the same sink that she did: "The thing is," Caballero declared, "that I walked in the same path as Miss O'Keeffe. I literally walked on the same floor she walked on."[65] He felt connected to her fame and talent just by working in the spaces she had worked decades earlier. According to another source, "[Caballero] had this obsession with O'Keeffe, and he wanted to talk about her all the time," and he thought he had "some kind of an astral relationship with O'Keeffe."[66]

Caballero even tried for years to get a book published about these connections—he fancied himself able to write the authoritative biography on O'Keeffe.[67] That never happened. But what did happen is that Caballero began to research absolutely everything pertaining to O'Keeffe in Canyon, building up an archive of photographs, memoirs, and ephemera.[68] Having access to the Art Department where O'Keeffe worked, he began to collect any object he found around the department that could possibly connect to O'Keeffe; he dug through every scrap of paper in the department looking for a drawing or note left behind, every book in the WT library for an inscription by the artist, and every old easel and paint brush, trying to find what he called "memorabilia" of the artist.[69]

In 1988, Caballero was the one who established the provenance required in the contract between Terry Lee Caballero and Peters for the sale of the Canyon Suite. He provided an affidavit that declared he was the link back to Ted Reid, who was the reason the Canyon Suite was still in Canyon and not with O'Keeffe herself—as so many of her other Canyon-era watercolors were.[70] Caballero claimed that in 1975 Reid gave him a package in his office at WT. Being the "gentleman" that he was—a descriptor that Caballero always insisted upon for himself, perhaps celebrating the translated meaning of his last name—he said that he took the package as a favor to Reid and stored it in some boxes that made their way from the WT campus to the garage at his home. Years later, in 1987, when Caballero was packing up to move out of his home, he claimed to have found the package again and gifted it to Terry Lee Caballero because Reid was her grandfather. She was married to Caballero's son C. T. (Charles Thomas) by that time, so the elder Caballero did not have to work hard to track down Terry Lee Caballero as a relative of Reid. On the contrary, he tells us that she was in the very garage where the items were allegedly found, helping her father-in-law pack up his belongings for his move. Terry Lee Caballero then, according to the affidavit, opened the package, discovering the collection of watercolors, and the two families decided to seek the expert advice of O'Keeffe gallerists and dealers in Santa Fe. A year later, they connected with Peters and the sale of the works was arranged.

OFFERING A THEORY

Because the Canyon Suite surfaced in West Texas, it seems reasonable that it was created there. But someone working in the Panhandle would not have had direct access to authentic O'Keeffe watercolors, since approximately half of her output, which included most of her early watercolors, remained in O'Keeffe's own collection and was transferred to the estate after her death. So how were the derivative works created? As with so many art forgeries, published color reproductions seem to have been the key.[71] I have tracked how most of the Canyon Suite paintings can be related to an authenticated work found in a publication in existence before 1988, when the collection's discovery was first announced. These publications include O'Keeffe's autobiography published with Viking Press in 1976, where large-scale color images of her *Evening Star* series, *Light Coming on the Plains II*,

Starlight Night, and *Canyon with Crows* (fig. 2.1) all appear—these correspond to the Canyon Suite's *Evening, Sunset*; *Light Coming on the Plains*; *Abstraction*; *Autumn on the Plains*; and *Landscape with Crows*.[72] Another is Jan Garden Castro's illustrated biography *The Art & Life of Georgia O'Keeffe*, published in 1985, which included color reproductions of *Pink and Green Mountains III*, *Portrait W - No. III* (fig. 2.2), *Tree and Picket Fence, Train at Night in the Desert*, and *Light Coming on the Plains No. I* (fig. 2.7), which correspond to the Canyon Suite works *Blue Hills* and *Purple Mountains*, *Portrait - W* (fig. 2.3), *Tree, Train Coming In*, and *First Light Coming on the Plains* (Fig. 2.6). Castro's book also includes black and white versions of O'Keeffe's charcoal drawing *Train at Night in the Desert* from 1916 and *Dark Abstraction* from 1924, which look similar to the Canyon Suite *Grey Abstraction* and *Abstraction, Black and Blue*.[73] The Museum of New Mexico in Santa Fe produced a catalogue for the exhibition *O'Keeffe Works on Paper* in 1985, which included the abstraction *Untitled (Red, Blue and Green)* (fig. 2.5) and *Nude XI*, which correspond to the Canyon Suite works *Abstraction, Sunset* (fig. 2.4) and *Standing Nude*, as well as *Tree* and *Portrait W - No. 1*, both of which also appeared in Castro's biography.[74]

This practice of making forgeries based on illustrated art books has been seen time and again. It was the key to the forgeries featured in Richard and Sally Price's book *Enigma Variations* published in 1997, the story of two anthropologists who discover that their own published books on the art of Black ex-slaves in French Guyana was used to create a set a forgeries sold to a new museum of Guyana's cultural history.[75] Another example of books being the key to a worldwide scandal of art forgeries is seen in the case of Elmyr de Hory, the faker of European modernist masters whose known works number more than one thousand, many of which still grace the walls of major art museums masquerading under the names of famous artists. The scandal of de Hory broke for the public when a large cache of his works was sold to Algur Meadows for the inaugural exhibit of his Meadows Museum in Dallas in 1965.[76] When art experts reviewed Meadows's newly acquired collection, they discovered that his Gauguins, Picassos, Matisses, Chagalls, and Modiglianis were all fake.[77]

By that time, the FBI was already on de Hory's trail, but he had escaped to the island of Ibiza, and he lived out his life there.[78] His fame as a great art forger was secured when his biography was penned by Clifford Irving, himself the forger of the autobiography of Howard Hughes, and when Orson Welles, the man responsible for the 1939 *War of the Worlds* radio broadcast that fooled a nation of listeners, produced a documentary on him. Irving and Welles were fascinated by de Hory's ability to fake out the world—two fakers tell the "real" story of another.

The selling of the Canyon Suite

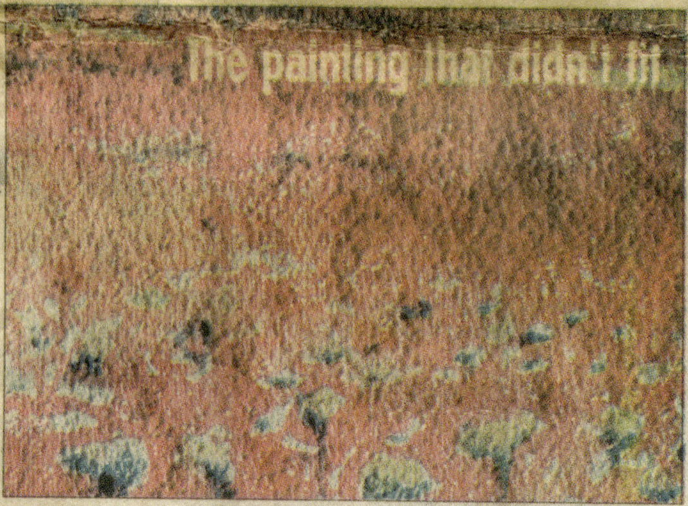

The painting that didn't fit

Courtesy, The Winterthur Library: Joseph Downs Collection of Manuscripts and Printed Ephemera

When Gerald Peters bought the Canyon Suite — paintings attributed to artist Georgia O'Keeffe during her time spent in Canyon, Texas — there were 29 watercolors. After discovering that the painting above was too recent to fit with the others, Peters removed it. R. Crosby Kemper Jr. says he bought 28 works without learning this painting had once been part of the group.

Figure 2.12. Image of the work removed from the Canyon Suite original collection, as published in the *Kansas City Star*, January 14, 2001.

But the point here is that de Hory pulled off his forgeries by working from published books. He would bring books with him wherever he traveled, posing as an Eastern European modern art collector who had fallen on hard times during World War II. When an interested buyer would ask de Hory if he had a Matisse, for instance, he would say, "Let me head back to my hotel room, where I have some of my collection, and see." He would disappear to his hotel room, open one of his books, take a piece of believably aged paper, and draw a work of art based on something reproduced in his books.[79] And de Hory did exactly what the O'Keeffe forger seems to have done. De Hory produced a subject that the artist already created: another woman with flowers by Picasso, or another woman on a couch by Modigliani. He rarely copied works directly, line by line, but instead, he would skillfully emulate the style and composition of a known and beloved artist in a way that looked entirely plausible to the experts. De Hory's works also looked believable to collectors in the Amarillo area, and I have published elsewhere on how his art defrauded Panhandle collectors.[80]

The same thing seems to have occurred with the Canyon Suite. The compositions, subjects, aspects of style, and origin story made sense. Peters and others knew O'Keeffe had painted Palo Duro Canyon, nude women, and portraits of someone named W—such subjects were part of her "way of thinking," as Peters put it. And they knew that O'Keeffe and Reid had a relationship. Therefore, when Terry Lee Caballero, the granddaughter of Reid, showed up in Santa Fe with a collection of watercolors similar to existing works by O'Keeffe, Peters and Hamilton found them believable.[81] According to news reports, Peters did pull out one work from the cache because he was suspicious of its authenticity. He claimed in the press that he had the works examined by a paper conservator and pulled out the single piece.[82] He went forward with the twenty-eight remaining works. The *Kansas City Star* later published this work in 2001 and indeed, it looks nothing like an O'Keeffe original (fig. 2.12).

In the end, no one went to jail for this scandal, and no fraud was legally proven. Peters made amends with Kemper, avoiding a lawsuit and criminal allegations. Peters also launched an investigation against Terry Lee Caballero, one that involved the FBI, but no crime was proven.[83] On the record, she claimed that she never knew the works were by O'Keeffe; she deferred to the opinion of Peters. He had been selling O'Keeffes for years, so the burden of proof was on him, she asserted.[84] To be sure, forgery is a very hard crime to prosecute; the authorities basically have to catch the forger in the middle of the act.[85]

At this point, I have proposed how the works were executed: through careful study and creative translation of O'Keeffe's originals from published reproductions. But who conducted this careful study and creative translation? One of the most likely suspects for the artist of the Canyon Suite is Emilio Caballero. My evidence for this hypothesis comes above all from the archives at WT, but also from having taught several classes on O'Keeffe and on fakes and forgeries and from having closely studied Caballero's work in person.

It is worth briefly reviewing Caballero's biography because outside of the region he is little-known. He was born in the United States in 1917 to Spanish immigrant parents who had lived in Cuba before settling in New Jersey. In 1937, Caballero moved to Amarillo, Texas, where he enrolled in classes at Amarillo Junior College (now Amarillo College) and earned an associate's degree in 1940.[86] The exact reason for his move to West Texas remains unclear, but the region quickly became a home for him. Caballero continued his studies at WT (then known as West Texas State College), where he earned his bachelor's degree in 1942. He served in the army during World War II, from 1943 to 1945, participating in both the European and the Pacific theaters of the war. He returned to the Texas Panhandle after the war and started teaching at Horace Mann Elementary and Junior High in downtown Amarillo between 1945 and 1947. During these years, Caballero held his first art exhibition at the Amarillo Public Library. In 1947, he took a job teaching art at his alma mater of WT. But around that time, he also enrolled at Columbia Teachers College in New York—the same institution where O'Keeffe studied in 1916—earning a master's degree in 1949. That year, he returned to WT, accepting a position as a faculty member. Between 1949 and 1955, Caballero completed his doctorate of education at Columbia, which allowed him to secure a full professorship at WT and the position of department chair. Not only had he studied art education at the same college in New York as O'Keeffe, but he had secured for himself the very position she had held.

As discussed above, these parallels between Caballero's life and O'Keeffe's life were not unnoticed by Caballero. He became infatuated with his biographical connections to her and began to amass items he found around the Art Department that could connect to O'Keeffe. And over the years, he tried to sell these items to dealers and gallerists. He even succeeded a few times.[87] By 1966, for instance, he had convinced local reporter Vivian Robinson to take several items he found to O'Keeffe in New Mexico to get her authentication for them.[88] Apparently, Robinson did succeed in securing a reception with O'Keeffe and in getting the artist to admit that a few of the works were hers, including portraits of a friend "from Columbia" done in 1915.[89] Then, when O'Keeffe tried to confiscate the works as her possessions, Robinson refused to give them over, claiming they were the "property" of her friend Caballero. The story continues with O'Keeffe refusing to sign the works because they were "no good," in her opinion.[90] Caballero later stated, "The storage room of things Isabel [Robinson, another of his teaching predecessors at WT, see fig. 4.7] had collected for many years . . . was cleaned out. . . . I collected a group of drawings and paintings that appealed to me from the things to be thrown out. I did not know at that time that among the things . . . would be some of Miss O'Keeffe's early work."[91] He describes his surprise here in finding O'Keeffe's works and objects, but we know that he was actively looking for them for years.

By the 1970s, Caballero had begun to consign other items that he had found in Canyon, claiming they were O'Keeffe originals. A document dated May 1970 shows Caballero sold two O'Keeffe paintings to the Collections Gallery in Santa Fe, and for those received a $500 check as part one of the sales price. Apparently, he never received part two of this sale. In a letter dated November 1978, dealer Andrew Smith sought further proof in order to buy several O'Keeffe works that Caballero was selling and asked him to declare in writing that O'Keeffe herself authenticated them.[92] But we know that Caballero never met O'Keeffe personally, so he was unable to do this. That same year in December, Smith purchased the works for $1,250, apparently without the requested authentication.

In 1985, Caballero once again tried to sell works by O'Keeffe, this time through Nat Owings, another gallerist in Santa Fe. As noted in a memo from Owings-Dewey Fine Art, items belonging to Mary Caballero, the wife of Emilio—including a watercolor of a still life with a candle, a second watercolor, a letter, and other documents—were being examined for purchase. According to one source, Owings vividly remembers going over the works laid out on the floor of his vacation home in Montana.[93] Owings, who continues to buy and sell works by O'Keeffe at his Santa Fe galleries to this day, remembered in an interview with a reporter: "They sent me reams of stuff and Isabel Robinson files that had never been opened. And in it, I found five watercolors in folders stuck in this pile of stuff that were clearly by O'Keeffe, one of which I still have. Stylistically, there's no question."[94] By 1986, Mary Caballero was in possession of a check for $3,000 for the sale of the candle still life. But like the Canyon Suite works, this still life and other works Owings-Dewey had purchased were not included in the 1999 catalogue raisonné.

However, the Canyon Suite was a sales attempt on a whole new level for Caballero and his family. This cache of paintings came to light suspiciously just after O'Keeffe's death in 1986. At that point, O'Keeffe could not deny the authenticity of the twenty-nine works, nor could Reid, who had also passed away by then. At that time, Caballero was no longer working at WT.[95] In fact, he had been forced into retirement from his department head position in 1975, when numerous members of the university faculty and administration brought claims against him for mismanagement and overall incompetence. What interests me most among these charges are the claims that he was being fraudulent in his administrative duties. For instance, he had added his son C. T. to the roster of a graduate art class and coerced a faculty member to give his son A-level grades although C. T. never even attended the classes. Newspaper articles describe nearly every aspect of the legal hearings that Caballero went through in the fall of 1975, including which faculty members claimed they were being forced to give false grades; one of them still worked in my department when I started there in 2010.[96]

Caballero was thus not above bending the rules for his own gain. We also discover that his son was an art student—perhaps not one who attended his classes regularly, but an art student nonetheless. C. T.'s obituary in 2014 even described him as "an accomplished artist."[97] So perhaps C. T. was the painter of the Canyon Suite, not his father. This possibility cannot be ruled out, and to this day some people in Canyon, who will remain unnamed, are convinced that it was C. T. who painted the fakes. But we have very little evidence of C. T.'s skill and style as an artist, so this contention would be hard to prove beyond a doubt.

In contrast, we have a great deal of evidence of Emilio Caballero's skills and style as an artist: he was a prolific producer of paintings, including watercolors and oil on paper, as well as some stunning enamel works on copper. Indeed, his best works, in my opinion, include his enamel on copper panels in the Blackburn Room of the Cornette Library at WT and in the laboratory suite at the Texas Tech Health Sciences Center in Amarillo (figs. 2.13 and 2.14). The Blackburn panels depict the Spanish conquistador Coronado "discovering" the High Plains of the Texas Panhandle, a story that had personal resonance for Caballero, with his Spanish heritage. According to two reporters writing for the *Kansas City Star*, Caballero "quickly point[ed] out" to them "that he [was] of Spanish heritage, not Mexican, a significant cultural distinction in Texas if you want to emphasize that you descended from conquerors, not the conquered."[98] In Caballero's panels, the narrative scenes of Coronado's conquest unfold in a panorama that spans the wall above shelves of Special Collections books, including books about O'Keeffe. And the Texas Tech panels depict a vibrant flower market with bouquets in the foreground beneath billowing white tents. These enamels stand out among Caballero's works both for their quality of production and for Caballero's confidence with the medium. While other works seem derivative and tentative, and his painting style varies eclectically from realistic to impressionistic to abstract, his enamels are bold in color, design, and execution. They have a layered appearance where the bright colors dance on the surface of the metal, while the ground looks almost spray-painted or stained in an exciting way that feels fresh and contemporary (figs. 2.15 and 2.16).

But the works that interest me most for this chapter are Caballero's works on paper, and there are many. WT has a collection of these works, and I have inspected them firsthand in classes with my students (see fig. 2.17). Our department put

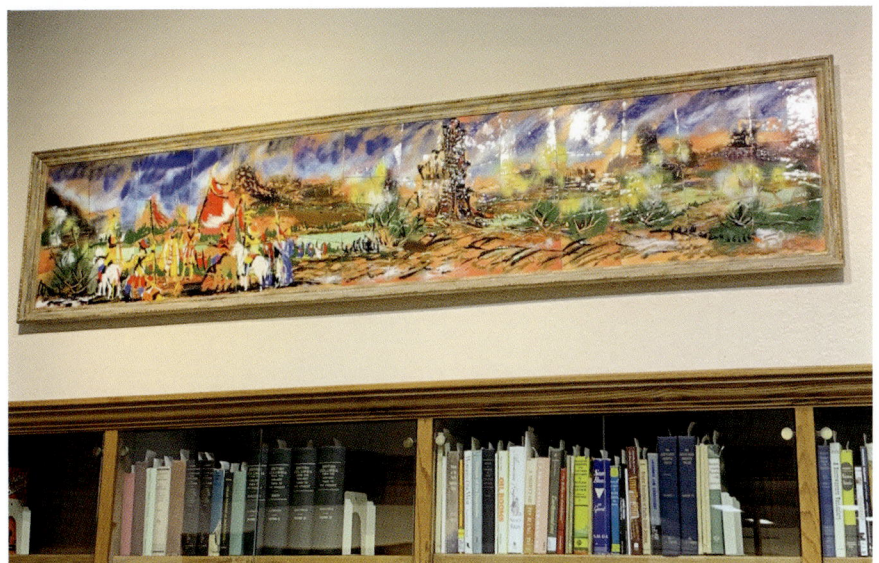

Figure 2.13. Emilio Caballero, *Untitled (Coronado's Expedition in West Texas)*, left panel, unknown date, enamel on copper, Blackburn Room, Cornette Library, West Texas A&M University. (Photo by author. With permission from the Emilio Caballero family.)

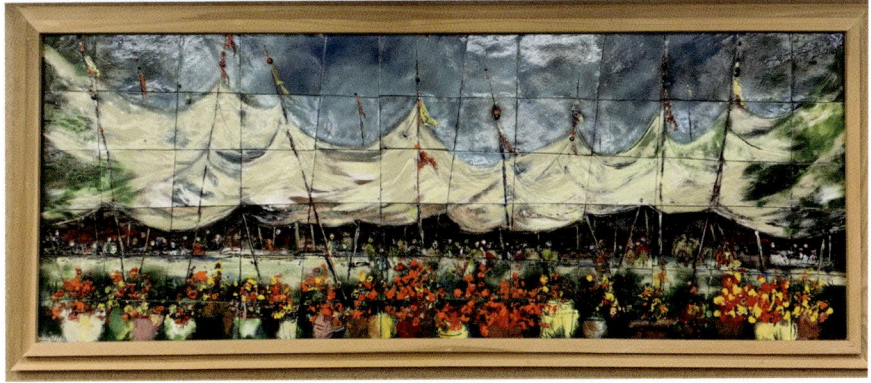

Figure 2.14. Emilio Caballero, *Flower Market*, unknown date, enamel on copper, University Public Art Collection, Texas Tech University, Texas Tech University Health Sciences Center, Amarillo, Texas. (Photo by author. With permission from the Emilio Caballero family.)

together an exhibition of these works in 2017 in our university art gallery, which I co-curated.[99] Most of the pieces are representational landscapes having very little in common with any of the more abstracted Canyon Suite paintings (figs. 2.18 and 2.19). But what stands out for me is the noticeable rough texture of their paper grounds (figs. 2.20 and 2.21), which converse with the similarly rough texture of several Canyon Suite paintings, such as *Autumn on the Plains, Train Coming In, Purple Mountains, Abstraction, Sunset* (fig. 2.4), and *Abstraction*, in both versions.

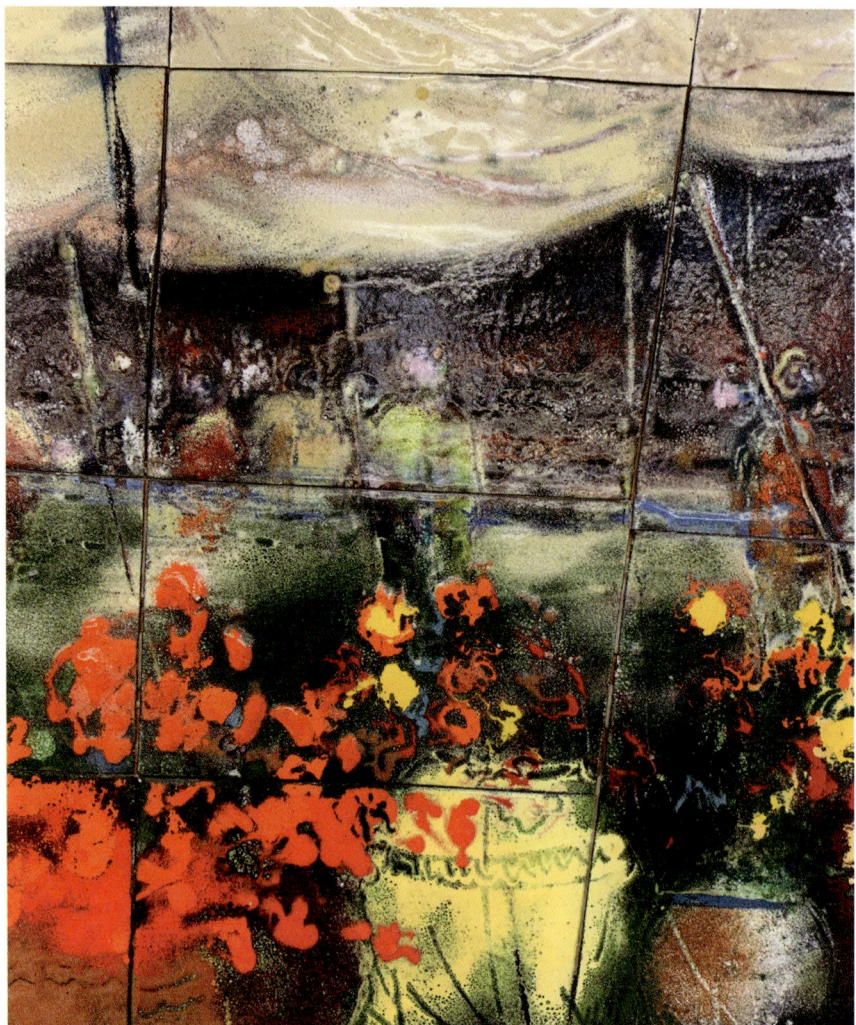

Figure 2.15. Emilio Caballero, *Flower Market*, detail.

Emilio Caballero, along with Terry Lee Caballero, was directly involved in the sale of the Canyon Suite to Peters. The sales contract drawn up on May 20, 1988, between Terry Lee Caballero and Peters specified that the former would provide a written provenance for the works, or, in other words, a declaration of how the watercolors made their way into her possession.[100] This provenance did not come from Terry Lee Caballero herself or describe any knowledge about her grandfather Ted Reid receiving gifts from O'Keeffe; it instead came from an affidavit written and signed by Emilio Caballero in June 1988. Caballero's statement declared that Reid in 1975 brought him a package "that would be of interest to [him] and

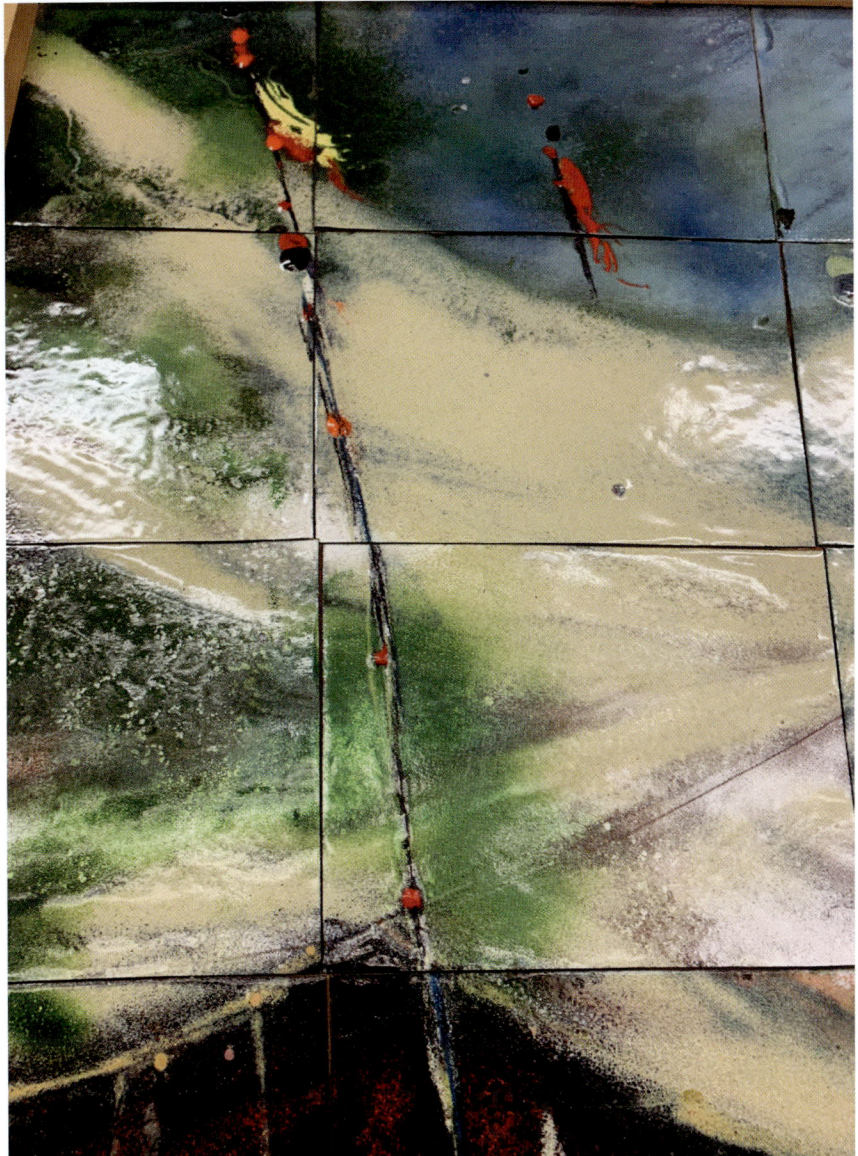

Figure 2.16. Emilio Caballero, *Flower Market*, detail.

that he wanted [Caballero] to have"—a gift that Caballero claimed never to have opened.[101] In a second version of his statement, this one quoted in a news article from 2000, Caballero changed his story slightly, claiming that Reid asked him to simply "hold" the package for him and not open it.[102] Caballero said that Reid "placed a carefully wrapped package in brown paper on his desk" and "asked if he might leave it with me until sometime at which it would be more convenient

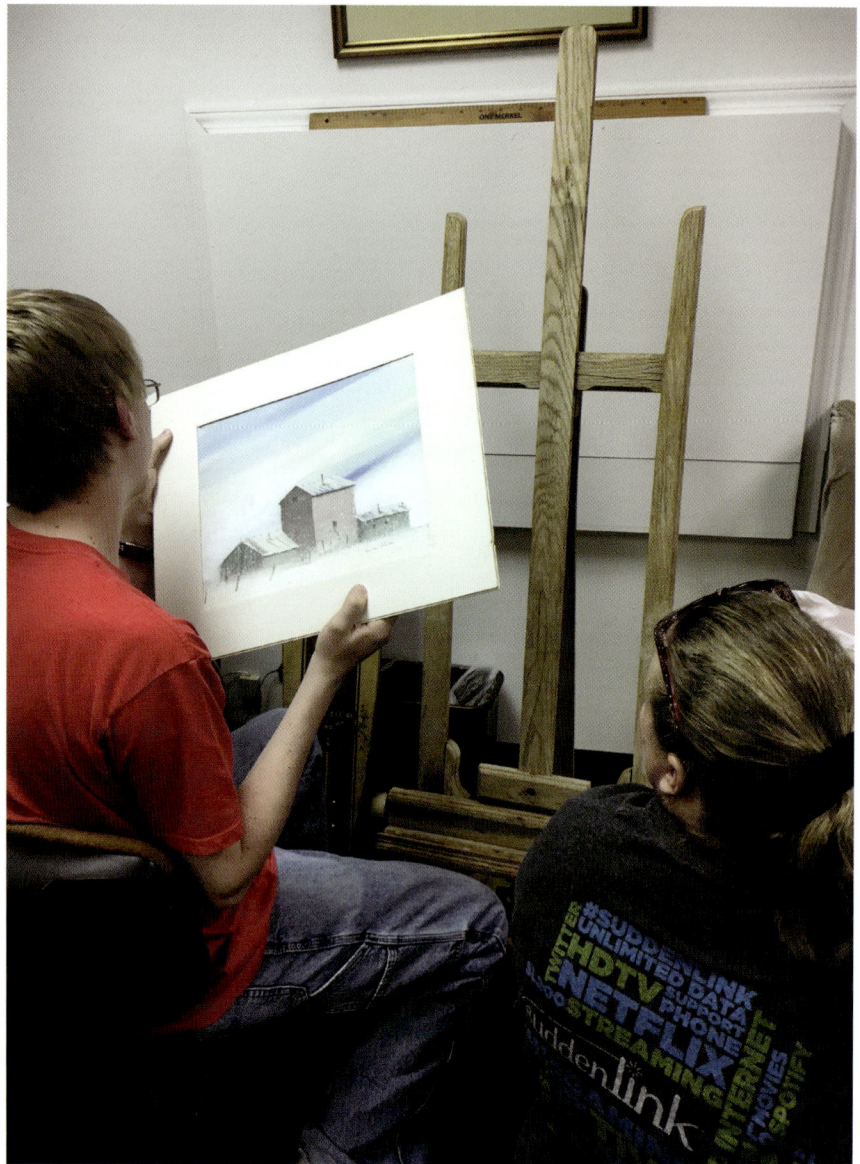

Figure 2.17. WT students examining works on paper by Emilio Caballero. (Photo by author. With permission from the Emilio Caballero family.)

for him to pick it up." He continued: "I took the package and put it in one of the cardboard boxes along with other personal items I had been moving from my office" and "eventually these boxes with Ted's package were taken home and stored in our garage." Caballero then explained that the package stayed at this location until his son and Terry Lee Caballero moved into the elder Caballero's former

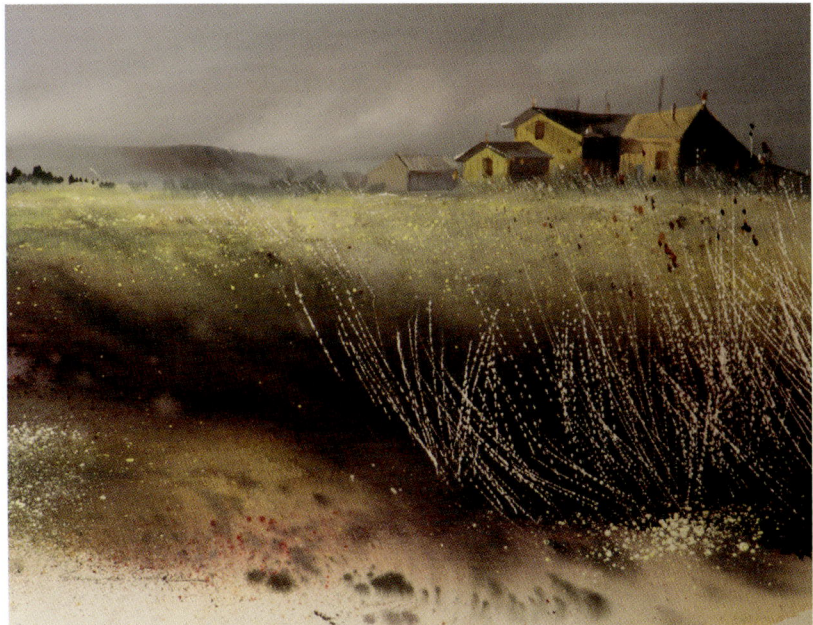

Figure 2.18. Emilio Caballero, *Untitled*, unknown date, oil on paper, 30 x 22 inches. University Collection, West Texas A&M University. (Photo by Rik Andersen. With permission from the Emilio Caballero family.)

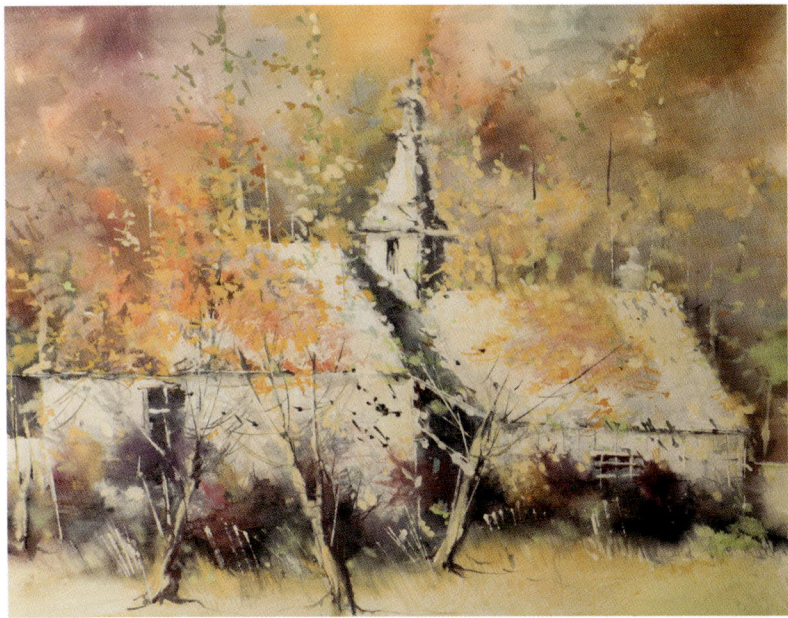

Figure 2.19. Emilio Caballero, *Untitled*, unknown date, oil on paper, 30 x 22 inches. University Collection, West Texas A&M University. (Photo by Rik Andersen. With permission from the Emilio Caballero Family.)

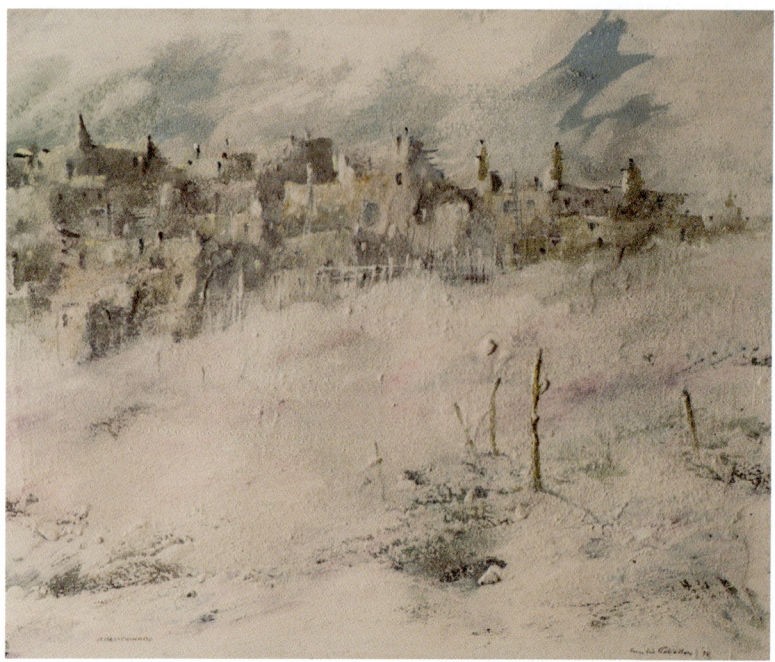

Figure 2.20. Emilio Caballero, *Untitled*, 1994, watercolor on paper, 30 x 24 inches. University Collection, West Texas A&M University. (Photo by Rik Andersen. With permission from the Emilio Caballero family.)

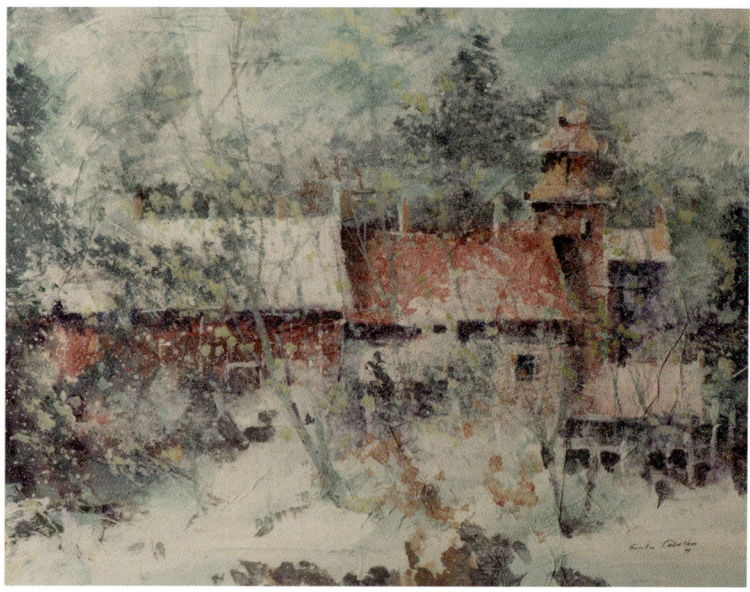

Figure 2.21. Emilio Caballero, *Untitled*, 1993, oil on paper, 32 x 30 inches. University Collection, West Texas A&M University. (Photo by Rik Andersen. With permission from the Emilio Caballero family.)

house. At that time, the Caballero family supposedly found the package, and Caballero felt "it was only logical and right that [he] give the package—which was never opened while in my possession—to Terry" as the granddaughter of Reid. In a notarized conveyance dated June 22, 1988, Caballero stated that he legally gifted the package to Terry Lee Caballero, relinquishing all his rights of ownership, and declared that he knew what was in the package: the twenty-nine watercolors, which he gave to his daughter-in-law for the remarkable price of $10.[103]

On September 16, 1988, a $640,000 check was issued to Terry Lee Caballero from the Peters Corporation for twenty-five works from the Canyon Suite.[104] By that date, the remaining four "option works" were added into the agreement, bought by Peters for the additional amount of $300,000, with the promise of closing the sale and transferring the money by May of the following year.[105] But first, we have a receipt dated September 22, 1988, drawn up by Caballero, showing that Terry Lee Caballero paid him $4,000 for "taxes and insurance."[106] This could be an innocent exchange of money between Caballero and his daughter-in law, helping him out with financial costs after he no longer had a job at WT. But the date of the exchange, the same year that Terry Lee Caballero came into all that money from selling the O'Keeffes allegedly inherited from her grandfather, seems suspicious. Also strange is the lack of any money gifted to any of Terry Lee Caballero's siblings or other members of the Reid family, a point that brought acute familial bitterness.[107]

In 1993, Caballero continued to try to sell another thirteen items he claimed were original O'Keeffes. In April of that year, he exchanged letters with Dion O'Wyatt of the John Adams Fund in New York—O'Wyatt calls Caballero by the familiar nickname "Milio."[108] O'Wyatt supplied Caballero with a copy of another letter he had sent to Lynes, the author of the O'Keeffe catalogue raisonné and leading scholar of the artist.[109] The letters discuss O'Wyatt "trying to deduce things" from Lynes about whether any of the works with a Caballero provenance would be included in the publication. O'Wyatt described how he promoted Caballero's expertise and "wealth of knowledge" to Lynes and how he tried to "trick her" into divulging information "using psychological slips." O'Wyatt tried to cajole Lynes into being sympathetic to Caballero's pieces. He acknowledged her contract commitment to not offer opinions about works of art except through the published catalogue raisonné founded on "fear of lawsuit" and promised several things if she would authenticate the Caballero works, including paying "her expenses."[110] Lynes was unswayed, as again none of these works entered the catalogue raisonné. According to the gallerist Owings in an interview with a reporter, "[The authors

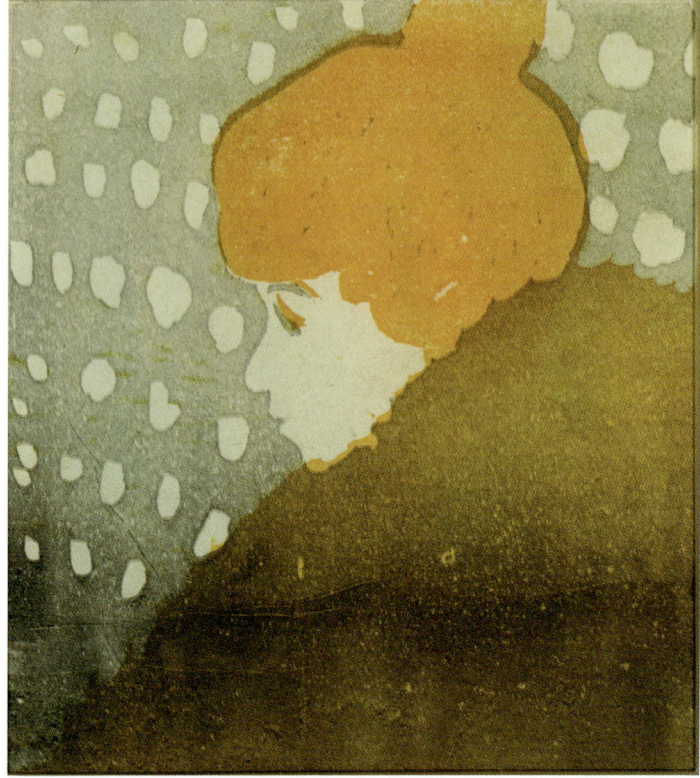

Figure 2.22. Georgia O'Keeffe, *Untitled (Portrait of Dorothy True)*, 1914–1915, linoleum block print, 7.375 x 6.75 inches. Private Collection. (© 2025 Georgia O'Keeffe Museum / Artists Rights Society (ARS), New York.)

of the raisonné] threw out the baby with the bath water. . . . They simply eliminated everything with a Caballero provenance."[111] And yet, given the evidence starting to stack up against the Canyon Suite, as the largest Caballero-connected cache of O'Keeffes, Lynes did not include any work that rigorous research and assessment determined not to be by O'Keeffe.

This exchange of letters involving O'Wyatt also shows that the Canyon Suite was not the single, idiosyncratic "lark" that Terry Lee Caballero claimed it to be in the press. Rather, Caballero and his family had been trying to sell anything and everything they could claim to be "O'Keeffes" since the 1960s. And among the unauthenticated works left out of the raisonné, twenty-nine of these were the Canyon Suite, plus all but one of the many others offered by Caballero. In other words, Caballero alone provided the largest number of unauthenticated O'Keeffes coming from one source.[112] Only one work ever sold by Caballero, the monoprint *Untitled (Portrait of Dorothy True)*, made it into the catalogue raisonné (fig.

2.22).[113] But Emilio Caballero and Terry Lee Caballero both repeatedly claimed they never directly represented their works for sale as O'Keeffes. As Terry said, "We did it as a lark. We just found these watercolors in a box in my father-in-law's garage when we were helping him move. And we were astonished because they looked so much like O'Keeffe. We never said they were by O'Keeffe. . . . They were nothing but pieces of paper until Juan Hamilton [O'Keeffe's assistant and heir] said they were [by O'Keeffe]. I knew how these things worked—I used to be an antiques dealer. But we weren't trying to deceive anyone."[114] But the contract Terry Lee Caballero signed for Peters declared that she believed "in good faith" the works were by O'Keeffe even before Hamilton had authenticated them.[115]

Ted Reid's son, J. W. Reid, gave a telling statement to the press in 2001 regarding his suspicions about Terry Lee Caballero's story. "I don't believe that story [of Caballero's] one bit," he said. "If [my dad] had that many works by O'Keeffe, he would have left them to his children. Or he would have given at least one of them to the school."[116] The younger Reid also questions why his father would have bothered to travel to Abiquiu with WT administrators in 1977 to request a painting donation from O'Keeffe if he already possessed one, let alone twenty-nine, which he could have just gifted to the school. He states, "I'm sure if my dad had any of those paintings then he would have given one to the college."[117] Caballero's successor as head of the Art Department, Steve Mayes, recalled in a 2001 interview that he had talked with Reid sometime between 1975 and 1983 (the year of Reid's death) about "a plan to create an O'Keeffe museum at West Texas" and that "he [Mayes] had lined up a commitment from a Texas foundation for $1 million if only a dozen works could be secured."[118] Again, had Reid actually been in possession of those O'Keeffe watercolors, he surely would have shared them in the context of these museum plans. And add to this the fact that O'Keeffe in 1917 only *almost* gifted Reid a single photograph, but in the end, she could not part with it, even for Reid. It was an image of her taken by Stieglitz in April 1917 when she returned to New York to see her first solo show at Gallery 291. O'Keeffe wrote: "I showed my face and hands to Ted this afternoon," referring to the photographs by Stieglitz. She continued: "He liked the smiling one because he likes me to laugh—likes me to have a good time, as he puts it—Finally liked the smile best—I almost gave it to him—Showing them to him was lots of fun."[119] According to her letters, O'Keeffe only briefly considered giving Reid an art gift, but decided against it. It is hard to believe that she would have casually gifted him so many of her watercolors in that same 1917 moment and that she would not have written about it.

By the time Minton donated the Reid Family Papers to WT in 2016, everyone directly involved in the Canyon Suite discovery and sale from her family—Caballero, Terry Lee Caballero, and her husband C. T. Caballero—had passed away, and Minton was trying to make sense of her family's complicated legacy. She admitted to me that she was confused about the whole affair, not knowing whom to trust. Both Minton and J. W. Reid have pointed out their surprise that Terry Lee Caballero did not share her $1.25 million with either of them, but rather kept it all to herself, sharing it only with her husband and likely his father—remember the $4,000 "taxes and insurance" money she gave him after she received her seller's check from Peters.[120]

This all demonstrates that if Ted Reid had more than two dozen priceless treasures created by his longtime friend and former girlfriend, he would not have wrapped them in brown paper and handed them over to Emilio Caballero. He would have lovingly preserved them in his family papers, as he did her letters, and likely gifted them to WT, as his granddaughter did years later. And if Caballero, with his obsessive interest in O'Keeffe, had received such a gift from a former boyfriend of O'Keeffe, he most certainly wouldn't have waited a whole decade to take a peek! But Caballero's answer to this was "I am a gentleman. I would never open anyone's package they had left with me for safekeeping."[121] Caballero was continually declaring the worth of his gentlemanly honor.[122] But the only evidence we have that Caballero and Reid were even friends, let alone close friends, is Caballero's own claims that the two "had long discussions about art over the many years" and got to know each other well when Reid was teaching aviation at WT.[123]

A THEORY OF FORGERY

Comparing Caballero to other known art forgers, we might draw some psychological parallels. The 2013 exhibition *Intent to Deceive: Fakes and Forgeries in the Art World* included "profiles" of five of the best-known twentieth-century forgers.[124] The commonalities of their profiles include a lack of institutional and art-world recognition as well as a resulting delight in duping those very institutions that overlooked their worth.[125] Caballero had a devoted regional following, but he remained entirely unknown beyond the Panhandle; he failed to garner the national acclaim of O'Keeffe. Moreover, Caballero must have felt acute disappointment when his attempts to publish his biography on O'Keeffe were dismissed and when the items he was selling as authentic O'Keeffes were rejected. Perhaps this lack of attention and these dismissals pushed him to desire revenge on the art world. If he did produce a set of O'Keeffes that fooled the leading O'Keeffe experts, he likely took a great deal of joy in his work being mistaken as hers.[126] As the *Intent to Deceive* exhibition argued, the "reality of art collecting is that relatively few artists are celebrated as masters, producing a strong incentive for forgers to duplicate famous works and to foist their copies as originals."[127]

Caballero longed to connect himself to O'Keeffe, and what better way to share in her recognition and fame than to duplicate her works and pass them off as authentic? The forgers highlighted in *Intent to Deceive* all displayed talent, charm, and audacity—qualities that Caballero possessed. According to Colette Loll, the curator of the exhibition, "Even though profit and greed are often assumed to be the underlying motive for forgery, the psychological underpinning of these grand deceptions is actually far more complex than a simple scheme for financial gain."[128] Moreover, according to William Casement, author of *The Many Faces of Art Forgery*, many forgers claim to have "an unusual connection with the artist being copied," whether that connection is based on spiritual and even "magical" relations or diligent study.[129] Caballero, according to local witnesses, saw his unique appreciation of O'Keeffe as founded in both of these bases; not only did he claim to have an "astral" connection to her, but he also apparently committed himself to studying her life and work.[130] To be sure, many forgers have believed in the authenticity of their "unusual connection" to the artists they are copying, making their imitations less fraudulent and more grounded in an honest, if self-constructed, belief system. Like a talented actor playing a role, they gain a special access that "allows them to 'be' another artist in a sense, to delve inside the other artist's works and way of fashioning them rather than merely observe from the outside."[131] We may never know if Caballero was a forger of O'Keeffe's art. But it is worth exploring this possibility to help us understand how forgeries unfold and what they reveal about the art world.

After the inauthenticity of the Canyon Suite was disclosed in 1999, another person claimed authorship of three of the watercolors and co-authorship with O'Keeffe on thirteen others: Jacobo Suazo. O'Keeffe had "fostered" and mentored Suazo in New Mexico in the 1940s and '50s.[132] Suazo had seen the Canyon Suite images reproduced in the press and said he recognized the works as his own. Having lived and studied with O'Keeffe, Suazo could well have produced copies of her early works in his own less-accomplished hand, especially given his access to the originals that O'Keeffe kept in her personal collection. But how would those works then make their way to the Panhandle of Texas? Again, the story just doesn't add up.

The Canyon Suite works were discovered, and therefore likely produced, in Canyon. Are they best described as fakes, forgeries, copies, or honest homages to

O'Keeffe?[133] The semantics of what we should call them, I argue, matter less than what we can learn from these objects and their story. We discover just how powerful O'Keeffe's presence has been and still is in West Texas—a place with few such claims to artistic fame, so the ones that do exist become hyperbolically significant, fetishized, monumental. A fetish is an overvalued object—a sexual, commercial, spiritual, or beautiful object, for instance.[134] Advertising commonly employs the power of the fetish, creating an elevated level of desire around an object, convincing viewers of its necessity and power.[135] According to Anne McClintock, the fetish is above all "an impassioned object."[136] A work of art is often fetishized because it is valued above and beyond its material components—valued for its relations to a beloved or "genius" artist, for its extreme rarity, or for its unique power to inspire. And once an art object is shown to be fraudulent or fake, that overvaluation of the fetish implodes and the object becomes suddenly worthless, meaningless. Art value fluctuates between overvaluation and undervaluation, fetishization and rejection. Nothing proves this more than when the works of art forgers such as Elmyr de Hory or Pei-Shen Qian themselves become fetish objects, desirable and collectible because of their new fame as once-successful fakes.[137] In the case of de Hory, for instance, there is a known market of "fake fakes" of his art—objects that some second forger has made and signed with the now famous name "Elmyr" to profit off the forger's fascinating story.[138] The art market therefore powers itself on desire and the risky but lucrative investment in fame and the claim of authenticity.[139]

O'Keeffe only lived in the Panhandle region for around thirty-seven months on and off, between 1912 and 1918—in other words, a little more than three years of her near-century-long life. But her legacy looms so large in the region that people have become obsessed with knowing about her, feeling close to her, becoming experts on her. Perhaps I should include myself in this group of West Texas O'Keeffe devotees. But what is needed for characterizing and furthering this important legacy is a basis in evidence in the archives and O'Keeffe's own words about herself. O'Keeffe should not have to bear the burden of forgers and copyists, but addressing the issue of the Canyon Suite, as I have done here, contributes to the history of art and illuminates new aspects of O'Keeffe's legacy, especially her complex connection to the Texas Panhandle.

CHAPTER 3

A FRANK LLOYD WRIGHT HOUSE FOR AMARILLO

Amarillo, Texas, has never been known as an architectural treasure trove. But looking with new eyes, we can discover that in its 130-plus years of existence, Amarillo boasts many architectural structures worthy of study. One of the most important, but least known either locally or nationally, is the Dorothy Ann and Sterling Kinney House designed by Frank Lloyd Wright in 1957 (fig. 3.1).[1] As a still privately owned residence built late in Wright's career, the Kinney House has been largely off the radar of Wright scholars, fans, and appreciators.[2] This chapter offers the first close art-historical reading of the home as a unique and impressive example of Wright's evolving style. But perhaps more importantly, it allows us to appreciate how a mainstream modernist architect like Wright can be looked at with fresh eyes when we take into account the specificity with which he worked in out-of-the-way places like the Texas Panhandle.

The Kinney House was one of Wright's Usonian designs, and one of only three Wright houses built in Texas.[3] The origin of this term "Usonian" is a bit of a mystery, but scholars believe Wright embraced it in reference to a "reformed American society," with the "U-S" referencing "United States," as opposed to

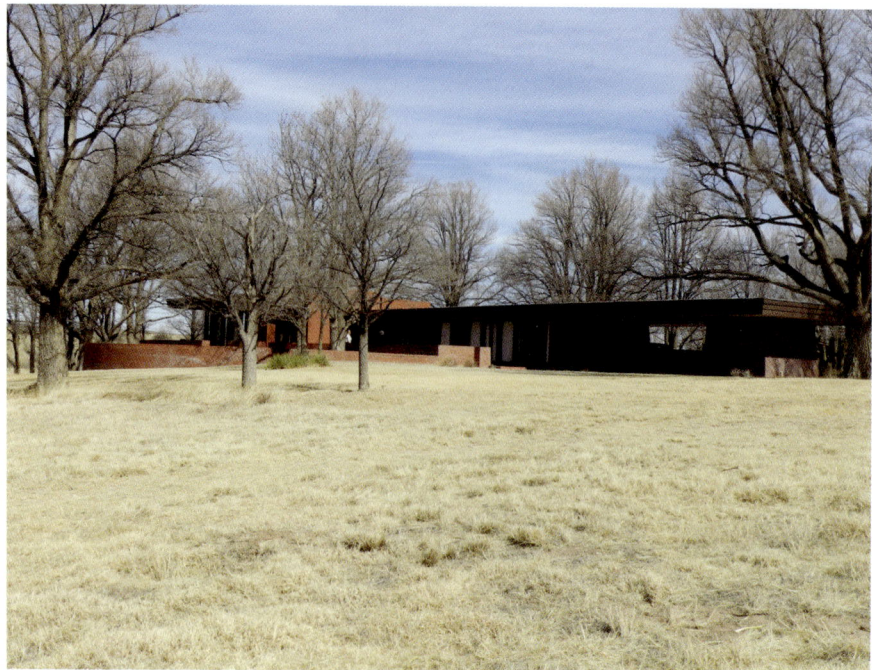

Figure 3.1. Frank Lloyd Wright, Dorothy Ann and Sterling Kinney House, Amarillo, Texas, 1957–61. (Photo by author.)

"American" which includes the Americas more broadly.[4] The construction of the Kinney House was completed in 1961 after the architect's death in 1959.[5] Wright was ninety years old at the time of its design, but the architect worked until the day he passed away with an "astonishing creativity" that belied any obvious old-age decline.[6] Wright's Usonian homes were originally meant to offer well-designed single-family dwellings on an affordable budget, around $5,500. But among the dozens of Usonians constructed between 1937 and 1959, including the Kinney residence, most exceeded this price tag.[7] The Usonians share numerous elements that define them as a genre of Wright's homes, all of which can be seen in the Kinney House. They generally have one story; a flat roof; a cantilevered carport (figs. 3.2 and 3.3)—apparently Wright coined this very term—built-in furniture; tall casement windows that soften the barrier between interior and exterior spaces (fig. 3.4); a central hearth (fig. 3.5); underfloor heating systems that eliminate ducts and radiators; a lack of an attic or basement; a foundation of a lightweight concrete slab; an open plan between living room, dining room, and kitchen; a lack of spaces for servants; and patios instead of porches.[8] As John Sergeant writes, "The relationships of the house mass to the carport and terrace, of the living areas to the central kitchen and bedroom wing, remained remarkably

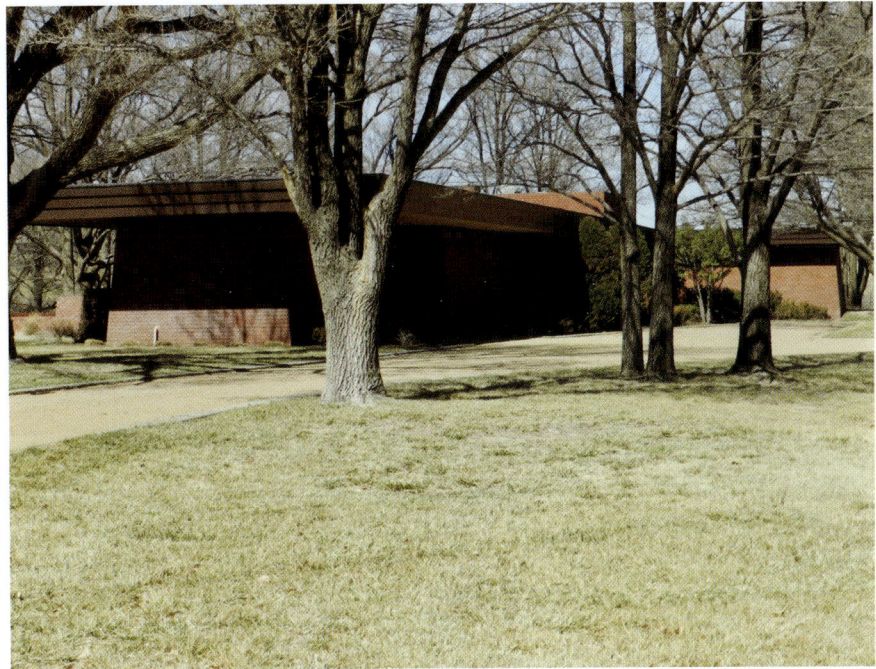

Figure 3.2. Kinney House, view of carport side of house. (Photo by author.)

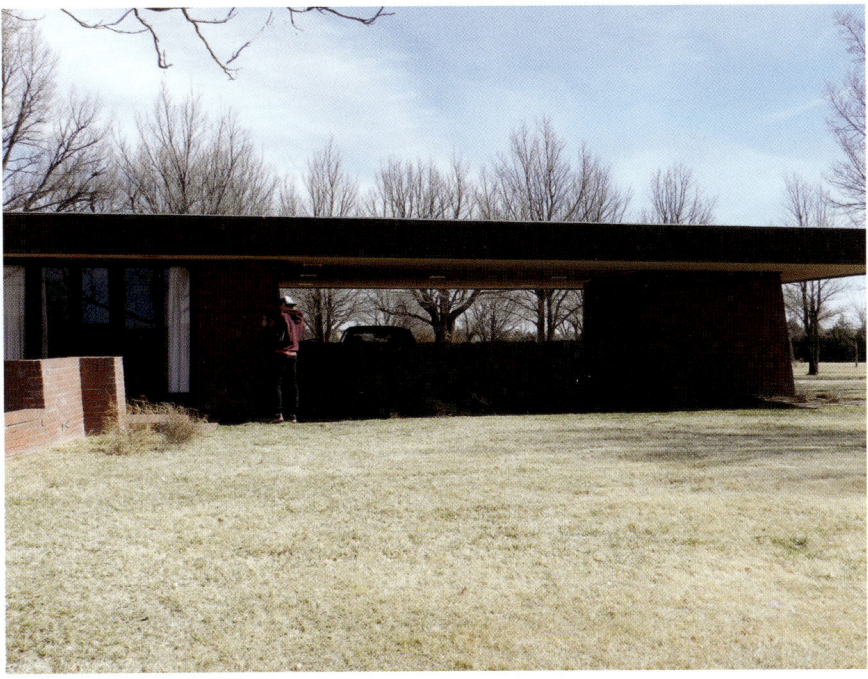

Figure 3.3. Kinney House, view of carport from rear. (Photo by author.)

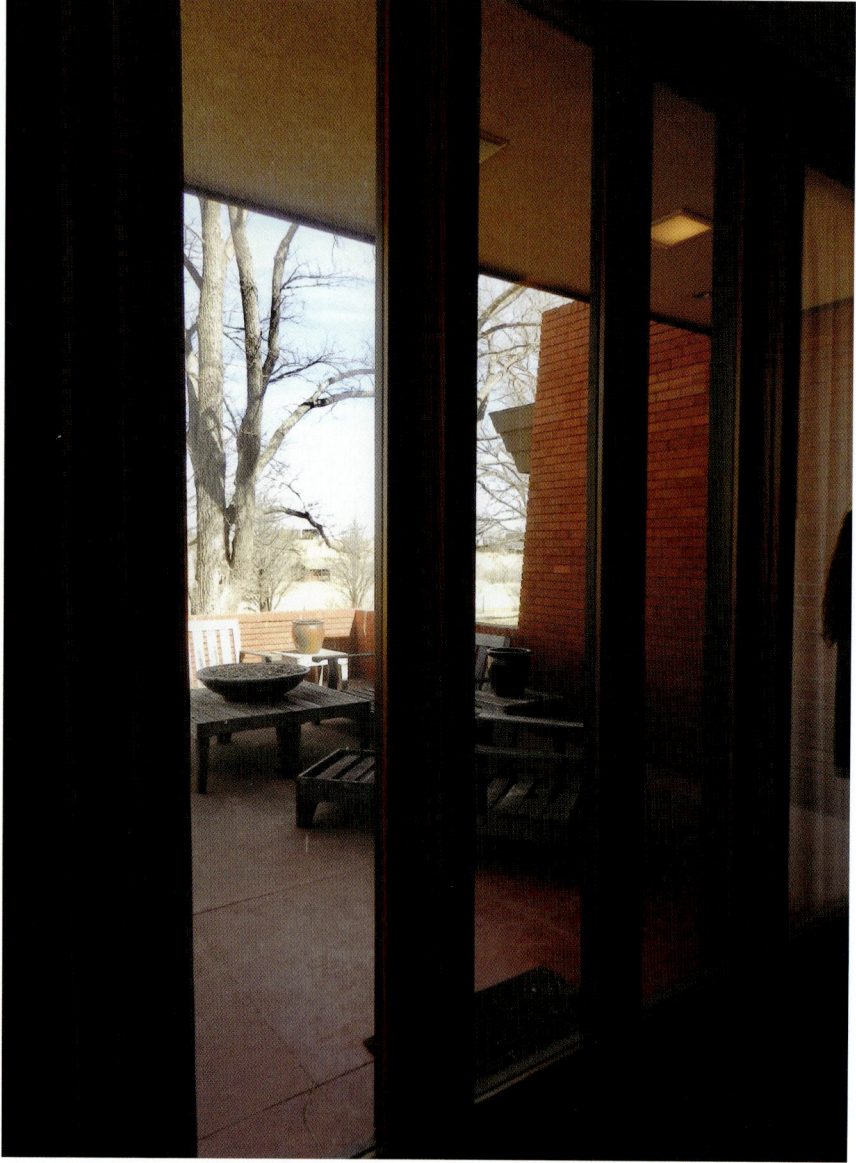

Figure 3.4. Kinney House, casement windows in living room, looking out onto patio. (Photo by author.)

constant" in the Usonian houses; and yet, the homes were also highly "varied to suit differing sites and clients." Sergeant continues: "Each house was different, yet each one used what Wright called the same 'grammar.'"[9]

The first Usonian home, the Herbert Jacobs House in Madison, Wisconsin, built in 1937, embraced a new kind of family dynamic in its design: "Mrs. Jacobs, by

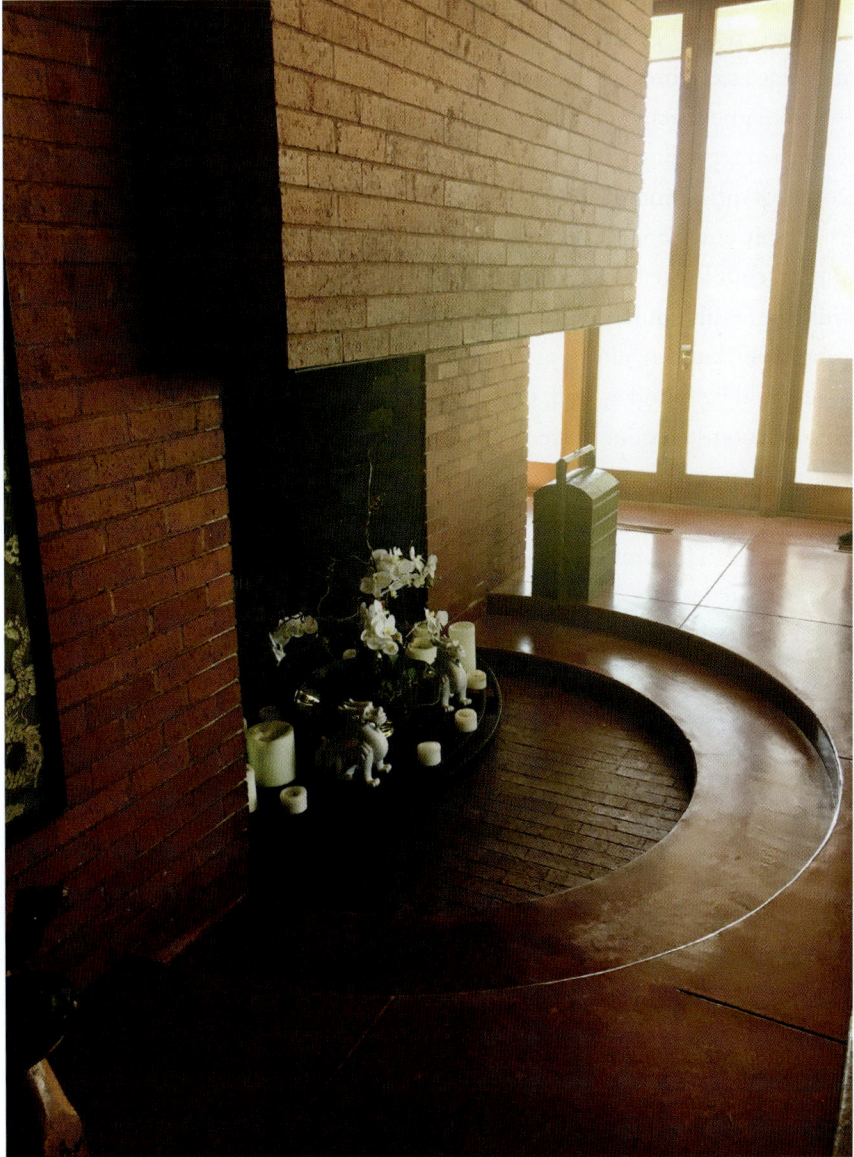

Figure 3.5. Kinney House, hearth. (Photo by author.)

contrast with earlier hostesses, was comparatively emancipated. From her kitchen (which Wright soon began to call the workplace [or 'work-space']), she could watch the children on the terrace, bring food to the table almost without moving, and join in conversation with the guests. This centralized position contrasts with the Prairie house kitchen, located in a corner of the house for the use of a servant or 'hired girl.'"[10] Though built two decades later than the Jacobs House, the Kinney

House continued this presumption of modern gender roles and family use, with its open concept between the kitchen, the small dining area, the living room, and the terrace seen through tall windows.

Usonian clients, including the Kinneys, tended to be more progressive and egalitarian regarding gender, with the wife often being an "efficient careerist."[11] Dorothy Ann Kinney had a law degree and was a practicing attorney in Amarillo. As Wright envisioned, the woman living in a Usonian home, including Mrs. Kinney, could take fewer steps and save their labor when managing the home, while the family could feel more togetherness sharing the flowing spaces between living room, kitchen, dining area, and patio. At the same time, areas of privacy and quiet could be found as well, in the separate bedroom wing, while the slab floor reduced room-to-room noise.[12] The Usonian homes did away with the formal, separated dining room of the earlier Prairie houses, as homelife and entertaining both became more informal in the United States around the middle of the twentieth century.[13] The Kinneys also fit the profile of Wright's Usonian buyers in being both educated professionals and active in the community.[14]

Like many of Wright's Usonian homes, the Kinney House is located not in the urban heart of Amarillo but rather on the fringes of the small city, northwest of downtown, where the streets begin to feel like country roads as they wind between short mesas, shallow creeks, and craggy canyons. Set back from the paved roadway, the home is located down a curving gravel-covered dead-end street, announced with a low stone gateway that opens onto a long driveway leading to the circle drive and the carport. As architectural historian Robert C. Twombly describes, the Usonian homes of Wright's design were "often in the country, on the edge of small cities, or in large, wooded lots, taking advantage of irregular and spectacular sites—hillsides, inclines, or lake shores."[15] Though Twombly does not discuss or even mention the Kinney House, its site fits his description.

The flat roof of the Kinney House contrasts with Wright's more famous Prairie Style developed in the early twentieth century (1901–1914) in gems like the Robie House in Chicago (1907). The Prairie Style homes had roofs with a shallow pitch that were hipped, not flat, and the house structures embraced a horizontal emphasis that mimicked the wide-open spaces of the American prairie.[16] In fact, however, the majority of Wright's Prairie houses were built on forested sites, rather than on the open prairie.[17] As both Thomas H. Beeby and Larzer Ziff argue, "prairie" was as much a mythical concept for Wright as it was a reference to a specific geographic climate or region, a "wild space awaiting a social life."[18] It drew upon nostalgic memories of Wright's childhood in rural Wisconsin but also spoke to the expectations of American Manifest Destiny and the "conquering" or "taming" of the Western frontier.[19] The horizontality of the Prairie houses suggests the spread of safety and shelter for US citizens across Middle America—at the expense, of course, of other people's safety and shelter[20]—even more perhaps than functioning as a mirror of the natural sites where they were built. The Prairie homes were also stacked vertically in ways that fit well into the rolling hills of the more humid portions of the Midwest, where tall trees grow in dense groves. "While firmly and obviously rooted to site," Twombly writes, "[the Prairie houses] also reach into space."[21]

A comparison between Wright's traditional Prairie Style homes and the Kinney House offers not only a view of the evolution of Wright's aesthetic into a mid-century-modern mode but also a reflection of the differences between the landscapes of the Midwest and the High Plains of West Texas.[22] The Midwest, at least the Upper Midwest where Wright lived much of his life, is verdant and thickly peppered with tall, densely-leaved trees, which create shade but block out the open sky and any views of an unobstructed horizon.[23] The High Plains, in contrast, are arid, golden rather than green, and filled with rough-hewn mesas and canyons (fig. 3.6). They are largely treeless except for around creek draws where smaller but hardy trees like locusts, cottonwoods, and elms grow best.[24] The site of the Kinney House includes just such a creek curving through it, allowing for a small collection of trees to thrive. And beyond that creek, the space opens outward bordered in the distance by squat mesas. When Wright finalized his design (fig. 3.7)—and apparently it went through at least two versions for which there are extant drawings[25]—he responded directly to this landscape of plains, creek beds, smaller hardy trees, and mesas. And he did so in an effective and creative way, one that has been overlooked by Wright connoisseurs but which is never missed by visitors to the home. According to Twombly, "Wright claimed that each of his designs could be built only on one particular spot, meaning that its setting was an integral part of the overall conception."[26] This is certainly true for the Kinney House in its relationship to its site, even if it was not always true for all of Wright's designs.[27]

Of the few publications that mention the Kinney House, those that do exist unfailingly note Wright's unique choice of a fifteen-degree "batter."[28] This architectural term describes how a strategically selected set of the vertical features of the home—walls, edges of overhanging eaves, and cabinetry (see, for instance, figs. 3.6, 3.8, 3.9, 3.11–13)—are pitched at a fifteen-degree angle from the vertical, an interesting and lovely effect that makes the Kinney House a true masterwork of modern design. With this batter, Wright produced a subtle lean to the structure of

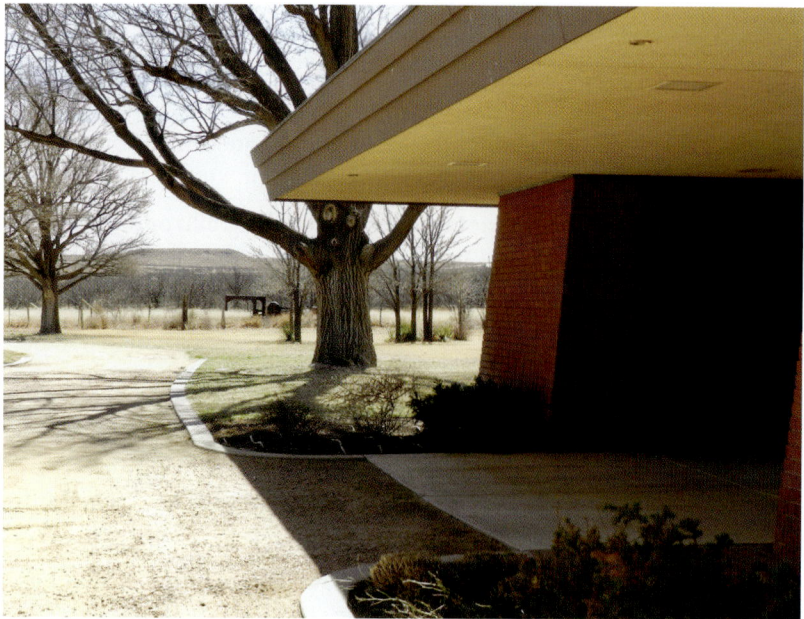

Figure 3.6. Kinney House, view of carport with batter and eave edge; trees and mesa in the distance. (Photo by author.)

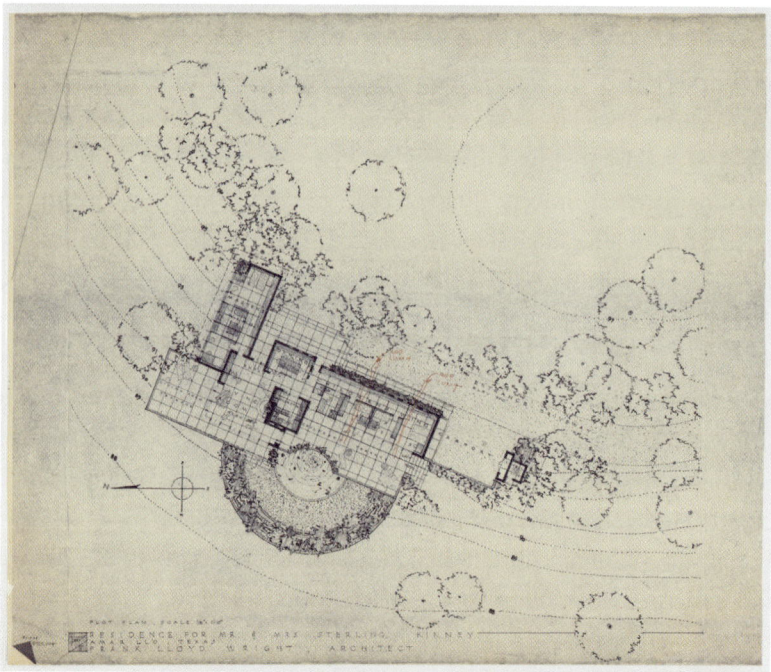

Figure 3.7. Frank Lloyd Wright, plan drawing for the Dorothy Ann and Sterling Kinney House, Amarillo. The Frank Lloyd Wright Foundation Archives. The Museum of Modern Art / Avery Architectural & Fine Arts Library, Columbia University, New York.

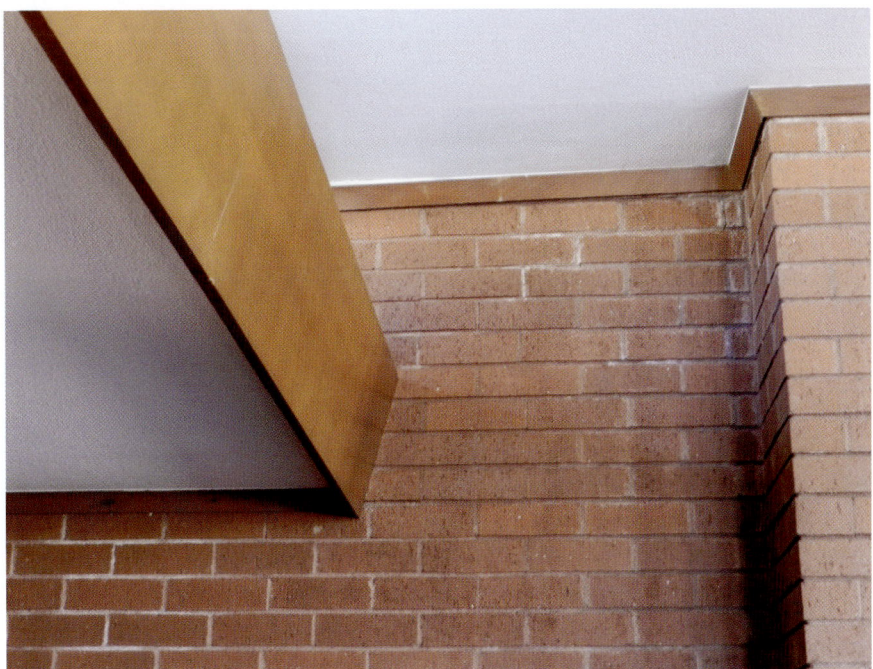

Figure 3.8. Kinney House, wood ceiling below clerestory in living room, showing batter. (Photo by author.)

the home that responds directly to its natural site, including the angles at which the shallow mesas rise in the distance (figs. 3.6 and 3.10) and the branches on those small trees, which jut out low from the trunk rather than high into the air like prairie trees (fig. 3.11). As Wright claimed, a good architect should be able to sketch trees "with their characteristics faithfully portrayed," showing their deep engagement with the shapes and forms of nature.[29] It appears that Wright paid close attention to those High Plains trees in Amarillo. An added dynamic to this play of angles in the home occurs when it shifts in directionality, as when the eave edges are leaning one direction from the vertical and the patio wall leans the other way (fig. 3.12).

According to Wright, "the integral character of extended vistas [is] gained by marrying buildings to ground levels, or blending them in with slopes and gardens; yes, it is in this new sense of earth as a great human good that we will move forward in the building of our new homes and great public buildings."[30] This philosophy plays out in the Kinney House design, where the structure is indeed married to the site, blended in with its particular elevation changes. Wright also believed that a house should respond to the natural patterns of its site and find an organization as if it were a "living being"; for Wright, nature was the only true guide of scale,

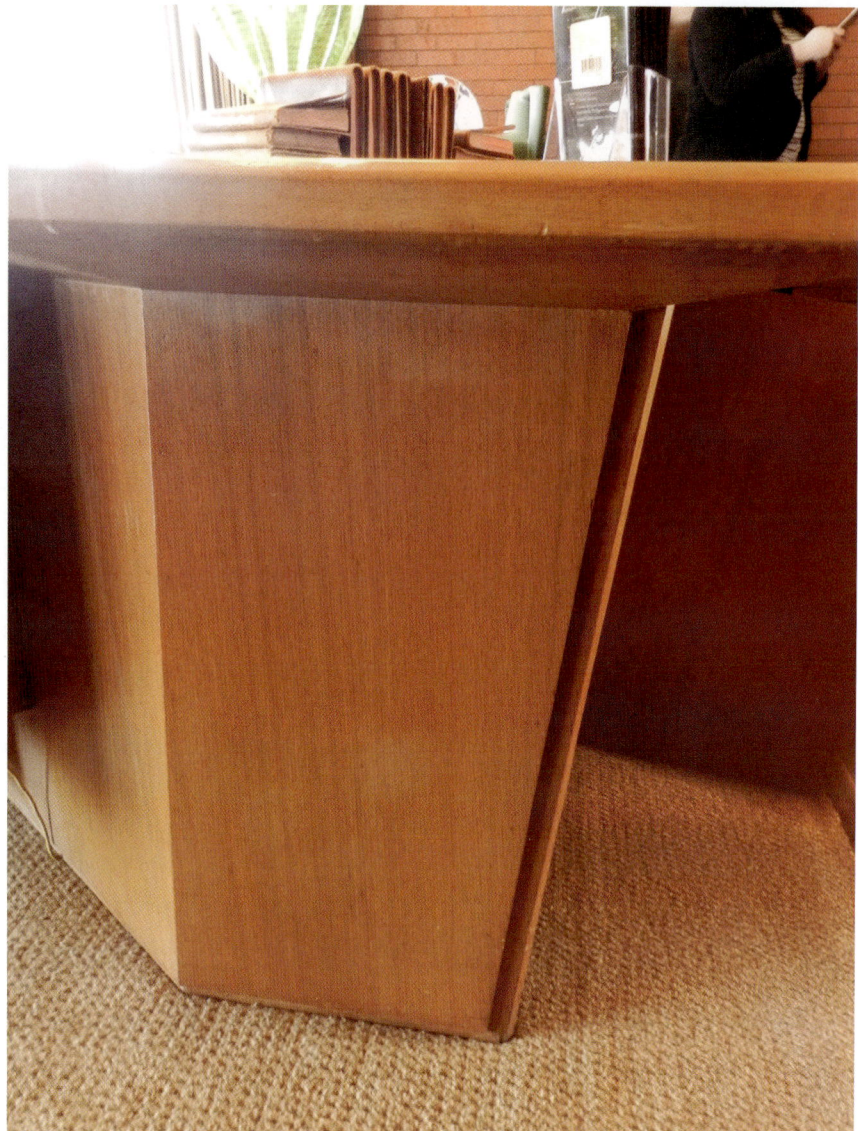

Figure 3.9. Kinney House, built-in furniture in living room. (Photo by author.)

proportions, and relations of parts to the whole, creating a "natural growth" in the construction that is quickly perceived by a person inhabiting it.[31] His theory of nature as a metaphor and guide plays out beautifully in the Kinney residence.

Wright used diagonals in other designs as well, especially in those set in the desert landscapes of the US West. For instance, his Death Valley project (1923–25), which was Wright's "first contact with the desert," resulted in the "application of

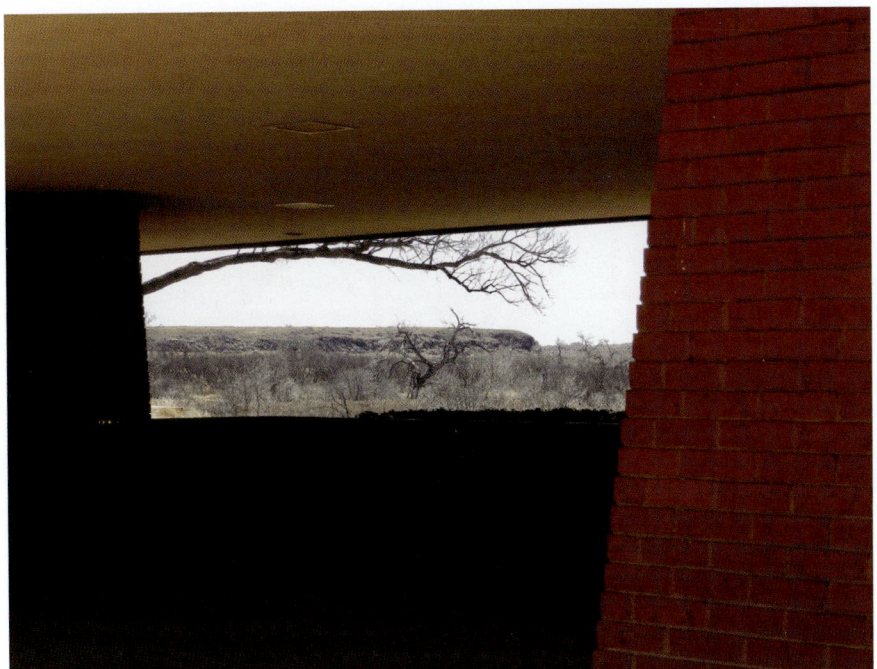

Figure 3.10. Kinney House, mesa in distance seen through carport opening. (Photo by author.)

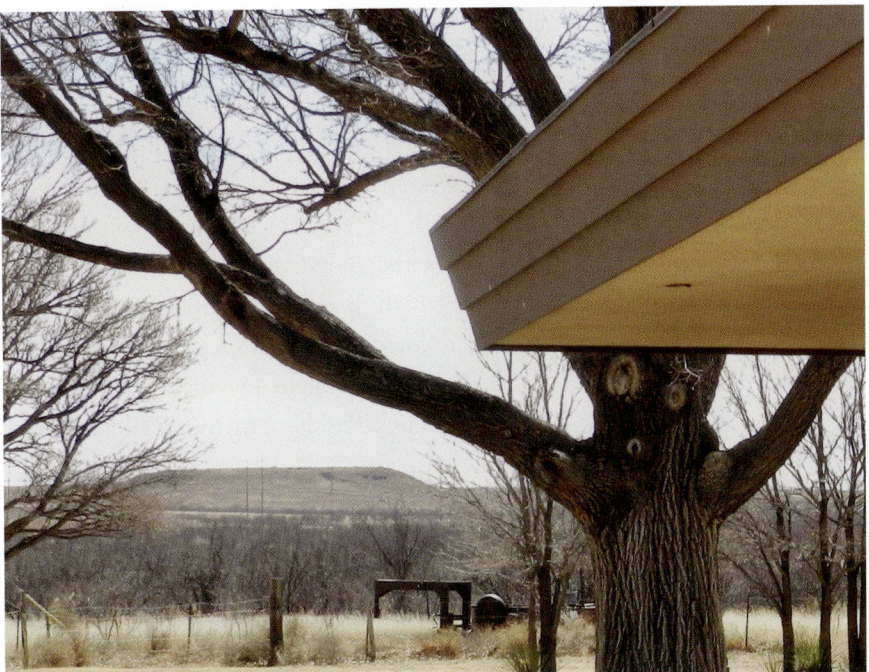

Figure 3.11. Kinney House, detail of tree branch angles with mesa in distance. (Photo by author.)

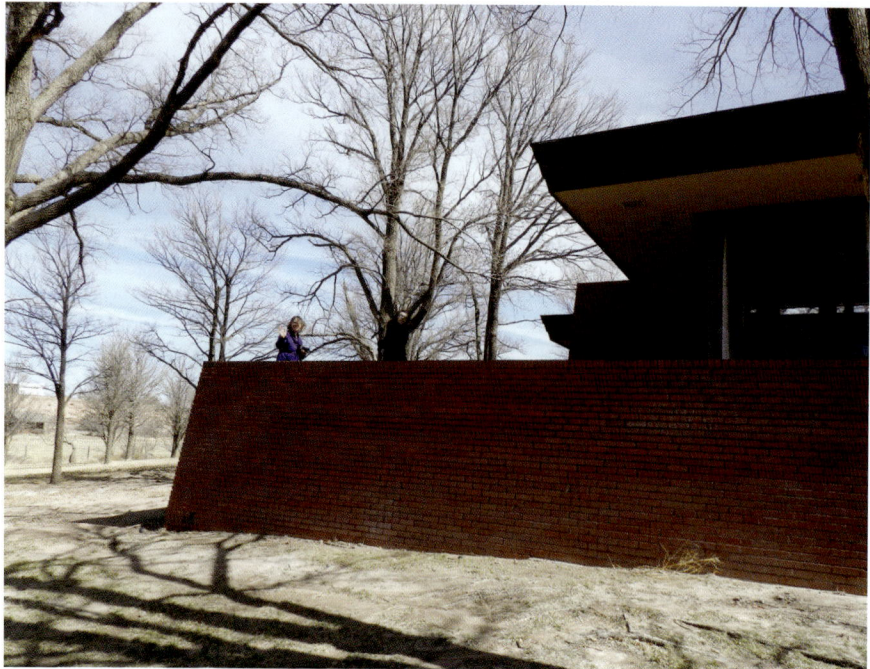

Figure 3.12. Kinney House, eave-edge angles contrasting with patio wall angle. (Photo by author.)

a diagonal axis to the overall scheme [that] allowed Wright to endow the continuous, low-lying forms of the connected structures with a sense of the ever-changing, imperceptibly shifting quality of the desert landscape itself."[32] Wright employed similarly dramatic diagonals in his designs for the Ocotillo camp compound near Phoenix (1929) and in Taliesin West in Scottsdale, Arizona.[33] These other examples of Wright's use of the diagonal, however, bring to light how specific the Kinney House diagonals are in Wright's design oeuvre. Unlike the more severe and dramatic diagonals inspired by the high desert landscapes of Death Valley and Scottsdale, the softer diagonals employed in Amarillo respond to the softer and subtle leans of the land of the High Plains. There, low mesas ease up from the horizon in contrast to the high mountains that shoot up more boldly vertical, more dynamically angled in the western deserts.

In addition to the leans keyed to the Amarillo landscape, Wright also added a soft stair-step design into many of these pitches in the Kinney House. For example, the cantilevered eave edges have three levels to them, creating the overall fifteen-degree angle but with a slight layered, stacked, and stepped aspect that also responds to the High Plains in a distinct and poetic way (figs. 3.11 and 3.13). Amarillo is set atop what is called the Llano Estacado, meaning "staked (or palisaded) plains," one

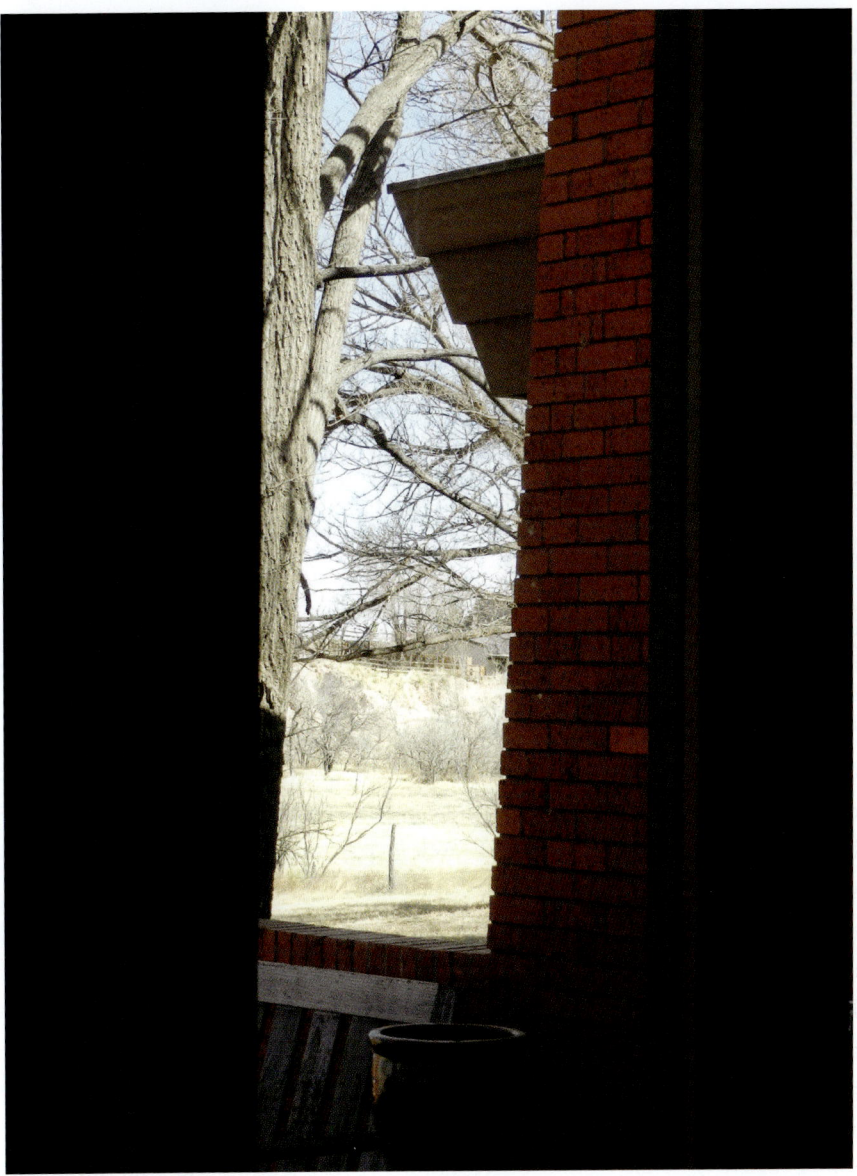

Figure 3.13. Kinney House, eave edge. (Photo by author.)

of the largest "tablelands" of the North American continent.[34] This broad sweep of high, flat, arid land sits on a layer of what is called the "caprock," which is not actually a rock layer in the traditional sense but a "'hard-pan' layer that developed a few feet below the ground as highly mineral subsoil particles cemented themselves together to form a rock-like layer that resists erosion."[35] Beneath the caprock runs the Ogallala Aquifer, a vast underground water reservoir that courses beneath the

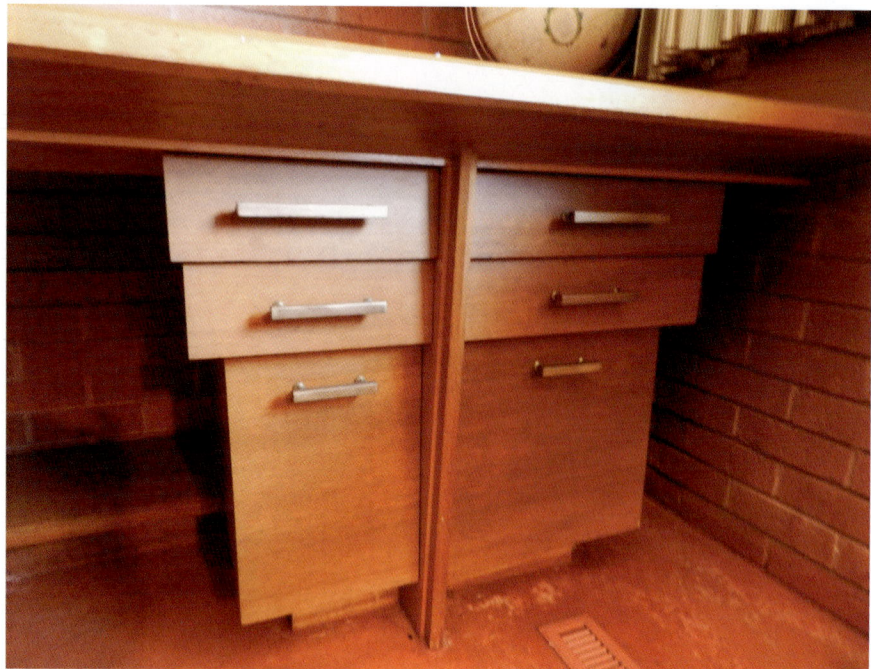

Figure 3.14. Kinney House, cabinet design. (Photo by author.)

plains of Middle America from Nebraska to West Texas.[36] In other words, the site of the Kinney House on the Llano Estacado is defined by this layering, which is captured creatively in the stacked and stair-step details of the home, including the highly original built-in cabinets (fig. 3.14).

Wright further played with this layered landscape in his window designs in the dining room and in a clerestory along the ceiling line of the main hallway (figs. 3.15 and 3.16). These windows are shaped by the brick masonry walls into an interesting orifice with a right angle on one side and a stair-step on the other. The patterned shapes of the dining room windows in the Kinney House are particularly prominent and central in the design because of the open floor plan, where the dining alcove is visible from the kitchen, living room, and patio. Are these stairs going up or down? Viewed from one direction, they descend as if inviting us to climb down into the nearby creek bed or to step down into an area canyon. In the Texas Panhandle, canyons often rip downward into the flat landscape like ditches or scars. When approaching the dramatic Palo Duro Canyon, for instance—second in size only to the Grand Canyon in Arizona, or at least that's what Panhandle residents claim—one sees flat plains for miles in every direction, and then suddenly the canyon appears beneath you, opening down into the earth.

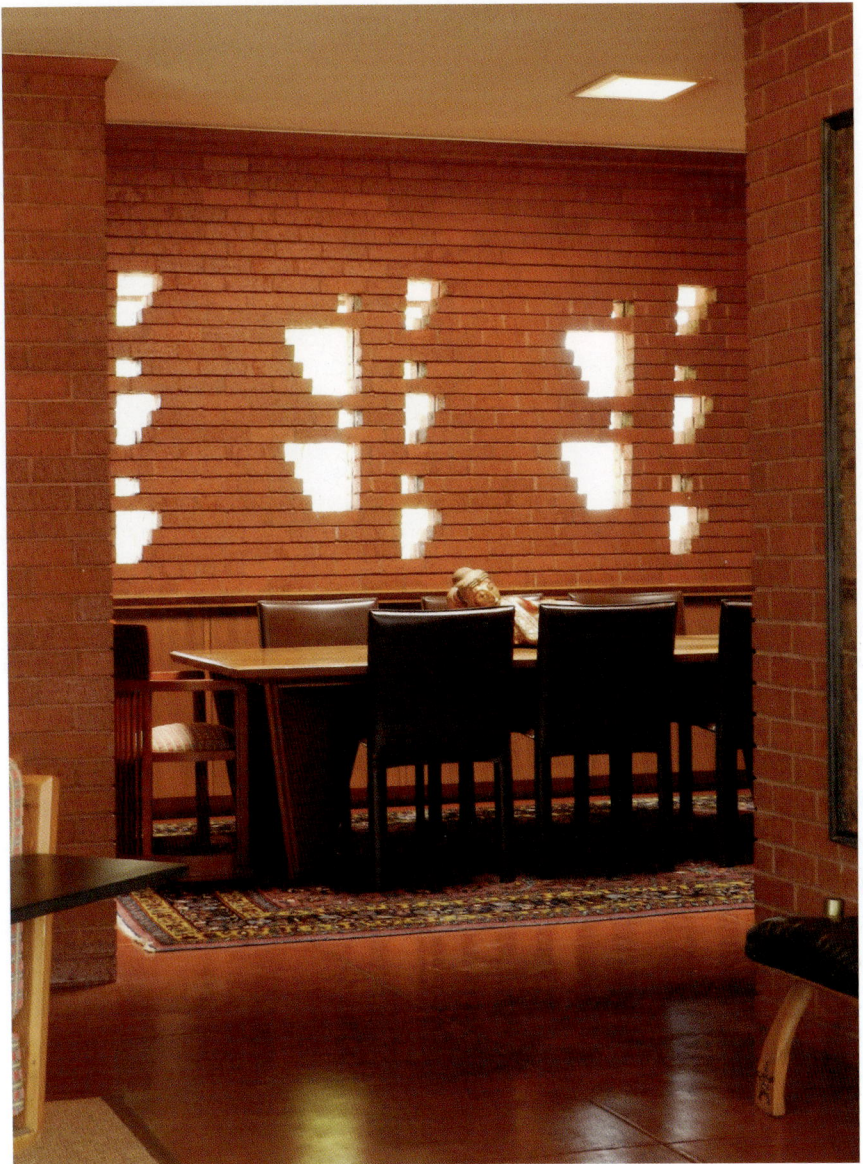

Figure 3.15. Kinney House, dining room with window design. (Photo by author.)

Viewed the other way, the warm red bricks forming the stair side of the windows offer an ascent, like a climb up the elevated mesas stacked and stepped at that same angle, and formed from the iron-rich, red-toned earth in a similar color.[37] To be sure, the Kinney House displays warm, reddish earth tones throughout its design, employing primarily medium-brown woods, mainly teak—a tropical rather than a local wood but one with the surface qualities and color that Wright preferred—as

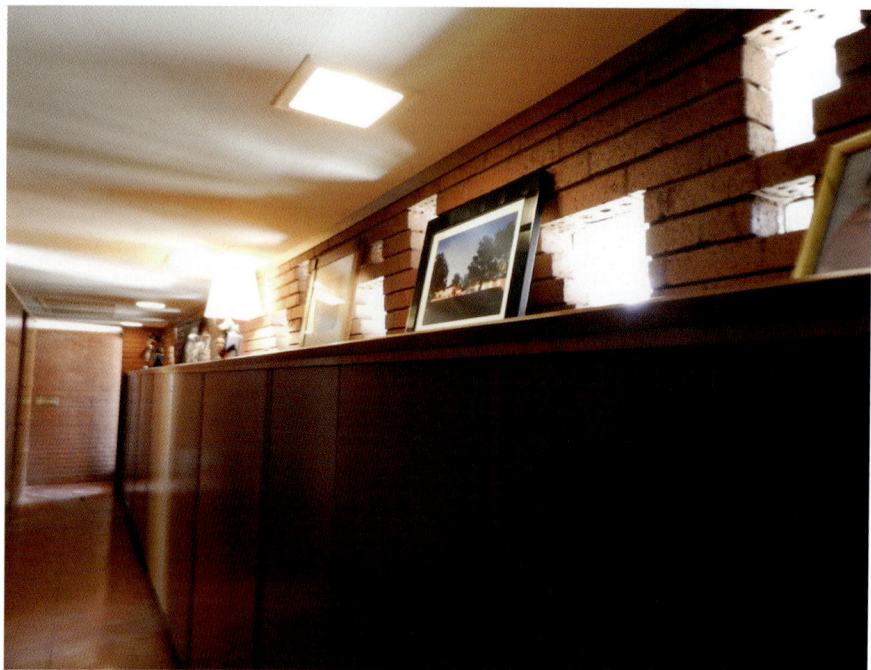

Figure 3.16. Kinney House, hallway clerestory with window design. (Photo by author.)

well as burnt-red bricks, hues that reflect the arid earth of the Llano Estacado and its canyonlands. Wright described how natural colors like the "soft, warm, optimistic tones of earths and autumn leaves" were preferable for him.[38] About brick, in particular, he wrote: "Make the walls of brick that the fire touched . . . choicest of all earth's hues. They will not rise rudely above the sod . . . but recognize the surface of the ground on which they stand, gently spreading there to a substantial base that makes the building seem more firm in its earth socket. Brick walls will carry with a profile of grace the protection of sheltering eaves."[39] This poetry in brick resonates vividly in the Kinney House.

At the same time, Wright's window designs for the Kinneys draw on motifs that had been popular since the Art Deco style swept through the United States in the 1920s and '30s. You can find the stepped pyramid motif on buildings across the country, including in New York City and Detroit, but especially in the Southwest, in cities such as Fort Worth and Albuquerque.[40] Wright's use of the stepped pyramid in the Kinney House, however, reflects more than just a generic modernist motif. I argue that it suggests aspects of the multicultural diversity of the Panhandle region and its connection to broader cultural traditions, including references to Mesoamerican, American Indian, Mexican, and early Euro-American aesthetics.

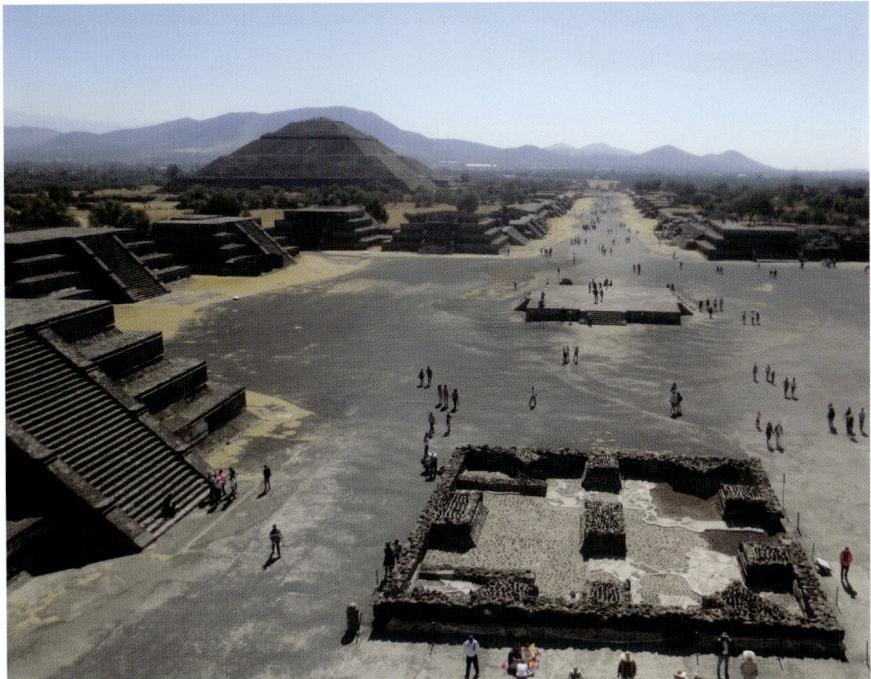

Figure 3.17. Pyramids at Teotihuacan, Mexico. (Photo by Jon Revett.)

With their stair-stepped sides, the window designs distinctly recall the stepped pyramids at Teotihuacan in what is now central Mexico, built between 1 and 500 CE (fig. 3.17). At that time, Teotihuacan was the largest city in Pre-Columbian America, and the design of the smaller pyramids surrounding the monumental Sun and Moon Pyramids, with their geometric stepped shapes, bears a striking resemblance to the windows at the Kinney House. Wright expressed his interest in Mesoamerican architecture in several writings, including his essay "A Testament," penned in 1957, the very year the Kinney House was designed. He wrote:

> I remember how as a boy, primitive American architecture—Toltec, Aztec, Mayan, Inca—stirred my wonder, excited my wishful admiration. I wished I might someday have money enough to go to Mexico, Guatemala, and Peru to join in excavating those long slumbering remains of lost cultures; mighty, primitive abstractions of man's nature—ancient arts of the Mayan, the Inca, the Toltec. Those great American abstractions were all earth-architectures: gigantic masses of masonry raised up on great stone-paved terrain, all planned as one mountain, one vast plateau lying there or made into the great mountain ranges themselves; those vast areas of paved earth walled in by stone construction. These were human

creations, cosmic as sun, moon, and stars! Nature? Yes, but the nature of the human being as he was then.[41]

The earthiness balanced with the spiritual transcendence that Wright saw in Mesoamerican forms comes through in the Kinney House windows.

Wright had drawn on Mayan and Aztec influences in earlier designs, especially in Los Angeles, including the Hollyhock House (1916) and the Charles Ennis House (1924). According to Neil Levine, the Hollyhock House was "built in the Hollywood section of Los Angeles at the first peak of excitement over that city's role in the motion picture industry," and its design "makes the house seem to be part of the [crown of Olive Hill], at once reinforcing the temple-like character of the precinct and calling to mind the ancient monuments of Mesoamerica and the Middle East."[42] Itself like an elaborate Hollywood stage set, the geometric details of the Hollyhock House seem both ancient and ultramodern in their lack of connection to any classical styles. Levine specifically and effectively compares the design of Hollyhock to the Mayan temples and palaces at Palenque, Uxmal, and Chichén Itzá, providing illustrations in his text for the reader to appreciate the direct influence from these Mesoamerican examples.[43] The Ennis House then similarly employed a pattern of rectangular cast-cement blocks that repeated a Mayan-inspired geometric design throughout the structure.[44] Even earlier, though, Wright had arguably drawn upon the Tlaloc mask form of Aztec origin for his Herman W. Winslow House in River Forest, Illinois, built in 1893; the geometric angled form of the mask seems to correspond to the façade design of the Winslow House, which somewhat strangely resembles rectangular eyes and an open maw like an Aztec deity.[45] But the Kinney House windows designed in 1957 seem a new iteration of Mesoamerican stylistic influence worth recognizing in Wright's oeuvre.

Another Panhandle aesthetic that Wright's windows, as well as the overall massing of the home's profile, both respond to—and one that has been largely erased from the landscape today—is that of the many adobe structures that stood in the vicinity of where the Kinney House was built. After the Civil War, in the mid-1870s, Hispanic sheepherders and their families started settling in an area near a convenient crossing of the Canadian River that became the town of Tascosa.[46] They built homes with adobe organized into plazas.[47] Like so many adobe structures throughout the US Southwest, these homes were geometric in their low-slung rectangularity while also softly organic given their earthen material molded into curves of natural dried-mud coloration. When two Anglo-American soldiers arrived in these plazas in 1874 during a hunting expedition, they apparently described them as sparkling like a "little city of diamonds and rubies in the morning sun."[48] To be sure, the terra-cotta walls of an adobe structure made from the iron-rich earth of the Canadian River Valley would have glowed red at sunrise and sunset.[49] The rusty red color of Wright's stair-stepped windows, along with their soft-edged rectangular shapes, seem to respond to this cultural and aesthetic history. But shortly after their arrival in the Texas Panhandle, the Hispanic settlers and their herds of sheep began to compete for the land with Anglo cattlemen who also wanted to graze their herds along the Canadian River and later set up ranches fenced with barbed wire.[50] By 1877, some 3,500 cattle had been brought to the area, and the first large-scale ranch, LIT, was established.[51] As these ranches were formed, the townsite of Tascosa expanded, adding such structures as blacksmith shops, saloons, hotels, and residences—all built in adobe.[52] Other settlers, including the German Jewish immigrant Ira Rinehart, who opened a general store in the town of Tascosa, built his family home in adobe, and still other adobe structures followed, including a school.[53] When the town was at its height of population, Mexican and Anglo families lived adjacent to one another and the space was dominated by a clearly Southwestern adobe aesthetic, not unlike Taos, New Mexico, today. However, when the railroad lines that were laid in the region in the 1880s and 1890s passed by Tascosa and crisscrossed instead at Amarillo, the settlement of Tascosa was largely abandoned.[54] In 1893, a devastating flood of the Canadian River left the town in ruins, destroying many of the adobe buildings, and those not washed away in the flood slowly collapsed and crumbled from neglect.[55]

As Amarillo grew following its establishment in 1887 with its first rail line, very few adobe structures were built there. Instead, milled wood and later brick and stone predominated, all of which could be delivered via railroad; the Southwestern flavor of Tascosa rather suddenly and dramatically shifted to more Eastern and Midwestern styles in the region, including in Amarillo, but also in the other emerging Panhandle towns of Channing, Dalhart, and Canadian.[56] An example of this shift can be seen in the Bivins Home, built in Amarillo starting in 1903 with its clear Colonial-style architecture (fig. 4.36). However, Wright's window designs in the Kinney House can remind us of that lost Southwestern adobe aesthetic in the region—something that should not be forgotten.

At the same time, Wright's fenestrations also recall Native American patterns and designs, including Plains Indian beadwork, Puebloan pottery (fig. 3.18), and Navajo textiles with their stark geometric patterns.[57] The area around the Kinney House was long a crossroads of Indigenous cultures, a "regular rendezvous" of peoples from the Southwest, the Midwest, and the Gulf Coast to Chihuahua

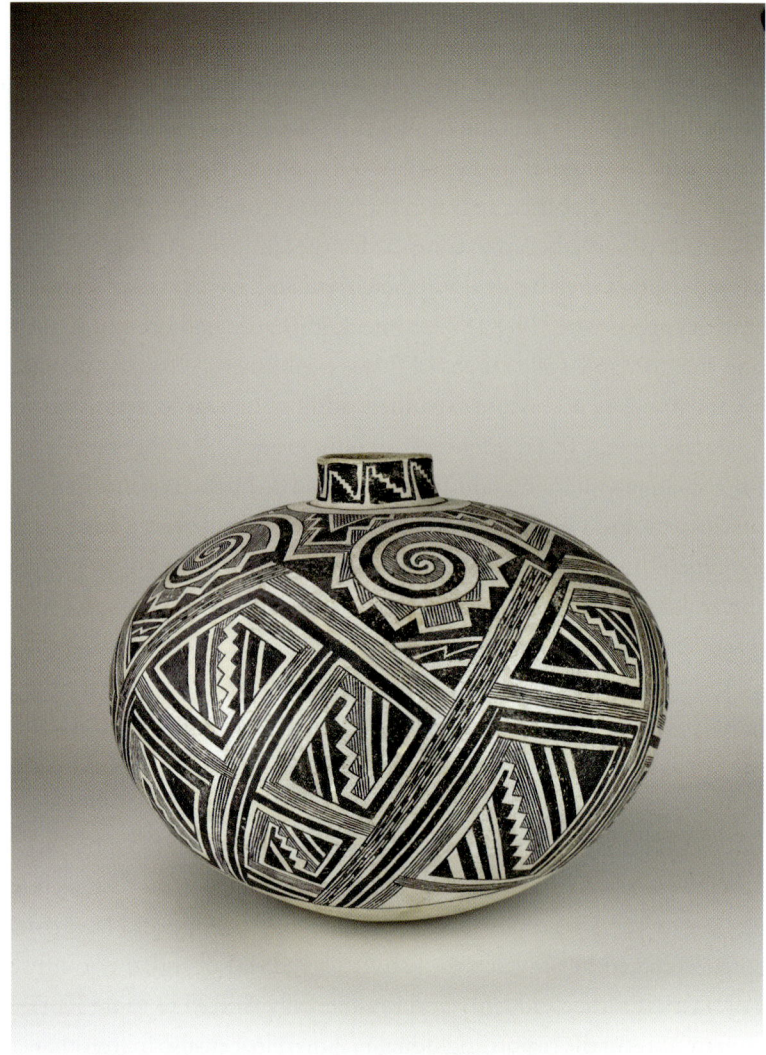

Figure 3.18. Olla, Tularosa black on white pottery, c. 1180, 13 x 17 inches. Museum of the Red River, Idabel, Oklahoma.

and what is now Mexico City.[58] The simplicity of the Kinney windows' geometry allows for a hybridity of references to Indigenous styles, one that registers the rich and diverse settlement history of the region, rather than any kind of direct quotation of native traditions. This layering of allusions to the multiple cultures—Indigenous, Hispanic, and Anglo—that have settled the Panhandle is among the

Kinney House design's most powerful aspects. Even if Wright did not overtly intend to evoke all these allusions, they nonetheless resonate strongly for visitors to the home. Knowing Wright's exact aesthetic intentions for the Amarillo home is nearly impossible because he wrote or spoke little about the home on the historical record and passed away while it was being built. But that should not stop us from allowing the potency of meanings in Wright's design to speak to its visitors now and into the future.

As mentioned above, the forms of the Kinney windows are anticlassical. Wright had long designed in styles that rejected traditional Beaux Arts classicism.[59] In the early 1900s, Wright turned to Japanese architecture, moving away from the dominant mode of the Greco-Roman temple with its columns, triangular pediments, domes and arches, and exact symmetry, which are still seen ubiquitously in turn-of-the-century US architecture—in homes, government buildings, college campuses, and art museums.[60] Wright first visited Japan in 1905, but even before then he was exposed to Japanese architecture at the 1893 World's Columbian Exposition in Chicago.[61] Responding to East Asian styles, Wright began to work with an asymmetrical balance rather than keeping the rigid symmetry of classicism, and he began to use wood as a primary material and emphasize the horizontal over the vertical.[62] According to author John Sergeant, asymmetry allowed him to produce the integration of an intellectual system on the one hand with the physical experience of space on the other:

> Wright was not concerned that the grid pattern should be symmetrical. This provided a means by which every element of the building could be coordinated into a whole. It also solved an endemic architectural problem, the potential divorce between the intellectual organization of the plan and the physical experience of an observer; with Wright, they became one and the same, concept and experience.[63]

Though his Prairie houses were the first iteration of these theories in home design, Wright continued them in his Usonian houses, including the Kinney House. For instance, he used "board and batten walls" in his Usonians that drew upon traditional Japanese wood architecture for their assembly methods (figs. 3.19 and 3.20), which created horizontal linear patterns and removed the need for the plastering, wallpapering, or painting of walls.[64] Another aspect of the Usonians that Wright drew from Asian influences includes the unfolding of spaces according to the human body's movement through them. As Sergeant explains, classical architecture can be understood "at once," but "organic architecture," which Wright

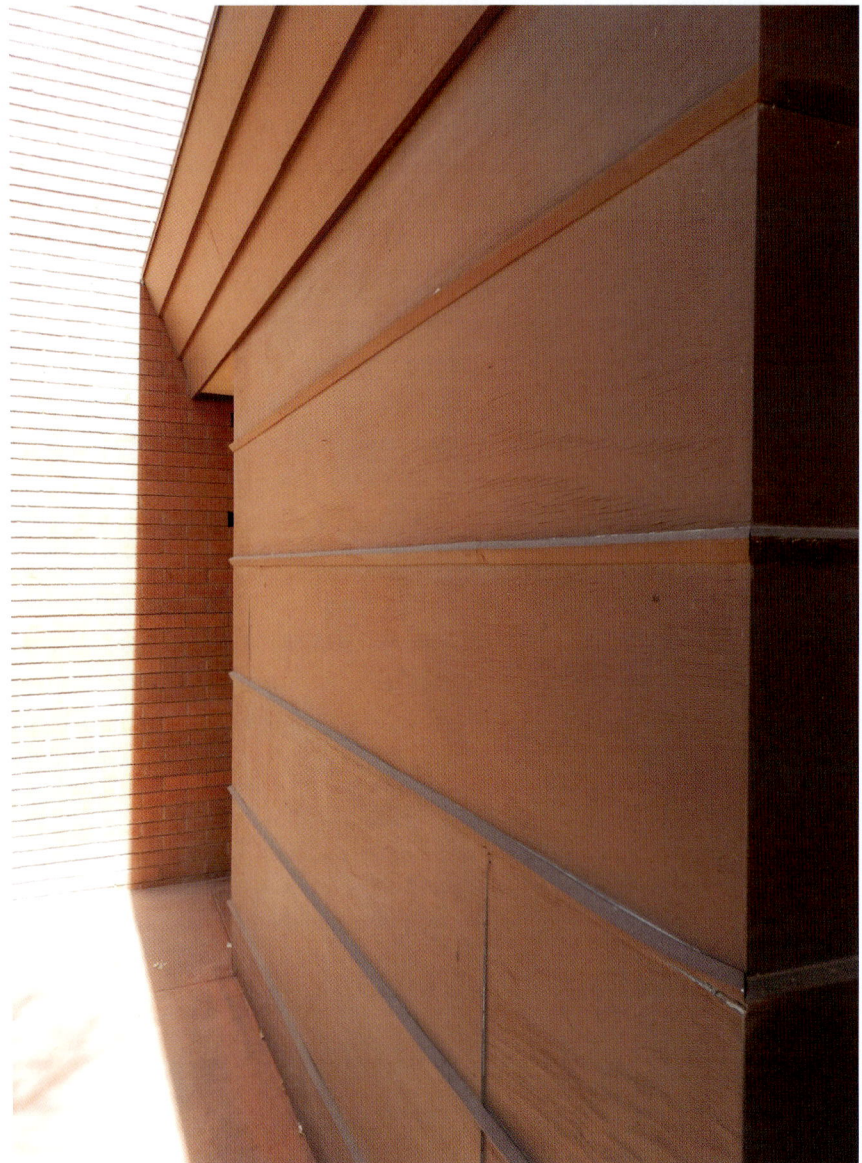

Figure 3.19. Kinney House, board and batten walls, exterior. (Photo by author.)

embraced, "engages the senses, since it can only be appreciated if the viewer walks around it and perceives the action of the time upon it and the mind because the physical is left purposely incomplete to be mentally resolved by the observer."[65] The Kinney House, with its balances of organic and geometric forms, its plays of light and shadow, its intersections of interior and exterior and of built structures and natural geography, demonstrates this Wrightian

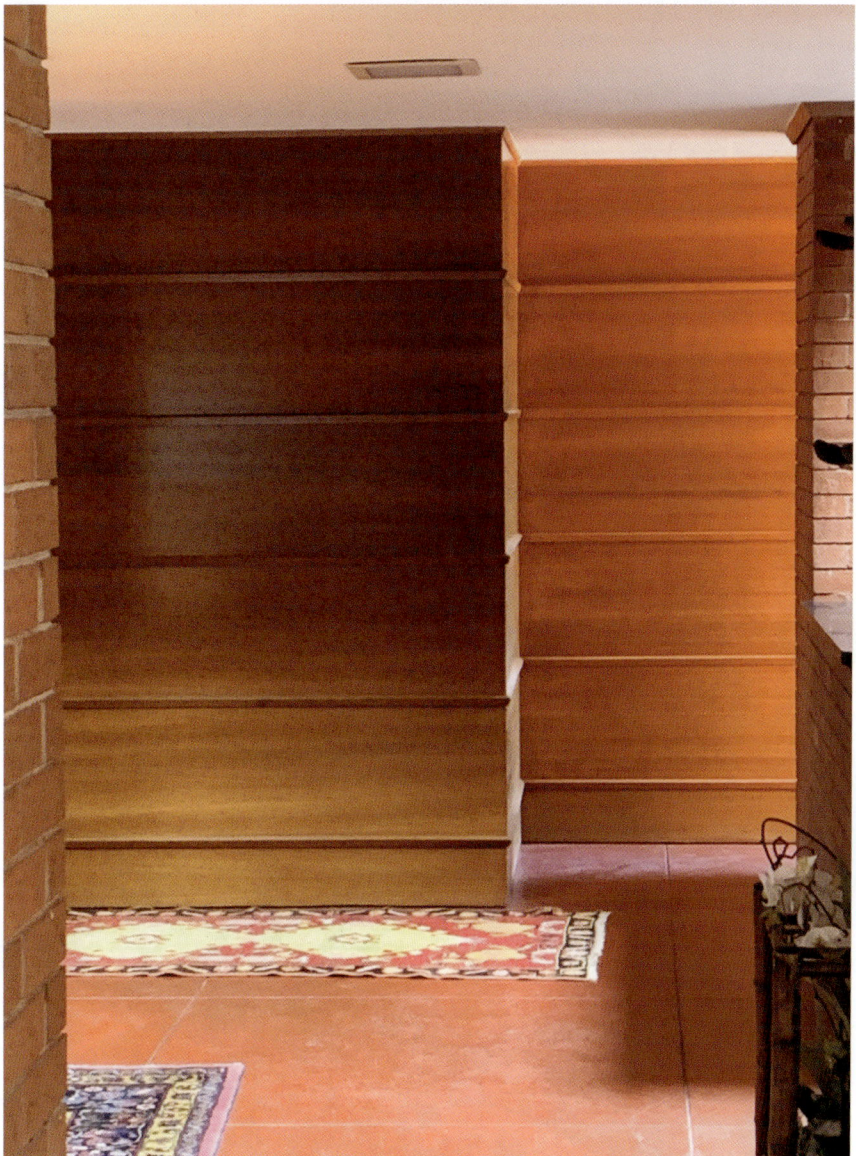

Figure 3.20. Kinney House, board and batten walls, interior. (Photo by author.)

concept of design: the not "all at once" but a journey across and through both time and space.[66]

Wright additionally incorporated the circle throughout the Kinney House design, a form most likely based on a response to the curving creek on the property. For instance, the outer garden wall forms just over 180 degrees of a circle (figs. 3.7 and 3.21), with a circular lily pond within it making the same arc of a circle with

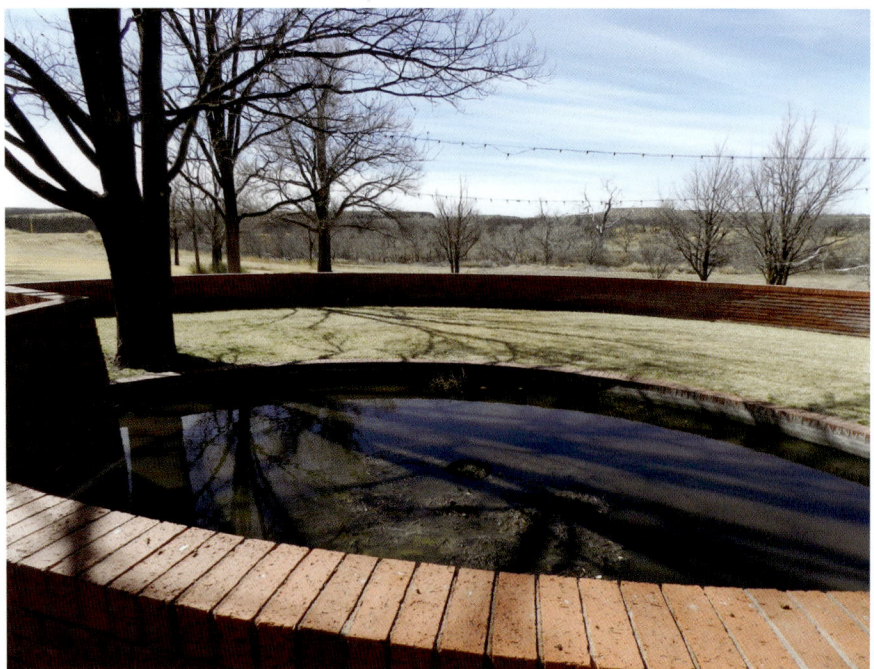

Figure 3.21. Kinney House, view of curving garden wall as seen past pond. (Photo by author.)

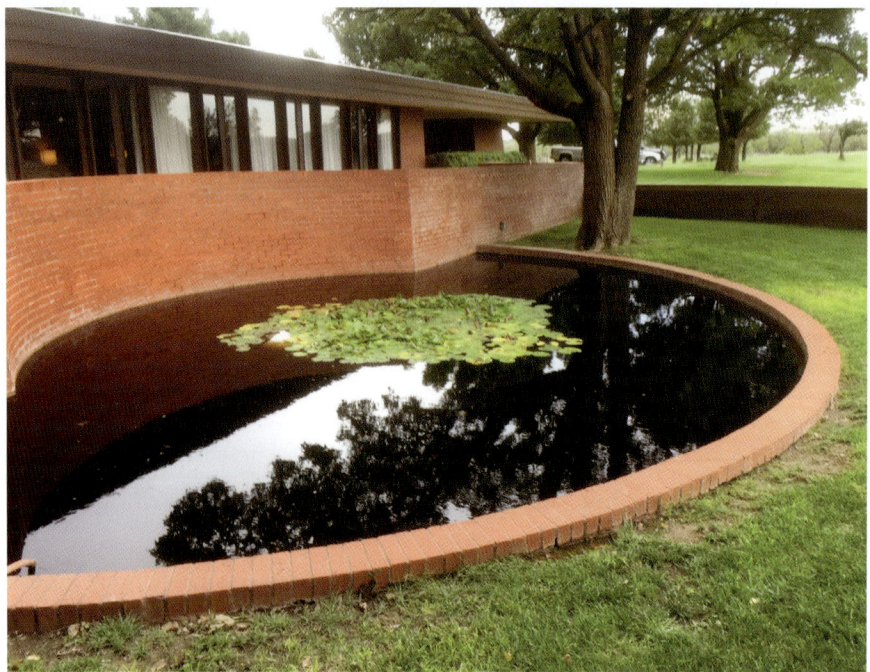

Figure 3.22. Kinney House, curving pond and inner wall design. (Photo by Charles Kitsman.)

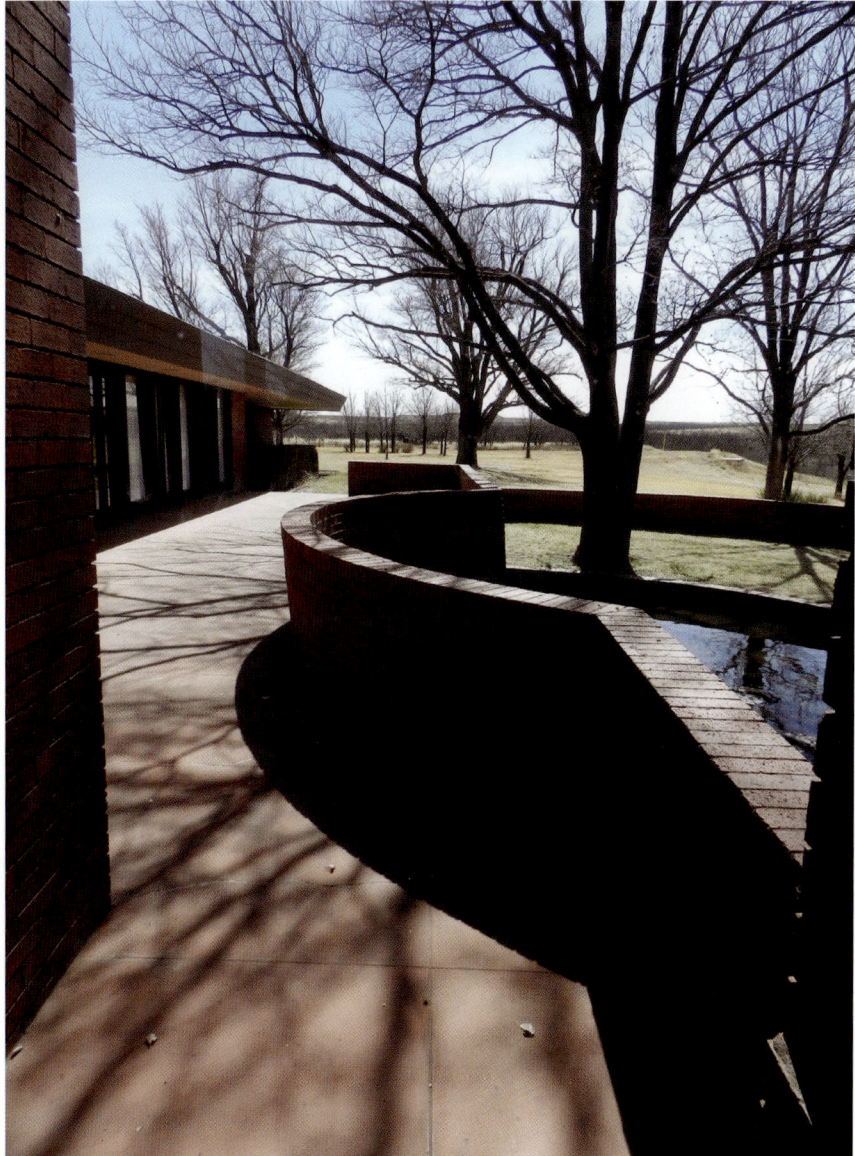

Figure 3.23. Kinney House, inner garden wall framing pond, with outer garden wall in distance. (Photo by author.)

a smaller radius (figs. 3.21 and 3.22). Then an inner garden wall responds in an opposite arc of an even smaller circle, but it also connects to straight portions of the wall on either side, forming a kind of keyhole shape that is playful and rhythmic, like a jazz melody (fig. 3.23). On the interior of the house, more curves create the hearth, with sunken circles framing the fireplace, which are then mirrored in the

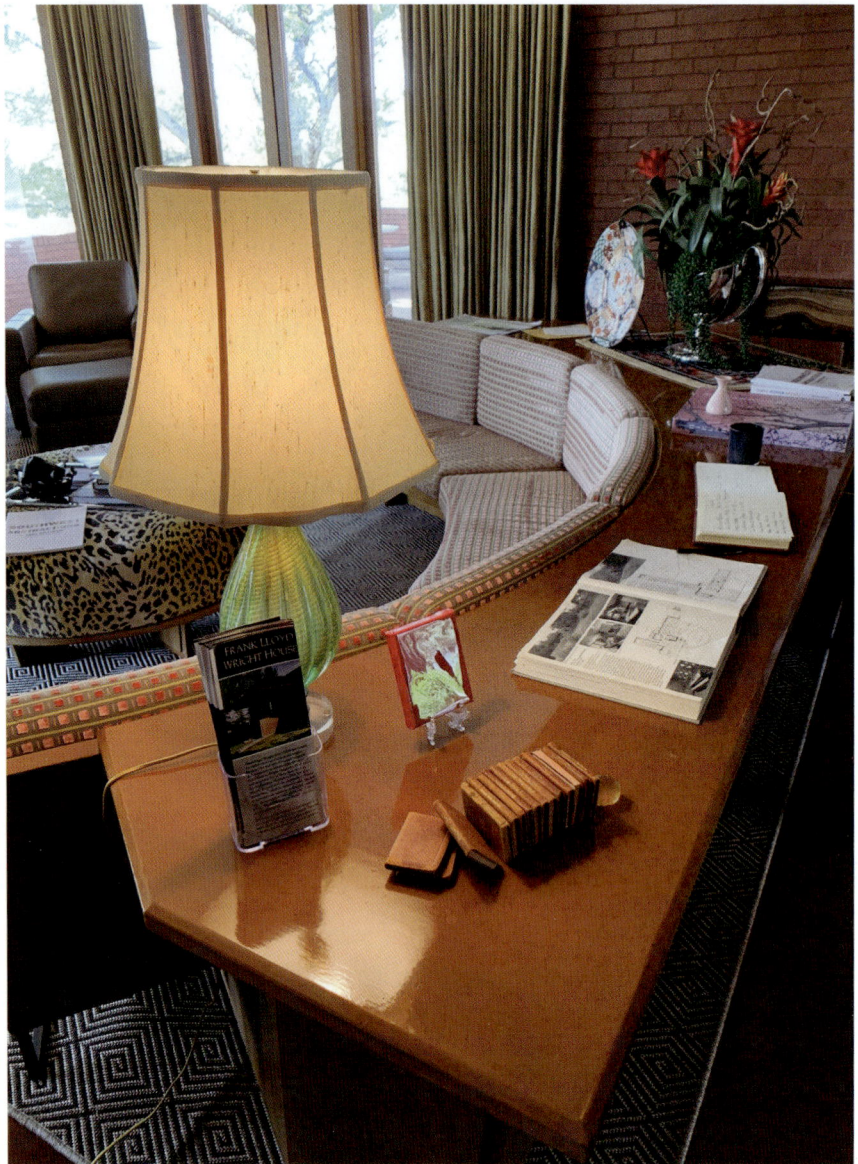

Figure 3.24. Kinney House, built-in cabinet and couch. (Photo by author.)

curving arc of the couch and a built-in cabinet (figs. 3.5 and 3.24).[67] This play of circular forms makes the house seem to breathe, in and out, with a life force that visitors can feel. The expanding and contracting circles are juxtaposed with the linear geometry of the home, including strategic placements of the fifteen-degree batter. These diagonal uprights are soft and ergonomic, like the lean of a body at rest against a wall (fig. 3.25). For example, the built-in cabinet fitted to the couch

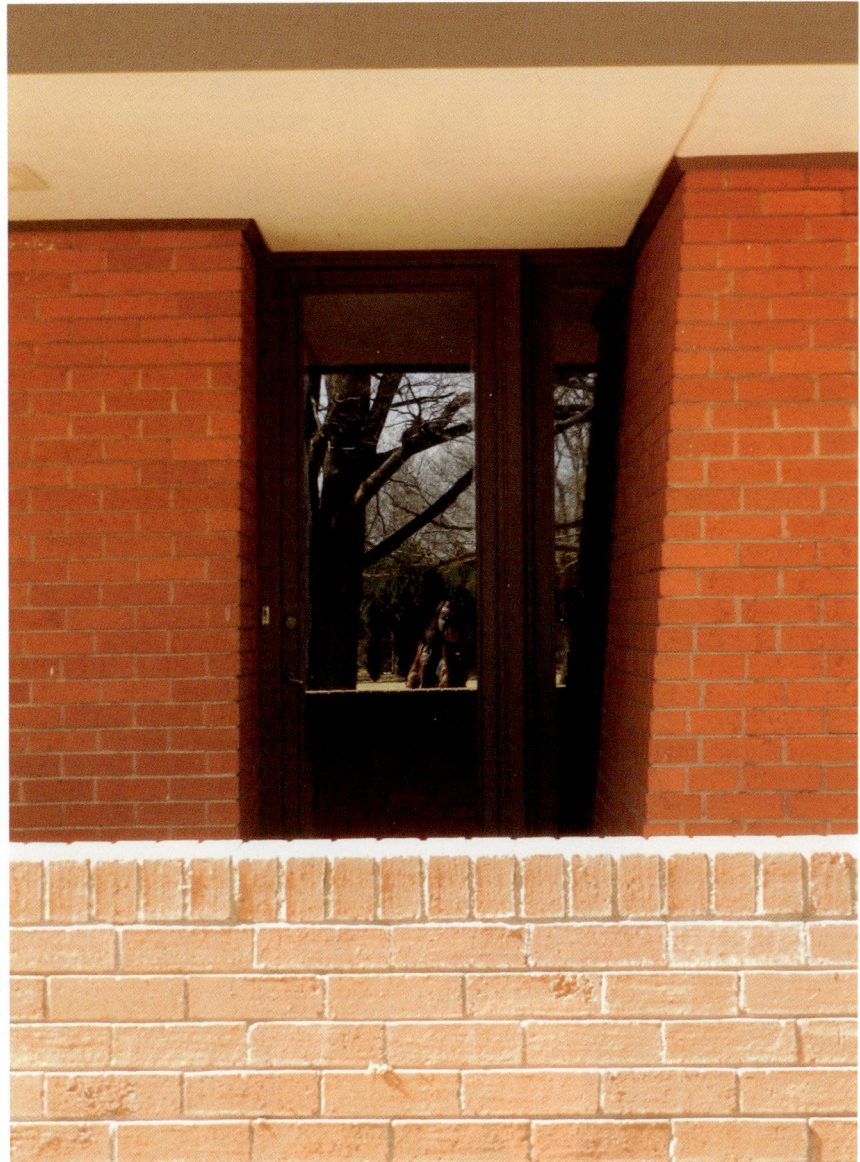

Figure 3.25. Kinney House, doorway with batter on right side. (Photo by author.)

curve has an opposite side that is angular, but without any hard-edged sharpness to undercut the organic aspects of the home (figs. 3.9 and 3.26). Likewise, the stair-stepped window openings are soft in their brick edges rather than harsh and overly machined (figs. 3.15 and 3.16).

This balance of organic and geometric, of nature and industry, parallels the careful balance of light and shadow created in the positive and negative spaces of

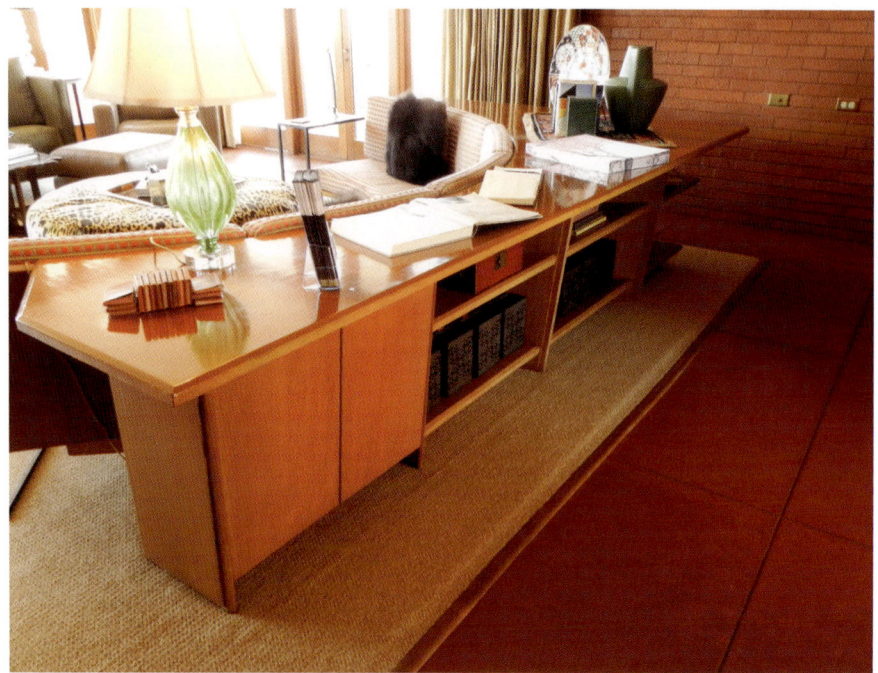

Figure 3.26. Kinney House, built-in cabinet in living room. (Photo by author.)

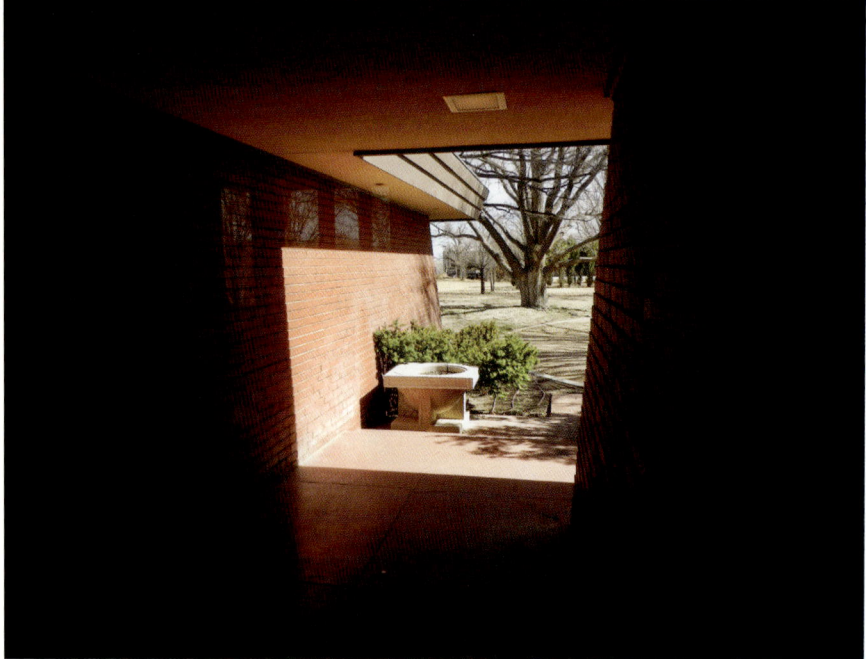

Figure 3.27. Kinney House, light and shadow in entryway. (Photo by author.)

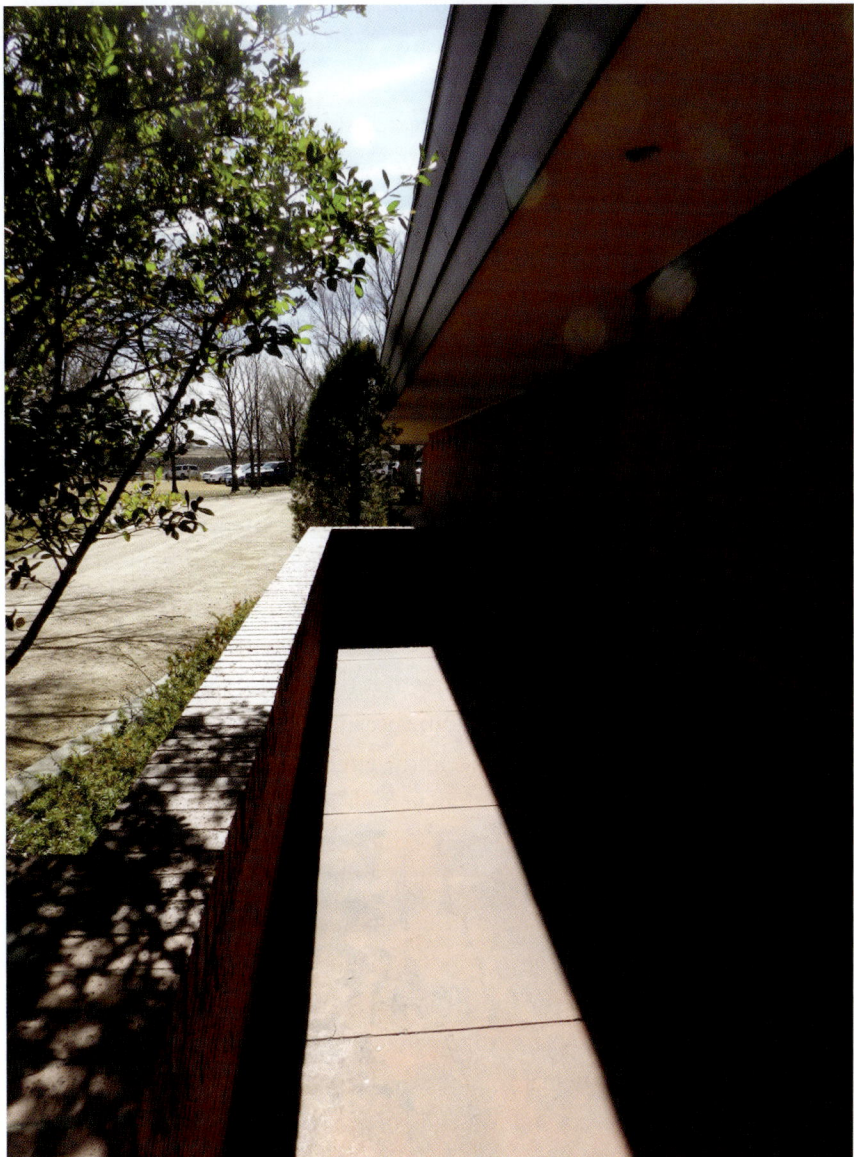

Figure 3.28. Kinney House, view of light and shadow patterns. (Photo by author.)

the home's design (fig. 3.27). On a bright, sunny day—and the Texas Panhandle has many of these—you can find an almost magical symphony of shade and illumi- nation throughout the structure, which in places even suggests the deep space per- spective of driving on the open road in the American West, where the wide-open nothingness of the land is balanced by the stark linearity of a long, straight road (fig. 3.28). These open-road angles were also celebrated by Ed Ruscha in his series of gas station images starting in the 1960s, as discussed in chapter 1 (figs. 1.23–25). By the 1930s, Wright had begun twice-yearly car trips between his two Taliesin sites in Wisconsin and Arizona, so he would have been acutely aware of these open-road vistas of the US West.[68] The rhythms created through light and shadow in the Kinney House are yet another way that Wright encourages the experientiality of space in his designs, through wandering discoveries and shifting perspectives, but those specifically responding to the wide-open West.[69]

CRITICAL REGIONALISM

The Kinney House in Amarillo—off the beaten path as a privately owned home in an isolated location on the High Plains—can be productively compared to two more famous homes that similarly reflect their natural and cultural locations, Georgia O'Keeffe's house in Abiquiu, New Mexico, and Wright's Fallingwater in Bear Run, Pennsylvania. O'Keeffe purchased the dilapidated adobe structure in Abiquiu in 1945 after a long period of negotiations with the Roman Catholic Diocese of Santa Fe, which owned the abandoned house.[70] Once the house was paid for, the artist worked with the help of Maria Chabot to repair the property and prepare it for residence. Chabot saw to it that O'Keeffe's many ideas about the place were realized.[71] In time, the house became a work of art in symbiosis with its site. This can be seen, for example, in the large picture windows of the house allowing views onto her gardens, with their built-in adobe *bancos*, where O'Keeffe placed the ever-growing rock collection she amassed throughout her life.[72]

Like Wright, O'Keeffe sought to collapse the distinct boundaries between interior and exterior in her home. O'Keeffe also demanded the installation of a Wrightian component—the corner window that he employed often in his Usonian homes, including the Kinney House (fig. 3.29). Wright's "corner-glazing" technique brings two window panes together at a right angle without the obstruction of a metal or wood divider to block the view of the exterior.[73] But O'Keeffe made this request of such a window design in a traditional adobe structure, a near architectural impossibility, but one that O'Keeffe pulled off with the addition of steel beams, including one at the corner of the two windows (fig. 3.30).[74] This corner window allowed the artist to see the Chama River Valley from her master bedroom, including a curving road around a hill in the distance that inspired numerous works of art (fig. 3.31).[75] In his writings, Wright described glass in terms that resonate with both O'Keeffe's house at Abiquiu and the Kinney House in Amarillo: "By means of glass, then, open reaches of the ground may enter into the building and the building interior may reach out and associate with these vistas

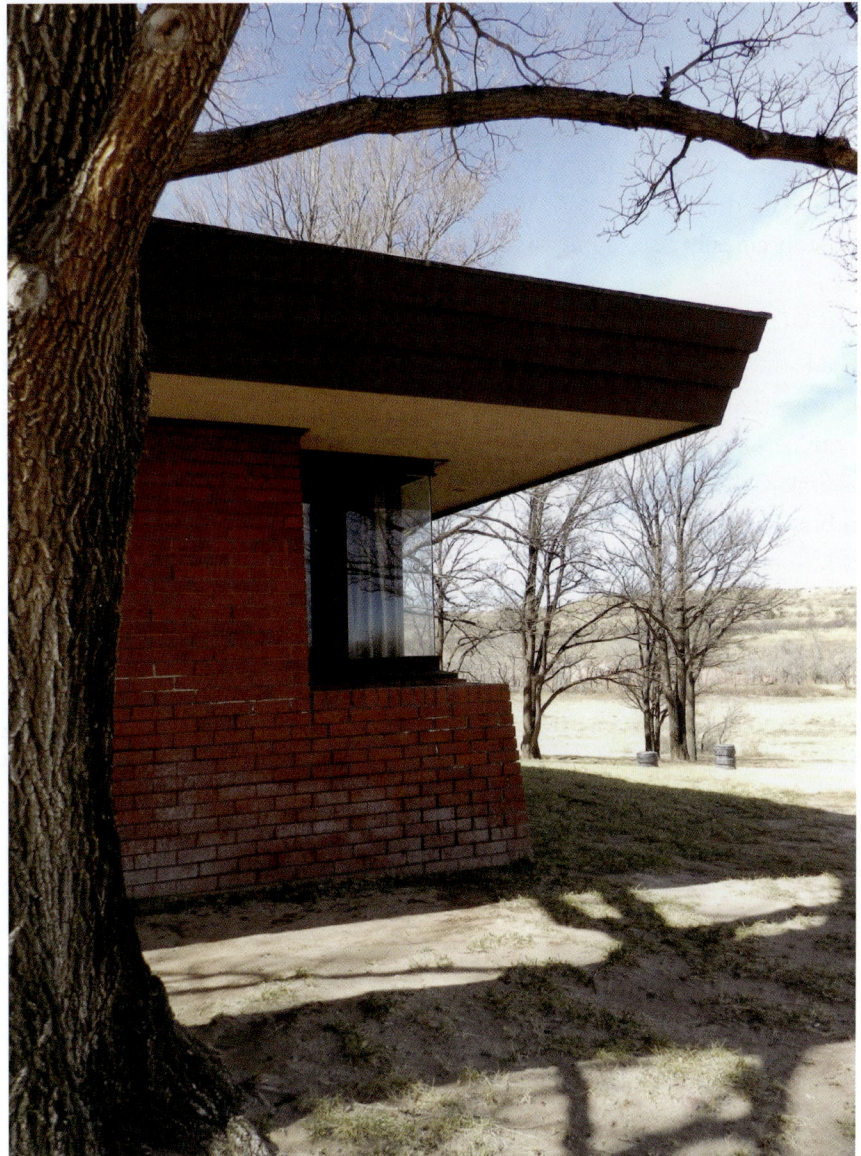

Figure 3.29. Kinney House, glazed corner. (Photo by author.)

of the ground. Ground and building will thus become more and more obviously directly related to each other in openness and intimacy; not only as environment but also as a good pattern or the good life lived in the building."[76]

Similarly, the plays of light and shadow, and of the organic and the geometric, in O'Keeffe's interior courtyard with "that wall with a door in it [that she] had to have," made famous by her many paintings of the space (figs. 3.32 and

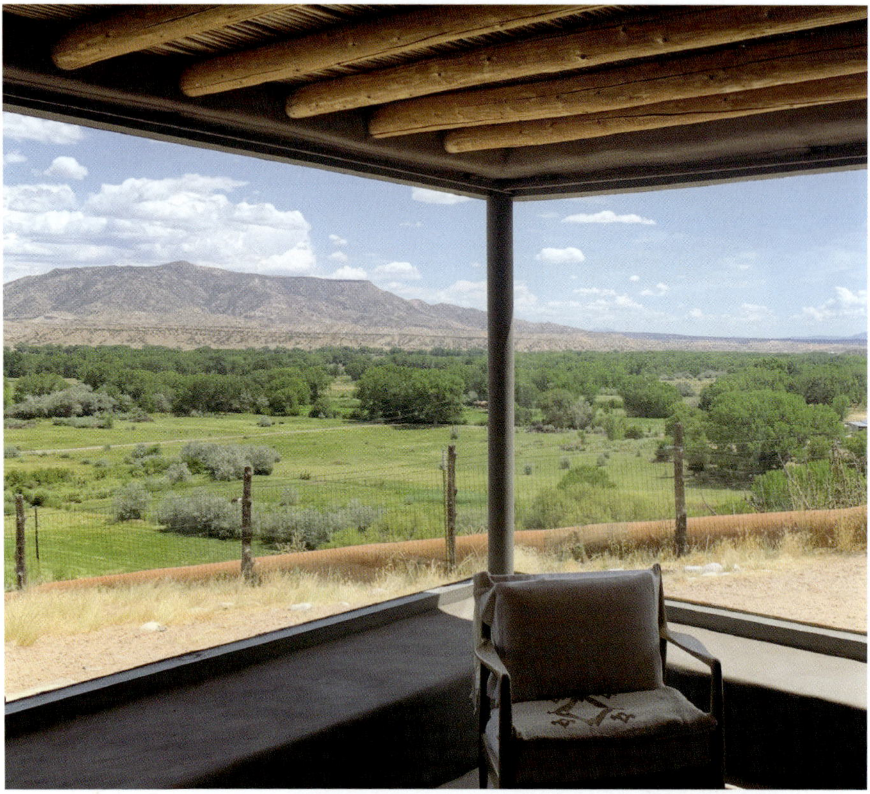

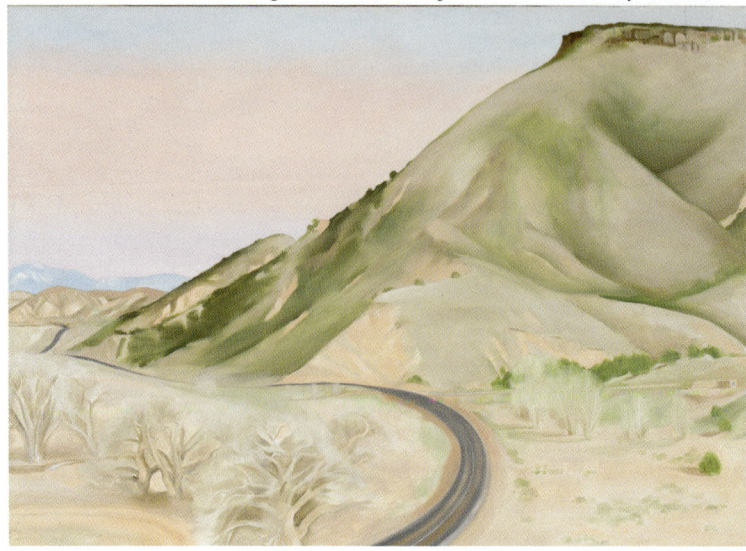

Figure 3.30. Corner window at Georgia O'Keeffe's Abiquiu House. (Photo by author.)

Figure 3.31. Georgia O'Keeffe, *Mesa and Road East II*, 1952, oil on canvas, 26 x 36.125 inches. Georgia O'Keeffe Museum. Gift of The Georgia O'Keeffe Foundation. (© 2025 Georgia O'Keeffe Museum [2006.5.235] / Artists Rights Society (ARS), New York.)

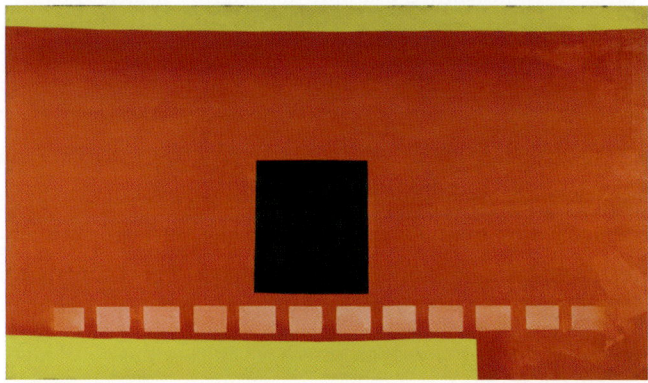

Figure 3.32. Georgia O'Keeffe, *Black Door with Red*, 1954, oil on canvas, 48 x 84 inches. Chrysler Art Museum. The Chrysler Museum, Norfolk, Virginia. Bequest of Walter P. Chrysler, Jr. (© 2025 Georgia O'Keeffe Museum / Artists Rights Society (ARS), New York.)

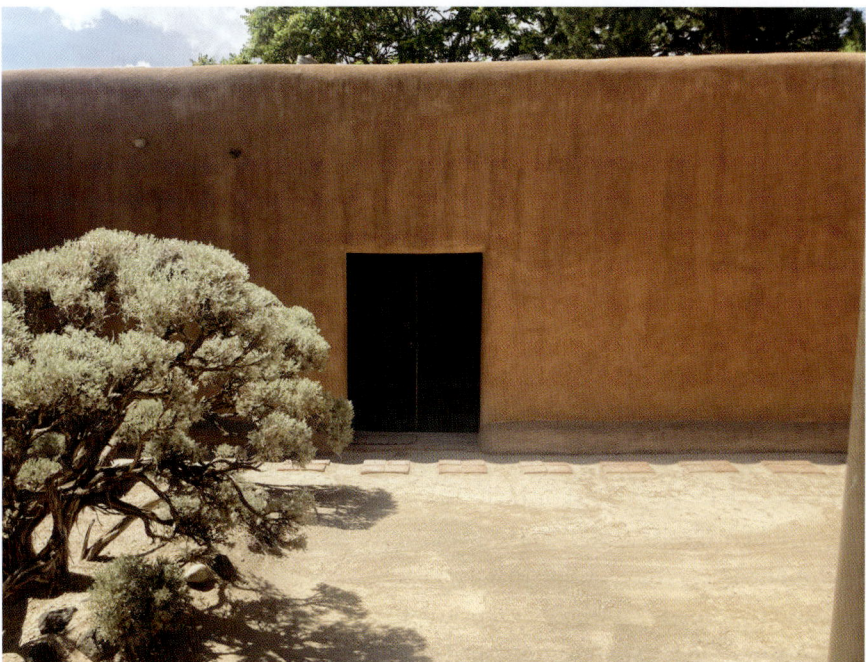

Figure 3.33. Patio door of Georgia O'Keeffe's house in Abiquiu, New Mexico. (Photo by Hollye Goddard.)

3.33), can likewise be compared to Wright's visual and formal rhythms of the Kinney House.[77] The square paving stones juxtaposed with the imperfect edges of O'Keeffe's adobe structure and shadowed wooden doorway in Abiquiu seem in conversation with how the rounded forms of the hearth and pond at the Kinney House balance the subtle lean of the house's diagonals and the light-shadow syncopations they create.

However, the most acclaimed example of Wright's ability to connect a house to its setting is Fallingwater, designed in 1936.[78] Wright nestled the dwelling into a forested hill directly atop a cascading waterfall. The stone used for parts of the structure mirrors the stones of the river, while the vertical stacking of the portions of Fallingwater—so distinct from Wright's more horizontally oriented Prairie Style— respond to the stacked rocky hillside of the setting. But, according to Sergeant, what is often overlooked with Fallingwater is the "strong contrast" between the house design and its natural setting, not its correspondence. He claims that the cantilevered forms composed of concrete horizontals with steel-framed glazing are in fact "inimical to the forms of the woods around it."[79] And in this construction, nature penetrates the field of the house as it does in no other design by Wright; it pierces the home almost violently, intrusively. Fallingwater was built "not as a family residence but a weekend entertainment retreat" for the family of a Pittsburgh millionaire, unlike the very livable and everyday design of Wright's Usonian homes.[80] The dramatic staging of Fallingwater offers a kind of antithesis to the practical efficiency and subtle beauty of a Usonian design like the Kinney House. But both structures nonetheless underscore Wright's contention that his designs were especially appropriate to their individual locations and their specific patrons.

Also comparable to Fallingwater, if much more subdued and functional, the Kinney House offers a unique dialogue with the widths and elevations of the land. Whether responding to the narrower widths and dramatic stacking of the Fallingwater site or to the wider widths and subtle layering of the Kinney House site, Wright was truly a master of the marriage of house to setting. Nature doesn't literally penetrate the interior of the Kinney House, but as with Fallingwater, nature acts as the "psychological foundation for the design."[81] Again, Wright's designs followed the principles of "organic philosophy," a construct to which Wright adhered throughout his career. According to architectural historian Edward Frank, "organic philosophy accepts the position that man is an experiencing being, or better yet, an experiencing becoming, whose nature is dynamic and therefore rejects the view of man divorced from the world and aloof from the flow of life."[82] The Kinney House offers a process of becoming for its owners and visitors.

The Usonian homes of the mid-twentieth century, including the Kinney House, captured a newly organic relationship with their sites. John Sergeant summarizes this relationship beautifully:

> These houses expressed a warmth and naturalness for which I was totally unprepared. I had come into contact with an architectural ability that I sensed had

generated the relationships with trees and contours and twists and turns, all of which gave me such enjoyment. I also found built-in seats where the building made me pause. I found soft lighting from within the fabric, and above all an extraordinary flowing, contained, and varied sense of space.[83]

The Kinney House displays all of this, and it demonstrates the truth of Sergeant's claim that "the need for a small, informal house was the greatest achievement of Wright's late architectural career."[84]

One theoretical perspective that has not often been connected to Wright's architecture, but which the Kinney House's unique specificity to its regional location calls to mind, is critical regionalism. According to Kenneth Frampton writing in 1983, critical regionalism reacts against the globalizing tendencies of International Style architecture—a kind of one-size-fits-all form for modern design, what Frampton describes as the "Megalopolitan development" of the "free standing high-rise and the serpentine freeway," for instance.[85] Frampton critiques this International Style as suffering from a "universal placelessness."[86] Instead, critical regionalism embraces local inflections of design, the "peculiarities of a particular place," but without falling into the trap of "sentimental regionalism," populism, or kitsch.[87] Wright's Kinney House is not a sentimental or simplistic reflection of Panhandle aesthetics—and as this volume articulates, such an aesthetics is by no means singular or homogeneous. Rather, the complex layering of references in the Kinney House designed by Wright embodies the very diversity of the Panhandle region, its history and its artistic developments. In his Kinney House design, Wright demonstrated what Frampton calls a "high level of critical self-consciousness" that responds to things like the "local light," the topography, and the structural modes familiar and functional in the region.[88] Frampton writes:

> It is possible to argue that in this last instance the specific culture of the region— that is to say, its history in both a geological and agricultural sense—becomes inscribed into the form and realization of the work. This inscription, which arises out of an "in-laying" the building into the site, has many levels of significance, for it has a capacity to embody, in built form, the prehistory of the place, its archaeological past and its subsequent cultivation and transformation across time. Through this layering into the site the idiosyncrasies of place find their expression without falling into sentimentality.[89]

Frampton's words here beautifully summarize Wright's accomplishments with the Amarillo Kinney House. It responds to the light, the climate, and the resources of the region, as well as its geological and agricultural developments, including the Llano Estacado land formation and the settlement of the land by various human groups over centuries. It embeds the very changes over time that the region has experienced—all into a formal design that simultaneously reads as clean, modern, and fresh. It demonstrates a "place-conscious poetic" that deserves recognition.[90]

As several Wright scholars have convincingly claimed, the Usonian home entered the US subconscious as nothing less than the prototype for the modern ranch house.[91] And Usonians were less regionally confined or defined than the Prairie house, and therefore all the more "American" because of it, allowing an easy adaptation to the unique and widely varied landscapes of the United States, including the High Plains of West Texas.[92] Wright's Usonian designs are "simultaneously lucid, deceivingly artless, and geometrically controlled," all of which are true of the Kinney House.[93] The year he designed the Kinney residence in Amarillo, Wright received no fewer than forty commissions, a record for his career. At the time, Wright supervised up to fifty or sixty apprentices who managed the projects with him; apparently Allen Lape "Davy" Davidson was the lead apprentice on the Kinney House.[94] In the 1950s, moreover, Wright designed plans for many grandiose structures that never got built, including a tower for the state of Illinois that included 528 floors, parking for 15,000 cars, and a landing pad for 75 helicopters.[95] And yet, he still found time to create a modest but subtly beautiful home well suited to its West Texas site. According to those working closely with him, Wright was "able to turn out a perfectly satisfactory Usonian house in a matter of hours," so the time commitment to design the Kinney House might not have been all that long.[96] But we do know that Wright visited the Kinney House site during the design stages, so he would have taken in the particulars of the setting and responded to them in his concept; according to Sergeant, Wright only rarely visited the sites of his Usonians into his later years, so his visit to the Kinney site is notable and important.[97] Of Wright's almost 800 designs across his career, close to 600 were houses, and he showed a lifelong "compulsion to build the perfect house."[98] We must put the Kinney House back into this context, recognizing that it is but one of many Wright homes designed and built but also acknowledging that it scores high on the scale of success.

According to the current homeowner, Robin Gilliland, Wright and Dorothy Ann Kinney had several heated arguments while the home was being designed and constructed.[99] Wright's difficult personality has been well documented: "he often made himself insufferable by demanding public adulation," and he was both convinced of his own genius and needed to be constantly reassured of it.[100] But because Mrs. Kinney was such a lover of Wright's work and was willing to pay for the home she wanted and hash out difficult compromises with Wright to produce a design she would love, Amarillo received a fine example of Wright's Usonian homes.

With Wright's designs, another thing that should be acknowledged is the amount of work they require in upkeep, and the Kinney House is no exception. Gilliland purchased the house from the estate of the Kinney family after both Sterling and Dorothy Ann had died. And she out-negotiated a buyer from London in the sale, claiming that only a person with direct knowledge of the region could effectively preserve the home.[101] According to her photographs, the property was in a severe state of disrepair. Ceilings were crumbling, wood surfaces had nicotine stains and cigarette burns, and the concrete floors were covered with chipped paint. Gilliland even has stories of combating snakes and snowstorms in her time as the home's owner. This case study of the Kinney House reminds us to attend to the ongoing status of Panhandle artworks, which, as we saw in chapter 1, are subject to decay, but a specific regional decay. Appreciating Frank Lloyd Wright's Kinney House in Amarillo can add to our understanding of the art culture of the region—a region that should be proud to claim a Wright design—but such an appreciation also adds a more nuanced reading of Wright's body of architectural design. He understood the subtle differences in each of the sites where he worked, and through him, we can discover those differences too.

CHAPTER 4

AVIATION: A HIDDEN AESTHETIC IN THE TEXAS PANHANDLE

n 1940, the Texas Panhandle was the location of an extravagant event focused on aviation. On April 13, the brothers Monte and Dick Ritchie hosted the first Aerial Roundup on the JA Ranch, which is adjacent to Palo Duro Canyon State Park. As the formal invitation declared (fig. 4.1), the guests' airplanes were to be their "brand of admittance" and no "groundlings" were "allowed."[1] No fewer than 102 planes landed on the three 3,000-foot ranch runways "graded and manicured to a king's taste" for this event, bringing 205 attendees (fig. 4.2).[2] One of the guests, for example, was the rancher and pilot Ted Reid, the "cowboy" whom Georgia O'Keeffe had fallen for during her years in Canyon, Texas, as discussed in chapter 2 (figs. 4.3 and 2.9).[3] The Ritchie brothers arranged for evening parking of their guests' planes at English Field in Amarillo—which itself has a fascinating history[4]—and for transportation of their attendees to the luxurious Herring Hotel for a happy hour followed by a banquet with dancing (fig. 4.4).[5] The invitation

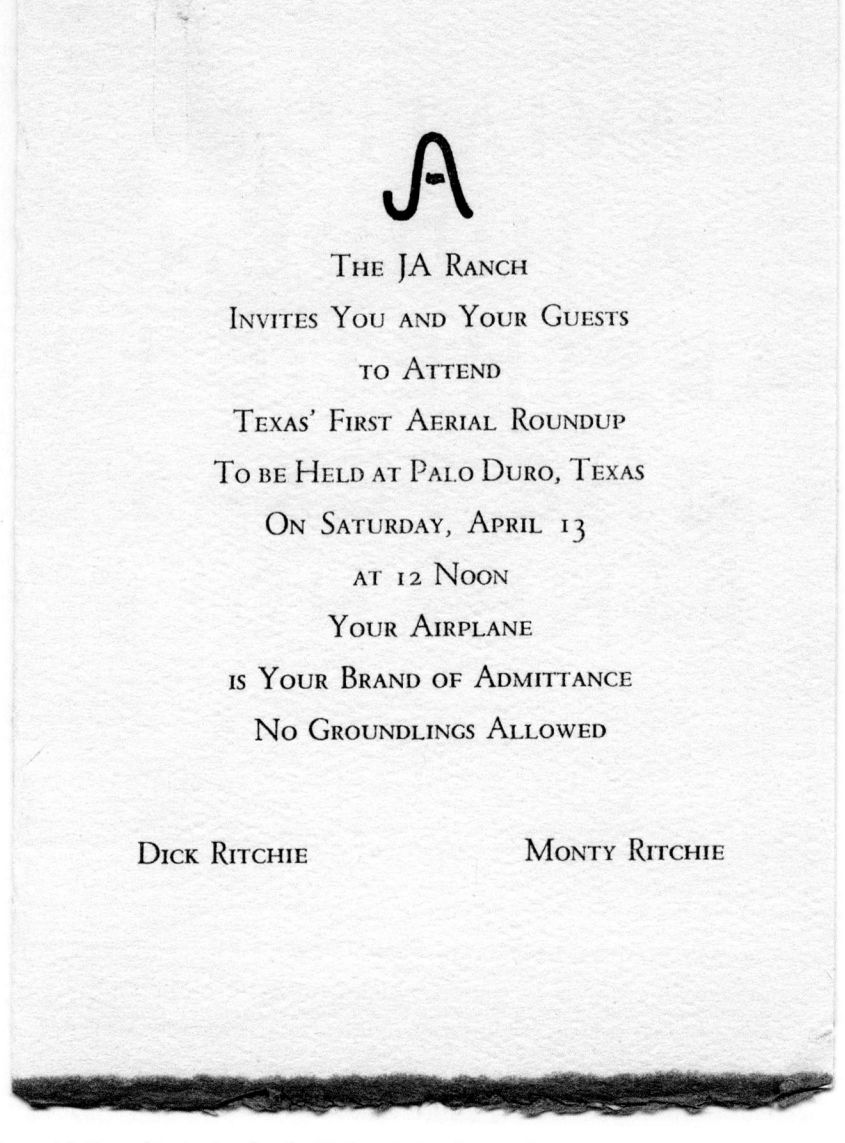

Figure 4.1. Formal invitation for the JA Ranch Aerial Roundup, 1940. John L. McCarty Papers, Panhandle-Plains Historical Museum, Canyon, Texas.

even promised "a date bureau available for unattached pilots," pointing to how the era's pilots were seen as some of the most eligible singles.[6]

Journalist Dick Martin, who held the title "News Aviation Editor" for the Amarillo newspaper, showing just how newsworthy flight was for the region in those years, described the roundup in exaggerative terms: "From far and near

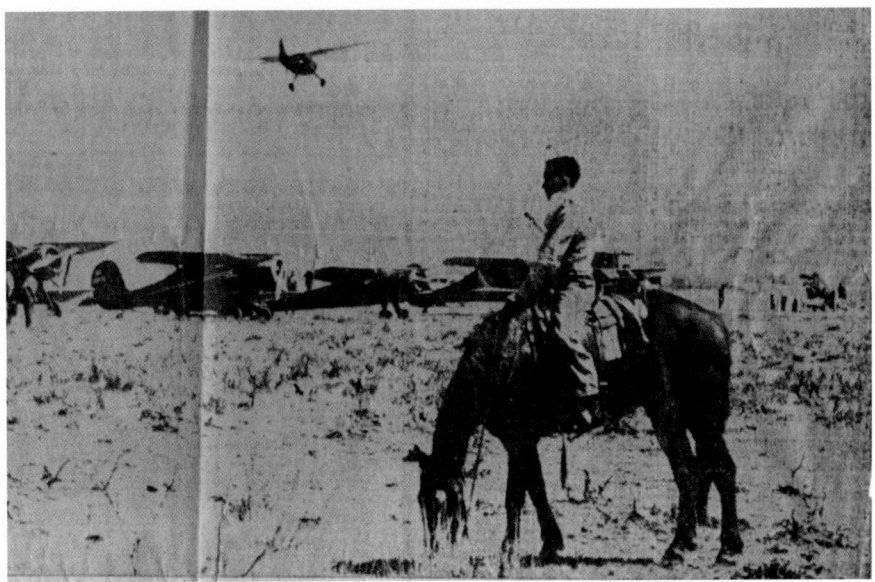

Figure 4.2. *Amarillo Sunday News and Globe* clipping, 1940. John L. McCarty Papers, Panhandle-Plains Historical Museum, Canyon, Texas.

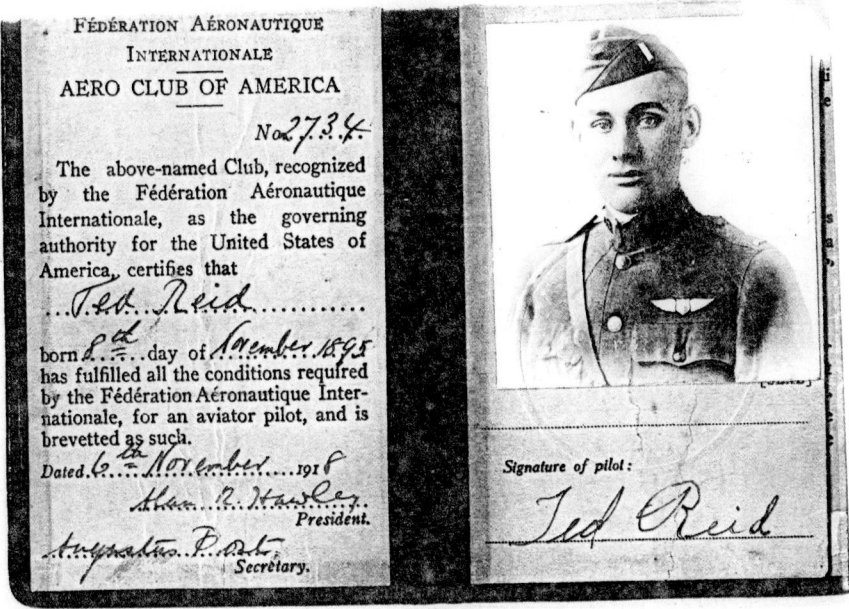

Figure 4.3. Ted Reid's Aero Club card, 1918. James Warren Ted Reid Aviation Papers, Panhandle-Plains Historical Museum, Canyon, Texas.

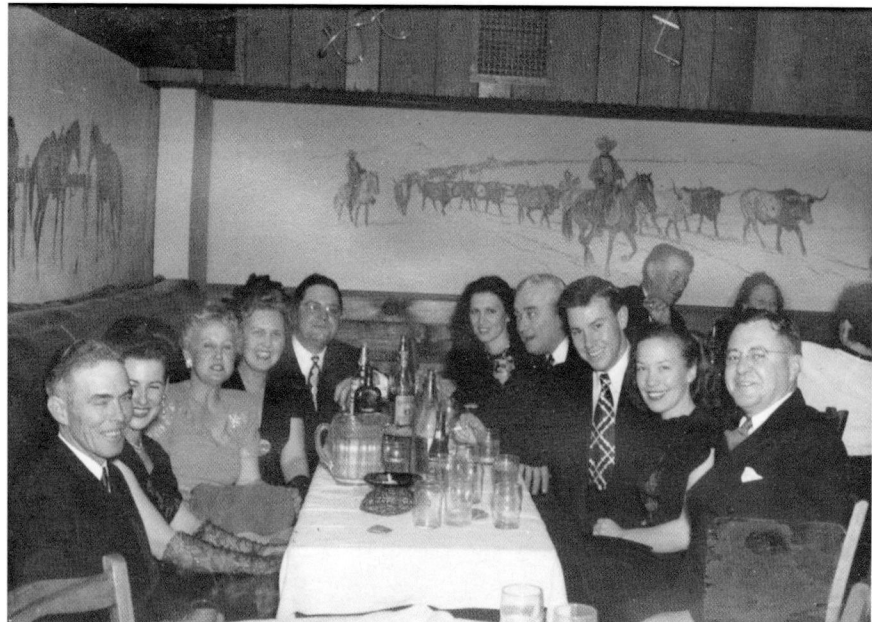

Figure 4.4. Unknown photographer, patrons of the Herring Hotel Old Tascosa Room, c. 1940. Panhandle-Plains Historical Museum, Canyon, Texas.

they came—big planes, little planes, single engine planes, twin-engined planes, new planes, old planes, shiny planes and dull veteran planes. All came roaring over the field, swung into the wind, and touched their wheels to the runway in rapid order."[7] Martin witnessed fifteen planes at once "circling above in a giant pinwheel of suspended action" that "filled the heavens with thunder." Clearly, the visual and auditory aspects of the Aerial Roundup event in the Panhandle were awe-inspiring for those present. But such aspects are now invisible, dissipated, hidden, long gone. This chapter will try to recreate some of these hidden aesthetics of Panhandle aviation, drawing on media from painting to architecture, sculpture, documentary photos, drawings, and mosaics.

Traditionally, the term "aesthetics" has described the appreciation of beauty, a branch of philosophy whose name derives from an ancient Greek word meaning sensory perception; in the eighteenth century, German philosophers, including Immanuel Kant, adapted the word to focus more on judgment of beauty and taste.[8] But for this chapter, I am using the term to represent the visual ecosystem, or ethos, that incorporates high art—painting, sculpture, and architecture, for instance—but also the spectacular practices that define and shape everyday life. For this definition, I draw upon visual studies scholarship, including the foundational work of Vanessa R. Schwartz, especially her monographs *Spectacular*

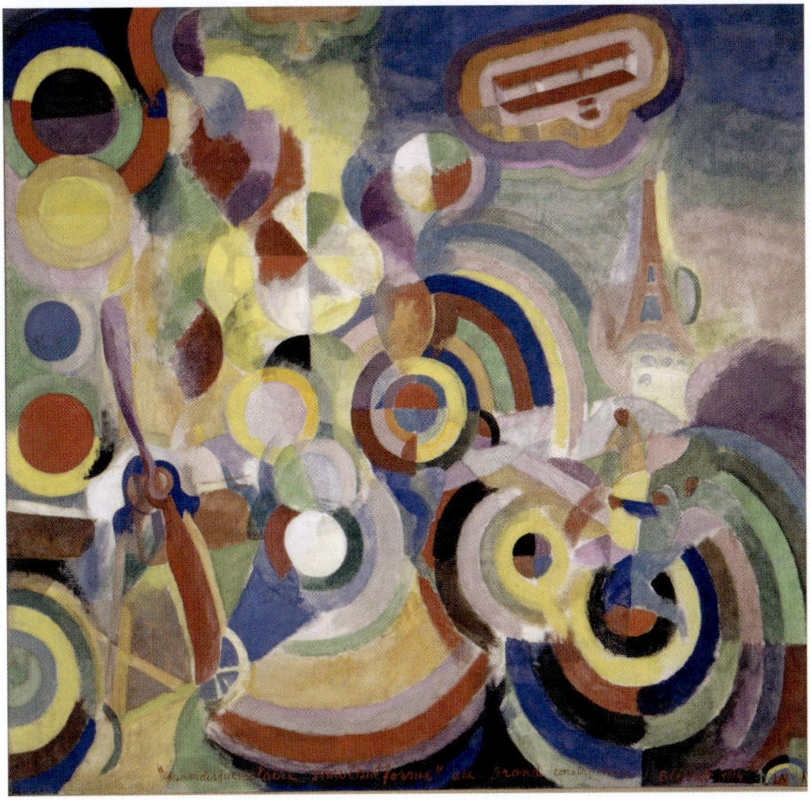

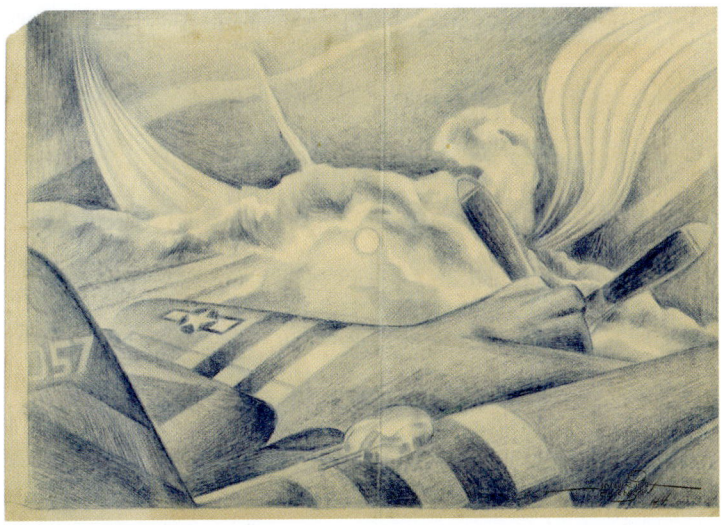

Figure 4.5. Robert Delaunay, *Homage to Blériot*, 1914, tempera on canvas, 98 x 99 inches (250 x 251 centimeters). Kunstmuseum, Basel, Switzerland.

Figure 4.6. Maurice Bernson, *Untitled (Bomber)*, 1944, colored pencil drawing on paper, 11 x 15 inches. Panhandle-Plains Historical Museum, Canyon, Texas.

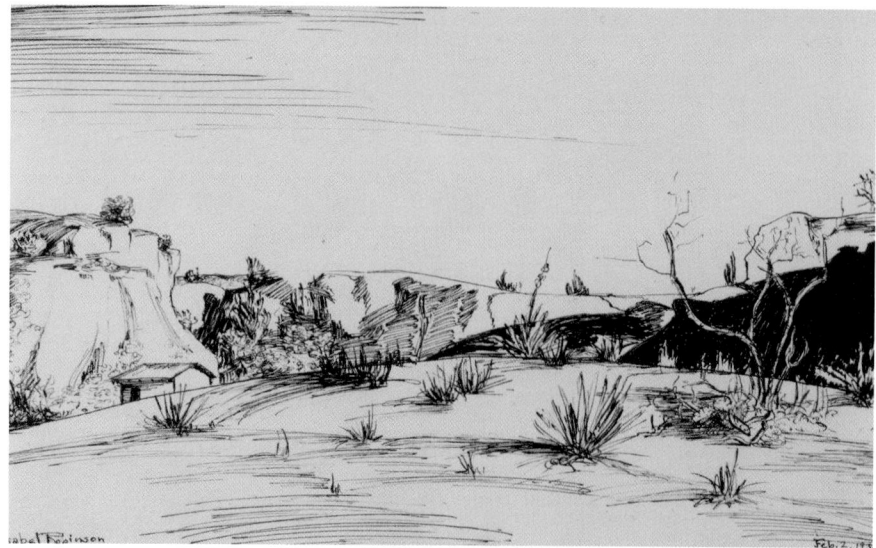

Figure 4.7. Isabel Robinson, *Untitled (Palo Duro Canyon)*, 1930, ink wash on paper, 7 x 11 inches. Panhandle-Plains Historical Museum, Canyon, Texas.

Realities: Early Mass Culture in Fin-de-Siècle France (1999) and *Jet Age Aesthetics: The Glamour of Media in Motion* (2020).[9] The former explores the visual entertainments of late nineteenth-century Paris, including wax museums, panoramas, dioramas, early cinema, and even spectatorship at the city morgue, and the latter examines the global "aesthetics" of the so-called jet age. My chapter takes a similar approach to understanding how aviation affected both the artistic developments and the spectacular entertainments of the region, from aerial roundups on ranches to the spectacles of airports and airshows.[10] In other words, the "aesthetics" of aviation in the Texas Panhandle encompass a broad spectrum of visual forms and experiences that responded to the technologies of flight.

When Dick Martin described the "pinwheel" of action that he viewed at the JA Ranch in April 1940, his words capture what was for him a stunning spectacle, but also one that left behind no material or visual trace. Alongside Martin's recorded words, we might look to the canonical modernist painting by French cubist Robert Delaunay *Homage to Blériot* from 1914, which celebrated a similar feat in aviation (fig. 4.5). Delaunay's composition captured the excitement of Louis Blériot's record-breaking flight across the English Channel in both its form and its color, embodying the whirling mechanics of airplanes in kaleidoscopic shapes and vivid rainbow pigments—not unlike Martin's pinwheel of planes above the JA.[11] Delaunay's colorful painting can be compared to another lesser-known work of aviation-inspired art by Panhandle artist and pilot Maurice Bernson (fig. 4.6).

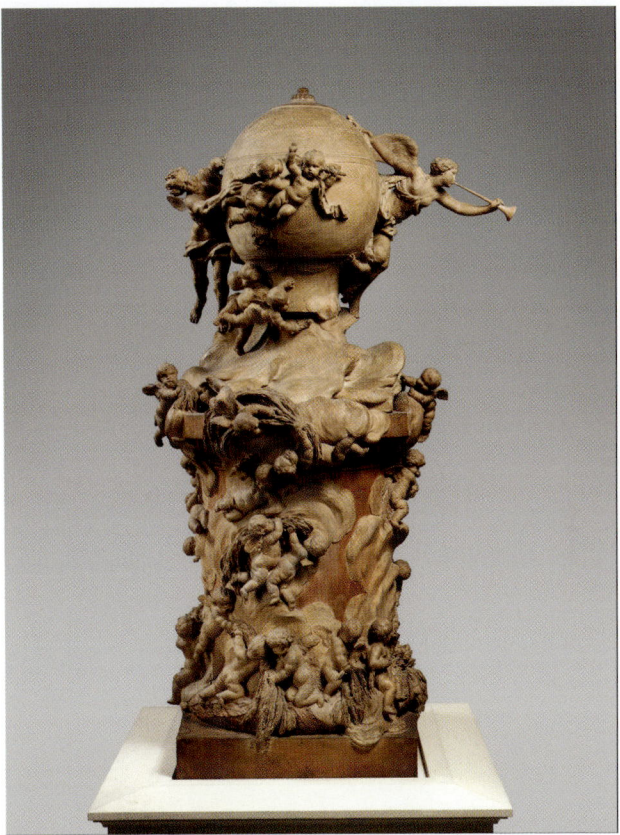

Figure 4.8. Clodion (Claude Michel), *Model for a Proposed Monument to Commemorate the Invention of the Balloon*, c. 1784, terra-cotta, 43.1258 x 24.75 x 20.375 inches. Metropolitan Museum of Art, New York. Purchase, Rogers Fund and Anonymous Gift, 1944.

Bernson was born in Canadian, Texas, in 1920 and he studied art at WT (then West Texas State College) in 1940, under the instruction of Isabel Robinson, a successor of Georgia O'Keeffe as head of the Art Department (fig. 4.7).[12]

During World War II, Bernson joined the US Army Air Corps, serving in the 394th Bombing Group and the 584th Squadron. He became a crew chief while he also painted designs on planes, and in his spare time, he created drawings such as the one reproduced here. This image rendered in blue pencil offers another visualization of that whirling spectacle Martin described. With its oblique perspective, Bernson's drawing places the viewer on the very wings of the bomber as the plane soars among the swirling clouds. To be sure, once aviation was possible, the ways of seeing and understanding the world, and of representing it in visual form, were dramatically shifting—and not just for Europeans like Blériot but for Texas Panhandle residents as well.

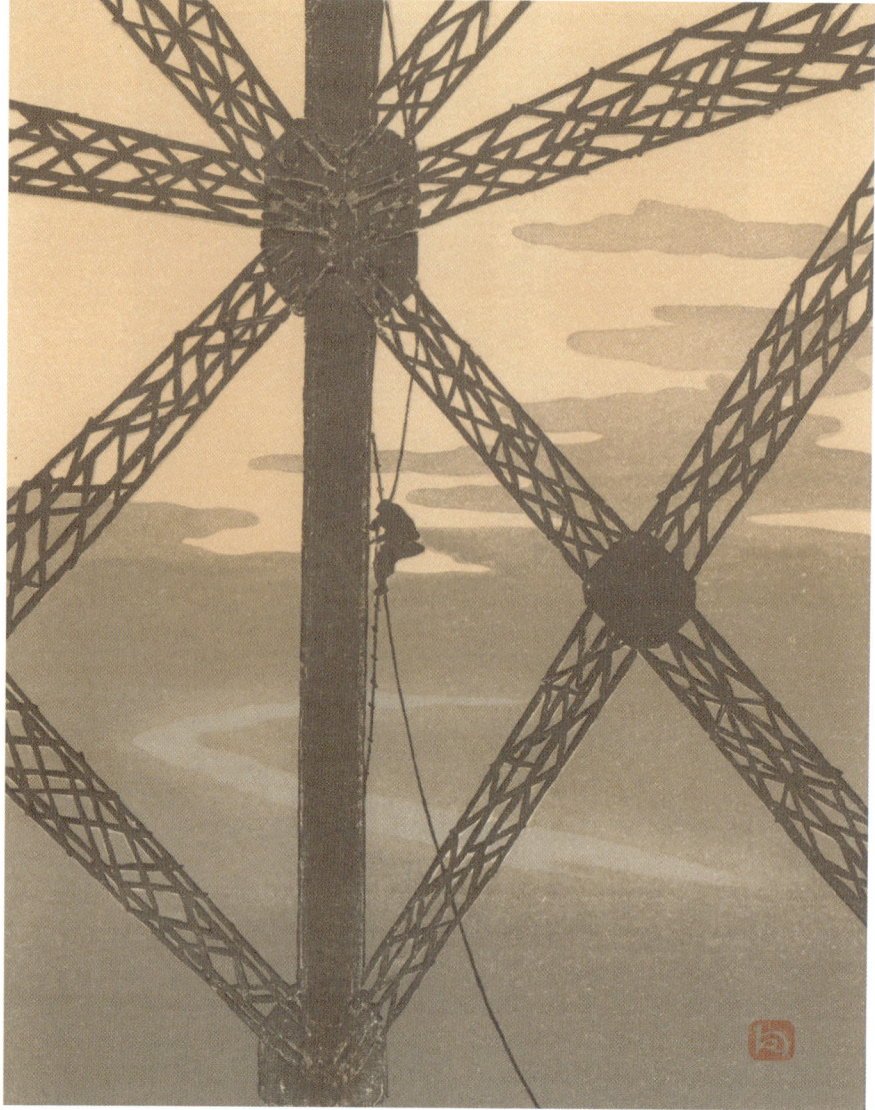

Figure 4.9. Henri Rivière, color lithograph from *Les Trente-six vues de la Tour Eiffel*, 1902. (Photo courtesy of the Harry Ransom Center, the University of Texas at Austin.)

The human conquest of the air, both physically and aesthetically, began around 1783 with the invention of the hot air balloon.[13] And by the 1889 World's Fair, over a million visitors rode up the Eiffel Tower to see Paris from high above.[14] Both advances inspired a plethora of artworks in response, from the 1784 terra-cotta monument maquette by Claude Michel, better known as "Clodion," which honored the invention of the balloon (fig. 4.8), to the photographs and prints of Henri Rivière, who visited the Eiffel Tower in 1889 during its construction and created

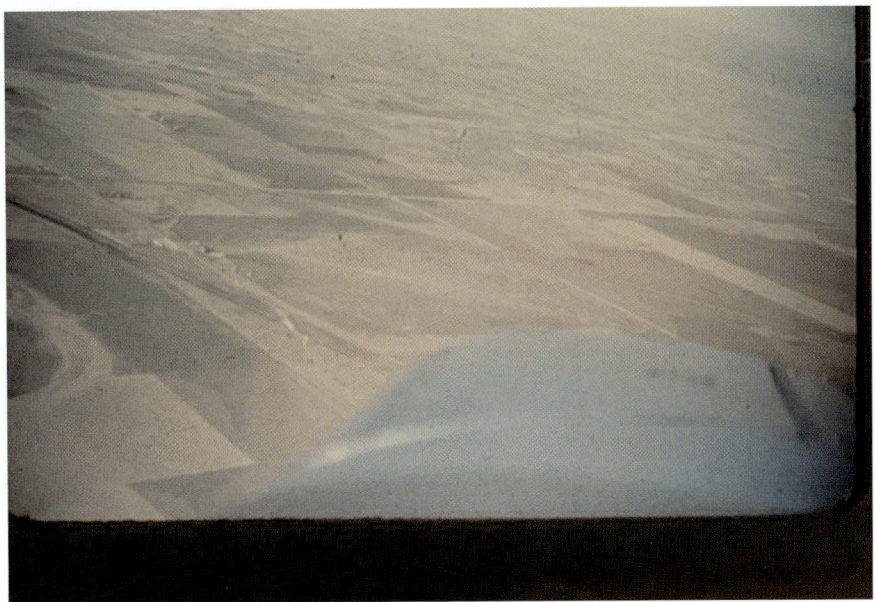

Figure 4.10. Colonel Leslie Neher, Aerial Photograph of English Field, 1944. Panhandle-Plains Historical Museum, Canyon, Texas.

aerial pictures from its heights (figs. 4.9).[15] Historian Jason Weems refers to this shift as "aeriality" or the "process of aerial seeing, picturing and thinking."[16]

Aeriality included the views of Paris from on high, but also views of the flat West Texas landscape as geometric grids of fenced ranches and fields of crops or the massive Palo Duro Canyon as a mere scar in the earth. For instance, Colonel Leslie Neher made an amazing collection of images from his plane in 1944, which are now in the archives of the Panhandle-Plains Historical Museum, including images that show not only the geometric patterns of the Southern Plains but also a plane's wing in a way that reminds us how the photographs were taken (fig. 4.10).[17] According to Weems, aeriality opened up previously understood land-scapes and presented them in radically new and exciting ways, especially on the rural Middle American plains.[18] These new views were both akin to a "god's eye" position of authority and an escapist feeling of not being beholden to gravity or social rules—both being powerful aspects of modernity and its pioneering spirit of exploration and expansion, especially in the United States.[19]

In the twentieth century, with the introduction of aviation and flight, aerial vision comprised not just the sensation of being elevated high above the ground, but also new sensory experiences of motion—the body moving up and down, right and left, and even in vertiginous swoops and loops—a physical and visual

125

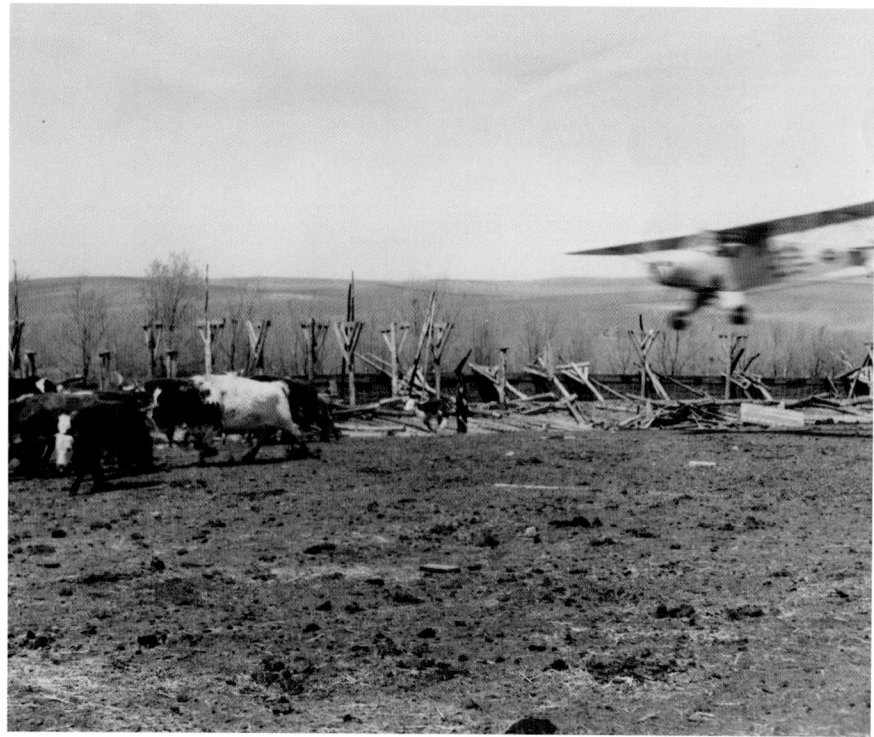

Figure 4.11. Unknown photographer, *Airplane and Cattle*, unknown date. Graham Plow Company Records, Panhandle-Plains Historical Museum, Canyon, Texas.

transformative sensation experienced by pilots and passengers alike in the era of barnstorming.[20] Those brave enough to pay for rides of aerobatic tricks in open planes, with the very real risk of crashing, experienced the extreme sport of their era.[21] But those new sensations of aeriality were not limited to trick pilots and planes, especially in the sprawling rural region of the Panhandle. Ranchers, cowboys, doctors, veterinarians—men and women alike—were maneuvering through the skies for both business and pleasure starting in the late 1920s.[22] For example, an extant photograph captures one rancher apparently "herding" cattle from his plane (fig. 4.11).[23] To be sure, "cowboying" from privately owned planes became a common thing in the area, both as a functional part of the ranching lifestyle and as a spectator sport. In his memoir *Pioneer Pilot from the Texas Panhandle: Stories of a Flier's Life*, George Christopher described barnstorming demonstrations in the 1930s where pilots would "bulldog a steer from the wing of a plane" in front of crowds of people. According to Christopher, a cowboy on a horse would direct the steer as the pilot swooped down to guide it, and the most difficult part was keeping the horse from panicking with the closeness of the plane—something only the best riders could do.[24]

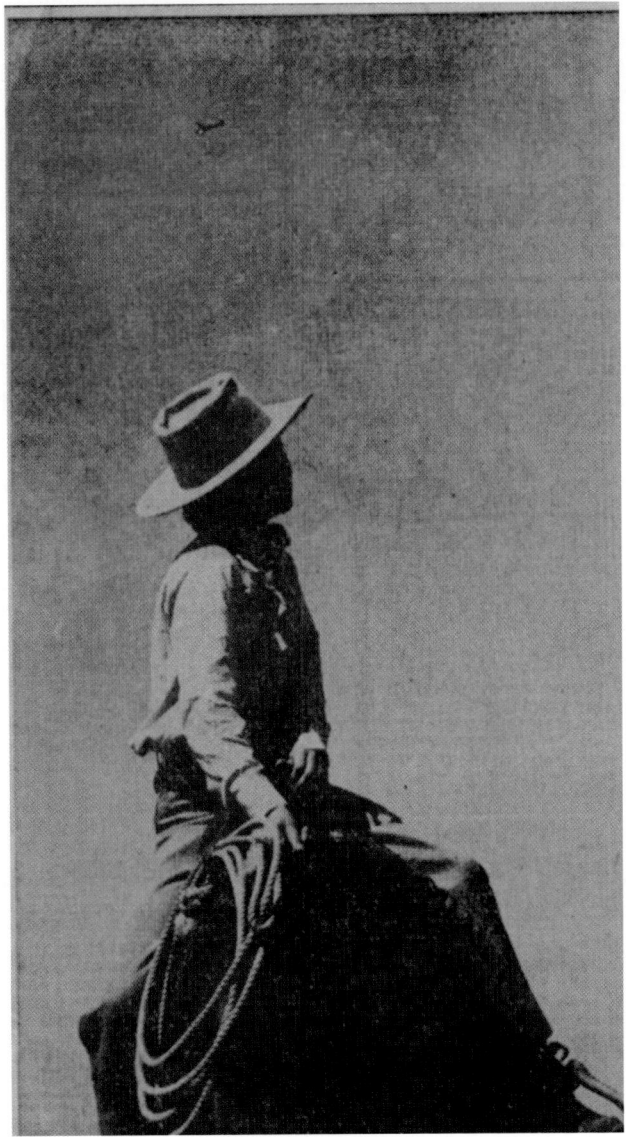

Figure 4.12. *Amarillo Sunday News and Globe* clipping, 1940. John L. McCarty Papers, Panhandle-Plains Historical Museum, Canyon, Texas.

The invitation to the JA Roundup in 1940 (fig. 4.1) also points to the practice of cowboying from planes. The invitation played upon nostalgia for former eras, the "good ol' days" of cowboys and cattle, while it emphasized that this "Old West" experience was now attainable only by airplane—"no groundlings allowed."[25] To be sure, tours of the "half million acres of the JA and its 25,000 head of cattle" were offered from the air during the roundup, and "cowboys [would] be glad to conduct" these tours. And as Martin wrote, "not one single collision" occurred, and the "ranch hands handled [the many planes] wonderfully," revealing how they were responsible for "rounding up" the airships much like cattle.[26] The cowboy-pilot had gained an important place in Panhandle history, just as cattle ranches had become their own centers of aviation shaped by the visual presence of both well-graded runways and planes. The JA Roundup invitation brags, "We feel it's a tribute to the advancement of aviation that an aerial roundup has replaced the traditional rodeo," again connecting planes to cattle, flight tricks to rodeo feats, and visual spectacles to aviation. Newspaper articles on the Aerial Roundup featured images of young girls and boys on horseback "casting their eyes aloft at the progress of the future," a progress that tied ranching directly to flight and its visual aesthetics (4.12).[27]

This intersection of Old West and New West centered upon aviation was further highlighted in a 1938 news article in the *Clovis* (New Mexico) *News Journal*, which argued that the modern cowboy was a pilot: "The cowboy's top horse today is an airplane. This 'old faithful' of the modern ranch rounds up wild horses, locates the stray calves, rides fences, brings buyers, rushes emergency supplies and, when business is done, takes the owner out for diversion."[28]

The author continued, describing how "plenty of young fellows will leap at the chance to be a cow pilot" and how "flying is a valuable aid to the man whose wealth is scattered through those nooks and crannies" when it is "no small responsibility keeping track of so much territory, so many cowhands, such big herds." Planes could deliver supplies quickly, could find a "stray in the snow," could drop feed from above, and could reach places even when roads were impassable. They transported ranch owners to the big-city stockyards to broker sales and took the "womenfolk" to complete their shopping errands, all pointing to the strategic and central role of the plane in everyday life on the twentieth-century American cattle ranch.[29]

However, lest we think that this link between aviation and masculine pastimes or labor were unique to the American West, Luke Seaber has shown that the "country sports" of hunting and fishing likewise intersected with aviation in interwar Britain as well.[30] Seaber explores how the traditional horsemanship and the pastime of the fox-hunt in particular became connected with flying as a practice in modern rural Britain, as country pilots took to flying planes much like the cowboys and cattlemen of the US West. As Seaber writes, "'Sport' here is used in what is now the old-fashioned sense, but was once perhaps its primary meaning, at least among the upper and upper-middle classes: outdoor country activity involved (at least as

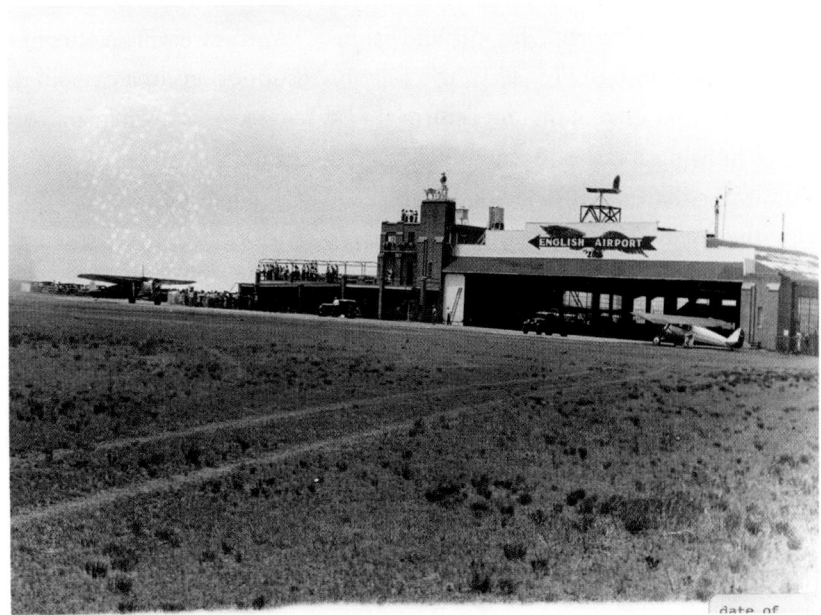

Figure 4.13. Unknown photographer, English Airport, Amarillo, Texas, c. 1933–35. Photographs of English Field Folder, Panhandle-Plains Historical Museum, Canyon, Texas.

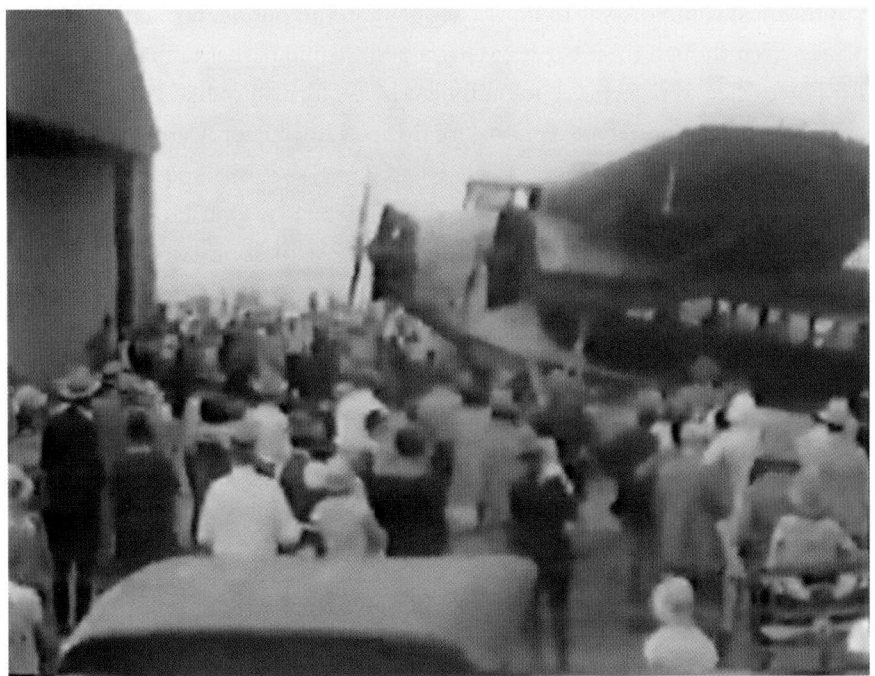

Figure 4.14. C. Don Hughes (filmmaker), first passenger plane arrival at English Field, film still, 1929. Panhandle-Plains Historical Museum, Canyon, Texas.

a goal, although often not as an achieved one) with the death of an animal – that is to say, the triad of huntin', shootin' and fishin'."[31] And as we will see later in this chapter with the instance of Julian and Billy Bivins shooting coyotes from their plane to rid their ranch of that predatorial threat, "cowboying" from planes often included hunting and shooting as much as herding animals.

Returning to the published photograph of an enthralled child viewing a plane during the JA Roundup (fig. 4.12), we are reminded that the excitement and entertainment of aviation in this interwar era involved spectators as much as pilots and passengers. Airports like English Field in Amarillo were not just spots to catch a plane but also places to watch aviation as a form of visual entertainment (fig. 4.13). One photo from the 1930s shows a crowd standing on the viewing deck of English Field, a practice one could find in airports from Amarillo to France and Britain. In *Jet Age Aesthetics*, Schwartz describes how crowds of people flocked to Orly Airport in Paris, viewing planes from the "public terrace," which included picnic areas and sandboxes for children—a practice seen in the Texas Panhandle as well.[32] Brett Holman defines the spectatorship of flight as "aerial theatre" and has shown that this "theatre" carried over to mock air battles viewed by British crowds in the hundreds of thousands between the wars.[33] He argues that spectatorship was the most common way to experience flight in this period, not actual flying in planes. Even though these battles were orchestrated in part as tests for the Royal Air Force, they were seen as entertainment by the British public.[34] Holman also points out how important cinema was for the spectatorship of aviation—a fact that became true in rural West Texas as well. For example, the visual spectacle of planes arriving at English Field was preserved on film when C. Don Hughes captured the first passenger plane to arrive there in 1929 (fig. 4.14), only two years after the silent film *Wings* won the Oscar for Best Picture, an award that demonstrated how the visual technology of film was by then a principal means of experiencing flight, optically and virtually, and also how flight had become a common part of modern life across the globe.[35]

AVIATION AND ARCHITECTURE

Aviation represented modernity not only in the forms of transportation and spectatorship but also in architectural design. The English Field building in Amarillo, like many other airports of the era, was constructed in an architectural style that specifically evoked machines and modern progress: namely Art Deco (fig. 4.15). The structure seen in this drawing—which burned in 1937—included Art Deco detailing defined by an emphasis on linearity and geometry that reacted against

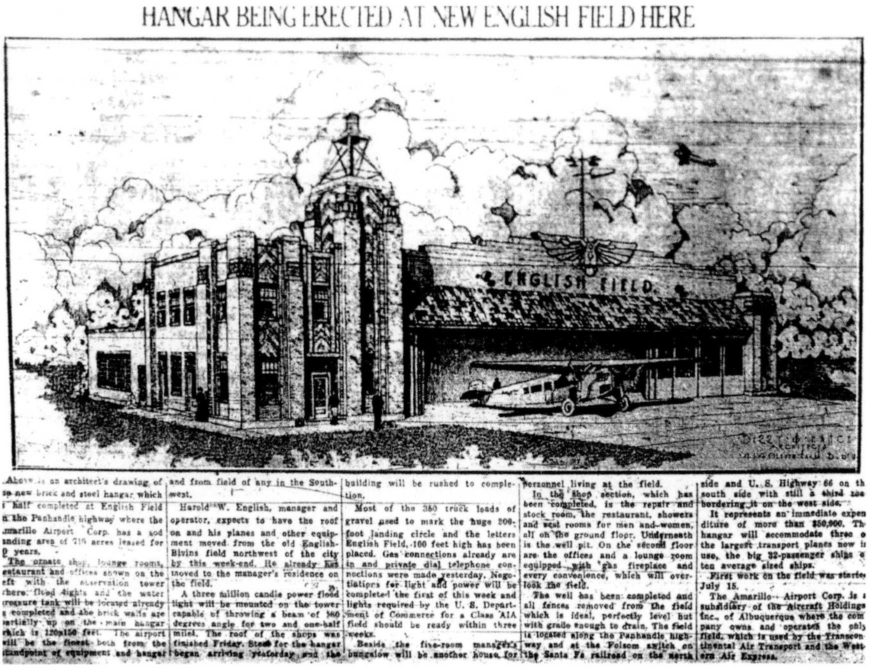

Figure 4.15. Drawing of the original English Field building (burned in 1937). Texas Air and Space Museum, Amarillo, Texas.

classical styles, while still holding onto traditional masonry massing; it was not yet the glass box architecture of the International Style that erased masonry with its steel frame and glass facing. In the 1920s and '30s, Art Deco was the leading modern style of commercial architecture in the United States, and we find this style in all major cities across the country, including New York, L.A., and Chicago, as well as in smaller cities such as Amarillo.[36]

Art Deco style allowed commercial buildings of all kinds—office buildings, theaters, hospitals, and apartment buildings, for instance—to declare themselves as "modern" in design, and in a language that appealed to the masses rather than to scholarly or artistic intellectuals. Art Deco was a popular style more than an avant-garde movement in the history of architecture. It used ornate surface decoration, sometimes organic plant forms or hard-edged geometric forms like zig zags, while also incorporating direct if abstracted references to modern technologies: automobile parts, electrical streaks, radio waves, movie camera parts, and aviation symbolism. The decorative accents on the first English Field building in Amarillo can be read in terms of aviation metaphors: plane propellers and wings, for instance, and in this, they are comparable to other airport buildings from the era, such as the New Orleans Lakefront Airport, built in 1934, with its central

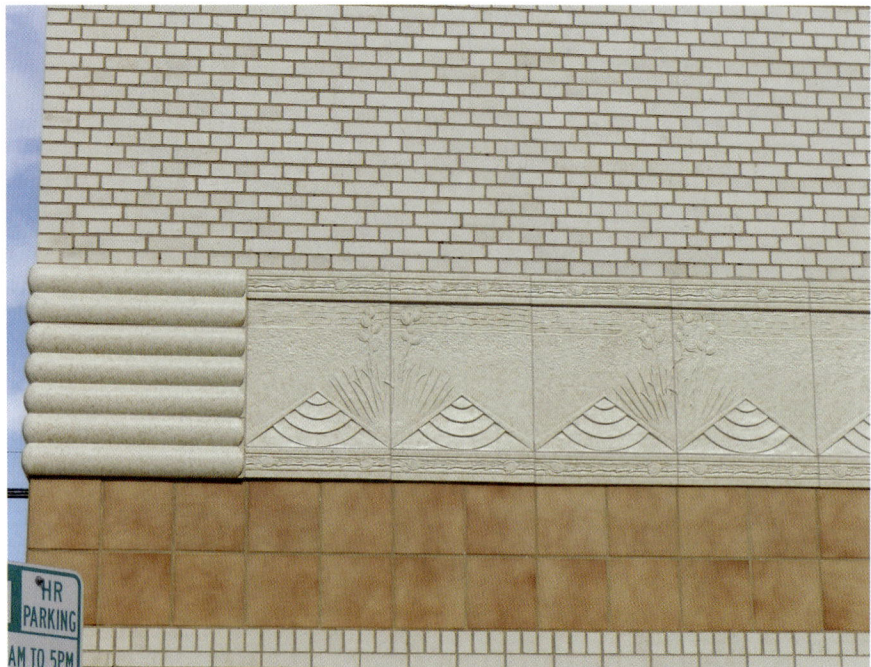

Figure 4.16. Guy Carlander (architect), detail of yucca design in cast concrete, White and Kirk Department Store, Amarillo, 1938. (Photo by author.)

winged human figure and propeller details.[37] At the same time, Art Deco architecture also embraced regional differences that pertained to specific geographic and cultural locations. Designs in the Texas Panhandle, for instance, displayed abstracted yucca plants, such as Guy Carlander's White and Kirk Department Store in Amarillo (fig. 4.16), or the fauna of the region that sculpted heads of wolves and buffalo on the façade of the Panhandle-Plains Historical Museum displays. Carlander was one of Amarillo's most prolific architects, opening his own firm in 1920 after having worked for the Santa Fe Railroad. In Amarillo and the surrounding region, he designed civic structures, office buildings, department stores, schools, railroad depots, hospitals, houses, power plants, a natatorium, and a country club—many of these with a modern Art Deco flavor.[38]

After the first iteration of the English Field main building burned in 1937, a new version was constructed by 1939, this time employing the latest variation of popular "modernistic" architecture: the Streamline Moderne style. This style had even more emphasis on machine-age technologies, including the increased aerodynamics of plane and automobile design in the 1930s (fig. 4.17). The new English Field building was comparable to Carlander's Amarillo Hardware Company building built in 1937 (fig. 4.18), with its flat surfaces, undecorated bands of windows,

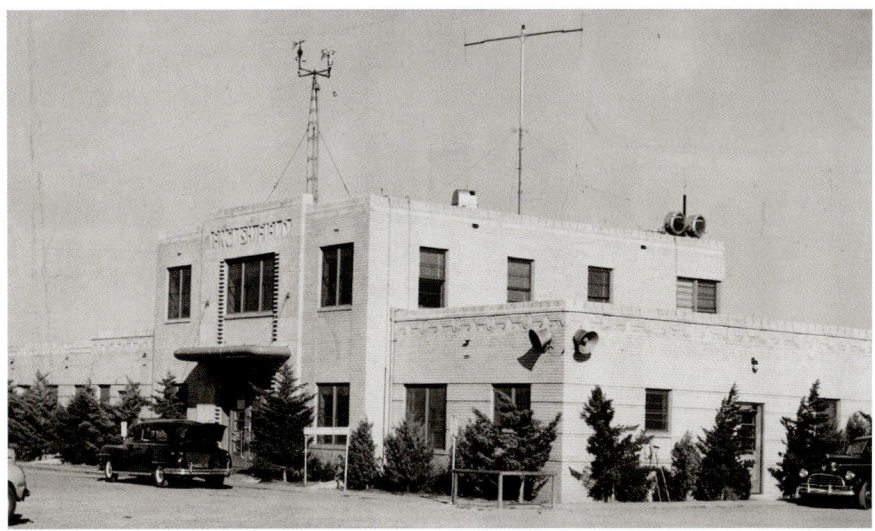

Figure 4.17. Rebuilt English Field, c. 1940. J. Howard Miller, staff photographer, *Amarillo Globe News*. Amarillo International Airport Folder, Panhandle-Plains Historical Museum, Canyon, Texas.

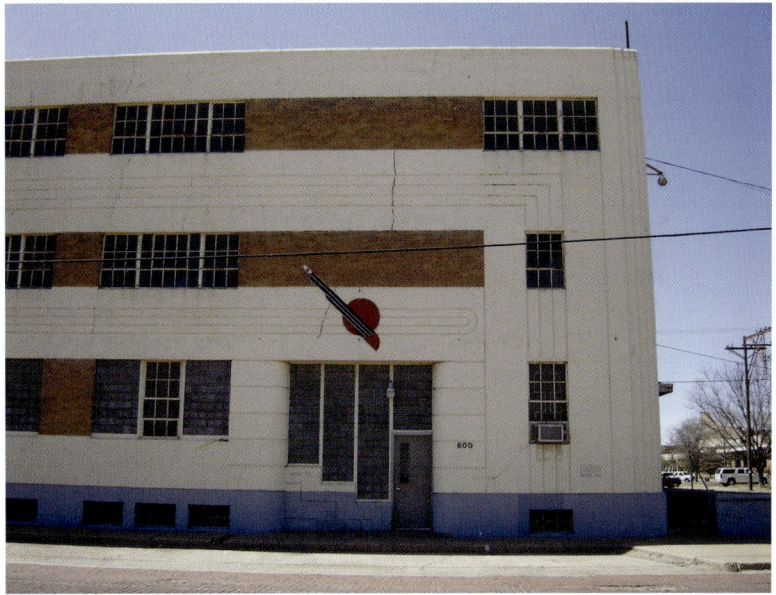

Figure 4.18. Guy Carlander (architect), Amarillo Hardware Company Building, 1938. (Photo by author.)

and linear detailing. The reworked English Field structure retained a decorative frieze like the original building, this time with designs of sunbursts and winged circles. The suspended overhang protecting the entrance comprised a tubular shape reminiscent of the increasingly sleek airplane bodies and other machine-inspired

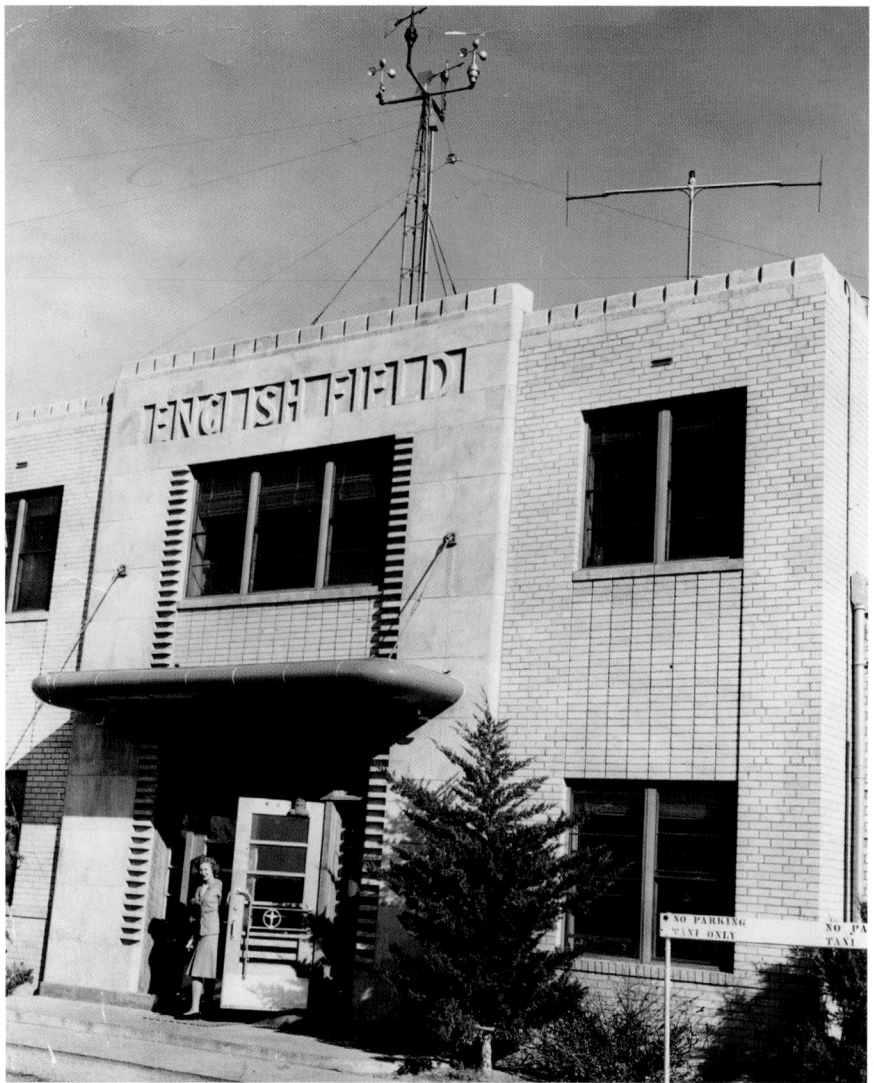

Figure 4.19. Rebuilt English Field, c. 1940. J. Howard Miller, staff photographer, *Amarillo Globe News*. Amarillo International Airport Folder, Panhandle-Plains Historical Museum, Canyon, Texas.

designs. And even the marquee that read "English Field" (fig. 4.19) took up modernistic text like so many buildings from the era, including Carlander's First Baptist Church and his Amarillo College Ordway Hall (figs. 4.20–21).

But perhaps the most striking architectural design responding to aviation was constructed by Maurice Bernson, the airline painter and artist mentioned above. After the war, Bernson continued his art studies at the renowned Cranbrook Academy in Michigan, among other schools. In 1955, Bernson was commissioned

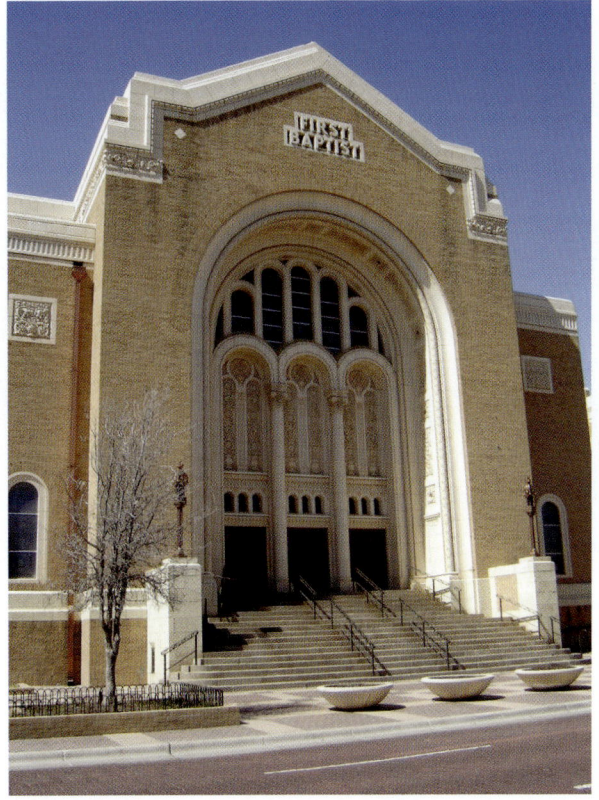

Figure 4.20. Guy Carlander (architect), First Baptist Church, Amarillo, 1930. (Photo by author.)

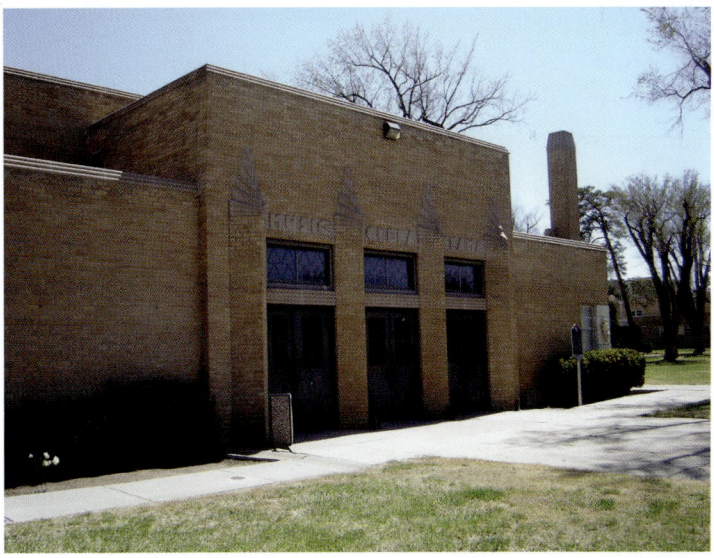

Figure 4.21. Guy Carlander (architect), Ordway Hall, Amarillo College, 1930. (Photo by author.)

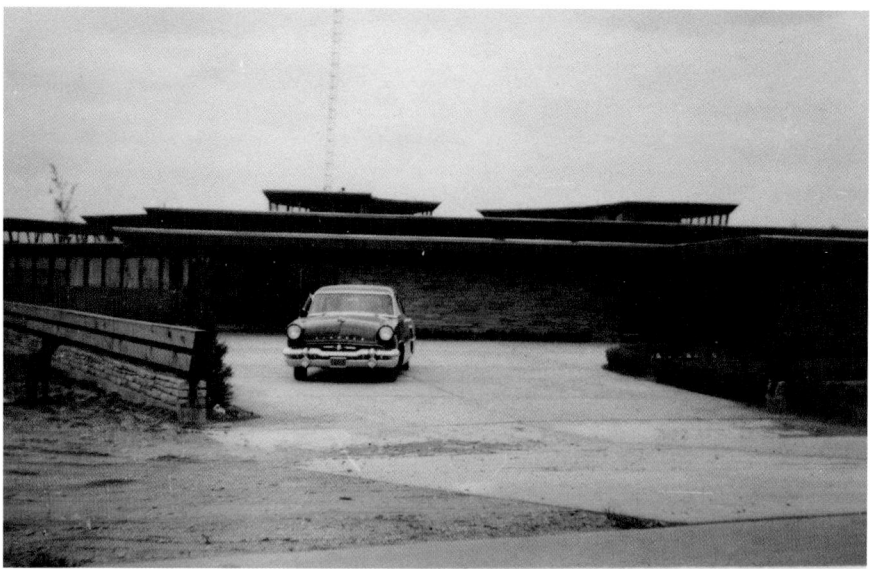

Figure 4.22. Maurice Bernson (architect), J. C. Daniels House, Pampa, Texas, 1955. Maurice Bernson Papers, Panhandle-Plains Historical Museum, Canyon, Texas.

as the architect of what became known as the "airport house" in Pampa, Texas (figs. 4.22–23).[39] A true mid-century modern gem but entirely off the radar of scholars and architecture lovers, this house was paid for by J. C. Daniels, the owner of a Lincoln-Mercury car dealership in Pampa and the founder of both a local radio station and newspaper—in other words, a leader in modern technology, transportation, and media.

Daniels wanted his house to be a showcase for his prized cars and feature a cutting-edge design.[40] Bernson's artistic vision produced a structure for Daniels that merged automotive and aviation modernity in an innovative way. The single-level house takes an overall U-shaped formation that wraps itself around an abstracted heart-shaped swimming pool in the back. On one side is a glass-enclosed carport to hold three cars—not unlike a dealership showroom. The overall structure of the house is topped with a continuous band of windows, making it appear that the flat roof hovers almost magically above the walls. According to one news article about the house, "the separation between walls and ceiling allows unobstructed flow of light and air. This openness with privacy gives a feeling of space without confinement—perhaps the most outstanding feature of the house."[41] Another reporter for the *Amarillo Daily News* wrote, "As houses go, [this example] is not outstanding – if you are willing to overlook the fact that the walls and ceiling do not meet." The reporter describes the unique design as "angular glass turrets"

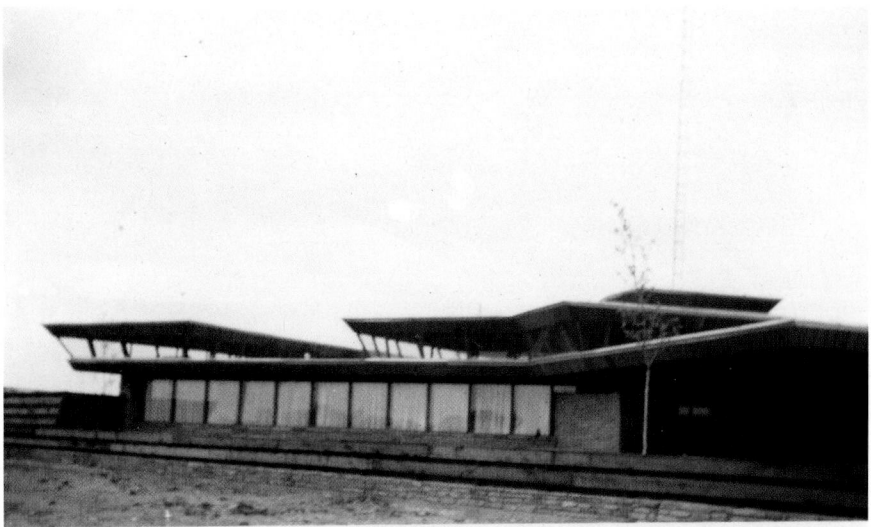

Figure 4.23. Maurice Bernson (architect), J. C. Daniels House, Pampa, Texas, 1955. Panhandle-Plains Historical Museum, Canyon, Texas.

that top the structure, offering "increased illumination and dramatic effects."[42] It is these turrets, I believe, that most reminded viewers of an airport design because they are quite reminiscent of air traffic control towers. Also like an airport, the house "zig zags" across its lot, unfolding fluidly rather than traditionally with the strict separation of rooms; it "has no actual beginning and no end; it just wanders. But the effect is not a rambling quality, but rather a kind of unity," again comparable to the latest airport terminals.[43]

As his notes on the design explain, Bernson wanted a space that "doesn't leave you feeling 'boxed in,'" but instead "allows freedom of movement void of oppressive confinement," one that feels "physically, intuitively and visually free."[44] This freedom of movement embodies the promises of modern transportation, not only the cars Daniels was selling but also the planes that had become a common way to travel, especially during the emerging jet age of the 1950s. The concept also ties to the "open road" freedom that so characterizes the ethos and aesthetics of the Texas Panhandle region. However, the jet age also brought its own "boxed in" sensations that are very different from the boundless freedom experienced by earlier pilots and passengers. Schwartz describes how the jet age was characterized by a distinct sense of motionless and sensationless travel—at least when the ride in the jet is at its best.[45] The visual views are minimized, both by the small airplane windows in jets and by the focus of passengers toward the interior of the plane rather than the surrounding air or land below. In contrast, however, airports continued to be

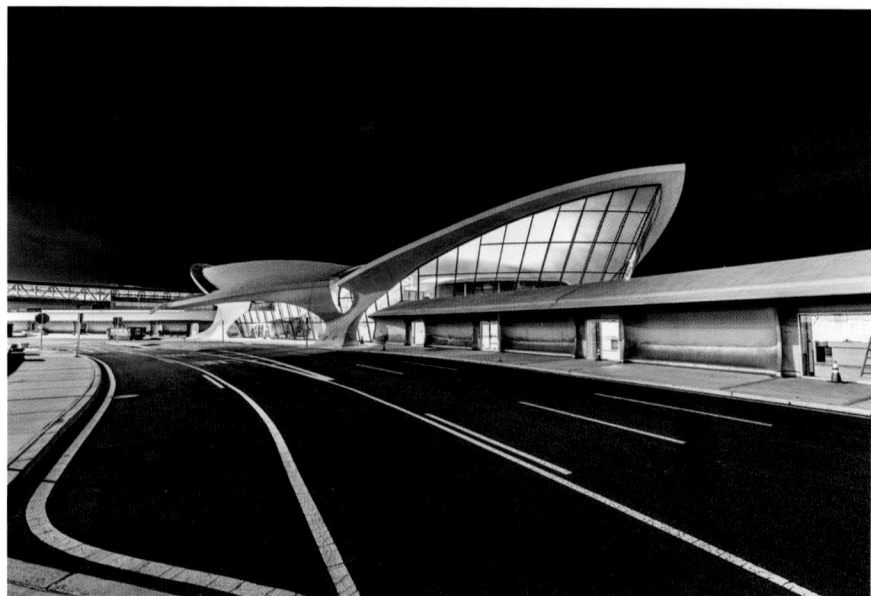

Figure 4.24. Eero Saarinen (architect), TWA Terminal, John F. Kennedy Airport (originally Idlewild), New York, 1962. (Photo by Max Touhey.)

environments for spectatorship, with windows and decks that allowed passengers and visitors alike to witness the thrill of flight.[46] It is this airport aesthetic—rather than the experience of flying in a jet—that helps explain why Bernson's design acquired its nickname: "airport house."

The most famous jet-age airport design to which we could compare Bernson's house in Pampa would be the TWA Terminal at John F. Kennedy (originally Idlewild) Airport in New York City designed by Eero Saarinen (fig. 4.24). However, the TWA Terminal was completed in 1962, years after the Bernson house was designed and constructed.[47] The point to make is that the jet-age "airport design" was a style that captured the imagination of architects from New York to West Texas—and not that Bernson was explicitly influenced by the famous Saarinen. What both designs have in common is the horizontal spread of the structure defined by adjacent glass windowpanes that make the buildings "antimonumental and in a constant state of becoming."[48] Schwartz uses this phrase to describe the design at LAX Airport, completed in 1961, but it perfectly describes the Bernson house as well.

In addition to his work as an architect on this house, Bernson also created abstract wall-mounted metal sculptures for the home that embraced themes of progress and flight, especially those with a sleek, linear jet-age aesthetic (fig. 4.25).[49]

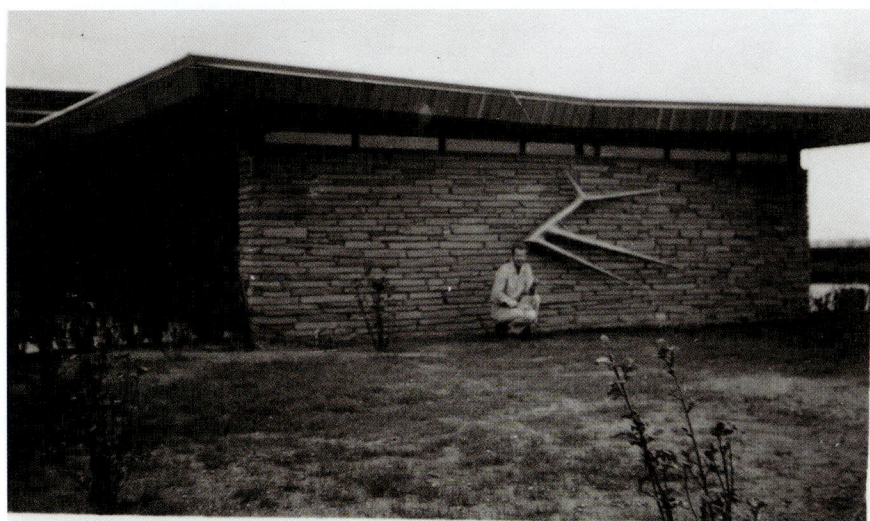

Figure 4.25. Maurice Bernson, sculpture on the J. C. Daniels House, Pampa, Texas, 1955. Panhandle-Plains Historical Museum, Canyon, Texas.

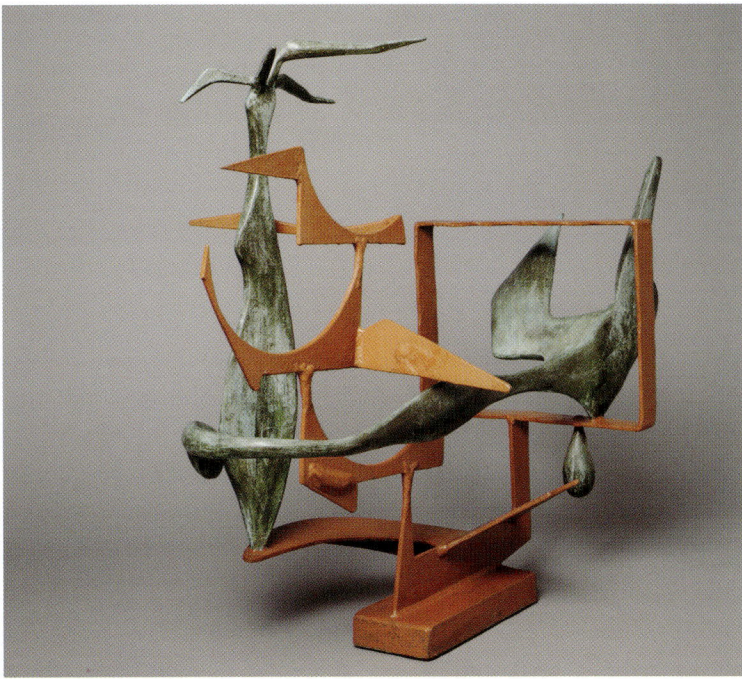

Figure 4.26. David Smith, *Flight*, 1951, welded and painted steel and cast bronze, 32.625 x 34 x 20.5 inches. Harvard Museums / Fogg Museum, Cambridge, Massachusetts, gift of Lois Orswell. Object Number 1994.21. (©2025 The Estate of David Smith / Licensed by VAGA at Artists Rights Society (ARS), New York. Photo: ©President and Fellows of Harvard College.)

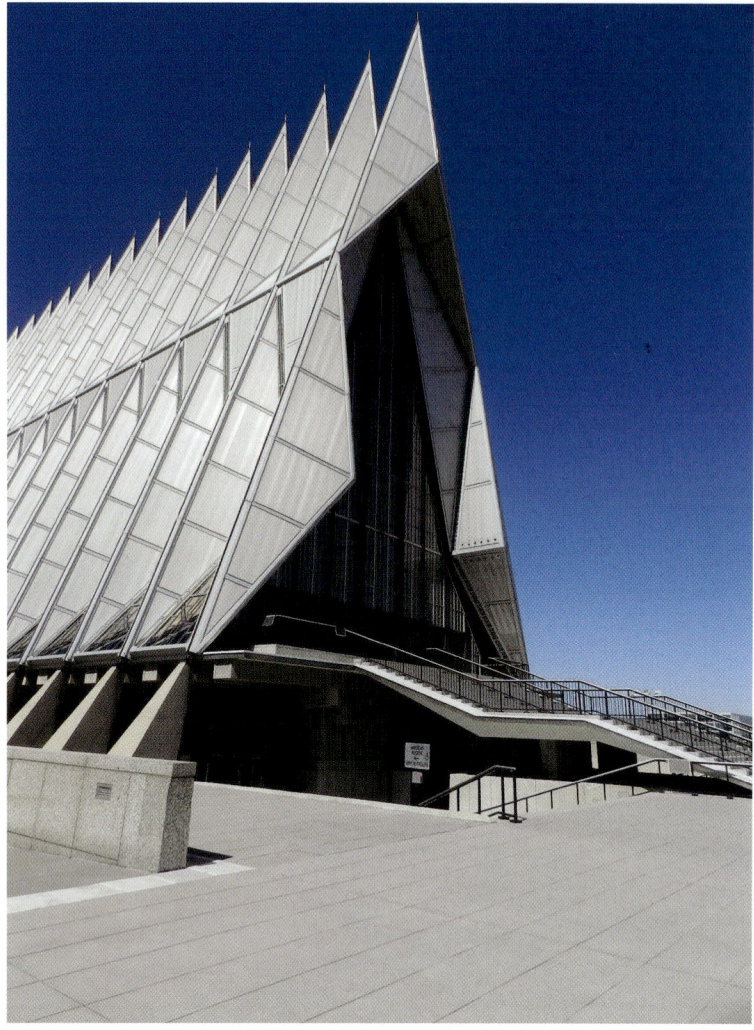

Figure 4.27. Skidmore, Owings, and Merrill (architects), Air Force Academy Chapel, 1962. (Photo by author.)

For instance, one that was mounted on the exterior brick wall of the home employs thin metal forms arranged in diagonal positions, mirroring the wings and noses of jets. Bernson's sculptures converse with other mid-century modern designs responding to jet-age flight—from David Smith's 1951 welded-steel and bronze sculpture *Flight* (fig. 4.26) to Skidmore, Owings, and Merrill's Air Force Academy Chapel completed in 1962 with its vertical pointed metallic forms (fig. 4.27).[50] The chapel's structure embodied the Air Force's commitment of "soaring to new heights" as a military branch, founded only a decade before, which embraced jet-age speed through the most advanced technology of aerospace engineering. A

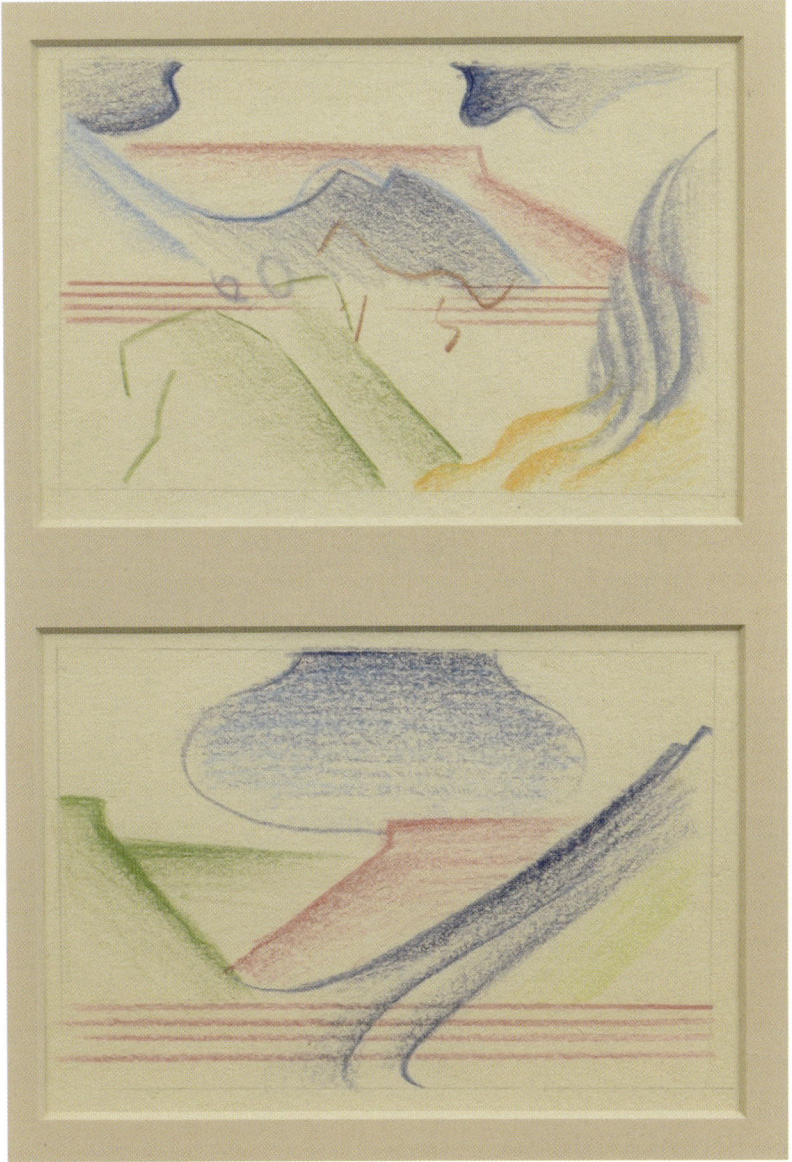

Figure 4.28. Maurice Bernson, *Untitled*, unknown date, pencil and crayon on pulp paper, 12 x 17.875 inches. Panhandle-Plains Historical Museum, Canyon, Texas.

drawing by Bernson now in the PPHM also corresponds to this jet-age aesthetic (fig. 4.28). Even when he renders two landscapes of canyonland mesas, including an abstracted but very clear horse, his lines zip and swoop like his sculptures for the Daniels's airport house in Pampa.[51]

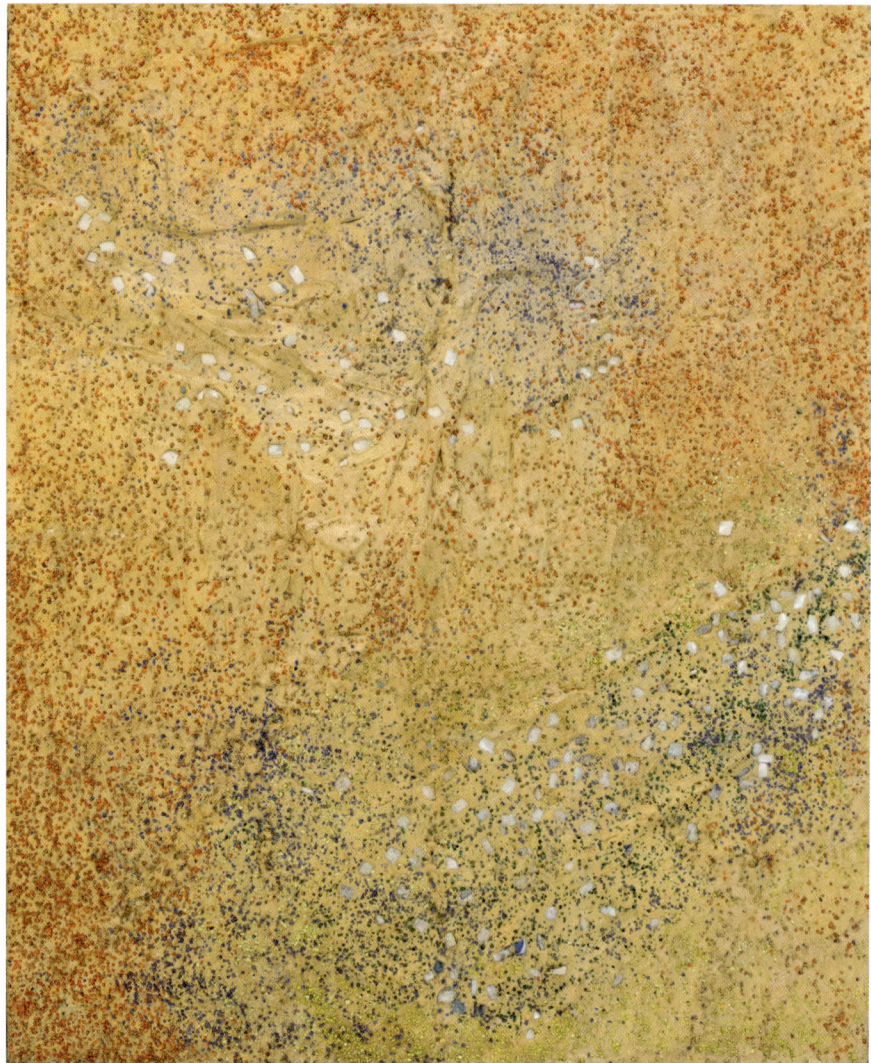

Figure 4.29. Jeanne Reynal, *Amarillo*, 1960, mosaic, mixed media. 72 x 60 inches. Eric Firestone Gallery. (©2025 Estate of Jeanne Reynal / Artists Rights Society (ARS), New York.)

AVIATION AESTHETICS

Bernson's designs show his response to the shift into a new aesthetic era shaped by the speed and design of jets. The airport house in Pampa, much like the other examples of aviation and aesthetics we explored in this chapter, embodies the way aviation challenged conventional vision and design in the Panhandle and opened it up to innovation and change. Both the conceptual promise and the bodily experience of flight undoubtedly expanded the perspective of pilots and passengers, just as it did for artists and designers. A pioneering mentality and a distinct energy for change in the region coincided with the embrace of flight. The belief in open-ended possibilities of making a life on the "frontier" aligned directly with the thrilling risks and exciting potentials of aviation. If the frontier is defined as an infinite notion of the future, something always to be explored and wrestled with but never entirely conquered, so is the conquest of the air.[52] At the same time, the rural and small-town idylls of the High Plains intersected directly with the big business capitalism of cattle ranching—and aviation was at the center of this intersection. The powerful nostalgia for the "good old days" of cowboys and the early years of ranching finds itself embraced alongside a commitment to the "New West" with a focus on modernity and a promising future. Such paradoxes of past and future, of old and new, are foundational to the identity of the region.[53]

Aviation experiences inspired still other jet-age artists to complete work connected to the Texas Panhandle. Mosaicist Jeanne Reynal captured what appears to be an aerial view of the arid canyonlands in her work *Amarillo* from 1960 (fig. 4.29), which was made immediately after her first plane flight to the region.[54] She took this trip from her home in New York City to participate in an all-women show in Amarillo at the Dord Fitz Gallery—a show that also included the art of sculptor Louise Nevelson and painter Elaine de Kooning, both New York–based colleagues of Reynal.[55] In *Amarillo*, we are perhaps reminded of Colonel Neher's image (fig. 4.10) with its similar variated earth tones displayed from a bird's-eye view that produces an abstract all-over aesthetic pattern—both compositions read as foundationally modernist, simultaneously non-objective and playfully representational, an ambiguity at the center of modern art. Artists and photographers captured a common sight for pilots and passengers flying in the region.

Like Reynal, Nevelson also flew via plane to and above Amarillo from New York. In the Texas Panhandle, she taught classes and courted patrons—and found aesthetic inspiration for her art.[56] While she began coating her wooden wall sculptures with cheap gold paint in response to the gilding of the faucets in Texas ranch houses, she also began working in steel, the same material as the planes that flew her across the country. Her large-scale, vertically oriented sculpture *Voyage* surges skyward, moving away from her more famous "walls" to forms that ascend in space (fig. 4.30). The most direct flight between New York and Amarillo, and the one that Nevelson took, was on TWA airlines. TWA was the first national airline to have a presence in Amarillo, and it had the longest-running service to the city.[57] Through TWA, artists like Reynal and Nevelson could get on a state-of-the-art jet in New York and get off that same plane in Amarillo. Once during her flight, Nevelson got a little tipsy and forgot to get off the plane in Amarillo; she fell asleep

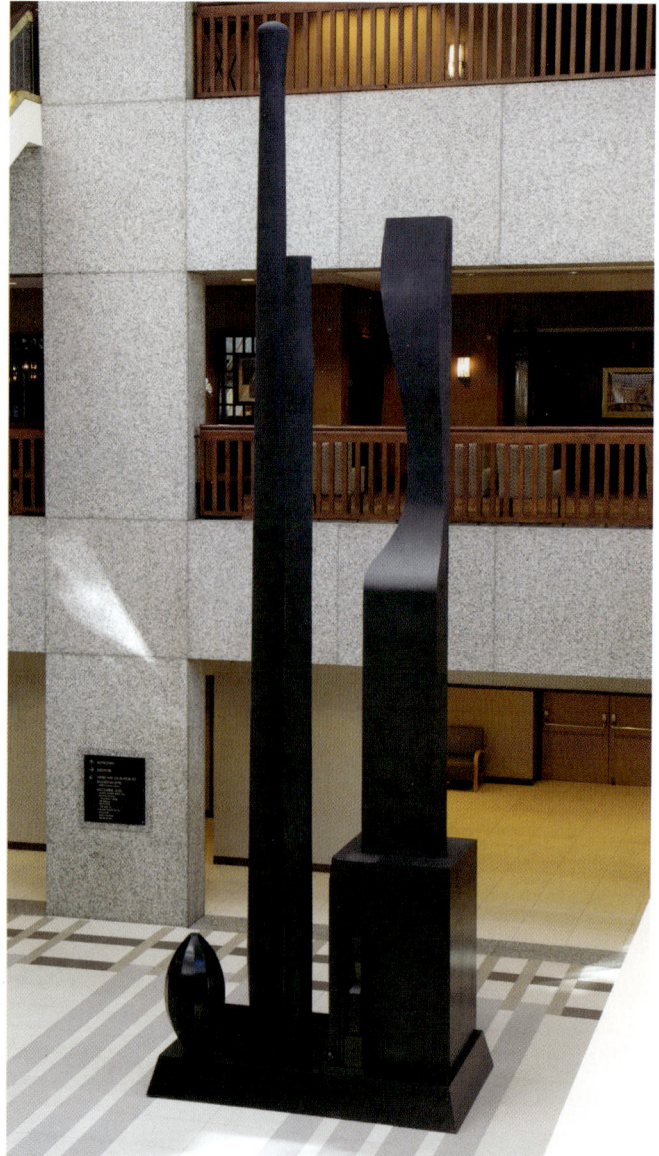

Figure 4.30. Louise Nevelson, *Voyage*, 1975, painted steel, 360 x 108 x 65.5 inches. Hallmark Art Collection, Hallmark Cards, Inc., Kansas City, Missouri. (©2025 Estate of Louise Nevelson / Artists Rights Society (ARS), New York.)

and woke up at the next stopover in Albuquerque instead. Though Nevelson's biography has been well traced by art historians, her aviation experiences have never been directly related to her artwork.[58] The trip between New York and Amarillo on TWA was not nonstop and included a layover in Kansas City. To be sure, the hub of TWA at mid-century was Kansas City, a place where

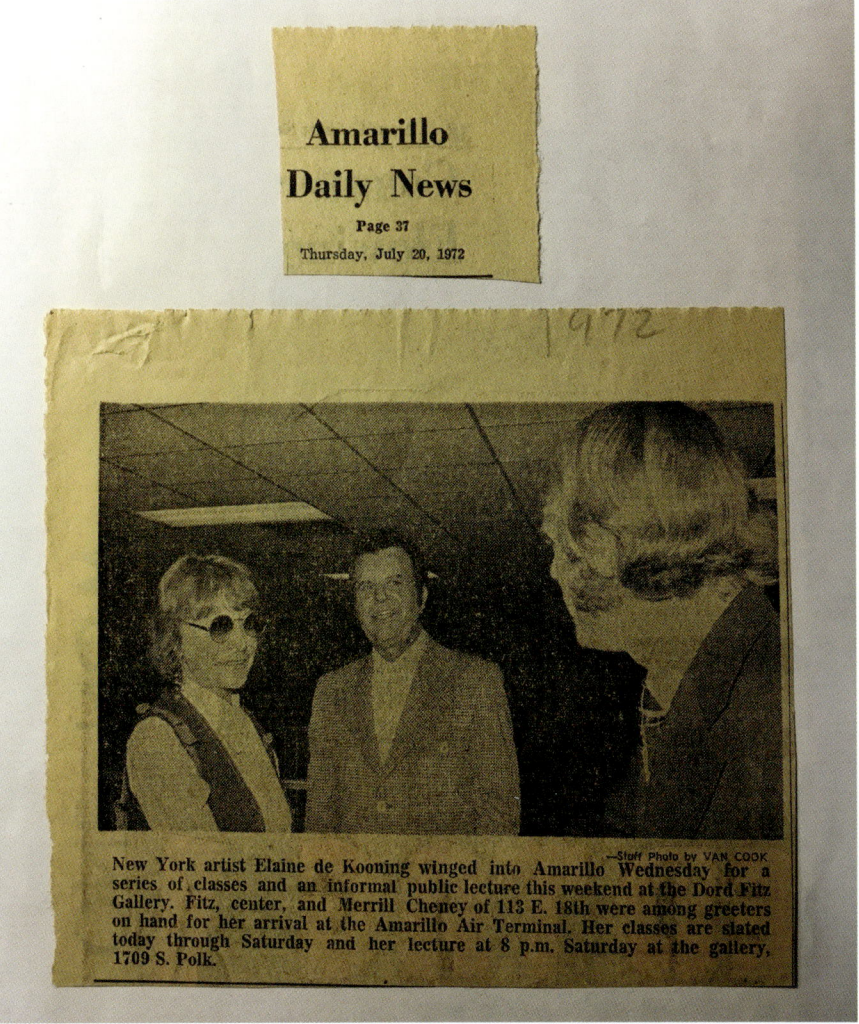

Figure 4.31. Elaine de Kooning with Dord Fitz and Merrill Cheney at the Amarillo Air Terminal. *Amarillo Daily News*, July 20, 1972. Van Cook, staff photographer. (Image courtesy of the Western History Collections, University of Oklahoma and the family of Dord Fitz.)

Nevelson also spent time and courted patrons, perhaps because of the several flights on this airline she took to the Texas Panhandle. Fittingly, Nevelson sold her soaring *Voyage* sculpture to the Hallmark Card Company based in Kansas City—again reminding us how deeply interconnected aviation and art histories of the United States have been.[59] Elaine de Kooning likewise sold a piece to Hallmark Card Company—one of her famous bull paintings—after she discovered Kansas City through her flight patterns between New York and West Texas.[60]

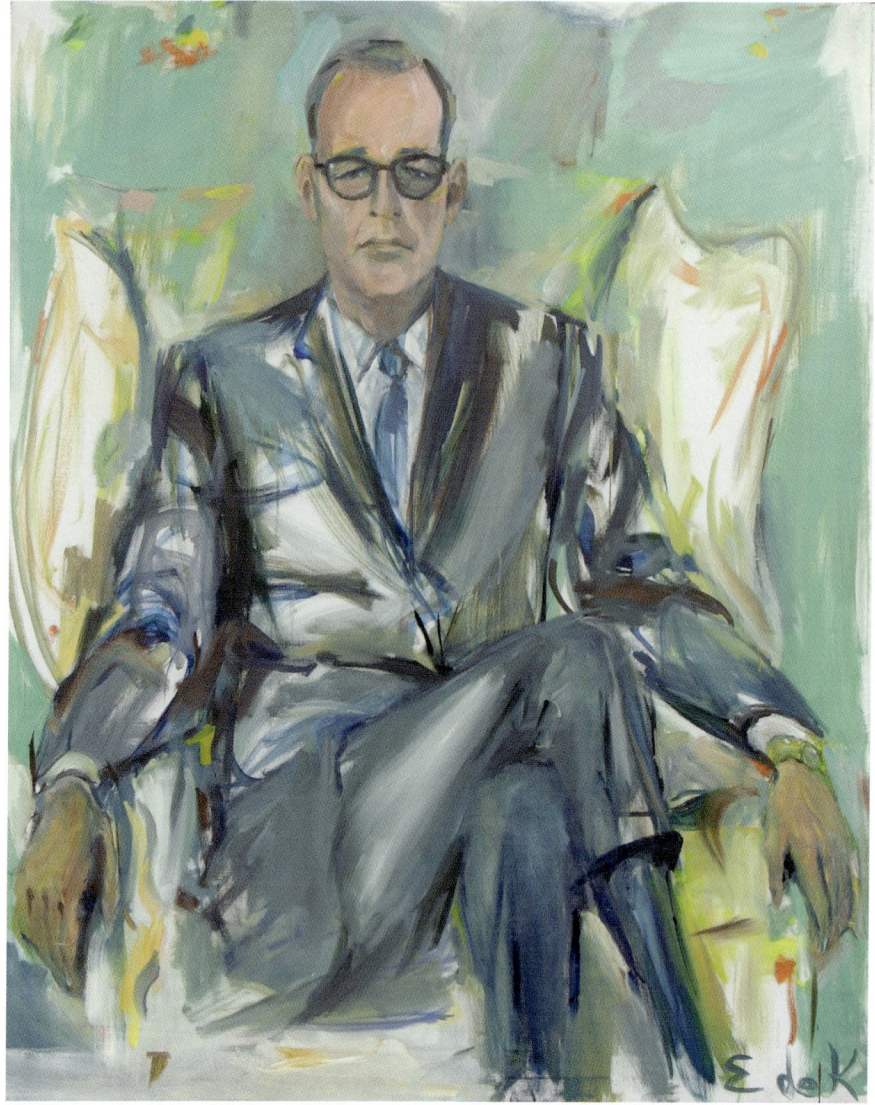

Figure 4.32. Elaine de Kooning, *Lee T. Bivins*, 1965–67, oil on canvas, 59.5 x 48 inches. Amarillo Museum of Art. Gift of the Bivins Foundation. (©Elaine de Kooning Trust.)

De Kooning traveled to Amarillo even more often than Reynal or Nevelson. She made the trip no fewer than sixteen times between 1957 and 1989 (fig. 4.31). But on none of these trips did she drive a car on Route 66 or, after 1968, on Interstate 40. Nor did she ever take a train, which would not have been her style—too crowded, too slow.[61] De Kooning, like Reynal and Nevelson, was a mid-century jet setter, and Amarillo always accommodated her modern lifestyle.[62] While she was in the area, de Kooning met and befriended a family of

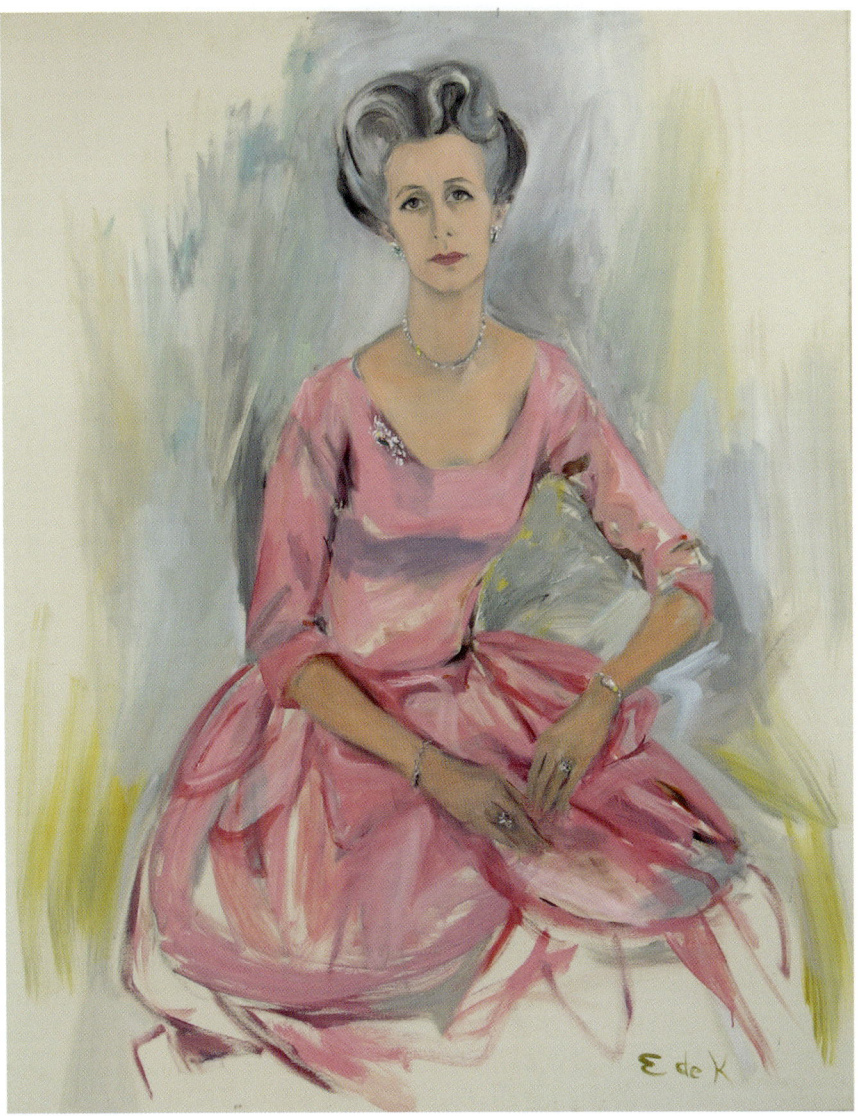

Figure 4.33. Elaine de Kooning, *Betty Teel Bivins*, 1965–67, oil on canvas, 60 x 48 inches. Amarillo Museum of Art. Gift of the Bivins Foundation. (©Elaine de Kooning Trust.)

leading developers of Amarillo's urbanity and artfulness, as well as aviation: the Bivins family. De Kooning painted portraits of Lee Truscott Bivins—a pilot himself—and his wife Betty Teel Bivins in the early 1960s (figs. 4.32–33), which are now in the permanent collection of the Amarillo Museum of Art, an institution founded by Lee's sister, Betty Bivins Childers. De Kooning also painted Childers several times, pieces that remain in the family's private collections (fig. 4.34).[63]

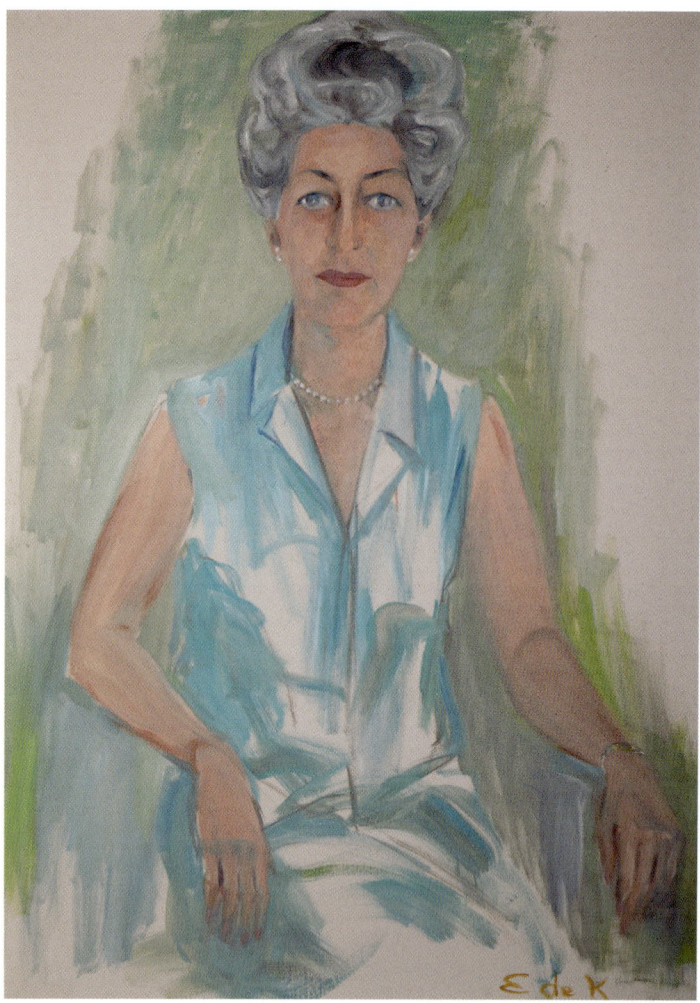

Figure 4.34. Elaine de Kooning, *Betty Bivins Childers*, c. 1965, oil on canvas, 48 x 36 inches. Collection of Claire and Paul Burney. (©Elaine de Kooning Trust.)

Over the years, de Kooning clearly appreciated and benefited from the many artistic investments of the Bivins family.[64] But the New York artist likely did not realize when she painted these family members that their grandfather Lee Bivins had been responsible for bringing aviation to Amarillo (fig. 4.35).[65] In other words, de Kooning's most supportive Western patrons also helped make it possible for her to fly to the Panhandle, comfortably and directly, from her New York home, just as they were responsible for instigating much aesthetic change to the city of Amarillo. Starting in 1903, the Bivins family constructed one of the first in-town mansions, a neoclassical beauty on the corner of Polk and Tenth Streets with its columned semicircular two-story portico and symmetrical structure. The house

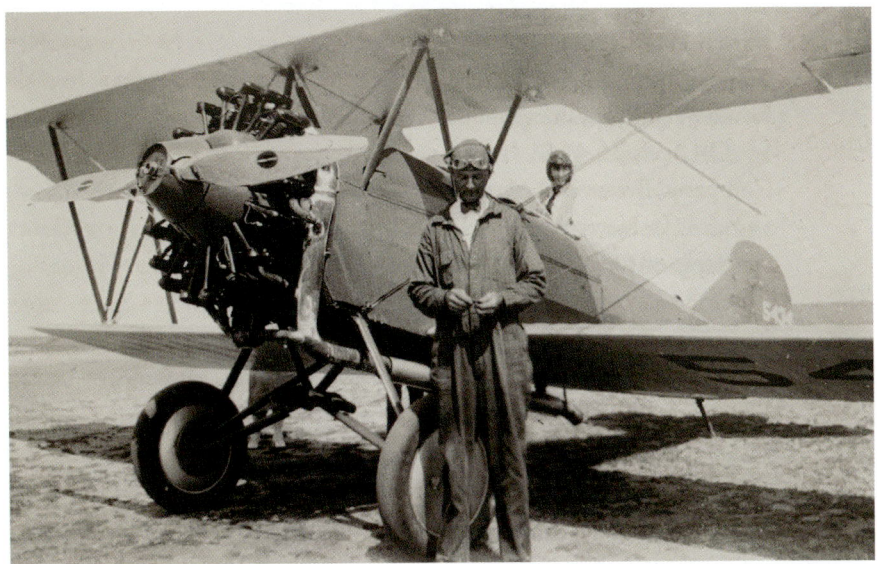

Figure 4.35. Unknown photographer, Lloyd Bivins (standing) and Lee Bivins (seated), c. 1920. Texas Air and Space Museum, Amarillo, Texas.

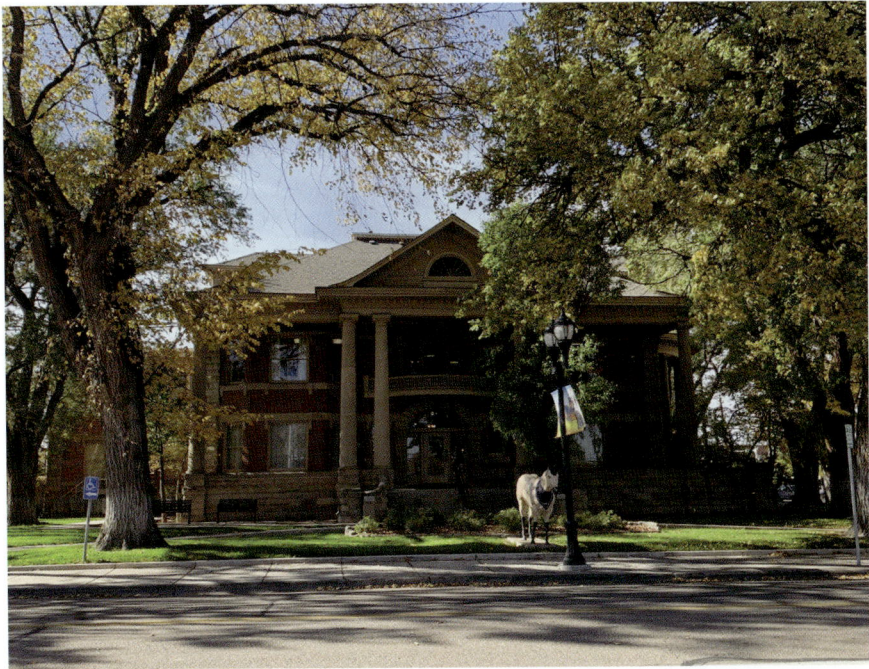

Figure 4.36. Bivins Home, now the Amarillo Chamber of Commerce, built 1903–06. (Photo by author.)

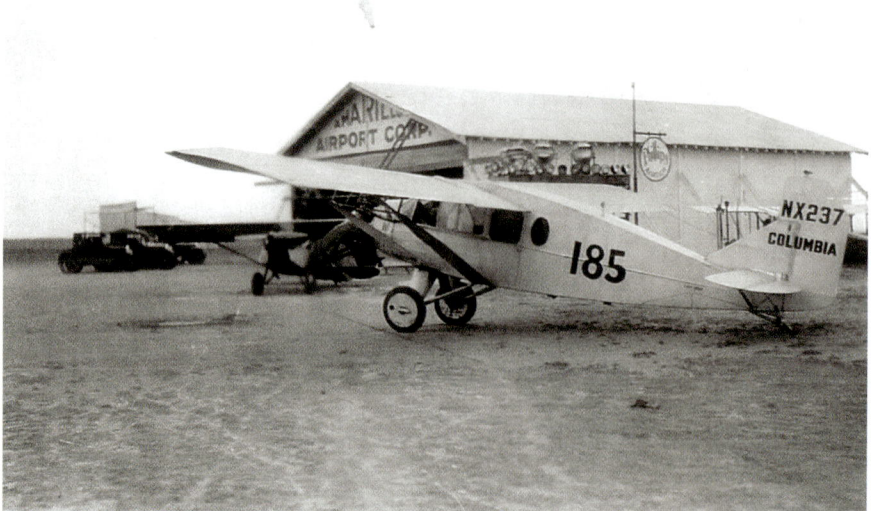

Figure 4.37. Unknown photographer, Bivins Field, c. 1920. Texas Air and Space Museum, Amarillo, Texas.

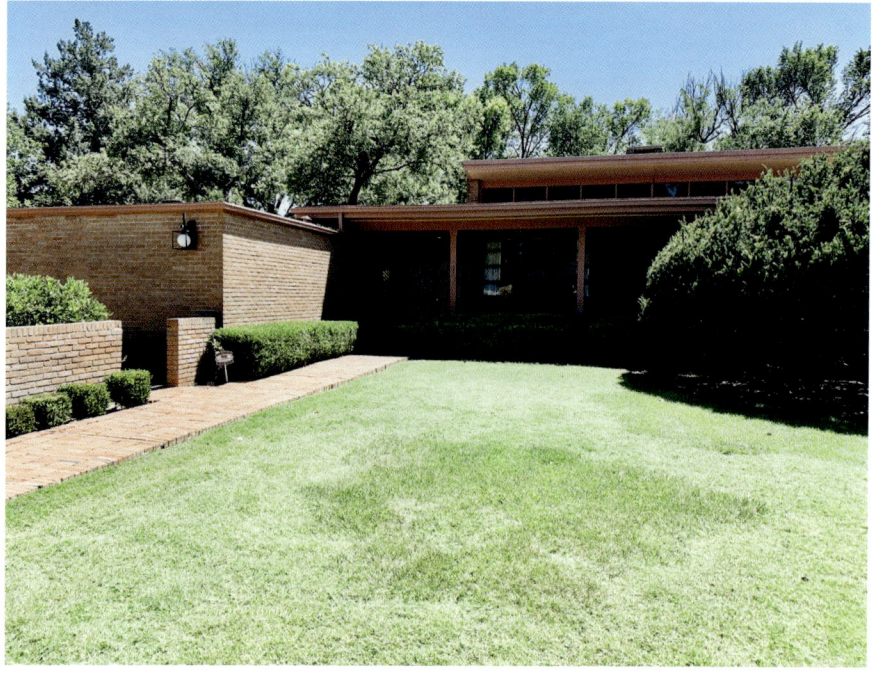

Figure 4.38. O'Neil Ford (architect), home in Bivins Neighborhood, Amarillo, 1952. (Photo by author.)

remains in the city's center and now serves as home of the Amarillo Chamber of Commerce (fig. 4.36).[66] It also functioned as the Mary E. Bivins Library between

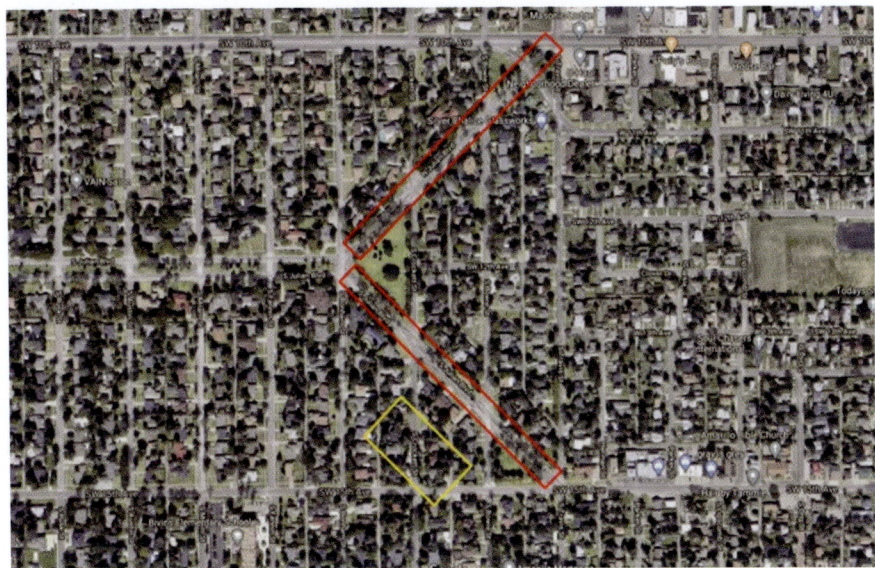

Figure 4.39. Bivins Neighborhood from satellite view, and (on right) with original runways in red and hangar in yellow. (Photo courtesy of Google Maps, TheBullAmarillo.com.)

1955 and 1976, and many Amarillo citizens remember writing their school reports in the home's spaces decorated with Tiffany glass, antique furniture, elaborate crown molding, and imported silk brocade draperies.[67]

Always an entrepreneur and visionary, Lee Bivins embraced the most advanced technologies of his time. He had one of the first telephones in Amarillo.[68] He was among the first to purchase a car and became one of the initial automobile dealers in town.[69] The Dodge Corporation even filmed Bivins's car travels for an advertising campaign in the 1920s, in his "Dodge car, with the LX brand painted on the doors . . . shown traversing rivers, climbing steep banks, and navigating tall grass."[70] As a civic leader, Bivins was largely responsible for the installation of brick paving on twenty-five city blocks in the 1910s, making it easier for cars to negotiate the urban spaces and setting the stage for Amarillo to become, in the words of historian Brian Ingrassia, a "car town as much as it was a cow town"—a history explored in chapter 1 of this volume.[71]

But in 1918, after Bivins witnessed aviators landing planes in a field outside the city, he decided that the next big thing Amarillo needed was a proper airfield.[72] The location of this original Amarillo airport developed by Bivins (fig. 4.37) is known today as the Bivins neighborhood, which is filled with lovely, substantial, single-family homes and treelined streets, including one by renowned Texas architect O'Neil Ford built in 1952 with jet-age aesthetics comparable to Bernson's

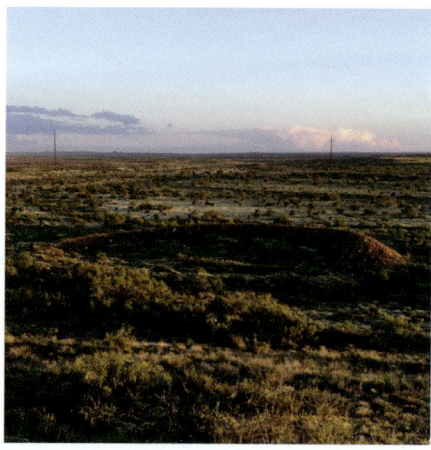

Figure 4.40. Robert Smithson, *Amarillo Ramp*, 1973, Amarillo, Texas. (©2025 Holt/Smithson Foundation / Licensed by Artists Rights Society (ARS), New York. Photo by Jon Revett.)

airport house in Pampa (fig. 4.38).[73] The main street through the Bivins sub-division is Julian Boulevard, named for Lee Bivins's son Julian Lee Bivins.[74] The eastern section of Julian Boulevard suddenly splits and forms a strange Y shape with North and South Julian making a perfect perpendicular to one another. This formation comes from the fact that those portions of the street were the original Bivins Airfield runways (fig. 4.39), offering perhaps the most striking example of the hidden aesthetics of aviation in the Texas Panhandle.[75]

The region's aesthetics were shaped not only by successful flights and the infra-structure to support them but also by plane crashes. Most famously, artist Robert Smithson died suddenly in a plane crash on July 20, 1973, near the Canadian River while he was surveying for his next land art piece, *Amarillo Ramp* (fig. 4.40).[76] This crash site is not far from where Julian Bivins and his son Billy also crashed while cowboying from their private plane in 1940. Worth noting is the way witnesses to both these crashes said they saw the planes dipping low and then stalling out before plunging into the ground.[77]

Julian had developed his interest in aviation at a young age and became involved with his father's air service business in the 1920s. But unlike Lee Bivins, who paid pilots to fly him, Julian became an expert pilot himself. He bought his first plane in Wichita, Kansas, in 1925—another Middle American aviation hub with a rich history of flight[78]—which he flew regularly between Amarillo and his ranchland near the Tascosa townsite, a location discussed in chapter 3 in light of its original adobe structures.[79] The Bivins family bought the Tascosa townsite as ranchland and built an airstrip there. The landing strip was not only used by members of the Bivins family but pilot instructor friends of Julian also used it during practice flights for students. Julian introduced his own sons, Oliver and Billy, to aviation early in their lives, and both passed their flying examinations with high marks. But in 1940, Julian and Billy were managing their ranch from the air—hunting coyotes to keep them from harming the cattle. Billy, twenty-two at the time, was at the controls while his father had a shotgun aimed at a coyote. According to the many news articles published about the crash, Billy dipped low so that his dad could take aim, the plane stalled out, he banked too hard, and ultimately couldn't gain altitude. Both men died on impact when the plane hit the ground.[80] A search party set out after dark that evening in cars and on horseback and found nothing. But the next morning, seven planes were sent up, including two of Julian's own planes flown by pilot friends, and from the air the wreckage was quickly discovered.

The crash of two members of the Bivins family was met with great public mourning, but the attitude of the regional populace was also one of admiration for the family's "progressive spirit" shown by their love of aviation.[81] One pilot wrote a moving statement in the local papers, asserting that despite this tragedy, he would not stop flying:

> That they died in the still spectacular crash of an airplane is lamentable—as all sudden death is. But their deaths are not going to halt or slow up flying in this area. . . . No longer does an air crash conjure up dark hints of a mysterious something that plucked the plane from the air. The public today is wiser and better educated on the subject of flying and airplanes. Where once there was ignorance and the attendant superstitious fear of the upper air there is now knowledge and understanding. Amarillo flying is going to miss Jude and Billy Bivins, for they had contributed generously to its growth with faith and money. But flying will continue as it did before the accident. People have come to know that where man creates a machine for himself so does that machine at times prove unmanageable. Jude and Billy, in that flier's Valhalla where there is never bad weather and you're always on the beam with a full tank, we salute you![82]

As this statement declared, the Texas Panhandle would continue to embrace flying as a way of life.

In a strange twist of fate relating to this crash in the Bivins family, Lee T. Bivins might never have married his wife Betty Teel Bivins—the two featured in those portraits by de Kooning (figs. 4.32 and 4.33)—if his cousin Billy had not crashed in 1940 with his father. At the time the plane went down, Betty Teel was engaged to Billy, who was the brother of her best friend Mary Miles Bivins; Betty was a junior at the University of Texas at Austin.[83] Lee T. Bivins, as mentioned above, like his uncles and cousins, had also become an avid aviator by that date. He joined the US Army Air Corps during World War II and after the war was stationed at Randolph Airfield in San Antonio as an instructor. Lee met Betty at Mary Miles's wedding, and when he was on leave from military duty in 1944 and had returned home to Amarillo, he proposed to Betty. The couple married in 1945, when Betty wore a wedding dress sewn from curtains because of war rationing and shortages.[84]

The famous plane crashes of Julian and Billy Bivins and Robert Smithson happened around an area near Canadian River breaks that stirs up dangerous air pockets. Both crashes occurred when the pilots and passengers flew above ranchland trying to scope out something on the ground—coyotes on the part of the Bivins and the staked-out site for an artistic earthwork on the part of Smithson—and both planes stalled out dangerously during this situation. Selma English, who was the wife of Harold English, namesake of English Field and a pilot herself, described this particular danger in an interview from 1981: "[I recall the] rough weather over the Canadian [River], and over in the rugged country or breaks. . . . I remember my first encounter with just a whirlwind in a small plane even then when you are close enough to the ground now that was not any semblance like a cyclone or a tornado, it was just a whirlwind and that can shake a little airplane around quite a bit."[85] George Christopher also recalled this particular site and its weather challenges. He described a "full blown line squall" around the Canadian and the turbulence that suddenly forced his plane downward.[86]

The crash that killed Smithson involved a two-engine Beechcraft Baron plane that art patron Stanley Marsh 3—discussed further in chapter 1—chartered for the artist's use.[87] It was Marsh's ranch that Smithson chose as the site of *Amarillo Ramp.* The crash occurred on the second date that the artist had gone up in the plane to survey the site from the air. During the first trip, on July 17, 1973, Marsh and his family members, including his children, were on board; on the second trip, it was just the artist, the pilot, and a photographer.[88] That second day, Smithson's wife, artist Nancy Holt, had opted out of the flight to shop for materials for her own piece of outdoor art that Marsh intended to sponsor. As Holt recalled years later, "It was strange because I was scheduled to go [up in the plane]. I normally liked flying over the site and seeing the results of the work . . . but since Stanley [Marsh] had expressed interest in my doing a work on his ranchland, I decided to go into Amarillo to get Sonotubes [concrete forms] to build a model. . . . I went

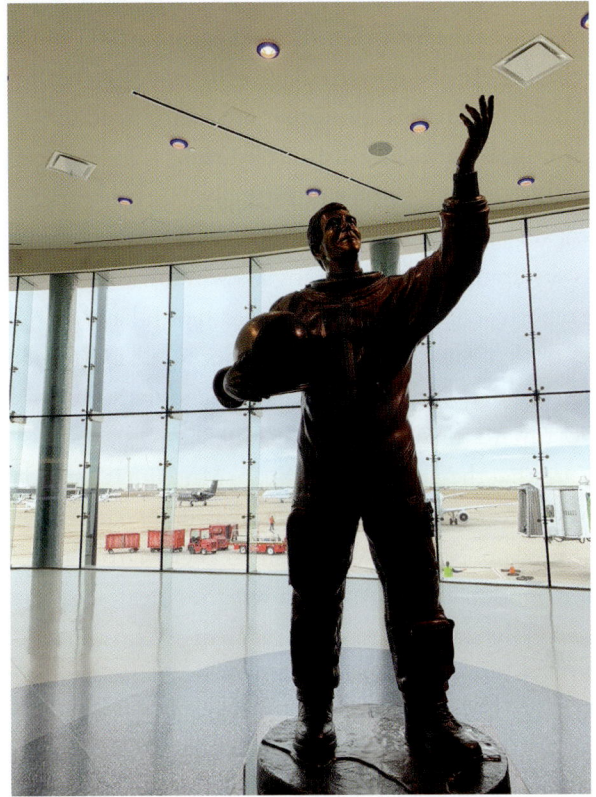

Figure 4.41. Mark Lundeen, *Rick Husband*, 2004, bronze. Rick Husband Amarillo International Airport. (Photo by author.)

into town; I didn't go up in the plane. It's as simple as that. It's auspicious because it turns out my art saved my life."[89]

One month after the crash, Holt returned to Amarillo along with two other artist-friends of Smithson's, Richard Serra and Tony Shafrazi, to construct *Amarillo Ramp* posthumously to Smithson's exact specifications. At this time, Holt and Serra also created the audio performance piece *Boomerang* using the television station that Marsh owned in Amarillo; the haunting repetition of Holt's echoing voice in the recording seems to embody the confusion and grief she felt in mourning her husband while also attempting to continue his legacy through the creation of *Amarillo Ramp*.[90] The plane crash in 1973 did not stop this major earth-art piece from having a presence in the Texas Panhandle; but the site, which can be visited to this day, is still thick with sadness and loss, even while it is striking in its relationship with the landscape and reactivated by visitors who find themselves there, not unlike a visit to the Frank Lloyd Wright Kinney House discussed in the last chapter.

One final aesthetic addition to Amarillo also responded to a tragic aviation crash—the explosion of the Space Shuttle *Columbia* in 2003, which killed seven astronauts, including Amarillo native Rick Husband.[91] Amarillo's airport was rededicated as the Rick Husband International Airport in 2003, and the next year, a life-sized bronze statue of Husband by Mark Lundeen was placed in the welcome area of the terminal (fig. 4.41). Fittingly, Husband's head on the statue is tilted upward, with his left arm outstretched as if to direct viewers toward the big West Texas sky, framed in huge clear glass window panels behind the piece. Much like the reporter commenting on the death of Julian and Billy Bivins, this statue reassures us that Amarillo's aviation legacy is one inextricably linked with visual aesthetics—both the creation of artworks and the spectatorship that lures the public's eyes toward the skies.

When we learn that the Texas Air and Space Museum is located not in a larger Texas city like Houston, Dallas, Fort Worth, Austin, or San Antonio, but rather in Amarillo, we need not be shocked. Newsman Dick Martin effused in 1940 that the first Aerial Roundup at the JA Ranch was the "greatest cavalcade of private aviation ever seen in the state of Texas," and as George Christopher observed in his memoir, "Amarillo is an airplane town."[92] Not only did the Texas Panhandle, with Amarillo at its center, have a thriving aviation culture, that culture was also highly visible and present for its citizens—for its pilots and passengers and its spectators, architects, artists, and photographers. According to historian James L. Haley, "Texans, perhaps because of the vast distances that were a part of their everyday life, were undoubtedly among the first people anywhere to appreciate the possibilities of flight," an observation that was especially applicable to the Panhandle.[93] Such statements begin to make perfect sense when the region's rich history of flight and its aesthetics are retrieved. More than the practical aspects of these "possibilities of flight," the region's love affair with aviation has distinctly shaped its artistic and spectacular developments. Not only have artists made their way to the region by plane, but artistic styles connected to the area have reflected and been inflected by flight. From the spectacle of aviation enjoyed by audiences at county fairs and airports to sculptures and architectural designs based on the materials and forms of airplanes and airports, we cannot but discover how truly foundational the history of aviation has been for the culture and identity of the area.

CONCLUSION

Now that I have shared these stories about the art and aesthetics of the Texas Panhandle, it is time to explore what they can mean for us. On the one hand, they illuminate the history, culture, and identity of a strange and fascinating region of the United States. But on the other, and perhaps even more importantly, they reveal not just how these histories are locally resonant but how they point to broader themes and ideas about time, place, people, and objects. They inflect our understanding of historical narratives of art and American identity, offering a fresh perspective not from the "outside" but from a newly recognized center. Not only is the Panhandle geographically central within the continental United States, it is also densely networked as a crossroads of trails, rails, roads, and flight paths. A focus on this area helps us reconceive our notions of "region" and "regional identity" with a more nuanced view. For example, we have seen how various theoretical perspectives can be applied to the understanding of this region. First, we have drawn from Jacques Derrida's writings on deconstruction to help conceptualize the profound engagement with decay by Panhandle artists and residents. Next, the scholarship on psychological profiling of art forgers highlighted for us how over-looked creators, especially when relegated to smaller art markets like the Panhandle, have sought out recognition and fame at the cost of ethics and legality. Then, we applied Kenneth Frampton's theories of critical regionalism to characterize Frank Lloyd Wright's unique ability to adapt designs to geographical, cultural, and histor-ical sites. And, finally, we pulled from scholarship in visual studies and modernity studies—in the contexts of France, Britain, and the United States—to describe the impact of aviation on area aesthetics. In other words, our local art stories coincide with and can be illuminated by perspectives of cultural theory.

Our stories have also revealed just how many artists have been inspired by the Panhandle—its land, climate, transportation technologies, and histories. This volume has recognized the most famous and renowned artists who have worked in the region, often briefly or intermittently: Georgia O'Keeffe, Frank Lloyd Wright, Ant Farm, Ed Ruscha, John Chamberlain, Robert Smithson, Nancy Holt, Louise Nevelson, Jeanne Reynal, and Elaine de Kooning. But we have also brought to light the underrecognized work of artists and architects who have lived and settled in the Panhandle: Maurice Bernson, Lightnin' McDuff, Guy Carlander, Emilio Caballero, Bob Lile, Jon Revett, and Matthew Williams.

We have likewise explored numerous historical trends and regional developments, including human settlement over centuries and conflicts among Indigenous peoples, sheepherders, and ranchers. We have examined ecological changes, from the eradication of the buffalo herds to the fires and drought that dominate and threaten the region today. This study has argued that decay is more than just decomposition of outdoor art works exposed to the harsh environment or the Frank Lloyd Wright house needing conservation and repair—although it is certainly that too. The reach of "decay" is also conceptual in the region of the Panhandle, with the legal issues surrounding the Canyon Suite case, for instance, or the manufactured decay of the fake art monument of McDuff's *Ozymandias*. Our focus on decay also leads to the recognition of several tragic deaths that have intersected with our art stories, including that of Dynamite Museum artist Brian Denecke, land artist Robert Smithson, ranching pilots Julian and Billy Bivins, and astronaut Rick Husband. At the same time, we have seen how this decay and loss did not result in an end to the region's creative productions and endeavors. To the contrary, as the artist Ruscha observed so poignantly, decay has provided a nutritional substance for new productions and innovations and new artistic creations. So, when Robin Gilliland worked with local craftsmen to bring the Kinney House back to a stable state so that future generations of visitors can enjoy this Frank Lloyd Wright design, we see such post-decay rejuvenation in action. Just like the seasonal cycles of brown into brighter colors that the Panhandle experiences year after year, visual artists and other creatives have continued to invest in the region's aesthetics, to be inspired by the Panhandle as place.

Our study has also demonstrated how central automobility and car culture have been for inspiring artistic responses. These include John Chamberlain's crushed car sculptures produced at Toad Hall in Amarillo, as well as Ant Farm's *Cadillac Ranch*, which not only comments on the rise and fall of the American automobile industry but also drew directly from the area, incorporating used cars bought in the Panhandle and placed in a cow pasture alongside a major cross-country interstate highway that connects Amarillo to the rest of the country. Even Frank Lloyd

Wright's carport design for the Kinney House, and his use of light and dark views that evoke the open road, point to the importance of car culture and its history in the region.

Beyond cars and highways, we have also recognized how transportation developments and infrastructure in the Panhandle have inspired artistic designs. While Chamberlain literally used car parts for his monumental sculptures, he also named some of them after the roads that shape the spaces of the Amarillo area: Crockett, Goliad, and Canyon Road, for instance. Chamberlain's works remind us that developing city spaces become an important shaper of regional aesthetics and that these spaces are embedded with works of art in ways we must recognize, just as the Dynamite Museum signs once peppered the streets of Amarillo even more densely than they do today, but their presence—current and historical—will ever be part of the urban fabric of the area. Likewise, Ruscha's art that we featured here is not about cars, but about gas stations, not only as the waystations for "gassing up" along the American road trip but also pinnacles of modern, efficient, functional, and "standardized" design. The gas station that forms the centerpiece of so much of Ruscha's Standard Oil Station series was the Amarillo station—reflecting the centrality of Amarillo in this canonical thread of pop art. We have also seen the highly innovative "airport house" by Bernson, which responded not only to the forms of jet planes in its sculptural accents but also to the airports that have become such key gateways in the daily lives of modern humans.

Finally, we explored how the wide-open spaces of the Panhandle's landscape have inspired so many artists, including Robert Smithson's literal use of the land to construct his *Amarillo Ramp,* Georgia O'Keeffe's watercolor reflections of the flat land at sunrise and sunset or the raw beauty of the canyonlands, Colonel Leslie Neher's photographs, and Jeanne Reynal's mosaics inspired by their views of the plains from above. The spaces of Amarillo also inspired Stanley Marsh 3 to hire an artist to construct a "Hollywood" type sign that read "Actual Size" on his ranch, just off busy Amarillo Boulevard. This work creatively responded to the unique and specific relationship of size and space in the Panhandle. Spaces are vast, humans are small; but the human impact is big, so what is the actual size of a human creation? In the end, we must admit that the aesthetics of the region are not bland and perfectly planar but, like the land itself, subtly contoured and layered—physically, geographically, historically, and conceptually.

An important narrative throughout this volume tracks the regional tensions and intersections of old and new, past and present; it explores how the "good old days" of the horse and cowboy live on in vibrant ways in the region and how they connect with distinct modernities, including car culture and aviation, artistic abstraction, avant-garde architecture, land art, pop art, conceptual art, collaborative installations of urban art, site-specific art, and more.

What we need to realize, though, is how those "good old days" of the "Old West" were themselves a modern iteration working alongside and against long-standing traditions. The cattle ranching industry, and the oil industry that followed, were novel imports that supplanted, often violently, the native ecology of the plains, with its tall grasses and grazing herds of buffalo, as well as its Indigenous people. The Texas Panhandle has never been a space that was fixed and stagnant but has always been a dynamic crossroads region full of hybridity, where even the horse was once a plentiful animal in ancient America and then reintroduced as a modern import from Europe; now it remains a central component of the Panhandle land and culture. These tensions between tradition and change complicate and enrich the history of the region, the nation, and the North American continent. Even the declarative modernity of Frank Lloyd Wright's Kinney House design was built upon the layered aesthetics of pre-conquest Mesoamerica, Southwestern settlement of Hispanic and Indigenous cultures, ranching adaptations, and centuries-old Asian traditions.

The art of the Panhandle is thus distinctly nonlinear in its development, reminding us that cyclical time and the regenerative cycles of creation and decay are a fundamental and foundational part of the area's cultural identity. The geographic isolation of the Panhandle region, where the closest big cities are hundreds of miles away, is counterbalanced by the profoundly networked connections of this region to places within and beyond the borders of the United States. I have traced many of these connections in this volume that made this area its own kind of center, rather than an outlying periphery. The Texas Panhandle boasts deep ties to the US Southwest, but also to Mexico, the Midwest, and the coasts, as New York artists found temporary but repeated welcome here or as Ruscha became a West Coast darling of pop art with aesthetics inspired by traveling through the Panhandle. Houses built in Pampa, Texas, strike up a vibrant dialogue with airports in L.A., New York, England, and France. I began this volume with the hope that I could convince readers of the value of the art and aesthetics of the Texas Panhandle. That is still one of my goals. But another goal is to show just how richly this art history connects to narratives beyond its boundaries and borders. In producing this volume, I have learned that isolation can coexist with connection and that the stories of the Panhandle can continue to unfold into the future, as long as we keep telling them.

NOTES

INTRODUCTION

1. On how this aerial view corresponded to modernist art, see Stanton Macdonald-Wright, "Influence of Aviation on Art: The Accentuation of Individuality," *Ace: The Aviation Magazine of the West*, September 1919, 11–13, 17; Robert Hughes, *The Shock of the New*, 2nd ed. (New York: McGraw Hill, 1991), 14; and Jason Weems, *Barnstorming the Prairies: How Aerial Vision Shaped the Midwest* (Minneapolis: University of Minnesota Press, 2015), especially 138.

2. On O'Keeffe's art from Texas, see especially Amy Von Lintel, *Georgia O'Keeffe Watercolors, 1916–1918* (Santa Fe: Radius Books and Georgia O'Keeffe Museum, 2016). This book features full-scale, beautifully color-matched reproductions of the artist's works created in Texas.

3. Amarillo's stretch of Route 66 has had a strong revival since I moved here in 2010. Fewer properties are vacant, and the businesses display a variety of goods and services, from antique shops, art galleries, boutiques, and bookshops to bars and breweries. Likewise, numerous buildings have become the sites of painted murals, adding even more color and art to the district.

4. Amy Von Lintel and Bonnie Roos, *Three Women Artists: Expanding Abstract Expressionism in the American West* (College Station: Texas A&M University Press, 2022); and Jon Revett, Ruth Pasquine, and Amy Von Lintel, *Southwest Abstractions of Emil Bisttram* (Canyon, TX: Panhandle-Plains Historical Museum, 2021). The Emil Bisttram collection featured in this exhibition was brought to Amarillo by the Frank Ladd family, who have long been art collectors and supporters of visual art in the Panhandle.

5. On the history of the Air Force Base and its closure, see Thomas E. Alexander, *The Stars were Big and Bright: The United States Army Air Forces and Texas During World War II* (Austin, TX: Eakin, 2000), 59–62. Alexander notes the "enormous economic and social impact" of the base on the city of Amarillo, the "millions of federal dollars" that flowed into the regional economy, with 17,000 jobs, civilian and military, on the base, plus 30,000 more off-base.

6. See Von Lintel and Roos, *Three Women Artists*, for instance, which discusses collectors and collections in Perryton and Spearman.

7. My approach is comparable to that of regionalist scholar-writer Zachary Michael Jack, whose many books about Iowa and the US Midwest have gained a wide audience while emerging as important touchstones for scholars. See, for example, *The Midwest Farmer's Daughter: In Search of an American Icon* (West Lafayette, IN: Purdue University Press, 2012). For this comparison and a clearer articulation of my methodology, I thank the anonymous reader who reviewed my book manuscript in early 2023 for Texas Tech University Press.

8. On this, see for instance, James Dennis, *Grant Wood: A Study in American Art and Culture* (Columbia: University of Missouri Press, 1975) and *Renegade Regionalists: The Modern Independence of Grant Wood, Thomas Hart Benton, and John Stuart Curry* (Madison: University of Wisconsin Press, 1998); and Wanda Corn, *Grant Wood: The Regionalist Vision* (New Haven: Yale University Press, 1983). "Regionalism" in art history has most often designated an artistic movement of US American art in the early twentieth century with an interest in the subject matter of the Midwest, including such artists as Grant Wood, based in Iowa, and Thomas Hart Benton, based in Missouri but who worked throughout Middle America, including West Texas (see Benton's painting *Boomtown* from 1928, now at the University of Rochester, which responded to the oil boom in the Panhandle town of Borger). However, Jason Weems opens up the term "regionalism" to signify "both a generalized notion of processes of thinking anchored in the culture shaped by a specific environment . . . and a more particular set of cultural expressions and political ideals associated with the regionalist movement of the 1920s and 30s." See Weems, *Barnstorming the Prairies,* xxiv.

CHAPTER 1

1. Ron Warnick, "Arsonist Torches One of the Cars at *Cadillac Ranch*," *Route 66 News*, September 9, 2019, https://www.route66news.com/2019/09/09/arsonist-torche s-one-of-the-cars-at-cadillac-ranch/.

2. On this figure, see Larry Edsall, "Changes Don't Alter the Essence of Cadillac Ranch," September 15, 2021, https://www.petersen.org/blog/cadillac-ranch.

3. On *Cadillac Ranch*, see Constance M. Lewallen and Steve Seid, *Ant Farm: 1968–1978* (Berkeley: University of California Press, 2004); and James Nesbit, *Second Site* (Princeton, NJ: Princeton University Press, 2021), 50–57. On land art, see Nesbit, *Second Site*; Miwon Kwon, *One Place after Another: Site-Specific Art and Locational Identity* (Cambridge, MA: MIT Press, 2002); Philipp Kaiser and Miwon Kwan, *Ends of the Earth: Land Art to 1974* (Los Angeles: Museum of Contemporary Art, 2012); Michael Lailach, *Land Art* (Cologne: Taschen, 2007); Suzaan Boettger, *Earthworks: Art and the Landscape of the Sixties* (Berkeley: University of California Press, 2002); and John Beardsley, *Earthworks and Beyond: Contemporary Art in the Landscape* (New York: Abbeville, 1989).

4. On Uncle Buddie's, see Chip Lord, Doug Michels, and Curtis Schreier, "Ant Farm Timeline," as reproduced in Lewallen and Seid, *Ant Farm*, 125–26.

5. Stanley Marsh preferred the number 3 to the Roman numeral. On the moving of *Cadillac Ranch* to the west, see Warnick, "Arsonist" and interview with Chip Lord, February 2015, when he was a visiting artist at WT. Lord described how he and the other Ant Farm members had not been consulted, but he also stated that the "collective memory" about the work has forgotten about the move anyway, making it not that relevant for the meaning and function of the work.

6. The "tragedy of the commons" economic principle—which states that individual users with open access to a resource will use that resource for their own self-interest and not for the greater good, depleting the resource—originated in 1833 with a pamphlet authored by British economist William Forster Lloyd. It was then popularized by the American economist Garrett Hardin in an article published in 1968. For a good summary of this principle, see Alexandra Spiliakos, "Tragedy of the Commons: What It Is & 5 Examples," *Harvard Business School Online*, February 6, 2019, https://online.hbs.edu/blog/post/tragedy-of-the-commons-impact-on-sustainability-issues.

7. The decline of the American automobile industry reached a nadir between 2007 and 2010. See, for example, Joshua Murray and Michael Schwartz, *Wrecked: How the American Automobile Industry Destroyed Its Capacity to Compete* (New York: Russell Sage Foundation, 2019).

8. According to Marsh, *Cadillac Ranch* was "'a monument to the American dream' of a boy growing up in the 1950s. A car, he once said, 'represented money; it was the first valuable thing we ever had. . . . It represented sex; it was where you had dates,' he added. 'And it represented getting away from home. And I assure you those were the three things that were on our minds when we were 16.'" See Bruce Weber, "Stanley Marsh, Cadillac Rancher, Dies at 76, Shadowed by Charges," *New York Times*, June 23, 2014, https://www.nytimes.com/2014/06/23/arts/design/stanley-marsh-patron-of-the-cadillac-ranch-dies-at-76.html.

9. James Nisbet argues that land art, especially in the West, is always embedded in "secondness" and that there is no such thing as "first nature" or "first time" that one can find with it. I am exploring how this "secondness" has particular resonance in Amarillo's art history, and how it is not limited to its land art productions. See Nisbet, *Second Site*, xvi–xxi, xxx–xxiii.

10. Lile claims that he never takes the paint directly off the cars. In the 1960s, Lile was working as a car salesman at a Ford dealership when he was introduced to art and art culture by local dealer and art educator Dord Fitz. Then, after years of making mosaic images from found paint chips of *Cadillac Ranch*, Lile learned that another artist was making jewelry called "Fordite" from the lacquer and enamel paint chips left behind in Ford auto plants. Lile appropriated this idea and began making jewelry from *Cadillac Ranch* paint chips, which he called "Cadilite." See, for instance, Dusty Reins, "Bob Lile: Cadilite Jewelry," *Dusty Reins Stories*, June 21, 2016, https://www.youtube.com/watch?v=5YUm9bkh4Yc as well as Anthony Arno, "Bob 'Crocodile' Lile," *Route 66 Podcast*, no. 38, April 14, 2021, https://www.youtube.com/watch?v=6M9pzCuZr-E. See also Thomas Warren, "Lile's Cadilite Brings Worldwide Attention to Amarillo," *Amarillo Pioneer*, May 28, 2018,

https://www.amarillopioneer.com/blog/2018/3/28/liles-cadilite-brings-worldwid e-attention-to-amarillo; and the website for Lile Art Gallery, see https://lile-gallery.com/.

11. On the climate of Amarillo, see "Climate Narrative for Amarillo," published by the National Weather Service, https://www.weather.gov/ama/climo_narrative.

12. On this use of the term "entropy," see Jack Flam, ed., *Robert Smithson: The Collected Writings* (Berkeley: University of California Press, 1996), especially "Entropy and the New Monuments (1966)," 10–23 and "Entropy Made Visible (1973)," 301–9. He defines it using the example of Humpty Dumpty, a "closed system which eventually deteriorates and starts to break apart and there's no way that you can really piece it back together again" (301).

13. For one of the most succinct statements of this view of the West, see Ben Mitchell's statement in *Andy Warhol's Dream America*, as quoted in heather ahtone, Faith Brower, and Seth Hopkins, *Warhol and the West* (Tacoma: Tacoma Art Museum; Berkeley: University of California Press, 2019), 12: "[T]he myth of the West, a kit bag of pervasive notions about history, national identity, sentiment and heroism. A stew cooked up in the kitchens of Hollywood, popular literature, and advertising, flavored with insistent tourism and chamber of commerce boosterism, its main ingredients are the idealization of colonization, a glorification of violence, and a malignant and insidious disregard of racism. Spoons in hand, we are still gathered around that pot today."

14. For a clear explanation of Derrida's complex ideas, I suggest Leonard Lawlor, "Jacques Derrida," in Edward N. Zalta, *The Stanford Encyclopedia of Philosophy*, https://plato.stanford.edu/entries/derrida/. This entry also provides bibliographic citations for the scores of publications Derrida completed in his lifetime.

15. Robert Smithson also articulated this aspect of time and the present in "Entropy and the New Monuments," in Flam, ed., *Robert Smithson*, 11. Smithson writes: "Time breaks down into many times," and says we should not ask "when" but "where" regarding time. He continues: "A million years is contained in a second, yet we tend to forget the second as soon as it happens." He also draws on some other deconstructivist notions, such as "the dislocation of meaning" (23).

16. On the exploitation and forced removal of First American populations during the expansion of Anglo-Americans across the prairie, see especially "Manifest Destiny and Indian Removal," Smithsonian Institution of American Art, https://ameri-canexperience.si.edu/wp-content/uploads/2015/02/Manifest-Destiny-and-Indian-Removal.pdf. On how the Indigenous populations were not "tragic victims" but rather "full-fledged historical actors who played a formative role in the making of early America," see Pekka Hämäläinen, *The Comanche Empire* (New Haven: Yale University Press, 2008), 6.

17. The Ant Farm members came back to celebrate the ten-, twenty-, and fifty-year anniversaries of *Cadillac Ranch*. On this, see the film made by Chip Lord at the twenty-year celebration: *Cadillac Ranch 1974/1994*. Likewise, Lord has come to WT twice to do guest artist's talks, once in 2015 and once in 2018, when he produced a

film with Hayden Pedigo called *Greetings from Amarillo*. On this, see "Ant Farm's Chip Lord Comes to Amarillo," *Glasstire*, October 12, 2018, https://glasstire. com/2018/10/12/ant-farms-chip-lord-comes-to-amarillo/. For the fifty-year celebration, the Amarillo Museum of Art hosted the exhibition *Cadillac Ranch at 50*, which ran from June 1 to August 25, 2024, and featured the photographs of Wyatt McSpadden and an artist talk by Lord.

18. F. T. Marinetti, "The Foundation and Manifesto of Futurism," *Le Figaro* (Paris), February 20, 1909.

19. Wyndham Lewis, "Vorticist Manifesto," *Blast* 1 (1914).

20. On the Sign Project, see Cindy Brzostowski, "The Dynamite Museum's Sign Project is Part Open Air Art Museum and Part Scavenger Hunt," *Roadtrippers Magazine*, July 21, 2020, https://roadtrippers.com/magazine/dynamite-museum-sign-projec t-texas/; and Jennifer S. Evans-Cowley and Jack L. Nasar, "Signs as Yard Art in Amarillo, Texas," *Geographical Review* 93 (January 2003): 97–113.

21. Jon Revett and Amy Von Lintel, *Yellow City Art* (Plainview, TX: Contemporary Art Museum Plainview, 2018).

22. For example, one group calling themselves "Erase Marsh Madness" called in 2015 for the *Cadillac Ranch* to be destroyed. See Ron Warnick, "Group Wants to Remove *Cadillac Ranch*," *Route 66 News*, October 31, 2015, https://www.route66news. com/2015/10/31/group-wants-to-remove-cadillac-ranch/.

23. See Paula Newton, "Artist Paints Over Amarillo's Mock Road Signs," *Glasstire*, July 8, 2013.

24. On this work, see the description of *Erased de Kooning Drawing* by Robert Rauschenberg on the San Francisco Museum of Modern Art website: https://www. sfmoma.org/artwork/98.298/.

25. According to a statement from Marsh representatives in the context of this case, the signs "belong to the property owner" once they are installed: "Toad Hall representatives would not comment on the story, saying only that if people want to get rid of the signs in their yards to call them at 359-1014, and they'll remove them free of charge. . . . But, they would prefer not having them painted over. While Stanley Marsh 3 paid for all the signs, they belong to the property owner and they can do whatever they want with them." See Newton, "Artist Paints Over." Even if Marsh stated that they "belonged" to property owners, a legal case of ownership was never brought to the courts so their status as property remains ambiguous.

26. On this, see Susan Bielstein, *Permissions, a Survival Guide: Blunt Talk about Art as Intellectual Property* (Chicago: University of Chicago Press, 2006), 29.

27. See Bielstein, *Permissions*, 57.

28. On architecture and habitability, see Bielstein, *Permissions*, 59–60.

29. Bielstein, *Permissions*, 57.

30. Marsh would transport the signs to a new home for an "owner" of a sign if he or she moved, for instance, again at no cost.

31. Marsh's property was called Toad Hall, a name that reflects his admiration of the character Mr. Toad from *The Wind in the Willows*. It was located in the northwest

corner of the crossroads of Amarillo Boulevard and Western Street. The property was part of the Frying Pan Ranch, founded in 1881 from the money made from a successful barbed-wire manufactory. On this history, see Paul H. Carlson, *Empire Builder in the Texas Panhandle: William Henry Bush* (College Station: Texas A&M University Press, 1996); and Skip Hollandsworth, "Big Feud at Cadillac Ranch," *Texas Monthly* (March 1996), https://www.texasmonthly.com/being-texan/ big-feud-at-cadillac-ranch/

32.   In 2017, Toad Hall was sold. See Ben Egel, "Former Stanley Marsh Land Toad Hall Under Development," *Amarillo Globe-News*, September 8, 2017, https://www. amarillo.com/story/news/local/2017/09/08/former-stanley-marsh-3-land-toa d-hall-under-development/13037938007/.

33.   Wendy Bush O'Brien Marsh, Stanley's wife, is the sister of Mary Emeny, founder of Mariposa Eco-Village. See http://www.mariposa.eco/.

34.   The mission of the initiative is "to maintain monumental works of art in the Amarillo area and to give WT students real world experience with public art. BIG ART will organize and fund student actions to help with generation, repair, and restoration of large-scale art works. This program is designed to expose art students to highly visible and/or monumental public art and its positive effect on the community." On this, see the white paper of the WT Foundation BIG ART Fund presented to donors in 2013, as shared with me by Jon Revett.

35.   The curatorial team for *Amarillo Entropy* included Gregg Ruppe, Alden Pinnel, Revett, and Williams.

36.   The signs were installed similarly at the *Yellow City Art* exhibition at the Contemporary Art Museum Plainview in 2019.

37.   Williams's Instagram handle is @dynamitemuseumofficial.

38.   On Matthew Williams, see Revett and Von Lintel, *Yellow City Art*, 47. Williams also runs the Invisible Genie Art Gallery in Amarillo.

39.   Julie Sylvester, ed., *John Chamberlain: A Catalogue Raisonné of the Sculpture, 1954– 1985* (New York: Hudson Hills Press; Los Angeles: Museum of Contemporary Art, Los Angeles, 1986), 130–35; and Marianne Stockebrand, *Chinati: The Vision of Donald Judd* (New Haven: Yale University Press, 2010), 110. On the Texas Pieces, see also Peter Schjeldahl, "Early Success: Can It Be Lived Down?" *New York Times*, December 9, 1973; and Mary King, "Bumper Crop of Auto Art," *St. Louis Post-Dispatch*, April 11, 1975.

40.   Julie Sylvester and John Chamberlain, "Auto/Bio: Conversations with John Chamberlain," in Sylvester, ed., *John Chamberlain*, 15.

41.   On Amarillo's history of automobility, see Brian M. Ingrassia, "Speed Attractions: Urban Mobility and Automotive Spectacle in Pre–World War I Amarillo," *Southwestern Historical Quarterly* 123 (July 2019): 60–86; and Nick Gerlich and Ellen Klinkel, *A Matter of Time: Route 66 Through the Lens of Change* (Norman: University of Oklahoma Press, 2019).

42.   Contract signed by John Chamberlain for Case Power and Equipment of Amarillo, dated January 1975, for a rental period from January 5 to February 5, Stanley Marsh

Family Papers. I thank Jon Revett for helping me obtain copies of these documents for my research.

43. On the history of the North American horse, see Dan Flores, *Wild New World: The Epic Story of Animals and People in America* (New York: W. W. Norton, 2022), 23–24, 201–3.

44. On how the horse was reintroduced onto the Great Plains by Europeans and became a central resource for Comanches in particular, but also how the final defeat of the Comanche Empire took place in 1875 in the Texas Panhandle, see Hämäläinen, *The Comanche Empire*, especially 25. He writes: "By the 1710s, only a generation after obtaining their first horses," Comanches began to use the horse not only for conquest raids but also for hunting and transporting goods for trade and use. "Their reach of trade was multiplied, as was their ability to wage war, plunder, and defend themselves. In almost an instant, the world became smaller and its resources more accessible. . . . [The] horse represented a new way to tap energy." See also Adam Duncan Harris, "George Catlin's Vision of the Great Plains," in *George Catlin's American Buffalo* (Washington, DC: Smithsonian American Art Museum, 2013), 6.

45. Sylvester and Chamberlain, "Auto/Bio: Conversations," 14.

46. On Marsh's complicated identity and performances, see Gary Cartwright, "Playboys of the Western Plains," *Texas Monthly*, March 1978, https://www.texasmonthly.com/true-crime/playboys-of-the-western-plains/; Jesse Katz, "A Case of Art Gone Astray?," *Los Angeles Times*, January 15, 1996, https://www.latimes.com/archives/la-xpm-1996-01-15-mn-24846-story.html; Rozalia Jovanovic, "Dude Ranch," *Oxford American*, July 15, 2013; Weber, "Stanley Marsh, Cadillac Rancher, Dies;" Skip Hollandsworth, "Darkness on the Plains," *Texas Monthly*, May 2013, 120–23, 206–12, https://www.texasmonthly.com/articles/darkness-on-the-plains/; "Stanley Marsh 3, the Infamous West Texas Eccentric, Has Died," *Texas Monthly*, June 17, 2014, https://www.texasmonthly.com/articles/stanley-marsh-3-the-infamous-west-texas-eccentric-has-died/; Kevin Welch and Karen Smith Welch, "Daring or Devious?," *Amarillo Globe-News*, June 21, 2014. On his twang, see the video produced by Chip Lord, *Cadillac Ranch 1974/1994*, https://vimeo.com/185560546.

47. See video mentioned in previous note.

48. Stanley Marsh 3 to Don and Julie Judd, September 28, 1972, Judd Foundation Archives.

49. As reproduced in Lewallen and Seid, *Ant Farm*, 66.

50. On the history of Frying Pan Ranch, see Carlson, *Empire Builder*.

51. The piece has been variously titled *Bushland-Marsh* and *Bushland-Marsh III*.

52. Stockebrand, *Chinati*, 120.

53. Stockebrand, *Chinati*, 124.

54. On this history, see Carlson, *Empire Builder*.

55. According to Shelley Smith at the Chinati foundation, the two works were lost in being transported to an exhibition on Wards Island in 1977. See email from Smith to Von Lintel, May 17, 2022. See also Richard A. Whitney to Leo Castelli, March 12, 1981, a letter regarding the lawsuit brought against United Van Bus Delivery Co.

for destroying *Canyon Road Shell* and *Capote's Peak*, and damaging *Chili Terlingua* and *Glasscock-Notrees*; and memo of phone conversation between John Chamberlain and Joe Bishop with Dia Art Foundation, July 20 and 21, 1978, Chamberlain, John - Questions, circa 1967–1983, Leo Castelli Gallery records, circa 1880–2000, bulk 1957–1999, Box 7, Folder 26, Archives of American Art, Smithsonian Institution (hereafter, Leo Castelli Gallery Records, AAA).

56. This show was *John Chamberlain: Recent Sculptures*, curated by James Harithas at the Contemporary Arts Museum Houston.

57. A 1979 sketch shows the intended installation, but in 1980 they were installed in the Wool and Mohair Building instead, for a total of twenty-two works. The Chamberlain Building was opened to the public in 1983 as the first accessible art installation at Chinati. See Stockebrand, *Chinati*, 110–14.

58. See Stanley Marsh 3 to Julie Sylvester, March 21, 1984, which included a catalogue raisonné form completed for *Harvey*, 1974, seven by six by ten feet. The letter is in the Stanley Marsh Family Papers. The number of Chamberlain's "Texas Pieces" is contested; the catalogue raisonné claims there are twelve pieces; Leo Castelli wrote a notarized affidavit for valuation of the series pieces that claims there were ten. See Leo Castelli, Affidavit, June 28, 1978, Leo Castelli Gallery Records, AAA.

59. McDuff began the sculpture in 1994 and completed it in 1996. The measurements of the statue include a base that is four by ten by twenty feet, which supports a left leg that is twenty-four feet tall and a right leg that is thirty-four feet tall. On the *Ozymandias* sculpture, see KassiAnne Fondow, "Ozymandias: Atmosphere Brings Sculpture to Glory," *The Prairie*, May 3, 2011; Atlas Obscura, "Ozymandias of Amarillo: A Texan Take on Shelley's Poem, Featuring Tube Socks," *Slate*, September 12, 2013, https://www.slate.com/blogs/atlas_obscura/2013/09/12/ozymandias_of_amarillo_a_sculptor_s_tetex_take_on_shelley_s_poem_featuring.html; Eva Lorraine Molina, "Ozymandias: A King, a Poem, and a Concrete Statue in a Cow Pasture," *Reporting Texas*, December 12, 2013, https://www.reportingtexas.com/ozymandias-a-king-a-poem-and-a-chunk-of-cement-in-a-cow-pasture/. On McDuff, see Larry Lemmons, "Lightnin' and Mr. Hyde," Panhandle Spirit, ABC 7 News, KVII-TV, May 12, 2016, https://www.youtube.com/watch?v=aX77ZyBpjdw; and "Amarillo Art," Panhandle Spirit, KVII-TV, Pronews 7, July 13, 2013, https://www.youtube.com/watch?v=CaRpMzIxbSA.

60. Called the "Canyon E-Way," this interstate highway was constructed between the mid-1970s and 1992. See "Economic Development of History of Interstate 27 in Texas," US Department of Transportation, Federal Highway Administration," November 3, 2008, https://planningtools.transportation.org/files/41.pdf.

61. This fake museum is the Amarillo Museum of Natural History. See the text on the plaque, which reads: "The visage (or face) was damaged by students from Lubbock after losing to Amarillo in a competition. A stone cast of it will be replaced when it is ready. The original is on display now in the Amarillo Museum of Natural History. Souvenir hunters have scraped off the bottom of the pedestal. Archaeologists have determined it was as Shelley described it."

62. I thank Renea Dauntes for this observation.

63. Apparently, they were never meant to be graffitied, and the first to paint them was a young artist in the employ of Marsh called "LBK" or "Long Board Kid." LBK painted white tube socks on the legs, and then McDuff sandblasted the added paint off and returned the legs to their original nude color. Within a few days, LBK painted the tube socks on again. According to an interview conducted with Renea Dauntes, McDuff "chuckled as he explained that it would be a constant battle with the kid if he kept sand-blasting it, so he left it. Not so much encouraging it, but giving in to a very determined sock painter."

64. Molina, "Ozymandias."

65. Molina, "Ozymandias."

66. Fondow, "Ozymandias."

67. Harris, "Catlin's Vision of the Great Plains," 19. The history of the bison and its extermination in the US West is not just one that involves Anglos and Indigenous communities. Hispanic settlers in the High Plains also hunted buffalo as part of their lifeways and livelihood, but not on the industrialized level that led to the massive stockpiling of thousands of hides that we see in figure 1.19. On this history of the *ciboleros* in the Texas Panhandle region, see Fabiola Cabeza de Baca, *We Fed Them Cactus*, 2nd ed. (Albuquerque: University of New Mexico Press, 1994), 39–46.

68. See Joyce Gibson Roach, "Goodnight, Mary Ann Dyer [Molly]," *Handbook of Texas Online*; J. Evetts Haley, *Charles Goodnight: Cowman and Plainsman*, rev. ed. (Norman: University of Oklahoma Press, 1981), as well as "Charles Goodnight Bison Herd," *All About Bison*, https://allaboutbison.com/bison-in-history/texas-history/charles-goodnight-bison-herd/. On private herds of buffalo, including the Goodnight herd, see Harris, "Catlin's Vision of the Great Plains," 20–21, 25–26, 28.

69. For more on the history of the extermination of the bison and the use of their hides for industrial purposes, see Tom McHugh, *The Time of the Buffalo* (Lincoln, NE: Bison Books, 1979); Andrew C. Isenberg, *The Destruction of the Bison: An Environmental History, 1750–1920* (New York: Cambridge University Press, 2000); and Harris, "Catlin's Vision of the Great Plains," 6, 18–19.

70. On how the landscape of the region has been "divided, fenced, irrigated, seeded, fertilized, and harvested for the benefit of humans" at the expense of the bison herds, see Harris, "Catlin's Vision of the Great Plains," 2.

71. See Chuck Lanehart, "The Second Battle of Adobe Walls," *Lubbock Avalanche-Journal*, July 5, 2019, https://www.lubbockonline.com/story/news/state/2019/07/06/caprock-chronicles-second-battle-of-adobe-walls/4752477007/; and "Adobe Walls, Second Battle of," *Handbook of Texas Online*, https://www.tshaonline.org/handbook/entries/adobe-walls-second-battle-of.

72. For a history of the end of the Comanche Empire, with the final battles in 1874 and the ultimate relocation of the Comanches and their allies onto reservations, see Hämäläinen, *Comanche Empire*, and Cabeza de Baca, *We Fed Them Cactus*, 47–50. On the history of Oklahoma from territories to statehood, see Dianna Everest, "Indian Territory," *The Encyclopedia of Oklahoma History and Culture*, https://

www.okhistory.org/publications/enc/entry?entry=IN018.

73. On O'Keeffe's short but formative time in West Texas, see Amy Von Lintel, *Georgia O'Keeffe's Wartime Texas Letters* (College Station: Texas A&M University Press, 2020) (hereafter OTL) and Von Lintel, *Georgia O'Keeffe Watercolors*.

74. On *Spiral Jetty*, see Robert Smithson, "Spiral Jetty (1972)," in Flam, ed., *Robert Smithson: The Collected Writings*, 143–53; George Baker et al., *Robert Smithson: Spiral Jetty* (Berkeley: University of California Press, 2005); Suzaan Boettger, *Inside the Spiral: The Passions of Robert Smithson* (Minneapolis: University of Minnesota Press, 2022); and Hikmet Sidney Loe, *The* Spiral Jetty *Encyclo: Exploring Robert Smithson's Earthwork Through Time and Space* (Salt Lake City: University of Utah Press, 2017).

75. See Flam, ed., *Robert Smithson: The Collected Writings*, especially "Entropy and the New Monuments," 10–23. Smithson writes: "In a rather roundabout way, many of the artists have provided a visible analog for the Second Law of Thermodynamics, which extrapolates the range of entropy by telling us energy is more easily lost than obtained" (11).

76. Ric Collier and Jim Edwards, "*Spiral Jetty*: The Re-Emergence," *Sculpture Magazine*, July 1, 2004.

77. Amy Von Lintel and Jon Revett, "Completing Smithson's Trilogy," in Elyse Goldberg, ed., *Robert Smithson in Texas* (New York: Estate of Robert Smithson and James Cohan Gallery, 2015), 11–32. See also Nisbet, *Second Site*, 57–60.

78. On mesquite growth in the region, see R. J. Ansley and P. W. Jacoby, "Manipulation of Fire Intensity to Achieve Mesquite Management Goals in North Texas," Tall Timbers Fire Ecology Conference Proceedings (1998), https://agrilife.org/vernon/files/2012/11/ANS1998-03-Ansley-and-Jacoby-TallTimbers20-195-204.pdf.

79. Ed Ruscha, *Twentysix Gasoline Stations* (Los Angeles: National Excelsior Press, 1963). On these back-and-forth trips, see Ed Ruscha, interview with author, October 2014; Neal Benezra, "Ed Ruscha: Painting and Artistic License"; Kerry Brougher, "Words as Landscape"; and Phyllis Rosenzweig, "Sixteen (and Counting): Ed Ruscha's Books," in Neal Benezra and Kerry Brougher, eds., *Ed Ruscha* (Washington, DC: Hirschhorn Museum and Sculpture Garden, 2000), 148 and 157–59, 163, 181.

80. Brougher, "Words as Landscape," 158.

81. The Amarillo Standard Oil Station was located at 4001 East Amarillo Boulevard.

82. Eleanor Antin, "Reading Ruscha," *Art in America* 61 (November–December 1973): 66; and as quoted in Rosenzweig, "Sixteen," in Benezra and Brougher, *Ed Ruscha*, 181.

83. Brougher, "Words as Landscape," 161. According to Yve-Alain Bois, Ruscha was a direct influence on Smithson's investigations into entropy. Bois writes: "Smithson, for whom entropy was the key concept and who spoke of it in almost every one of his texts, never hid his debt to Ruscha, particularly in his books." See Yve-Alain Bois, "L/Liquid Words," in Yve-Alain Bois and Rosalind E. Krauss, eds., *Formless: A User's Guide* (New York: Zone Books, 1997), 129; and as quoted in Rosenzweig, "Sixteen," 182.

84. On this work, see Christian Müller, *Ed Ruscha: Los Angeles Apartments* (Basel: Kunstmuseum Basel, 2013), 16.

85. Müller, *Ed Ruscha*, 16; and Ralph Rugoff, "Heavenly Noise," in James Ellroy et al., *Ed Ruscha: Fifty Years of Painting* (London: Hayward, 2009), 14.

86. Brougher, "Words as Landscape," 160–61.

87. Brougher, "Words as Landscape," 162.

88. Ruscha, as quoted in Ulrich Wilmes, "Once Upon a Time in the Present," in Ellroy et al., *Ed Ruscha*, 47.

89. Brougher, "Words as Landscape," 161.

90. Benezra and Brougher, *Ed Ruscha*, 205.

91. Benezra and Brougher, *Ed Ruscha*, 154. Art critic Dave Hickey also saw these fire paintings as "an assault on institutions that dispense 'standards' and serve 'norms.'" See Dave Hickey, "Available Light," in Dave Hickey and Peter Plagens, *The Works of Ed Ruscha* (San Francisco: San Francisco Museum of Modern Art, 1982), 24; and as quoted in Rugoff, "Heavenly Noise," 17. On this painting as demonstrating a "hearty spirit of resistance and even protest," see also Alexandra Schwartz, "A History Without Words," in Ellroy et al., *Ed Ruscha*, 33.

92. Alastair Gee and Dani Anguiano, "Last Day in Paradise: The Untold Story of How a Fire Swallowed a Town," *The Guardian*, December 20, 2018, https://www.theguardian.com/environment/2018/dec/20/last-day-in-paradise-california-deadliest-fire-untold-story-survivors.

CHAPTER 2

1. On these press accounts, see Jeffrey Hogrefe, "Counterfeit O'Keeffes," *D Magazine*, July 1, 2000, https://www.dmagazine.com/publications/d-magazine/2000/july/the-case-of-the-counterfeit-okeeffes/; Annabelle Massey Helber, "Faked Out: Art Maven Gerald Peters Tries to Get to the Bottom of the 'Canyon Suite,'" *Dallas Observer*, February 17, 2000, https://www.dallasobserver.com/news/faked-out-6396240; Jo Ann Lewis, "The Curious Case of the Spurious O'Keeffes," *Washington Post*, August 6, 2000, https://www.washingtonpost.com/archive/lifestyle/2000/08/06/the-curious-case-of-the-spurious-okeeffes/f92feb73-0746-4621-89d5-7d179c6305fb/; Jo Ann Lewis, "The Art That Went from Boon to Bust," *Washington Post*, December 3, 1999, https://www.washingtonpost.com/wp-srv/style/feed/a11324-1999dec3.htm; Gretchen Reynolds, "If It's Not an O'Keeffe, Exactly What Is It?," *New York Times*, March 7, 2000, https://www.nytimes.com/2000/03/07/arts/arts-in-america-if-it-s-not-an-o-keeffe-exactly-what-is-it.html; and Jack Becker, "Caprock Chronicles: The Mystery of the Canyon Suite," *Lubbock Avalanche-Journal*, December 19, 2020, https://www.lubbockonline.com/story/news/history/2020/12/19/caprock-chronicles-a-canyon-suite/3935451001/.

2. On O'Keeffe's time in Canyon, see especially OTL; Von Lintel, *Georgia O'Keeffe Watercolors*; and Paul H. Carlson and John T. Becker, *Georgia O'Keeffe in Texas: A Guide* (Austin, TX: State House Press, 2012).

3. The museums included, in addition to the Kemper in Kansas City, the Phillips Academy (Andover, Massachusetts); Denver Art Museum; Mariana Kistler Beach Museum of Art, Kansas State University; Taylor Museum, Colorado Springs Fine Arts Center; St. Louis Art Museum; and McNay Art Museum, San Antonio. See Lewis, "Curious Case"; and Sharyn R. Udall, *O'Keeffe and Texas* (San Antonio: McNay Art Museum, 1998).

4. See, for instance, *Georgia O'Keeffe Canyon Suite* (Kansas City: Kemper Museum of Contemporary Art and Design, Kansas City Art Institute, 1994), with an introductory essay by Barbara J. Bloemink; Dana Self, *Intimate Landscapes: The Canyon Suite of Georgia O'Keeffe* (New York: Universe, in association with the Kemper Museum of Contemporary Art & Design, 1997); and Udall, *O'Keeffe and Texas*. Charles Eldredge, Hall Distinguished Professor of American Art at the University of Kansas and former director of the Smithsonian's American Art Museum, was also commissioned by Peters to write a twenty-page essay extolling the Canyon Suite's importance in helping us "better appreciate the artist's working methods at a crucial point early in her career." See Lewis, "Curious Case."

5. The documentary was titled *Georgia O'Keeffe: The Plains on Paper*. On this planned project, I cite my conversations with Joyce Herring in Santa Fe, New Mexico, in 2016. Herring worked for PBS when the documentary was being prepared.

6. Barbara Buhler Lynes, ed., *Georgia O'Keeffe: Catalogue Raisonné*, 2 vols. (Washington, DC: National Gallery of Art, 1999). On the definition of this volume as "the definitive, chronological, two-volume, twenty-pound book listing all [O'Keeffe's] accepted works and the history of their ownership from the time they left the artist's hands to the present. . . . The art market's bible on the artist," see Lewis, "Curious Case."

7. Kemper received a letter in December 1999 from Ruth E. Fine, curator of modern prints and drawings at the National Gallery, and Elizabeth Glassman, president of the Georgia O'Keeffe Foundation in Santa Fe, notifying him that his Canyon Suite paintings would not be included in the *Catalogue Raisonné*. The letter included a printed description of the criteria for works on paper used to determine the authenticity of O'Keeffe's pieces for the publication. Kemper suggested at the time that this refusal to include the works was retaliation against him for acquiring the works for his own museum instead of donating them to the National Gallery. See Hogrefe, "Counterfeit O'Keeffes"; Lewis, "Curious Case"; and Lewis, "Boon to Bust."

8. In 1993, J. Carter Brown, director of the National Gallery of Art in Washington, called the works "a national treasure," and was urging Kemper to buy them and to gift them to the National Gallery. See Lewis, "Curious Case"; Reynolds, "Not an O'Keeffe"; and Helber, "Faked Out."

9. On this, see Udall, *O'Keeffe and Texas*.

10. On Peters and the history of his gallery, see especially Mike McGraw and Steve Paul, "Success, Disputes Mark Art Dealer's Business," *Kansas City Star*, January 14, 2001; and https://gpgallery.com/.

11. The work is *Maple and Cedar, Lake George*, oil on canvas, 1922, https://www. kemperart.org/collection/maple-and-cedar-lake-george. Peters said: "I didn't have

to give it back to him legally, but ethically I felt obliged. This kind of thing has never happened to me, and I always said if it did I would honor my word as a dealer, which is that everything I sell is guaranteed to be what I sell it as." See Hogrefe, "Counterfeit O'Keeffes." On the extra painting from Peters's own collection, see Lewis, "Curious Case."

12. Lewis, "Curious Case." As Peters declared, "Juan was the man." Peters explained why even a verbal confirmation from Hamilton carried so much weight at the time: "He'd virtually lived with O'Keeffe for 14 years, and his knowledge of her work exceeded anyone's. The fact that he was fooled is my tough luck."

13. See the May 20, 1988, contract, signed by the seller Terry Lee Caballero and the purchaser Gerald P. Peters III, of the Peters Corporation, Reid-Caballero Family Papers, Cornette Library Special Collections, West Texas A&M University (hereafter cited as RCFP).

14. The contract also stated that the seller Lee Caballero was still able to keep the original $10,000 regardless of Hamilton's opinion.

15. This $10,000 payment came to Hamilton from Peters in the form of a Native American pot. However, according to two reporters for the *Kansas City Star* who interviewed Hamilton after the works were left out of the catalogue raisonné, Hamilton had struggled with authenticating some of them, feeling some were "not right." See Steve Paul and Mike McGraw, "Art of the Deal: The Selling of the Canyon Suite," *Kansas City Star*, January 14, 2001. On the practice of collecting a fee for authentication of a work of art, see Tom Flynn, "Art Forgery: A Crime on the Rise?," in Colette Loll, *Intent to Deceive: Fakes and Forgeries in the Art World* (Washington, DC: International Arts & Artists, 2013).

16. On this list of experts taken in by the fakes, see Lewis, "Curious Case." On experts who did not believe the works were good enough to be by O'Keeffe, or were somehow "off" or "wrong," see Paul and McGraw, "The Art of the Deal."

17. Hogrefe, "Counterfeit O'Keeffes."

18. Reynolds, "Not an O'Keeffe."

19. See reproductions of these nudes in Von Lintel, *O'Keeffe Watercolors*.

20. On Watkins, see Sarah Greenough, *My Faraway One: Selected Letters of Georgia O'Keeffe and Alfred Stieglitz, 1915–1933*, vol. 1 (New Haven: Yale University Press, 2011), 136n294: "Kindred Marion Watkins was a married man with two children who worked at the Connell Motor Company in Amarillo." See also OTL, 98–99, 101–4, 107, 120–22, 129, 133, 165.

21. On the Transcendental Painting Group, see Michael Duncan et al., *Another World: The Transcendental Painting Group* (New York: DelMonico Books, 2021); Christopher M. Scheer, Sarah Victoria Turner, and James G. Mansell, *Enchanted Modernities: Theosophy, the Arts, and the American West* (Somerset, UK: Fulgur, 2019), 40–51; and Gilbert Vicario et al. *Agnes Pelton: Desert Transcendentalist* (Phoenix: Phoenix Art Museum and Hirmer, 2019), as well as Revett, Pasquine, and Von Lintel, *Emil Bisttram*.

22. The titles of the Canyon Suite works were assigned by Peters in collaboration with

Charles Eldredge. Eldredge was paid for his scholarly labor regarding the Canyon Suite paintings. See Paul and McGraw, "Art of the Deal."

23. Samantha Friedman, ed., *Georgia O'Keeffe: To See Takes Time* (New York: Museum of Modern Art, 2023).

24. Judith C. Walsh, "Paper Study," in Lynes, ed., *O'Keeffe: Catalogue Raisonné*, 1: 25–26, as well as Lewis, "Curious Case."

25. Walsh, "Paper Study," 25–26; and Hogrefe, "Counterfeit O'Keeffes."

26. As the catalogue raisonné demonstrates, roughly 95 percent of O'Keeffe's works on paper from the 1910s were "on a student-grade paper identified as Bockingford cartridge paper," and of "cream color, of medium thickness and machine made, with a slightly fuzzy surface." See also Walsh, "Paper Survey," and Lewis, "Curious Case."

27. This exhibition was *Georgia O'Keeffe's Far Wide Texas*, which ran from April to October 2016 at the O'Keeffe Museum. Published in the context of the show was a book that featured in full size and beautifully color-matched reproductions the artist's authenticated Texas watercolors, including pieces like *Light Coming on the Plains* series that couldn't travel for the exhibition. See Von Lintel, *Georgia O'Keeffe Watercolors*.

28. Lewis, "Curious Case."

29. On this shift, see the biographies of O'Keeffe, including Roxana Robinson, *Georgia O'Keeffe: A Life*, 2nd ed. (Waltham, MA: Brandeis University Press, 2020).

30. On her Lake George years, for instance, see Erin B. Coe, Gwendolyn Owens, and Bruce Robertson, *Modern Nature: Georgia O'Keeffe and Lake George* (New York: Thames and Hudson, 2013).

31. She did return to watercolors late in life, after she went almost completely blind from macular degeneration. See works like her *Untitled (Abstraction Red Wave with Circle)*, from 1979, featured on the Georgia O'Keeffe Museum Facebook page on February 19, 2020. The post reads: "When macular degeneration seriously reduced Georgia O'Keeffe's eyesight, she still produced drawings with beautiful abstract marks inspired by her study of Japanese and Chinese styles of calligraphy. With the aid of an assistant, she created over 40 watercolors on paper, each consisting of just a few strokes and dots from a wide brush. These markings and the ways they define and interact with the white spaces around them form a late-life bookend to the 1910's abstractions that opened O'Keeffe's career." https://www.facebook.com/photo?fbid=10157759381535560&set=a.10150162854965560

32. O'Keeffe to Stieglitz, postmarked March 18, 1917, as transcribed in OTL. In a later letter from May 1, 1917, she described him as "Tall and thin—muscles like iron . . . good-natured—funny kid—has such funny kinks in his brain—I like him—Some way or other." See OTL, 101.

33. O'Keeffe to Stieglitz, November 13, 1916, OTL, 62.

34. On Reid fixing the heel in her shoe with needle and thread, see O'Keeffe to Stieglitz, postmarked March 18, 1917; on Ted tying her package up like a calf, see O'Keeffe to Stieglitz, postmarked June 25, 1917, OTL, 88, 113.

35. On this dancing, see O'Keeffe to Stieglitz, October 18, 1917, OTL, 128.

36. O'Keeffe to Stieglitz, postmarked June 22, 1917, OTL, 111–12.

37. A. Kirk Knott, interview with Ted Reid, April 26, 1978, CS 1970-19/10a, PPHMRC. On Reid's biography, see OTL, 179n23.

38. On this, see OTL, especially 93–94.

39. O'Keeffe to Stieglitz, October 18, 1917, OTL, 128.

40. See OTL, 105. See also her letter from June 16, 1917, when Ted asks her if she still likes him and she said yes, and her letter from June 19, 1917, when she says Ted is a "piece of the outdoors, gets my honesty at a queer angle." See OTL, 111.

41. See OTL, 107.

42. See, for instance, O'Keeffe to Stieglitz, May 1, 1917; May 9, 1917; August 6, 1917, OTL, 100–101, 105, 117–18.

43. O'Keeffe wrote of Ruby: "[Ted] came in late with an older brother and a girl he always trotted around here from habit, I think—She was from near his home—a really nice—loveable sort of girl. . . . I believe he is trying to like Ruby because he can't see me within reach—It seems I never saw such a live—seething piece of humanity—making such an effort to manage it. . . . I told him he ought to marry Ruby or leave her alone. . . . If he would marry her—it would be all right—knowing he was forgetting." O'Keeffe to Stieglitz, October 18, 1917, OTL, 127–28.

44. O'Keeffe to Stieglitz, October 18, 1917, OTL, 127.

45. O'Keeffe described Ted being "at the station—going to war—aviation" in a letter to Paul Strand written on November 15, 1917. She repeated a similar phrase in a December 7 letter to Stieglitz: "Ted met me at the station—bent on aviation." The exact date of his departure is not clear, but it was presumably around December 7, 1917. On December 28, 1917, O'Keeffe wrote: "Even Ted—he isn't himself any more. . . . Partly—maybe mostly—my fault—Engaged to Ruby." See OTL, 131, 136, 141, 201n16.

46. Whether this virus was related to the Spanish flu is an interesting question. O'Keeffe began having symptoms in November 1917 and the first cases of Spanish flu were not recorded until March 1918. But those first recordings were in Fort Riley, Kansas, a place within a 500-mile radius of Canyon, Texas. The possibility that earlier cases existed in the region but went undiagnosed and unreported is not impossible, a possibility we saw with the recent Covid epidemic. On the Spanish flu, see Laura Spinney, *Pale Rider: The Spanish Flu of 1918 and How It Changed the World* (New York: PublicAffairs, 2018); Catherine Arnold, *Pandemic 1918: Eyewitness Accounts from the Greatest Medical Holocaust in Modern History* (New York: St. Martin's Griffin, 2020); Gina Kolata, *Flu: The Story of the Great Influenza Pandemic of 1918 and the Search for the Virus That Caused It* (New York: Atria, 2001); and John M. Barry, *The Great Influenza: The Epic Story of the Deadliest Pandemic in History* (New York: Viking, 2004).

47. Georgia O'Keeffe to Ted Reid, postmarked May 8, 1946, RCFP.

48. O'Keeffe to Reid, postmarked May 10, 1946, RCFP.

49. One source on this encounter is Anita Pollitzer, who describes Reid coming to the opening and O'Keeffe asking him why he "dropped her like a hotcake" back in

Canyon. Pollitzer also quotes Reid saying, "Did you ever see the rain with Georgia? Did you ever see her watch a great storm? I knew and loved that country well and here for the first time was someone who felt the same way about it. There was never anyone in the world like her in her appreciation of such things. She always wanted the best and there wasn't any camouflage in her." See Anita Pollitzer, *A Woman on Paper: Georgia O'Keeffe* (New York: Simon and Schuster, 1988), 153–54.

50. O'Keeffe to Reid, postmarked August 17, 1951, RCFP.

51. On O'Keeffe carefully curating her reputation through photography, for example, see Susan Danly, *Georgia O'Keeffe and the Camera: The Art of Identity* (New Haven: Yale University Press, 2008).

52. O'Keeffe to Reid, postmarked April 1978, RCFP. In another similar letter, postmarked March 7, 1971, O'Keeffe sent Reid an invite to her retrospective at the San Francisco Museum of Art, along with the note, "These are my new telephone numbers, I had to change numbers because of various bothersome calls. *Please keep them confidential.*" On this note was a handwritten annotation with the date and time "3 o'clock Tuesday 23." It is tempting to think this meant they met in person following Reid's receipt of this invitation, but we have no further proof. See photocopy of this invitation and note in the file "Ted Reid Correspondence (1917–77)" in the Georgia O'Keeffe Research Center, Santa Fe. The files note that those photocopies were taken when Rebecca Reid Wheeler, Ted Reid's granddaughter and Minton's cousin, came to the O'Keeffe Research Center to try to sell the original correspondence materials in June 2012.

53. Barbara Buhler Lynes and Agapita Judy Lopez describe how, after her move to New Mexico, O'Keeffe became "known as a recluse and a loner." They also describe how annoyed she would get when visitors arrived unannounced at her homes there. See Barbara Buhler Lynes and Agapita Judy Lopez, *Georgia O'Keeffe and Her Houses: Ghost Ranch and Abiquiu* (New York: Abrams, in association with the Georgia O'Keeffe Museum, 2012).

54. Georgia O'Keeffe to Marcelete Reid Dana, April 21, and June 1, 1969, RCFP. In a charming, if slightly grumpy, way, O'Keeffe responded to the first letter that she didn't know who Marcelete was and that she "seldom [went] to the opera." In the second letter, she apologizes that she cannot attend the opera because she is "miserable with shingles" but tells Marcelete to "come and spend an hour with [her]" when she is in town.

55. See Reid Ted Correspondence, O'Keeffe Research Center.

56. Postcard dated November 9, 1949, addressed to Ted Reid, Canyon, TX. The photograph on the postcard shows a view of Route 66 with the Triangle Motel in Amarillo. Reid Ted Correspondence, O'Keeffe Research Center.

57. Interview with Jan Minton, Santa Fe, Summer 2016.

58. O'Keeffe to Stieglitz, August 6, 1917, OTL, 118.

59. Mike McGraw and Steve Paul, "A Strange Saga: Texas Connections Keep Watercolors Shrouded in Mystery," *Kansas City Star*, January 14, 2001.

60. This statement is part of what appears to be the draft of a 1977 speech given at WT

by Sherman, a photocopy of which is in the Reid Ted Correspondence, O'Keeffe Research Center.

61. On this sale, see Greenough, *My Faraway One*, 138, and 138n298.

62. On how it was difficult for her to find time and space to work given her teaching obligations in Canyon, see OTL, especially 126–27, 130, 145.

63. Apparently, even Peters recognized that the works seemed to be "works in progress" and that was why she "could have decided to leave them behind" in Canyon. See Hogrefe, "Counterfeit O'Keeffes."

64. On the "20 incidents" Caballero had identified where his life and O'Keeffe's life were parallel, see Hogrefe, "Counterfeit O'Keeffes."

65. On these claims, see Hogrefe, "Counterfeit O'Keeffes."

66. This observation was made by John Norton, a Santa Fe art collector who knew Caballero; it appears in McGraw and Paul, "A Strange Saga."

67. The notes and manuscript of this biography by Caballero are not extant, as far as I have found. The RCFP does not include any manuscript drafts, and only a few notes that may relate to his authorship of this volume. Caballero was also attempting to write and publish a book titled *Watercolor Painting* in 1964, but he never accomplished this goal. See "Dr. Emilio Caballero Named to Royal Society of Art," *Canyon News*, July 23, 1964.

68. See RCFP.

69. I even have in my office an easel that Caballero was convinced that O'Keeffe used in her teaching.

70. Many of O'Keeffe's Texas watercolors are in the collection of the Georgia O'Keeffe Museum in Santa Fe, having been part of the artist's personal collection and then part of her estate after her death. On her collection, see Barbara Buhler Lynes and Russell Bowman, *O'Keeffe's O'Keeffes: The Artist's Collection* (New York: Thames and Hudson, 2001).

71. On the complex definitions of "forgery," see Sándor Radnóti, *The Fake: Forgery and Its Place in Art*, trans. Ervin Dunai (New York: Rowman & Littlefield, 1999), 14, 43–44, 116. One definition argues that "forgery of a work of art is an object falsely purporting to have the history of production requisite for the (or an) original of the work." Another version states that "forgery is an applied art that relies for effect on the surface attraction of *another* work, or another style, flattering the eye by pretending to be exactly *that*" (italics in original). In other words, it pretends to be something it is not and it claims a "false pedigree" and a "place in history it does not deserve."

72. Georgia O'Keeffe, *Georgia O'Keeffe* (New York: Viking, 1976), figs. 6, 13, 88.

73. Jan Garden Castro, *The Art & Life of Georgia O'Keeffe* (New York: Crown Trade, 1985), 4, 20 (reproduced upside down), 21, 165, 50, and 90. Her two other versions of *Light Coming on the Plains* were reproduced in black and white.

74. See David Turner, *O'Keeffe Works on Paper* (Santa Fe: Museum of New Mexico; Albuquerque: University of New Mexico Press, 1985). Also reproduced in this catalogue was the MoMA version of *Train at Night in the Desert*.

75. Richard Price and Sally Price, *Enigma Variations* (Cambridge, MA: Harvard University Press, 1997).

76. See "Remembering William Jordan at SMU," on the Meadows School of the Arts website, https://www.smu.edu/Meadows/NewsAndEvents/News/201 8/180202-RememberingBillJordan. On Elmyr de Hory, see Orson Welles's film from 1973 *F for Fake* and the recent documentary *Real Fake: The Art, Life, and Crimes of Elmyr de Hory* (2017), as well as Clifford Irving, *Fake! The Story of Elmyr de Hory, the Greatest Art Forger of Our Time* (New York: McGraw Hill, 1969); and Mark Forgy, *The Forger's Apprentice: Life with the World's Most Notorious Artist* (Scotts Valley, CA: CreateSpace, 2012). Elmyr committed suicide in Ibiza in 1976; his works were purchased by dealers and collectors in North and South America, Europe, Africa, and Asia.

77. Other artists that Meadows bought that were forged by de Hory included Pierre Bonnard, Maurice Vlaminck, and Raoul Dufy.

78. The FBI had been on his trail since 1955, when the Fogg Museum at Harvard University detected one of his forgeries in their collection. De Hory's trial following the Meadows scandal was supposed to be held in France, but Spain (where Ibiza was located) did not have an extradition agreement with France, so he escaped trial there.

79. On de Hory's methods, see Forgy, *The Forger's Apprentice*, 38, 45–54, 68–71, 96, 108. Another interesting trick de Hory used was to remove a tipped-in or glued-in photograph in old art books and replace it with a new photograph of a painting or drawing he just made, but with a subject that would still match the printed title in caption on that page in the art book.

80. Amy Von Lintel, "West Texas Gets Taken by Art Fraud," Parts 1 and 2, Caprock Chronicles, *Lubbock Avalanche-Journal*, October 4 and October 26, 2018, https:// www.lubbockonline.com/story/news/state/2019/10/05/caprock-chronicle s-west-texas-gets-taken-by-art-fraud-part-1/2607715007/.

81. Hamilton's role in O'Keeffe's life and her estate after her death is controversial and contested by historians. He entered O'Keeffe's life in 1973, and by the time of her death, had taken over management of her affairs and secured his role as director of her estate. See, for instance, Paul and McGraw, "The Art of the Deal," and Charlotte Cowles, "Exclusive: Georgia O'Keeffe's Younger Man," *Harper's Bazaar*, February 14, 2016, https://www.harpersbazaar.com/culture/features/a14033/ georgia-okeeffe-0316/.

82. According to newspaper sources, Peters claimed that he had the works tested by paper conservator Keiko Keyes, who had doubts about one work. Peters withdrew that work from the collection. See Hogrefe, "Counterfeit O'Keeffes"; Lewis, "Curious Case"; and Paul and McGraw, "Art of the Deal." More research needs to be done on Keyes's participation in the review of the Canyon Suite; her papers exist and should be consulted by future researchers.

83. In 2000, the FBI office in Albuquerque opened an investigation under the leadership of Doug Beldon.

84. Lewis, "Curious Case."

85. See, for instance, Dara Moskowitz Grumdahl, "Con Artistry: The Real Story of How the World's Most Notorious Art Collection Wound Up in Minnesota," *Mpls St. Paul Magazine*, March 21, 2014, https://mspmag.com/arts-and-culture/con-artistry/. "Fraud in painting is actually difficult to prove. It is not illegal to paint in the style of Picasso or Rembrandt or Raphael. . . . What is illegal is to sell art as something it's not. That's fraud." On the largely unregulated, informal nature of the art market that makes it highly susceptible to criminal manipulation and forgery, see Flynn, "Art Forgery: A Crime on the Rise?" See also William Casement, "Criminality" and "Mitigated Culpability and Alternative Economics," in *The Many Faces of Art Forgery: From the Dark Side to Shades of Gray* (New York: Rowman & Littlefield, 2022), 160–84, and 213. Casement writes: "Because art forgery is not written into legal codes as a crime, the act is typically charged as a form of fraud (often involving mail or wire fraud), and perhaps other charges are added such as money laundering and (in the United States) tax evasion."

86. On this early biography, see especially "Dr. Emilio Caballero Named to Royal Society"; Brad Newman, "Impressions by Caballero," *Amarillo Globe-News*, March 5, 2011, written in the context of an exhibition of Caballero's work at the Art Center in Dumas, Texas; and Michael Grauer, "Emilio Caballero: Artista y Maestro en El Llano," http://www.tfaoi.com/aa/3aa/3aa24.htm , written in the context of an exhibition of the artist's work at PPHM from September 2001 to February 2002.

87. On Caballero's connections to the scandal, I have built upon the research of my graduate student Michaela Wegman, whose semester paper for my Fakes and Forgeries course in Spring 2020, "Case File: Dr. Emilio Caballero," laid important groundwork for this chapter. I also thank my students Taryin Tovar and Chelsea Minton for their careful reading and interpretation of the unpublished memoir of Caballero, included in the RCFP.

88. Vivian Robinson to Emilio Caballero, August 1, 1966, RCFP. Robinson also spoke with Hogrefe about this trip to see O'Keeffe in New Mexico. According to Hogrefe, "Robinson told me that when O'Keeffe opened the door, she grabbed the drawings and went back into her house and refused to come out. Robinson wouldn't leave until O'Keeffe gave her the drawings back." Robinson claimed that O'Keeffe said three of the four drawings were hers. On Robinson's visit, see also McGraw and Paul, "A Strange Saga."

89. Columbia here could refer to Columbia Teachers College in New York, where O'Keeffe took courses in 1915, or Columbia College in South Carolina, where O'Keeffe taught in 1915.

90. Lewis, "Curious Case."

91. Lewis, "Curious Case."

92. On this 1978 sale, see McGraw and Paul, "A Strange Saga."

93. Lewis, "Curious Case."

94. Lewis, "Curious Case."

95. Caballero's "retirement date" from WT is somewhat unclear. He retired from his department head position, possibly under some coercion, in January 1975. After

losing a trial to get reinstated in that position in the fall of 1975, he continued to serve as a faculty member and art professor at WT until 1979, when his retirement was announced at WT and in the local paper, but he continued to claim an affiliation with WT even after this date. See Newman, "Impressions by Caballero"; and "Caballero Has Busy Schedule," *Canyon News*, April 2, 1980.

96. See, for instance, "Caballero Hearing Begins Today Before University Committee," *Canyon News*, September 25, 1975, and "Committee Backs Watkins on Ruling," *Canyon Sunday News*, September 28, 1975.

97. See "Charles Thomas Caballero Obituary," published by the Boxwell Brothers Funeral Home in Amarillo, April 7, 2014.

98. McGraw and Paul, "A Strange Saga."

99. The exhibition was titled *Architecture, Nature, and Abstraction: Emilio Caballero at WTAMU*. It hung in the Dord Fitz Formal Art Gallery in 2017.

100. This contract stated that $10,000 would be given to Terry Lee Caballero upon signing, with $40,000 to be held with Peters's lawyers until closing. On closing of the sale of those twenty-five works, she would receive an additional $600,000. The contract also acknowledged the remaining four "Option Works" of which Peters was to have first right of refusal. It noted that the sales price included reproduction rights on the works, likely so that Peters could promote their resale. Third, it noted that Peters didn't have to pay any sales tax on the objects because of their intent to be resold, as per New Mexico tax law. On this contract, see RCFP.

101. See affidavit dated June 3, 1988, signed Emilio Caballero, RCFP. On this version of the affidavit, see also Lewis, "Curious Case."

102. Hogrefe, "Counterfeit O'Keeffes," as well as Lewis, "Curious Case."

103. "Letter of Conveyance," dated June 22, 1988, signed by Emilio Caballero, RCFP.

104. A copy of this check is in the RCFP.

105. See addendum dated September 16, 1988, again signed by Terry Lee Caballero and this time by Jack C. Lippincott, treasurer of the Peters Corporation, RCFP.

106. The memo dated September 22, 1988, reads, "Received from Charles and Terry the sum of four thousand ($4000) – Mary and Emilio Caballero. For taxes and insurance." See RCFP. This money was transferred only six days after Terry signed the contract for the remaining "Option Works" with Peters.

107. Lewis, "Curious Case" and McGraw and Paul, "A Strange Saga."

108. Dion O'Wyatt to Emilio Caballero, April 21, 1993, RCFP.

109. Dion O'Wyatt to Barbara Lynes, March 7, 1993, RCFP.

110. On the increasing reluctance of experts to offer opinions for fear of litigation by disgruntled collectors, see Flynn, "Art Forgery: A Crime on the Rise?" and "Collectors, Artists and Lawyers: Fear of Litigation Is Hobbling the Art Market," *The Economist*, November 24, 2012, https://www.economist.com/business/2012/11/24/collectors-artists-and-lawyers; Grossman, LLP, "Three Recent Suits Exemplify Some of the Legal Issues Surrounding Art Authentication," *Art Law Blog*, April 7, 2014, https://www.grossmanllp.com/three-recent-suits-exemplify-some-of-the-legal-issues-surrounding-art-authentication, as well as Charles and Thomas Danziger,

"On the Case: Exploring Real World Art Law Issues," *Artnet*, April 23, 2014, https://news.artnet.com/market/on-the-case-exploring-real-world-art-law-issues-11677.

111. Lewis, "Curious Case."

112. According to the press, there were 250 inauthentic works. See Lewis, "Curious Case" and Reynolds, "Not an O'Keeffe."

113. On this, see Hogrefe, "Counterfeit O'Keeffes." Caballero had claimed that he "discovered [the work] in one of the closets of the art department at West Texas." Peters had taken this work to O'Keeffe who authenticated it, but he also identified the sitter as her former classmate True.

114. Lewis, "Curious Case."

115. This discrepancy was pointed out too by McGraw and Paul in "A Strange Saga." Caballero also claimed, when speaking with Hogrefe, that he never "represented anything that he sold as O'Keeffes" but only that they "*could* be by O'Keeffe," a statement that became "his mantra." Hogrefe, "Counterfeit O'Keeffes."

116. Lewis, "Curious Case." In other instances, the Reid family denied ever having, or knowing that Ted Reid had, any O'Keeffes. See McGraw and Paul, "A Strange Saga."

117. McGraw and Paul, "A Strange Saga."

118. McGraw and Paul, "A Strange Saga."

119. O'Keeffe to Stieglitz, postmarked June 19, 1917, OTL, 111.

120. Minton interview and McGraw and Paul, "A Strange Saga."

121. Hogrefe, "Counterfeit O'Keeffes."

122. Caballero made this claim to Hogrefe. Caballero also said that Ted Reid denied being O'Keeffe's "boyfriend," because he "was a gentleman of the first order." Hogrefe, "Counterfeit O'Keeffes." This gentlemanly persona was also central to Elmyr de Hory's identity and served him well as a forger. On this, see Forgy, *The Forger's Apprentice*, especially 8, 50, 76, as well as Casement, *Many Faces of Art Forgery*, 154.

123. McGraw and Paul, "A Strange Saga." The authors likewise question the lack of evidence of the fifty-year friendship that Caballero claimed to have had with Reid. On Reid's teaching of aviation at WT, see Patrick Diepen, "Regional Aviation in the Space Between," a paper delivered at the Space Between Annual Conference in June 2023 at WT.

124. "About the Exhibition," in Loll, *Intent to Deceive*.

125. Colette Loll explains, "In profiling their lives and careers, this exhibition points to common and recurring patterns: frustrated artistic ambitions, chaotic personal lives, and a contempt for the art market and its 'experts.'" See Colette Loll, "Curator Statement," *Intent to Deceive*. For more on the highly complicated profiles of art forgers, and a nuanced interpretation of them, see Casement, "The Mind of the Forger," *Many Faces of Art Forgery*, 147–60. See also Radnóti, *The Fake*, 21–23.

126. As Radnóti argues, "on the one hand [forgery] unveils the snobbery and conceit of art lovers and collectors motivated externally, and on the other, it relativizes the expertise of the professionals." Radnóti, *The Fake*, 26.

127. Loll, *Intent to Deceive*.

128. Loll, "Curator Statement," *Intent to Deceive*.

129. Casement, *Many Faces of Art Forgery*, 157–58.

130. On this "astral" connection, see note 66 above.

131. Casement, *Many Faces of Art Forgery*, 159. The belief in the making of copies as a near miraculous way to demonstrate artistic skill dates back to ancient Greece, and played out in Renaissance Italy, with tales of artists showing their God-given talents in art by faking out viewers—perhaps most famously Michelangelo creating a work believed to be an authentic ancient Greek original. See Radnóti, *The Fake*, 1–16.

132. Hogrefe, "Counterfeit O'Keeffes," and Reynolds, "If It's Not an O'Keeffe."

133. On the fluidity of these and other forgery-related terms, see Radnóti, *The Fake*, 46–47.

134. For an excellent discussion of the rich and complex history of the fetish as a concept, including the early notions of the fetish, magic, and witchcraft, as well as the modern theories of Sigmund Freud, Jacques Lacan, and Karl Marx, see Anne McClintock, *Imperial Leather: Race, Gender, and Sexuality in the Colonial Context* (New York: Routledge, 1995), 184–95, 208, 230. See also William Pietz, "Fetish," in *Critical Terms for Art History*, eds. Robert S. Nelson and Richard Shiff, 2nd ed. (Chicago: University of Chicago Press, 2003), 306–17.

135. On advertising and fetishism, see especially Anne McClintock, "Soft-Soaping Empire: Commodity Racism and Imperial Advertising," in *Imperial Leather*, 207–31.

136. McClintock, *Imperial Leather*, 184–85.

137. On Pei-Shen Qian, who was the forger for the Knoedler Gallery scandal, see the documentary *Made You Look: A True Story about Fake Art* (Netflix, 2020); Patricia Cohen and William K. Rashbaum, "One Queens Painter Created Forgeries That Sold for Millions, U.S. Says," *New York Times*, August 15, 2013, https://www.nytimes.com/2013/08/16/nyregion/one-queens-painter-created-forgeries-that-sold-for-millions-us-says.html; and Brian Boucher, "Oops! A New Documentary About the Knoedler Fakes Scandal Accidentally Included an Artist's Trick Image as Real," *Artnet*, March 5, 2021, https://news.artnet.com/art-world/knoedler-pollock-documentary-fake-image-1948673. On both de Hory and Qian as well as other forgers, see Loll, *Intent to Deceive*.

138. On these "fake fakes," I have conducted interviews and exchanged emails with Mark Forgy. See also Johannes Rod, "Fake Fakes in the Forger's Oeuvre," posted on the blog "Elmyrstory" hosted by Mark Forgy, December 4, 2010, https://elmyrstory.wordpress.com/2010/12/04/fake-fakes-in-the-forger%E2%80%99s-oeuvre/; Grumdahl, "Con Artistry"; and Casement, *Many Faces of Art Forgery*, 167.

139. On the increasingly high risk–high return market for art forgery, see Flynn, "Art Forgery: A Crime on the Rise?" He writes: "The art object is ever more commonly treated as an investable commodity to be speculated upon, to provide a hedge against inflation, to act as a safe store of wealth or as a risk-reducing component within a judiciously diversified investment portfolio."

CHAPTER 3

1. The original owners of the home were both attorneys who met in law school at the

University of Texas at Austin. Wright designed another home for clients named Kinney, and the two houses have been mistaken for one another in discussions about Wright. The Patrick Kinney House was completed in 1953 in Lancaster, Wisconsin. See the Frank Lloyd Wright Foundation website: https://franklloydwright.org/site/kinney-house/. This website does not mention or discuss the Amarillo Kinney House.

2. When a book of Wright's writings was published in 1960, for instance, it included a map of locations of houses designed by Wright, as well as a list of his "executed works." The map shows nothing built in West Texas, and the list does not include the Kinney House in Amarillo. The home was still under construction, so perhaps it was left out because it was not yet "executed," but the omission has perpetuated the tendency to overlook and ignore the house in Wright scholarship. See Edgar Kaufmann and Ben Raeburn, eds., *Frank Lloyd Wright: Writings and Buildings* (New York: Horizon, 1960), 328–46. During the drafting of this chapter, an article-length study on the Kinney House was published, on which I consulted. This article offers a good overview of the aesthetics and style of the home and includes beautiful and detailed color reproductions by the magazine's photographer Angelina Marie—some of the first published photographs that do the structure justice. See Jason Boyett, "Unbelievably Rare: The Sterling Kinney House, Designed by Frank Lloyd Wright," *Brick & Elm*, March–April 2023, 38–47.

3. The others are the John Gillin House in Dallas built in 1950 and the William Thaxton House in Bunker Hill built in 1953. See Alan Weintraub and Alan Hess, *Frank Lloyd Wright: The Houses* (New York: Rizzoli, 2005), 531, 533.

4. John Sergeant, *Frank Lloyd Wright's Usonian Houses: The Case for Organic Architecture* (New York: Watson-Guptill, 1984), 16, 183. The Herbert Jacobs House was designed in 1936 and completed in 1937 at 1,500 square feet with a cost of $5,500. On the Jacobs House and the origin of "Usonian," see also Robert C. Twombly, *Frank Lloyd Wright: An Interpretive Biography* (New York: Harper and Row, 1973), 191–93; Meryle Secrest, *Frank Lloyd Wright: A Biography* (Chicago: University of Chicago Press, 1992), 448; and Kaufmann and Raeburn, eds., *Writings and Buildings*, 50, 294–96; Frank Lloyd Wright, *An Autobiography* (New York: Duell, Sloan, and Pearce, 1943), 25, 489–94; Brendan Gill, *Many Masks: A Life of Frank Lloyd Wright* (New York: G. P. Putnam's Sons, 1987), 386–94; and Bruce Brooks Pfeiffer and Yukio Futagawa, *Frank Lloyd Wright: Usonian Houses*, Global Architecture Traveler, no. 5 (Tokyo: A.D.A., 2002). The Jacobs House, like the Kinney House, was designed in an L-format, or a "tadpole" or "polliwog" format, which was one of the five styles of Usonian floorplans. The others were diagonal, in-line, hexagonal, and raised. See Sergeant, *Usonian Houses*, 41. On the Usonians, see also Alan Hess, "Utopia Promised," in Weintraub and Hess, *The Houses*, 229–36; and David Larkin and Bruce Brooks Pfeiffer, eds., *Frank Lloyd Wright: The Masterworks* (New York: Rizzoli, 1993), 143–49, 164–73.

5. It was completed by Taliesin Associated Architects (TAA) under the direction of Allen Lape "Davy" Davidson in 1961. See Weintraub and Hess, *The Houses*, 535.

TAA was a firm created by Wright to carry on his legacy after his death; it was housed in Taliesin West and disbanded in 2003.

6. Secrest, *Frank Lloyd Wright*, 554.

7. On the quickly increasing cost of the Usonian designs that exceeded $5,500, see Sergeant, *Usonian Houses*, 138.

8. Twombly, *Frank Lloyd Wright*, 191–94. On Wright coining the term "carport," see for example Sue Miklovic, "The Surprisingly Interesting History of the Carport," *North Baltimore Express*, September 6, 2019, https://www.thenbxpress.com/the-surprisingly-interesting-history-of-the-carport/.

9. Sergeant, *Usonian Houses*, 12–13.

10. Sergeant, *Usonian Houses*, 19. Sergeant continues, comparing the kitchen to a "service core like a ship's galley, with all walls used for storage or appliances," another point of comparison with the Kinney House. On the kitchen as "work-space," see Twombly, *Frank Lloyd Wright*, 200; and Edgar Kaufmann, ed., *An American Architecture: Frank Lloyd Wright* (New York: Horizon Press, 1955), 175.

11. Twombly, *Frank Lloyd Wright*, 200. On Wright's theories of gender roles and his interest in gender equality, see Gwendolyn Wright, "Architectural Practice and Social Vision in Wright's Early Designs," in Carol R. Bolon, Robert S. Nelson, and Linda Seidel, eds., *The Nature of Frank Lloyd Wright* (Chicago: University of Chicago Press, 1988), 102–3.

12. Twombly, *Frank Lloyd Wright*, 202.

13. Twombly, *Frank Lloyd Wright*, 200–202.

14. Sergeant, *Usonian Houses*, 139.

15. Twombly, *Frank Lloyd Wright*, 195.

16. On the Prairie Style, also called "Prairie Architecture," see Twombly, *Frank Lloyd Wright*, 57–76, 87; Kaufmann and Raeburn, eds., *Writings and Buildings*, 38–55; Bolon, Nelson, and Seidel, *Nature of Frank Lloyd Wright*; and Larkin and Pfeiffer, *Masterworks*, 35–61, 76–103. Wright was born in the Midwest where he saw the prairie ideal—a "mythic terrain" more than a geographical region—in the farmland of his birthplace in Wisconsin. See Donald Hoffmann, "Meeting Nature Face to Face," and Thomas H. Beeby, "Wright and Landscape: A Mythical Interpretation," in Bolon, Nelson, and Seidel, *Nature of Frank Lloyd Wright*, 93, and 154.

17. Weintraub and Hess, *The Houses*, 59.

18. Beeby, "Wright and Landscape," and Larzer Ziff, "The Prairie in Literary Culture and the Prairie Style of Frank Lloyd Wright," in Bolon, Nelson, and Seidel, *Nature of Frank Lloyd Wright*, 180–81, 183. On the prairie as a region, see also Weems, *Barnstorming the Prairies*, xx.

19. Beeby, "Wright and Landscape," 155–68. See also Wright, *An Autobiography*, especially the first few sections on "family" that celebrate his pioneering roots as his ancestors settled on "virgin American soil."

20. See "Manifest Destiny and Indian Removal."

21. Twombly, *Frank Lloyd Wright*, 60. On this verticality, see also Beeby, "Wright and Landscape," 168–69.

22. On Wright's creative dialogue with other mid-century modern designers, see Twombly, *Frank Lloyd Wright*, 195–96.

23. About the prairie, Wright wrote: "the gently rolling or level prairies of our great Middle West; the great rolling prairies where every detail of elevation becomes exaggerated; every tree towers above the great calm plains of flowered surfaces as the plain lies serene beneath a wonderful unlimited sweep of the sky." Kaufmann, ed., *An American Architecture*, 193.

24. See "Trees for the Texas Panhandle," Randall County Master Gardener Society of the Texas A&M AgriLife Extension Service, https://txmg.org/randall/ staying-connected/gardening-with-the-masters/gardening-tips-2/trees-for-the-texas-panhandle/ and "Texas Ecoregions: High Plains," Trees of Texas, Texas A&M Forest Service, http://texastreeid.tamu.edu/content/texasEcoRegions/HighPlains/.

25. On these drawings, see various auction websites and blog posts, including https:// fineart.ha.com/itm/works-on-paper/frank-lloyd-wright-american-1867-195 9-drawings-of-the-mr-and-mrs-sterling-e-kinney-house-three-works-1955ink- /a/5355-67055.s and http://wrightchat.savewright.org/viewtopic.php?t=11544.

26. Twombly, *Frank Lloyd Wright*, 197.

27. Weintraub explores how many of Wright's designs, especially houses, were recycled from earlier drawings and plans that were not completed, so a house originally designed for Hawaii was actually built in California, or one for Minnesota was built in New York, belying his claims of a perfect one-to-one relationship between site and structure. See Weintraub and Hess, *The Houses*, 14.

28. "Restored Usonian House in Amarillo Once Again Shows Wrightian Touch," *Texas Architecture*, July–August 2009, 10, 14. Wright also used a similar angled batter in the Fawcett House in Los Banos, California, built between 1959 and 1961 and the C. Leigh Stevens House, Auldbrass Plantation, built in 1939, and a stepped batter in the Harold Price Sr. House in Paradise Valley, Arizona (1954). See Hess, "Utopia Promised," 233; Weintraub and Hess, *The Houses*, 533; and Larkin and Pfeiffer, *Masterworks*, 188–97, 248–52.

29. Hoffmann, "Meeting Nature," 95.

30. Kaufmann, ed., *An American Architecture*, 106.

31. Hoffmann, "Meeting Nature," 93–94.

32. Neil Levine, *The Architecture of Frank Lloyd Wright* (Princeton, NJ: Princeton University Press, 1996), 174–75, 184–85. Wright always referred to the project as the A. M. Johnson Desert Compound and Shrine. On Wright's love of and inspiration from the Western US deserts, see Wright, *An Autobiography*, 306, 314.

33. On Ocotillo, see Levine, *Frank Lloyd Wright*, 201–6. At times, Wright spelled the name of this project "Ocatilla," including on some of his drawings. On Taliesin West, see Levine, *Frank Lloyd Wright*, 254–97; and Larkin and Pfeiffer, *Masterworks*, 294–307.

34. Art Leatherwood, "Llano Estacado," *Handbook of Texas Online*, https://www.tsha-online.org/handbook/entries/llano-estacado. According to Leatherwood, "It is part of what was known to early explorers and settlers as the Great American Desert, a

semiarid region with average annual precipitation of eighteen to twenty inches. The soils are almost universally dark brown to reddish brown sands, sandy loams, and clay loams." The idea of staked or palisaded came from the appearance of the region being on "high ground" like the sides of a military fort.

35. H. Bailey Carroll, "Caprock," *Handbook of Texas Online*, https://www.tshaonline.org/handbook/entries/caprock. Also on this "staked" land of the Llano and its resulting "wide open spaces," see Cabeza de Baca, *We Fed Them Cactus*, 5.

36. On the Ogallala, see R. F. Diffendal Jr., "Ogallala Aquifer," *Encyclopedia of the Great Plains*, http://plainshumanities.unl.edu/encyclopedia/doc/egp.wat.018

37. Another Wright house with similar stair-stepped brick designs, but in the fireplaces rather than the windows, can be seen in the Harold Price Sr. House in Paradise Valley, Arizona, constructed in 1954. On these elements, see Larkin and Pfeiffer, *Masterworks*, 251–53.

38. Twombly, *Frank Lloyd Wright*, 87.

39. Kaufmann, ed., *An American Architecture*, 108.

40. See, for instance, the City Hall in Buffalo, New York; Union Trust Building in Detroit; Wichita High School in Wichita, Kansas; the Texas & Pacific Warehouse in Fort Worth; and the Federal Building in Albuquerque. On these Art Deco designs, see Carla Breeze, *American Art Deco* (New York: W.W. Norton, 2003), 74–5, 130–33, 164–66; and Carla Breeze, *Pueblo Deco* (New York: Rizzoli, 1990), 21–25, 76.

41. Kaufmann and Raeburn, eds., *Writings and Buildings*, 21–22. Levine explains, too, how "Precolumbian architecture represented for Wright, as he later wrote, a repository of 'might,' of 'strength,' of 'gigantic power' and 'force.'" He continues: "As a 'greater elemental architecture than anything on record anywhere else,' it offered the archetypal image of permanence 'made one with the . . . land.'" See Levine, *Frank Lloyd Wright*, 140–41.

42. Levine, *Frank Lloyd Wright*, 125, 128.

43. Levine, *Frank Lloyd Wright*, 139–40.

44. On the Ennis House, see Weintraub and Hess, *The Houses*, 14, 182, 214, 233–34, 458. Sadly, the cement blocks are quickly crumbling as the material ages.

45. See Vincent Scully, "Introduction," in Bolon, Nelson, and Seidel, *Nature of Frank Lloyd Wright*, xix, 29. Scully refers to Tlaloc as "the Mayan rain god," when it is in fact the Aztec rain deity, "Tlaloc" being a Nahuatl word. On Tlaloc, see Richard F. Townsend and Trent Barnes, "Tetzcotzingo," *Grove Art Online* (2003), https://doi-org.databases.wtamu.edu/10.1093/gao/9781884446054.article.T084009 and "Tlaloc," *Encyclopedia Britannica*, https://www.britannica.com/topic/Tlaloc.

46. These included the families of Justo and Ventrual Borregos, Juan Domínguez, Casimero Romero, Agapito Sandoval, as well as those by the names of Salinas, Trujillo, Váldez, Ortega, Chávez, Tecolote, García, Sierna, and Tafolla. See John L. McCarty, *Maverick Town: The Story of Old Tascosa*, enlarged ed. (Norman: University of Oklahoma Press), 16, 39; Pauline Durrett Robertson and R. L. Robertson, *Tascosa: Historic Site in the Texas Panhandle*, 2nd ed. (Amarillo, TX: Paramount, 1995); Frederick Nolan, *Tascosa: Its Life and Gaudy Times* (Lubbock: Texas Tech

University Press, 2007), 9–11, 17; José Ynocencio Romero, "Spanish Sheepmen on the Canadian at Old Tascosa," as told to Ernest R. Archambeau, *Panhandle-Plains Historical Review* 19 (1946): 45–72; A. J. Taylor, "New Mexican Pastores and Priests in the Texas Panhandle, 1876–1915," *Panhandle-Plains Historical Review* 56 (1984): 65–79; and Paul H. Carlson, *Texas Woollybacks: The Range Sheep and Goat Industry* (College Station: Texas A&M University Press, 1982). See also chapter 4 of this volume, note 79.

47. McCarty, *Maverick Town*, 40: "These had grown to be large plazas modeled after the fashion of the day and very similar to some Indian and Mexican villages of the Southwest today."

48. McCarty, *Maverick Town*, 17.

49. On this "red earth" of the region and the building material of adobe, see Cabeza de Baca, *We Fed Them Cactus*, 2, 53.

50. McCarty for instance describes how Charles Goodnight made an arrangement with Casimero Romero to divide up the land, with Romero staying near the Canadian River and Goodnight moving south toward the Palo Duro Canyon. McCarty, *Maverick Town*, 37.

51. McCarty, *Maverick Town*, 43. On the other ranches that followed, including that of Lee Bivins, whose family is discussed in chapter 4 of this volume, see McCarty, *Maverick Town*, 44–50; and Robertson and Robertson, *Tascosa*.

52. McCarty, *Maverick Town*, 46.

53. McCarty, *Maverick Town*, 53–55, 59–60, 180–81; and Nolan, *Tascosa*, 59–60. For historical photographs of these adobe structures, see reproductions, for instance, in Robertson and Robertson, *Tascosa*, and Nolan, *Tascosa*, 201, 264–65.

54. See McCarty, "How a Town Dies," in *Maverick Town*, 229–57; Nolan, *Tascosa*, 237–39; and Robertson and Robertson, *Tascosa*, 46–48.

55. McCarty, *Maverick Town*, 250–51, 257; Nolan, *Tascosa*, 259; and Robertson and Robertson, *Tascosa*, 46–48.

56. See Nolan, *Tascosa*, 152, 224, 239–40, 250, 256.

57. On Wright's inspiration from Navajo sand paintings, Shoshone woven baskets, and Pueblo pottery, kivas, and cliff dwellings, see Levine, *Frank Lloyd Wright*, 144, 188–89. On the definition of the "Southwest" as a region, and one that included a complex history of cultural contestations, a "dynamic world of vibrant societies," see Hämäläinen, *The Comanche Empire*, 8–11.

58. On this, see McCarty, *Maverick Town*, 7.

59. On Wright's views on Beaux Arts styles, see Frank Lloyd Wright, "To the Students of the Beaux Arts Institute of Design: All Departments," in Wright, *An Autobiography*, 396–98.

60. On neoclassical architecture in turn-of-the-century America, see Elise Madeleine Ciregna, "Neo-Classicism in the U.S.A.," *Grove Art Online*, September 22, 2015, https://doi.org/10.1093/gao/9781884446054.article.T2283859.

61. Secrest, *Frank Lloyd Wright*, 185–86.

62. On Wright's use of wood inspired by Japanese architecture, see Kaufmann, ed., *An*

American Architecture, 108–9. On Wright's colonialist and discriminatory views of Japan and Japanese people, see Julia Meech-Pekarik, "Frank Lloyd Wright's Other Passion," in Bolon, Nelson, and Seidel, *Nature of Frank Lloyd Wright*, 145–46.

63. Sergeant, *Usonian Houses*, 184.

64. Sergeant, *Usonian Houses*, 19; and Twombly, *Frank Lloyd Wright*, 193.

65. Sergeant, *Usonian Houses*, 14. Levine also discusses how Wright's space was "processional" and was designed to operate like a "journey" for those existing within it. See Levine, *Frank Lloyd Wright*, 274.

66. This experiential architecture could be connected to phenomenology. See, for instance, Maurice Merleau-Ponty, *Phenomenology of Perception*, trans. Colin Smith (London: Routledge, 1981), especially 151. For a discussion of the shift from Cartesianism and empiricism to phenomenology, especially regarding the fields of aesthetics and art history, see Amelia Jones, "Body," in Robert S. Nelson and Richard Shiff, eds., *Critical Terms for Art History*, 2nd ed. (Chicago: University of Chicago Press, 2003), 251–66; and Amelia Jones, *Body Art: Performing the Subject* (Minneapolis: University of Minnesota Press, 1998), 40–43. See also Martin Jay, *Downcast Eyes: The Denigration of Vision in Twentieth-century French Thought* (Berkeley: University of California Press, 1993).

67. In other Usonian homes, Wright also used systems of geometric forms, such as the circular forms in the plans of the Jester House in Palos Verdes, California (1938) and the Friedman House in Pleasantville, New York (1950), or the triangular forms in the Sundt House in Madison, Wisconsin (1941). See Sergeant, *Usonian Houses*, 36, 88, and 187; and Hess, "Utopia Promised," 233.

68. Hess, "Utopia Promised," 231. On these car trips, see also Wright, *An Autobiography*, 315. He wrote: "For the homeward drive [to Taliesin East] we acquired a used Packard sport Phaeton wide open to the sky."

69. Sergeant, *Usonian Houses*, 185.

70. Lynes and Lopez, *Georgia O'Keeffe and Her Houses*, 10, 112. She paid $500 for the house and $2,500 as a contribution to the church. Parts of the home dated from the 1700s.

71. On Chabot's role at Abiquiu, see Lynes and Lopez, *O'Keeffe and Her Houses*; and Barbara Buhler Lynes and Ann Paden, eds., *Maria Chabot – Georgia O'Keeffe: Correspondence, 1941–1949* (Santa Fe: Georgia O'Keeffe Museum Research Center; Albuquerque: University of Mexico Press, 2003), 343.

72. Lynes and Lopez, *O'Keeffe and Her Houses*, 177.

73. Sergeant, *Usonian Houses*, 28; and Hess, "Utopia Promised," 233.

74. Lynes and Lopez, *O'Keeffe and Her Houses*, 242–43; and Lynes and Paden, eds., *Chabot – O'Keeffe: Correspondence*, especially 343.

75. Lynes and Lopez, *O'Keeffe and Her Houses*, 242–47. O'Keeffe wrote: "Two walls of my room in the Abiquiu house are glass and from one window I see the road toward Española, Santa Fe, and the world. The road fascinates me with its ups and downs and finally its wide sweep as it speeds toward the wall of my hilltop to go past me."

76. Kaufmann, ed., *An American Architecture*, 105.

77. Lynes and Lopez, *O'Keeffe and Her Houses*, 12, 145, 149. O'Keeffe wrote: "When I first saw the Abiquiu house it was a ruin with an adobe wall around the garden broken in a couple of places by falling trees. As I climbed and walked about in the ruin, I found a patio with a very pretty well house and bucket to draw up water. It was a good-sized patio with a long wall with a door on one side. That wall with a door in it was something I had to have. . . . That door is what made me buy this house. I waited ten years to get the house, because of that door. I used to climb over the wall, just to look at that door." She made eighteen paintings of the wall and door between 1948 and 1956.

78. Sergeant, *Usonian Houses*, 185; and Secrest, *Frank Lloyd Wright*, 416–25. On the incredible acclaim and success of Fallingwater as a modern masterwork, see also Twombly, *Frank Lloyd Wright*, 204–7; and Levine, *Frank Lloyd Wright*, 224–53.

79. Sergeant, *Usonian Houses*, 185.

80. Twombly, *Frank Lloyd Wright*, 205.

81. Sergeant, *Usonian Houses*, 185.

82. Sergeant, *Usonian Houses*, 14.

83. Sergeant, *Usonian Houses*, 12.

84. Sergeant, *Usonian Houses*, 14.

85. Kenneth Frampton, "Towards a Critical Regionalism: Six Points for an Architecture of Resistance," in Hal Foster, *The Anti-Aesthetic: Essays on Postmodern Culture*, 2nd ed. (New York: New Press, 1999), 17.

86. Frampton, "Critical Regionalism," 24.

87. Frampton, "Critical Regionalism," 21.

88. Frampton, "Critical Regionalism," 21.

89. Frampton, "Critical Regionalism," 26.

90. Frampton, "Critical Regionalism," 27.

91. Sergeant, *Frank Lloyd Wright*, 140; Twombly, *Usonian Houses*, 193; and Secrest, *Frank Lloyd Wright*, 449.

92. Twombly, *Frank Lloyd Wright*, 195.

93. Sergeant, *Usonian Houses*, 186.

94. Hess, "Utopia Promised," 235; and Weintraub and Hess, *The Houses*, 535.

95. Twombly, *Frank Lloyd Wright*, 261; and Bruce Brooks Pfeiffer, *Frank Lloyd Wright Drawings: Masterworks from the Frank Lloyd Wright Archives* (New York: Harry N. Abrams, 1990), 117–19. On the other unbuilt structures, see Twombly, *Frank Lloyd Wright*, 260–81.

96. Hess, "Utopia Promised," 235.

97. Sergeant, *Usonian Houses*, 108.

98. Twombly, *Frank Lloyd Wright*, 33. Wright completed 430 of his designs during his lifetime; 260 of them were houses. See Weintraub and Hess, *The Houses*, 13.

99. Interview with Robin Gilliland, March 5, 2018. Gilliland purchased the house in 2004.

100. Twombly, *Frank Lloyd Wright*, 190, 223–24. See also Levine, *Frank Lloyd Wright*, xiv.

101. On this, see Boyett, "Unbelievably Rare," 40, and interviews between Gilliland and the author, March 2018 and February 2023.

CHAPTER 4

1. Invitation, "JA Ranch Aerial Roundup," John L. McCarty Papers, LMC, Box 6, Folder 50, PPHMRC.

2. See "Many Sign JA Ranch Guest Book at Aerial Roundup" and Dick Martin, "Aerial Roundup at JA Success," clippings, "JA Ranch Aerial Roundup," McCarty Papers, as well as Dick Martin, "Hangar Gas," *Amarillo Sunday News Globe*, April 7, 1940, 64; and "Flying Party at JA Ranch Saturday," *Amarillo Daily News*, April 12, 1940, 23. Attendees included folks from towns across the Texas Panhandle and other Texas cities (Dallas, Houston, Wichita Falls, Fort Worth, and San Antonio), as well as Wichita, Kansas, and several cities in Oklahoma and New Mexico and even as far away as Pennsylvania. Also present were leaders in the aviation industry, such as the presidents of Cessna and Beechcraft, US Army aviators, Civil Aeronautics Authority officials, and editors of aviation magazines.

3. Reid was listed in the news articles on the roundup, but he also logged his visit to the JA Ranch in his Pilot Book. See James Warren "Ted" Reid Aviation Papers, 1980-173/1, Folder 2, PPHMRC. Reid's role in the military was with the Army Air Corps, and he served in both World Wars with distinction. As his granddaughter Jan Minton fondly remembers, Reid repaired Curtiss "Jennys" with what he called "banana glue" for the army during World War I, a material that produced some interesting hallucinatory effects. Reid's first solo flight was June 18, 1918, and he received one of the first pilot licenses issued in the Panhandle. Reid also served in the army reserves and taught flying lessons in the region, including courses of navigation and aviation at the West Texas State Airport in the 1940s. On the campus airport at WT, see the conference paper delivered by Patrick Diepen, "Regional Aviation in the Space Between," in June 2023 at the Space Between Conference at WT, as well as University Scrapbook, J. A. Hill Papers. One 1942 photograph (PW 1 1974-168/1.1) features CPT Trainees who will complete their primary course in aviation and includes J. W. "Ted" Reid of Dumas as instructor of navigation.

4. See, for instance, Anna Boydstun, "A Brief History of Aviation in Amarillo and the Texas Panhandle," published online through the Texas Air and Space Museum in Amarillo, https://www.youtube.com/watch?v=So6c3gXo3b4; Tonya L. Johnson, "History Buffs Given Keys to English Field," *Amarillo Globe-News*, August 16, 1996, "English Field" Folder, *Amarillo Globe-News* Collection, PPHMRC; and interview of Selma Caroline Olsen English by Frederick W. Rathjen, August 1, 1981, 1990-44/1, PPHMRC. Boydstun is also completing a dissertation on Amarillo's aviation history at Liberty University. See Anna K. Boydstun, "Amarillo in Flight: 'Queen City of the Plains' Conquers Frontier Skies, 1919–1939" (PhD diss., Liberty University, forthcoming).

5. According to the press, ninety-five planes were housed at English Field that evening,

and 175 people attended the Herring Hotel banquet. On the Herring Hotel, see Nick Gerlich, "Amarillo's Grandest Hotel," in Gerlich and Klinkel, *A Matter of Time*, 105.

6.   Martin reiterated this in his article: "Any young lady desiring a date with a handsome flier is urged to get in touch with this column any time after 2PM on weekdays and give us her name and address. These chaps coming in are going to be the cream of the private fliers from over the Southwest, and we understand they're all mighty attractive fellows, girls." See Martin, "Hangar Gas."

7.   Martin, "Aerial Roundup at JA Success."

8.   Oleg V. Bychkov and Anne Sheppard, trans., *Greek and Roman Aesthetics* (Cambridge, UK: Cambridge University Press, 2010); and Robert Wicks, *European Aesthetics: A Critical Introduction from Kant to Derrida* (London: Oneworld, 2013).

9.   Vanessa R. Schwartz, *Spectacular Realities: Early Mass Culture in Fin-de-Siècle Paris* (Berkeley: University of California Press, 1999) and *Jet Age Aesthetic: The lamour of Media in Motion* (New Haven: Yale University Press, 2020). See also Vanessa R. Schwartz and Jeannene Przyblyski, eds., *The Nineteenth-Century Visual Culture Reader* (New York: Routledge, 2004). Other studies of aviation and its "aesthetics" include literature along with visual art in their purview: for example, see Michael McClusky and Luke Seaber, eds., *Aviation in Literature and Culture of Interwar Britain* (London: Palgrave Macmillan, 2020).

10.   Schwartz writes: "To imagine the jet age as having an aesthetic is a way of envisioning the period's creative and aesthetic force and drive. Fine art movements of the period . . . also fit within its purview. But the footprint of the jet age aesthetic is far larger, shaping and encompassing the more general sensory regime." Schwartz, *Jet Age Aesthetic*, 10–11.

11.   On Louis Blériot's flight, see Robert Wohl, *A Passion for Wings: Aviation and the Western Imagination, 1908–1918* (New Haven: Yale University Press, 1994), 53–66. On Delaunay's representation of this flight in his paintings, see Wohl, *Passion for Wings*, 178–200.

12.   See Frances Hofsess, "Roomy House Tops in Ease: Canadian Artist Designs House in Pampa," clipping from unknown newspaper, June 14, 1955, Maurice Bernson Papers, PPHMRC.

13.   On the history of the hot air balloon, see Weems, *Barnstorming the Prairies*, 49; and Dan G. Ruggles, "The Perils of Ballooning," *Dallas Morning News*, September 14, 1930, clipping, "Aviation" Folder, PPHMRC.

14.   On the Eiffel Tower, see Phillip Dennis Cate, *The Eiffel Tower: A Tour de Force* (New York: Grolier Club, 1989); and Miriam R. Levin, *When the Eiffel Tower Was New: French Visions of Progress at the Centennial of the Revolution* (South Hadley, MA: Mount Holyoke College Art Museum, 1989). On aviation history in the United States, see especially Joseph Corn, *The Winged Gospel: America's Romance with Aviation, 1900–1950* (New York: Oxford University Press, 1983; and Jennifer Van Vleck, *Empire of the Air: Aviation and American Ascendancy* (Cambridge, MA: Harvard University Press, 2013).

15. On Henri Rivière's views of the Eiffel Tower, see especially Amy Von Lintel, "Camera to Crayon: A Reconsideration of Henri Rivière's Two Series on the Eiffel Tower" (MA thesis, Southern Methodist University, 2003).

16. Weems, *Barnstorming the Prairies*, x.

17. See Col. Leslie Neher Collection, 1981-27/1-18, PPHMRC. On how this view changed significantly in the jet age, with a turn inward toward the inside of the plane, producing an effect of motionless and sensationless travel, see Schwartz, *Jet Age Aesthetic*, 10. This feeling of sensationless travel could not have been more different from the plane experiences in the barnstorming era of Amarillo's aviation heyday.

18. Weems, *Barnstorming the Prairies*, xvi.

19. Weems, *Barnstorming the Prairies*, xvii. On how changing transportation has provided novel visual experiences, like the "panoramic vision" introduced by trains in the nineteenth century, early aerial vision in the US Midwest, and the jet in the mid to late twentieth, see Wolfgang Schivelbusch, *The Railroad Journey: The Industrialization of Time and Space in the Nineteenth Century* (Berkeley: University of California Press, 1986); Weems, *Barnstorming the Prairies*; Wohl, *A Passion for Wings*; and Schwartz, *Jet Age Aesthetic*.

20. According to historian Jason Weems, barnstorming could be described as "hyperkinetic displays of maneuverability, speed, and daring," in which "audiences were encouraged to focus on the fantastic and even irrational aspects of aviation," not unlike a roller coaster: Weems, *Barnstorming the Prairies*, 132. For a first-person description of barnstorming adventures, see George William Christopher, *Pioneer Pilot from the Texas Panhandle: Stories from a Flier's Life* (El Paso: self-published, 1992), especially 26–27, 34–37, a copy of which is in PPHMRC. For instance, one "game" that was played from the air involved throwing a roll of toilet paper out of the plane and then seeing how many times the pilot could cut the material with the plane's wings before the roll hit the ground. For photographic images of these trick flights, including playing tennis on the wings of planes, see *OX5 Aviation Pioneers* (Dallas, TX: private publisher, 1985), a copy of which is in the PPHMRC. See also Ray Franks and Jay Ketelle, *Amarillo Texas: The First Hundred Years 1887–1987* (Amarillo: Ray Franks Publishing Ranch, 1986), entry 32; and Jeanne S. Archer, *Touching Lives: The Lasting Legacy of the Bivins Family* (Orion, MI: Tell Studios, 2009), 84.

21. On this transformative sensation, see Weems, *Barnstorming the Prairies*, xiii. On the frequency of crashes, and the very real risk of death, see Weems, *Barnstorming the Prairies*, 131–32; and Wohl, *Passion for Wings*, 133.

22. An example of one doctor is Major Matthew P. Houseal of Amarillo, who flew his Luscombe around rural communities in the region to render medical services. Houseal also served as a US Navy jet pilot, as a member of the Army Reserves, and spent eleven months at a climate research station in Antarctica. He was one of five tragically killed on May 11, 2009, by an army sergeant at a mental health clinic at Camp Liberty in Iraq. I thank his child Ixchel Houseal for sharing this information with me. For examples of veterinarians, see Dr. James "Doc" Tucker of Tulia, who

owned a Cessna and flew around to area ranches for on-site treatment. I thank Walt Henson for sharing this information about Dr. Tucker. On the women pilots of the region, see especially Selma English, who was the first woman to fly solo in the Panhandle; Marcelete Reid, the daughter of Ted Reid, who learned to fly at eighteen years old; Amy Smallwood and Mrs. L. K. Bray of Pampa; and Berneta Bivins, who had begun taking lessons before her husband and son died in the 1940 crash. Berneta continued to take lessons after 1940, bought herself a plane, and did aerial observations of her ranchland as her husband had before her; her plane was confiscated for the war effort during World War II, but she bought herself another, and even learned to fly a helicopter. See Selma English interview; "Ruby Marcelete Reid Dana," *Canyon News*, June 25, 2013; Archer, *Touching Lives*, 163–64; and "Mrs. Bray Is 2nd Pampa Woman to Make Solo Hop," clipping, "Aviation," PPHMRC.

23. The efficacy of actually herding cattle from a plane has been questioned in conversations I have had with both scholars and ranchers. There is much evidence that ranchers flew their planes over their ranchlands to survey their herds, to find a lost animal, or even to remove unwanted predators by shooting them from the air. But the actual "cowboying" as in herding the animals from place to place by plane was probably not a widespread practice.

24. Christopher, *Pioneer Pilot*, 39.

25. Invitation, "JA Ranch Aerial Roundup." Attendees were served a "chuck wagon barbecue" composed of 800 pounds of prime beef, a meal the hosts claimed to be a "delicacy peculiar to the ranch cook" that had "reached perfection on the cattle ranch."

26. Martin, "Aerial Roundup at JA Success."

27. Clipping from the *Amarillo Sunday News and Globe*, Folder "JA Ranch Aerial Roundup," McCarty Papers.

28. Chas. J. Belden, "Wyoming's Flying Cowboys," *Clovis* (New Mexico) *News Journal*, May 29, 1938, "Aviation," clippings, PPHMRC.

29. Belden, "Wyoming's Flying Cowboys."

30. On this, see Kate Macdonald and Luke Seaber, "Introduction," John Llewelyn Rhys, *England Is My Village and the World Owes Me a Living* (Bath: Handheld Press, 2022), vii–xxiii, xiv–xv. See also papers given by Seaber at the British Association for Modernist Studies Conference (Bristol, 2022) and the Space Between Conference (Canyon, Texas, 2023), which he kindly shared with me.

31. Luke Seaber, "Huntin', Shootin', Fishin', and Flyin': Aviation as a Country Sport in the 1930s," a paper delivered at the Space Between Conference in Canyon, Texas, in June 2023.

32. Schwartz, *Jet Age Aesthetic*. The Croydon Airport in Britain was likewise "a popular tourist destination" because of its modern buildings and the spectatorship of the planes landing and taking off, often delivering celebrities that crowds gathered to see. See McClusky and Seaber, eds., *Aviation in Literature and Culture of Interwar Britain*, 10.

33. Brett Holman, "Spectre and Spectacle: Mock Air Raids as Aerial Theatre in Interwar

Britain," in McClusky and Seaber, eds., *Aviation in Literature and Culture of Interwar Britain*, 227–50.

34. Holman, "Spectre and Spectacle," 229.

35. See video 1985-48/13, PPHMRC. On how aviation spectacles entertained urban audiences in the jet age, see Schwartz, *Jet Age Aesthetic*, 7–8.

36. On Art Deco, see Breeze, *American Art Deco*, and Carla Breeze, *L.A. Deco* (New York: Rizzoli, 1991); and David Gebhard, *The National Trust Guide to Art Deco in America* (New York: John Wiley & Sons, 1996), which includes chapters on six regions and forty-five states in the United States.

37. See Terry Moyle, *Art Deco Airports: Dream Designs of the 1920s and 1930s* (London: New Holland, 2016).

38. The one piece of biographical writing on Carlander is an unpublished manuscript penned by the architect's nephew Kenneth Carlander, a copy of which is in the Carlander Papers at the Amarillo Public Library, Downtown Branch. My own forthcoming monograph *Guy Carlander: Amarillo's Architect* will be the first published scholarly study on Carlander.

39. On the house gaining the designation of "airport house," see "'Airport' House in Pampa Bought in Auction Sale," undated clipping in Maurice Bernson Papers.

40. On Daniels, see Hofsess, "Roomy House Tops in Ease."

41. Hofsess, "Roomy House Tops in Ease."

42. Jerry Searcy, "Unorthodox Design Puts Emphasis on Lighting: Homes of Interest in the Area," *Amarillo Daily News*, January 27, 1964, Maurice Bernson Papers. See also "Parent Education Plans Home Tour," *Pampa Daily News*, April 14, 1957, clipping in Maurice Bernson Papers.

43. Searcy, "Unorthodox Design."

44. See Maurice Bernson, "Creation of the J. C. Daniels Home, Pampa, Texas," unpublished typed notes, Maurice Bernson Papers.

45. Schwartz, *Jet Age Aesthetic*.

46. Schwartz, *Jet Age Aesthetic*. Of course, aviation had been a spectacular entertainment from the earliest days of flight. On this, see Wohl, *Passion for Wings*, especially 25, 36, 43, 51, 57, 103.

47. Saarinen received the commission in 1956, and the building was completed by 1962. Schwartz, *Jet Age Aesthetic*, 79.

48. Schwartz, *Jet Age Aesthetic*, 46.

49. On these sculptures that are variously cited as bronze and brass, see Hofsess, "Roomy House Tops in Ease" and Searcy, "Unorthodox Design."

50. On mid-century sculptors fascinated with flight, see Louise Siddons, *Centering Modernism: J. Jay McVicker and Postwar American Art* (Norman: University of Oklahoma Press, 2018), 11–12.

51. I thank Deana Craighead for helping me see the jet-age aesthetic of this work when it hung in the exhibition *From the Edge of the Plains* at PPHM in 2023, which Craighead curated.

52. On how the frontier was first defined by Frederick Jackson Turner as "an ethnocentric

and narcissistic rendition of the European takeover of North America," but revisionist scholars of frontier and borderland studies have repositioned the concept as a "zone of cultural interpenetration," a socially charged space of "messy, eclectic contact points" where cultures competed for resources and land, see Hämäläinen, *The Comanche Empire*, 7. Here, I use the term more as a conceptual promise of growth, but the layers of meaning in "frontier" are important to recognize.

53. Working with colleagues in the region, I have been aiming to conceptualize the "new west" to help frame our teaching, scholarship, and art exhibitions. For example, we hosted the exhibition *Art of the New West* in September 2013 at Process Art House in Amarillo, and we explored this concept in our scholarship on Emil Bisttram for the show *Southwest Abstractions of Emil Bisttram* in 2021–22 at PPHM. See, for instance, Revett, Pasquine, and Von Lintel, *Emil Bisttram*.

54. On Reynal's visits to Amarillo, see Von Lintel and Roos, *Three Women Artists*, chapter 2.

55. On this 1960 show, see Amy Von Lintel and Bonnie Roos, "Abstract Expressionism in Amarillo, Texas: *The Women: Tops in Art* Exhibition in 1960," *Woman's Art Journal* 42, no. 2 (Fall 2021): 12–21; and Von Lintel and Roos, *Three Women Artists*.

56. See especially Von Lintel and Roos, *Three Women Artists*, chapter 3.

57. Beginning as Transcontinental and Western Air, and renamed Trans World Airlines in 1950, TWA served Amarillo continuously until 1983. The route in the 1930s ran from Los Angeles to Kansas City—the TWA hub between 1931 and 1964—and terminated in New York City, with Amarillo as a major stop serving both passengers and airmail deliveries. Beginning in 1931, Amarillo was a stop on a coast-to-coast route that took thirty-six hours operated by Transcontinental and Western. Between the 1930s and the 1970s, Amarillo was networked via aviation routes to at least two dozen cities across the United States. On the history of TWA, see especially the Trans World Airlines (TWA) Records (K0453), 1929–2002, State Historical Society of Missouri Research Center, Kansas City, Missouri. On Amarillo as a flight hub for Middle America, see also Christopher, *Pioneer Pilot*. On these routes, see archival photographs in the Texas Air and Space Museum, Amarillo, Texas, and as featured in Boydstun, "A Brief History of Aviation in Amarillo."

58. See, for instance, Laurie Wilson, *Louise Nevelson: Light and Shadow* (New York: Thames and Hudson, 2016); and Laurie Lisle, *Louise Nevelson: A Passionate Life* (New York: Summit, 1990).

59. On Hallmark's art collection, see https://www.hallmarkartcollection.com/.

60. Elaine de Kooning's abstraction *Veronica* (oil on canvas, c. 1959) was purchased in 1960 as part of the Fifth International Hallmark Art Awards. I thank Erin Dodson, curator of the Hallmark Art Collection, for sending me several archival documents on these works.

61. On de Kooning's trips to the US Southwest, see Von Lintel and Roos, *Three Women Artists*, chapter 1. She did learn to drive in New Mexico and bought a car that she drove by herself back to New York, a trip she described with great excitement. See Elaine de Kooning to Dord Fitz, [1959?], box 1, folder 10, Dord Fitz Collection,

Western History Collections, University of Oklahoma.

62. On the definition of the "jet set," see Schwartz, *Jet Age Aesthetic*, 99–103, 110–11. Schwartz describes how this identity is "amorphous" but can be characterized as glamorous, mobile, traveling often via the most up-to-date transportation—the jet—and appearing in the media as photographable modern trendsetters. Elaine de Kooning had a fashionable nomadism, and one that took her often between New York and the West, aligning her with the mid-century "jet set."

63. Childers also served as the first woman board member of Amarillo College and a member of the Texas Art Alliance, roles that inspired her vision for the development of Amarillo Art Center, which became Amarillo Museum of Art. She established herself as a major art collector, purchasing the work of Nevelson, Jane Freilicher, Jane Wilson, and Dorothy Hood, in addition to de Kooning. See Archer, *Touching Lives*, 187–88; Von Lintel and Roos, *Three Women Artists*; and Von Lintel and Roos, "Abstract Expressionism in Amarillo."

64. On the multigenerational Bivins family as art collectors, see also Von Lintel and Roos, *Three Women Artists*.

65. Bivins never became a pilot himself; rather, he hired a pilot, Fred Hinds, to teach his chauffeur and cousin, Lloyd Bivins, to fly so that Lloyd could serve as his personal pilot. The life of Lee Bivins has been well traced. See for instance H. Allen Anderson, "Bivins, Lee," *Handbook of Texas Online*, https://www.tshaonline.org/handbook/entries/bivins-lee; Della Tyler Key, *In the Cattle Country: History of Potter County, 1887–1966* (Amarillo: Tyler-Berkley, 1961; 2nd ed., Wichita Falls: Nortex, 1972); and Archer, *Touching Lives*.

66. Archer, *Touching Lives*, 32. Numerous legends surround the home, including the fact that its cost is still a mystery because Bivins hired cowboys for construction and paid them in cash each day.

67. The home had five bedrooms on the second story, each with its own sink, an impressive modern convenience. On the home's history and design, see Archer, *Touching Lives*, 30–33; and *Amarillo Historic Building Survey*, published 1981, 84. On the history of the Amarillo Public Library, see Franks and Ketelle, *Amarillo Texas*, entry 95; and Archer, *Touching Lives*, 114–15.

68. Archer, *Touching Lives*, 67.

69. Archer, *Touching Lives*, 68–69.

70. Archer, *Touching Lives*, 70.

71. Ingrassia, "Speed Attractions," 86. Bivins served as city alderman and city commissioner from 1906, and it was in these roles that he helped pass the brick street ordinance. See Archer, *Touching Lives*, 90.

72. Along with other investors, including W. K. Whipple and Henry Earl Fuqua, Bivins founded the Panhandle Aerial Service and Transportation Company and served as the company president, retaining financial control. The company constructed an airfield complete with two runways and a $30,000 six-plane hangar—the only hangar between Fort Worth and Denver at the time—as well as a flight school to train pilots. They operated Curtiss JN-4 "Canucks," which were two-seater prop planes,

and offered charter services and "barnstorming." See Boydstun, "A Brief History of Aviation."

73. On O'Neil Ford, see Kathryn E. O'Rourke and Ben Koush, *Home Heat Money God: Texas and Modern Architecture* (Austin: University of Texas Press, 2024).

74. Julian Lee or "Jude" Bivins was born in 1896.

75. See Boyett, "High Plains Visionaries." The Bivins neighborhood as a former airfield is not unique in the United States; rather, there are numerous other examples of such airfields that succumbed to the growth of towns and cities. On this, see John Zimmerman, "Abandoned Airfields: History in our Midst," *Air Facts*, January 31, 2013, https://airfactsjournal.com/2013/01/abandoned-airfields-history-in-our-midst/. See also Paul Freeman's website "Abandoned and Little-Known Airfields," http://www.airfields-freeman.com/.

76. Steve LaPrade and Ben Keck, "Plane Crash Takes 3 Lives," *Amarillo Globe-News*, July 21, 1973; and Von Lintel and Revett, "Completing Smithson's Trilogy."

77. Von Lintel and Revett, "Completing Smithson's Trilogy," 14.

78. Wichita was the "Air Capital of the World" in the 1930s, a center for both commercial and military aerospace production. See Siddons, *Centering Modernism*, 153; and Craig Miner, "A Roar from the Sky: Air-Mindedness in Wichita, 1908–1950," *Journal of the West* 30 (January 1991): 37–44.

79. Located northwest of Amarillo near the Canadian River on ranchland acquired by Bivins's father around 1900, Tascosa became the county seat of Oldham County in 1880 and gained the designation of the "Cowboy Capital of the Plains." But when the railroad was constructed on the other side of the Canadian River from the town, it steadily declined until it was basically a deserted ghost town by the time Julian moved his family there. Today it has become the site of Boys Ranch, a residential community for at-risk children. See McCarty, *Maverick Town*; "Tascosa, TX," *Handbook of Texas Online*, https://www.tshaonline.org/handbook/entries/tascosa-tx; Robertson and Robertson, *Tascosa*; and the Boys Ranch website at https://www.calfarley.org/. See also chapter 3 of this volume.

80. The news articles describing the crash featured gruesome details about the positions of the bodies and the need to use a hacksaw to remove the bodies from the fuselage. See "Julian Bivins, Son Killed in Air Crash: Bodies Found in Wreck 12 Miles North of Town," *Amarillo Globe*, May 24, 1940; "Julian Bivins and Son Killed in Plane Wreck," undated clipping, scrapbook, Bivins Family Papers; and "Bivins Funeral Rites Planned this Afternoon," *Amarillo Daily News*, May 25, 1940, "Bivins Family," clippings, PPHMRC. See also Archer, *Touching Lives*, 160–61.

81. See "Throngs Gather for Tribute to Bivins and Sons," undated clipping, scrapbook, Bivins Family Papers, PPHMRC.

82. "In Memoriam," undated clipping, scrapbook, Bivins Family Papers, PPHMRC.

83. Archer, *Touching Lives*, 226; and "J. L. Bivins and Son Will Be Buried Together Today," undated clipping, scrapbook, Bivins Family Papers, PPHMRC.

84. Archer, *Touching Lives*, 229. Betty Teel Bivins, like Betty Bivins Childers, continued life as a strong single woman and mother after the death of Lee in a tragic drowning

incident in Peru in 1972. For instance, she became the first woman board member of the First National Bank, filling the position Lee's death left open. She took banking courses at WT to prepare for her position, and later served on the WT Board of Regents and on the museum board at Amarillo Museum of Art, among many other similar positions for area nonprofit organizations. See Archer, *Touching Lives*, 253–54.

85. Interview of Selma Caroline Olsen English by Frederick W. Rathjen, August 1, 1981, 1990-44/1, PPHMRC.

86. Christopher, *Pioneer Pilot*, 53.

87. Von Lintel and Revett, "Completing Smithson's Trilogy," 13.

88. The pilot was Gale Ray Rogers, age twenty-six, and the photographer was twenty-three-year-old Richard I. Curtain.

89. As quoted in Von Lintel and Revett, "Completing Smithson's Trilogy," 14.

90. On *Boomerang*, see Alena J. Williams, ed., *Nancy Holt: Sightlines* (Berkeley: University of California Press, 2011).

91. Boydstun, "A Brief History of Aviation in Amarillo." On Husband, see Evelyn Husband, *High Calling: The Courageous Life and Faith of Space Shuttle* Columbia *Commander Rick Husband* (Nashville, TN: Thomas Nelson, 2003).

92. Christopher, *Pioneer Pilot*, 42. This same phrase was the caption on a photo of English Airport in Folder 2-30, "Photographs of English Field," LMC 26, PPHMRC.

93. James L. Haley, *Texas: From Spindletop Through World War II* (New York: St. Martin's, 1993), 63. Amarillo's commitment to air travel was not a rare occurrence in the state of Texas, where vast spaces separated the developing urban areas. The first flights in Texas apparently occurred in 1909 in Dallas at the Texas State Fair, and then in 1910 aviator Otto Brodie gave demonstrations to Dallas viewers in his Curtiss plane. Around the same time, at Fort Sam Houston near San Antonio, Lieutenant Benjamin Foulois—after having only forty-four minutes of instruction from the Wright brothers—taught himself to fly. Foulois also flew patrols on the US-Mexico border in 1916. On this see, Haley, *Texas*, 65, 95.

BIBLIOGRAPHY

ABBREVIATIONS

OTL: *Georgia O'Keeffe's Wartime Texas Letters* (2020), by Amy Von Lintel

PPHM: Panhandle-Plains Historical Museum

PPHMRC: Panhandle-Plains Historical Museum Research Center

RCFP: Reid-Caballero Family Papers

WT: West Texas State Normal College (1910 to 1923), West Texas State College (1949 to 1963), West Texas State University (1963 to 1993), West Texas A&M University (1993 to today)

ARCHIVES

Archives of American Art, Smithsonian Institution, Washington, DC
    Leo Castelli Gallery Records
Cornette Library Special Collections, West Texas A&M University, Canyon, TX
    Reid-Caballero Family Papers
Georgia O'Keeffe Research Center, Santa Fe, NM
    Ted Reid Correspondence (1917–77)
Hallmark Art Collection Papers, Kansas City, MO
Judd Foundation Archives, Marfa, TX
Panhandle-Plains Historical Museum Research Center, Canyon, TX
    Amarillo Army Air Field Yearbook, 1943
    Amarillo Globe-News Collection
    Aviation Folder
    Bivins Family Papers
    Col. Leslie Neher Collection, 1981-27/1-18
    J. A. Hill Papers
    James Warren "Ted" Reid Aviation Papers, 1980-173/1
    John L. McCarty Papers
    Maurice Bernson Papers
Stanley Marsh Family Papers, Private Holdings

Texas Air and Space Museum Collections, Amarillo, TX

Trans World Airlines (TWA) Records (K0453), State Historical Society of Missouri Research Center, Kansas City, MO

PUBLISHED SOURCES

"Adobe Walls, Second Battle of." *Handbook of Texas Online.* https://www.tshaonline.org/ handbook/entries/adobe-walls-second-battle-of.

ahtone, heather, Faith Brower, and Seth Hopkins. *Warhol and the West.* Tacoma: Tacoma Art Museum; Berkeley: University of California Press, 2019.

Alexander, Thomas E. *The Stars were Big and Bright: The United States Army Air Forces and Texas During World War II.* Austin, TX: Eakin, 2000.

Allston, Tom. "Air, Space Museum Seeks Public Support." *Amarillo Globe-News,* February 6, 1998.

Amarillo Historic Building Survey. Amarillo: Charles Hall Page and Associates, 1981.

Anderson, H. Allen. "Bivins, Lee." *Handbook of Texas Online.* https://www.tshaonline. org/handbook/entries/bivins-lee.

Ansley, R. J., and P. W. Jacoby. "Manipulation of Fire Intensity to Achieve Mesquite Management Goals in North Texas." Tall Timbers Fire Ecology Conference Proceedings. 1998. https://agrilife.org/vernon/files/2012/11/ANS1998-03-Ansley-an d-Jacoby-TallTimbers20-195-204.pdf.

"Ant Farm's Chip Lord Comes to Amarillo." *Glasstire,* October 12, 2018. https://glasstire. com/2018/10/12/ant-farms-chip-lord-comes-to-amarillo/.

Antin, Eleanor. "Reading Ruscha." *Art in America* 61 (November–December 1973): 64–71.

Archambeau, Ernest R. "Spanish Sheepmen on the Canadian at Old Tascosa." *Panhandle-Plains Historical Review* 19 (1946): 45–72.

Archer, Jeanne S. *Touching Lives: The Lasting Legacy of the Bivins Family.* Orion, MI: Tell Studios, 2009.

Arno, Anthony. "Bob 'Crocodile' Lile." *Route 66 Podcast,* no. 38, April 14, 2021. https:// www.youtube.com/watch?v=6M9pzCuZr-E.

Arnold, Catherine. *Pandemic 1918: Eyewitness Accounts from the Greatest Medical Holocaust in Modern History.* New York: St. Martin's Griffin, 2020.

Atlas Obscura (blog). "Ozymandias of Amarillo: A Texan Take on Shelley's Poem, Featuring Tube Socks." *Slate,* September 12, 2013. https://www.slate.com/blogs/ atlas_obscura/2013/09/12/ozymandias_of_amarillo_a_sculptor_s_texan_take_on_ shelley_s_poem_featuring.html.

Baker, George, et al. *Robert Smithson:* Spiral Jetty. Berkeley: University of California Press, 2005.

Barry, John M. *The Great Influenza: The Epic Story of the Deadliest Pandemic in History.* New York: Viking, 2004.

Beardsley, John. *Earthworks and Beyond: Contemporary Art in the Landscape.* New York: Abbeville, 1989.

Becker, Jack. "Caprock Chronicles: The Mystery of the Canyon Suite." *Lubbock*

Avalanche-Journal, December 19, 2020. https://www.lubbockonline.com/story/news/history/2020/12/19/caprock-chronicles-a-canyon-suite/3935451001/.

Beeby, Thomas H. "Wright and Landscape: A Mythical Interpretation." In *The Nature of Frank Lloyd Wright*, edited by Carol R. Bolon, Robert S. Nelson, and Linda Seidel, 154–72. Chicago: University of Chicago Press, 1988.

Belden, Chas. J. "Wyoming's Flying Cowboys." *Clovis* (New Mexico) *News Journal*, May 29, 1938.

Benezra, Neal. "Ed Ruscha: Painting and Artistic License." In *Ed Ruscha*, Neal Benezra and Kerry Brougher, 145–56. Washington, DC: Hirschhorn Museum and Sculpture Garden, 2000.

Benezra, Neal, and Kerry Brougher. *Ed Ruscha*. Washington, DC: Hirschhorn Museum and Sculpture Garden, 2000.

Benjamin, Walter. "The Work of Art in the Age of Mechanical Reproduction." In *Illuminations: Essays and Reflections*, edited by Hannah Arendt, translated by Harry Zahn, 217–51. New York: Schocken, 1968. Reprint, 2007.

Bielstein, Susan. *Permissions, a Survival Guide: Blunt Talk about Art as Intellectual Property*. Chicago: University of Chicago Press, 2006.

"Bivins Funeral Rites Planned this Afternoon." *Amarillo Daily News*, May 25, 1940.

Bloemink, Barbara J. *Georgia O'Keeffe Canyon Suite*. Kansas City: Kemper Museum of Contemporary Art and Design and Kansas City Art Institute, 1994.

Boettger, Suzaan. *Earthworks: Art and the Landscape of the Sixties*. Berkeley: University of California Press, 2002.

———. *Inside the Spiral: The Passions of Robert Smithson*. Minneapolis: University of Minnesota Press, 2022.

Boetzkes, Amanda. *Plastic Capitalism: Contemporary Art and the Drive to Waste*. Cambridge, MA: MIT Press, 2019.

Bois, Yve-Alain. "Liquid Words." In *Formless: A User's Guide*, edited by Yve-Alain Bois and Rosalind E. Krauss, 124–32. New York: Zone Books, 1997.

Bolon, Carol R., Robert S. Nelson, and Linda Seidel, eds. *The Nature of Frank Lloyd Wright*. Chicago: University of Chicago Press, 1988.

Boucher, Brian. "Oops! A New Documentary About the Knoedler Fakes Scandal Accidentally Included an Artist's Trick Image as Real." *Artnet*, March 5, 2021. https://news.artnet.com/art-world/knoedler-pollock-documentary-fake-image-1948673.

Boydstun, Anna. "A Brief History of Aviation in Amarillo and the Texas Panhandle" [video]. Texas Air and Space Museum, Amarillo. https://www.youtube.com/watch?v=So6c3gXo3b4.

Boyett, Jason. "High Plains Visionaries." *Amarillo Globe-News*, May 18, 2018. https://www.amarillo.com/story/lifestyle/magazine/2018/05/18/cover-story-high-plains-visionaries/12195125007/.

———. "Unbelievably Rare: The Sterling Kinney House, Designed by Frank Lloyd Wright." *Brick & Elm*, March–April 2023, 38–47.

Breeze, Carla. *American Art Deco: Architecture and Regionalism*. New York: W. W. Norton, 2003.

———. *LA Deco*. New York: Rizzoli, 1991.

———. *New York Deco*. New York: Rizzoli, 1993.

———. *Pueblo Deco*. New York: Rizzoli, 1990.

Brougher, Kerry. "Words as Landscape." In *Ed Ruscha*, Neal Benezra and Kerry Brougher, 157–76. Washington, DC: Hirschhorn Museum and Sculpture Garden, 2000.

Brzostowski, Cindy. "The Dynamite Museum's Sign Project Is Part Open Air Art Museum and Part Scavenger Hunt." *Roadtrippers Magazine*, July 21, 2020. https://roadtrippers.com/magazine/dynamite-museum-sign-project-texas/.

Bychkov, Oleg V., and Anne Sheppard, trans. *Greek and Roman Aesthetics*. Texts in the History of Philosophy Series. Cambridge: Cambridge University Press, 2010.

"Caballero Has Busy Schedule." *Canyon News*, April 2, 1980.

"Caballero Hearing Begins Today Before University Committee." *Canyon News*, September 25, 1975.

Cabeza de Baca, Fabiola. *We Fed Them Cactus*. 2nd ed. Albuquerque: University of New Mexico Press, 1994.

Carlson, Paul H. *Amarillo: The Story of a Western Town*. Lubbock: Texas Tech University Press, 2006.

———. *Empire Builder in the Texas Panhandle: William Henry Bush*. College Station: Texas A&M University Press, 1996.

——— *Texas Woollybacks: The Range Sheep and Goat Industry*. College Station: Texas A&M University Press, 1982.

Carlson, Paul H., and John T. Becker. *Georgia O'Keeffe in Texas: A Guide*. Austin, TX: State House Press, 2012.

Carroll, H. Bailey. "Caprock." *Handbook of Texas Online*. https://www.tshaonline.org/handbook/entries/caprock.

Cartwright, Gary. "Playboys of the Western Plains." *Texas Monthly*, March 1978. https://www.texasmonthly.com/true-crime/playboys-of-the-western-plains/.

Casement, William. *The Many Faces of Art Forgery: From the Dark Side to Shades of Gray*. New York: Rowman & Littlefield, 2022.

Castro, Jan Garden. *The Art & Life of Georgia O'Keeffe*. New York: Crown Trade, 1985.

Cate, Phillip Dennis. *The Eiffel Tower: A Tour de Force*. New York: Grolier Club, 1989.

"Charles Goodnight Bison Herd." All About Bison. https://allaboutbison.com/bison-in-history/texas-history/charles-goodnight-bison-herd/.

"Charles Thomas Caballero Obituary." Boxwell Brothers Funeral Home, Amarillo, April 7, 2014.

Christopher, George William. *Pioneer Pilot from the Texas Panhandle: Stories from a Flier's Life*. El Paso: self-published, 1992.

Ciregna, Elise Madeleine. "Neo-Classicism in the U.S.A." *Grove Art Online*, September 22, 2015. https://doi.org/10.1093/gao/9781884446054.article.T2283859.

"Climate Narrative for Amarillo." National Weather Service. https://www.weather.gov/ama/climo_narrative.

Coe, Erin B., Gwendolyn Owens, and Bruce Robertson. *Modern Nature: Georgia O'Keeffe and Lake George*. New York: Thames and Hudson, 2013.

Cohen, Patricia, and William K. Rashbaum. "One Queens Painter Created Forgeries That Sold for Millions, U.S. Says." *New York Times*, August 15, 2013. https://www.nytimes.com/2013/08/16/nyregion/one-queens-painter-created-forgeries-that-sold-for-millions-us-says.html.

"Collectors, Artists and Lawyers: Fear of Litigation is Hobbling the Art Market." *The Economist*, November 24, 2012. https://www.economist.com/business/2012/11/24/collectors-artists-and-lawyers.

Collier, Ric, and Jim Edwards. "*Spiral Jetty*: The Re-Emergence." *Sculpture Magazine*, July 1, 2004. https://sculpturemagazine.art/spiral-jetty-the-re-emergence/.

"Committee Backs Watkins on Ruling." *Canyon Sunday News*, September 28, 1975.

Corn, Joseph. *The Winged Gospel: America's Romance with Aviation, 1900–1950*. New York: Oxford University Press, 1983.

Corn, Wanda. *Grant Wood: The Regionalist Vision*. New Haven: Yale University Press, 1983.

Cowles, Charlotte. "Exclusive: Georgia O'Keeffe's Younger Man." *Harper's Bazaar*, February 14, 2016. https://www.harpersbazaar.com/culture/features/a14033/georgia-okeeffe-0316/.

Curtis, Cathy. *A Generous Vision: The Creative Life of Elaine de Kooning*. New York: Oxford University Press, 2019.

Danly, Susan. *Georgia O'Keeffe and the Camera: The Art of Identity*. New Haven: Yale University Press, 2008.

Danziger, Charles, and Thomas Danziger. "On the Case: Exploring Real World Art Law Issues." *Artnet*, April 23, 2014. https://news.artnet.com/market/on-the-case-exploring-real-world-art-law-issues-11677.

Dennis, James. *Grant Wood: A Study in American Art and Culture*. Columbia: University of Missouri Press, 1975.

———. *Renegade Regionalists: The Modern Independence of Grant Wood, Thomas Hart Benton, and John Stuart Curry*. Madison: University of Wisconsin Press, 1998.

Diffendal, R. F., Jr. "Ogalalla Aquifer." *Encyclopedia of the Great Plains*. http://plainshumanities.unl.edu/encyclopedia/doc/egp.wat.018.

"Dr. Emilio Caballero Named to Royal Society of Art." *Canyon News*, July 23, 1964.

Duncan, Michael, et al. *Another World: The Transcendental Painting Group*. New York: DelMonico Books, 2021.

"Economic Development of History of Interstate 27 in Texas." US Department of Transportation, Federal Highway Administration." November 3, 2008. https://planningtools.transportation.org/files/41.pdf.

Edsall, Larry. "Changes Don't Alter the Essence of Cadillac Ranch." September 15, 2021. https://www.petersen.org/blog/cadillac-ranch.

Egel, Ben. "Former Stanley Marsh Land Toad Hall Under Development." *Amarillo Globe-News*, September 8, 2017. https://www.amarillo.com/story/news/local/2017/09/08/former-stanley-marsh-3-land-toad-hall-under-development/13037938007/.

Ellroy, James, et al. *Ed Ruscha: Fifty Years of Painting*. London: Hayward, 2009.

Evans-Cowley, Jennifer S., and Jack L. Nasar. "Signs as Yard Art in Amarillo, Texas." *Geographical Review* 93 (January 2003): 97–113.

Everest, Dianna. "Indian Territory." *The Encyclopedia of Oklahoma History and Culture.* https://www.okhistory.org/publications/enc/entry?entry=IN018.

Flam, Jack, ed. *Robert Smithson: The Collected Writings.* Berkeley: University of California Press, 1996.

Flores, Dan. *Wild New World: The Epic Story of Animals and People in America.* New York: W. W. Norton, 2022.

Flynn, Tom. "Art Forgery: A Crime on the Rise?" In Colette Loll, *Intent to Deceive: Fakes and Forgeries in the Art World.* Washington, DC: International Arts & Artists, 2013. https://theartssociety.org/events/short-history-fakes-and-forgeries.

Fondow, KassiAnne. "Ozymandias: Atmosphere Brings Sculpture to Glory." *The Prairie*, May 3, 2011.

Forgy, Mark. *The Forger's Apprentice: Life with the World's Most Notorious Artist.* Scotts Valley, CA: CreateSpace, 2012.

Frampton, Kenneth. "Towards a Critical Regionalism: Six Points for an Architecture of Resistance." In *The Anti-Aesthetic: Essays on Postmodern Culture.* 2nd ed. Edited by Hal Foster, 16–30. New York: New Press, 1999.

Franks, Ray, and Jay Ketelle. *Amarillo Texas: The First Hundred Years 1887–1987, a Picture Postcard History.* Amarillo: Ray Franks Publishing Ranch, 1986.

Friedman, Samantha, ed. *Georgia O'Keeffe: To See Takes Time.* New York: Museum of Modern Art, 2023.

Gebhard, David. *The National Trust Guide to Art Deco in America.* New York: John Wiley & Sons, 1996.

Gee, Alastair, and Dani Anguiano. "Last Day in Paradise: The Untold Story of How a Fire Swallowed a Town." *The Guardian*, December 20, 2018. https://www.theguardian.com/environment/2018/dec/20/last-day-in-paradise-california-deadliest-fire-untold-story-survivors.

Gerlich, Nick, and Ellen Klinkel. *A Matter of Time: Route 66 Through the Lens of Change.* Norman: University of Oklahoma Press, 2019.

Gill, Brendan. *Many Masks: A Life of Frank Lloyd Wright.* New York: G. P. Putnam's Sons, 1987.

Grauer, Michael. "Emilio Caballero: Artista y Maestro en El Llano." Panhandle-Plains Historical Museum, 2001. https://tfaoi.org/aa/3aa/3aa24.htm.

Greenough, Sarah. *My Faraway One: Selected Letters of Georgia O'Keeffe and Alfred Stieglitz, 1915–1933*, vol. 1. New Haven: Yale University Press, 2011.

Grossman, LLP. "Three Recent Suits Exemplify Some of the Legal Issues Surrounding Art Authentication." *Art Law Blog*, April 7, 2014. https://www.grossmanllp.com/three-recent-suits-exemplify-some-of-the-legal-issues-surrounding-art-authentication.

Grumdahl, Dara Moskowitz. "Con Artistry: The Real Story of How the World's Most Notorious Art Collection Wound Up in Minnesota." *Mpls St. Paul Magazine*, March 21, 2014. https://mspmag.com/arts-and-culture/con-artistry/.

Haley, J. Evetts. *Charles Goodnight: Cowman and Plainsman.* Revised ed. Norman:

University of Oklahoma Press, 1981.

Haley, James L. *Texas: From Spindletop Through World War II.* New York: St. Martin's, 1993.

Hämäläinen, Pekka. *The Comanche Empire.* New Haven: Yale University Press, 2008.

Harris, Adam Duncan. "George Catlin's Vision of the Great Plains." In *George Catlin's American Buffalo*, 1–32. Washington, DC: Smithsonian American Art Museum, 2013.

Helber, Annabelle Massey. "Faked Out: Art Maven Gerald Peters Tries to Get to the Bottom of the 'Canyon Suite.'" *Dallas Observer*, February 17, 2000. https://www.dallasobserver.com/news/faked-out-6396240.

Hess, Alan. "Utopia Promised." In *Frank Lloyd Wright: The Houses*, edited by Alan Weintraub and Alan Hess, 229–36. New York: Rizzoli, 2005.

Heuer, Christopher P., and Rebecca Zorach, eds. *Ecologies, Agents, Terrains.* Williamstown, MA: Clark Art Institute; New Haven: Yale University Press, 2018.

Hickey, Dave, and Peter Plagens. *The Works of Ed Ruscha.* San Francisco: San Francisco Museum of Modern Art, 1982.

Hoffmann, Donald. "Meeting Nature Face to Face." In *The Nature of Frank Lloyd Wright*, edited by Carol R. Bolon, Robert S. Nelson, and Linda Seidel, 85–97. Chicago: University of Chicago Press, 1988.

Hogrefe, Jeffrey. "The Case of the Counterfeit O'Keeffes." *D Magazine*, July 1, 2000. https://www.dmagazine.com/publications/d-magazine/2000/july/the-case-of-the-counterfeit-okeeffes/.

Hollandsworth, Skip. "Big Feud at Cadillac Ranch." *Texas Monthly*, March 1996. https://www.texasmonthly.com/being-texan/big-feud-at-cadillac-ranch/.

———. "Darkness on the Plains." *Texas Monthly*, May 2013: 120–23, 206–12. https://www.texasmonthly.com/articles/darkness-on-the-plains/.

———. "Stanley Marsh 3, the Infamous West Texas Eccentric, Has Died." *Texas Monthly*, June 17, 2014. https://www.texasmonthly.com/articles/stanley-marsh-3-the-infamous-west-texas-eccentric-has-died/.

Holman, Brett. "Spectre and Spectacle: Mock Air Raids as Aerial Theatre in Interwar Britain." In *Aviation in Literature and Culture of Interwar Britain*, edited by Michael McClusky and Luke Seaber, 227–50. Studies in Mobilities, Literature, and Culture Series. London: Palgrave Macmillan, 2020.

Hoving, Thomas. *False Impressions: The Hunt for Big-Time Art Fakes.* New York: Touchstone, 1997.

Hughes, Robert. *The Shock of the New.* 2nd ed. New York: McGraw Hill, 1991.

Husband, Evelyn. *High Calling: The Courageous Life and Faith of Space Shuttle* Columbia *Commander Rick Husband.* Nashville, TN: Thomas Nelson, 2003.

Ingrassia, Brian M. "Speed Attractions: Urban Mobility and Automotive Spectacle in Pre–World War I Amarillo." *Southwestern Historical Quarterly* 123 (July 2019): 60–86.

Irving, Clifford. *Fake! The Story of Elmyr de Hory, the Greatest Art Forger of Our Time.* New York: McGraw Hill, 1969.

Isenberg, Andrew C. *The Destruction of the Bison: An Environmental History, 1750–1920.* New York: Cambridge University press, 2000.

Jack, Zachary Michael. *The Midwest Farmer's Daughter: In Search of an American Icon.* West Lafayette, IN: Purdue University Press, 2012.

Jay, Martin. *Downcast Eyes: The Denigration of Vision in Twentieth-Century French Thought.* Berkeley: University of California Press, 1993.

Johnson, Tonya L. "History Buffs Given Keys to English Field." *Amarillo Globe-News,* August 16, 1996.

Jones, Amelia. "Body." In *Critical Terms for Art History.* 2nd ed. Edited by Robert S. Nelson and Richard Shiff, 251–66. Chicago: University of Chicago Press, 2003.

———. *Body Art: Performing the Subject.* Minneapolis: University of Minnesota Press, 1998.

Jovanovic, Rozalia. "Dude Ranch." *Oxford American,* July 15, 2013.

"Julian Bivins, Son Killed in Air Crash: Bodies Found in Wreck 12 Miles North of Town." *Amarillo Globe,* May 24, 1940.

Kaiser, Philipp, and Miwon Kwon. *Ends of the Earth: Land Art to 1974.* Los Angeles: Museum of Contemporary Art, 2012.

Katz, Jesse. "A Case of Art Gone Astray?" *Los Angeles Times,* January 15, 1996. https://www.latimes.com/archives/la-xpm-1996-01-15-mn-24846-story.html.

Kaufmann, Edgar, ed. *An American Architecture: Frank Lloyd Wright.* New York: Horizon Press, 1955.

Kaufmann, Edgar, and Ben Raeburn, eds. *Frank Lloyd Wright: Writings and Buildings.* New York: Horizon, 1960.

Key, Della Tyler. *In the Cattle Country: History of Potter County, 1887–1966.* Amarillo: Tyler-Berkley, 1961. 2nd ed. Wichita Falls: Nortex, 1972.

King, Mary. "Bumper Crop of Auto Art." *St. Louis Post-Dispatch,* April 11, 1975.

Kolata, Gina. *Flu: The Story of the Great Influenza Pandemic of 1918 and the Search for the Virus That Caused It.* New York: Atria, 2001.

Kuhlman, Marty. *Always WT: West Texas A&M University, a Centennial History.* Stillwater, OK: New Forums, 2010.

Kurz, Otto. *Fakes: A Handbook for Collectors and Students.* London: Faber & Faber, 1948.

Kwon, Miwon. *One Place after Another: Site-Specific Art and Locational Identity.* Cambridge, MA: MIT Press, 2002.

Lailach, Michael. *Land Art.* Cologne: Taschen, 2007.

Lanehart, Chuck. "The Second Battle of Adobe Walls." *Lubbock Avalanche-Journal,* July 5, 2019. https://www.lubbockonline.com/story/news/state/2019/07/06/caprock-chronicles-second-battle-of-adobe-walls/4752477007/.

LaPrade, Steve, and Ben Keck. "Plane Crash Takes 3 Lives." *Amarillo Globe-News,* July 21, 1973.

Larkin, David, and Bruce Brooks Pfeiffer, eds. *Frank Lloyd Wright: The Masterworks.* New York: Rizzoli, 1993.

Lawlor, Leonard. "Jacques Derrida." In *The Stanford Encyclopedia of Philosophy* (online), Edward N. Zalta. https://plato.stanford.edu/entries/derrida/.

Leatherwood, Art. "Llano Estacado." *Handbook of Texas Online.* https://www.tshaonline.org/handbook/entries/llano-estacado.

Lemmons, Larry. "Amarillo Art." Panhandle Spirit, KVII-TV, Pronews 7, July 13, 2013. https://www.youtube.com/watch?v=CaRpMzIxbSA.

———. "Lightnin' and Mr. Hyde." Panhandle Spirit, ABC 7 News, KVII-TV, May 12, 2016. https://www.youtube.com/watch?v=aX77ZyBpjdw.

Lenain, Thierry. *Art Forgery: The History of a Modern Obsession.* London: Reaktion, 2011.

Levin, Miriam R. *When the Eiffel Tower Was New: French Visions of Progress at the Centennial of the Revolution.* South Hadley, MA: Mount Holyoke College Art Museum, 1989.

Levine, Neil. *The Architecture of Frank Lloyd Wright.* Princeton, NJ: Princeton University Press, 1996.

Lewallen, Constance M., and Steve Seid. *Ant Farm: 1968–1978.* Berkeley: University of California Press, 2004.

Lewis, Jo Ann. "The Art That Went from Boon to Bust." *Washington Post*, December 3, 1999. https://www.washingtonpost.com/wp-srv/style/feed/a11324-1999dec3.htm.

———. "The Curious Case of the Spurious O'Keeffes." *Washington Post*, August 6, 2000. https://www.washingtonpost.com/archive/lifestyle/2000/08/06/the-curious-case-of-the-spurious-okeeffes/f92feb73-0746-4621-89d5-7d179c6305fb/.

Lewis, Wyndham. "Vorticist Manifesto." *Blast* 1 (1914).

Lisle, Laurie. *Louise Nevelson: A Passionate Life.* New York: Summit, 1990.

Loe, Hikmet Sidney. *The Spiral Jetty Encyclo: Exploring Robert Smithson's Earthwork Through Time and Space.* Salt Lake City: University of Utah Press, 2017.

Loll, Colette. "Curator Statement." In Colette Loll, *Intent to Deceive: Fakes and Forgeries in the Art World.* Washington, DC: International Arts & Artists, 2013.

Lord, Chip. "Cadillac Ranch 1974/1994." https://vimeo.com/185560546.

Lynes, Barbara Buhler, ed. *Georgia O'Keeffe: Catalogue Raisonné.* 2 vols. Washington, DC: National Gallery of Art, 1999.

Lynes, Barbara Buhler, and Russell Bowman. *O'Keeffe's O'Keeffes: The Artist's Collection.* New York: Thames and Hudson, 2001.

Lynes, Barbara Buhler, and Agapita Judy Lopez. *Georgia O'Keeffe and Her Houses: Ghost Ranch and Abiquiu.* New York: Abrams, in association with the Georgia O'Keeffe Museum, 2012.

Lynes, Barbara Buhler, and Ann Paden, eds. *Maria Chabot – Georgia O'Keeffe: Correspondence, 1941–1949.* Santa Fe: Georgia O'Keeffe Museum Research Center; Albuquerque: University of Mexico Press, 2003.

Macdonald, Kate, and Luke Seaber. Introduction to *England Is My Village and The World Owes Me a Living*, John Llewelyn Rhys, vii–xxiii. Bath: Handheld Press, 2022.

Macdonald-Wright, Stanton. "Influence of Aviation on Art: The Accentuation of Individuality." *Ace: The Aviation Magazine of the West*, September 1919, 11–13, 17.

MacLean, Alex S. *Designs on the Land: Exploring America from the Air.* New York: Thames and Hudson, 2003.

"Manifest Destiny and Indian Removal." Smithsonian Institution of American Art. https://americanexperience.si.edu/wp-content/uploads/2015/02/Manifest-Destiny-and-Indian-Removal.pdf.

Marinetti, F. T. "The Foundation and Manifesto of Futurism." *Le Figaro* (Paris), February 20, 1909.

Martin, Dick. "Flying Party at JA Ranch Saturday." *Amarillo Daily News*, April 12, 1940.

———. "Hangar Gas." *Amarillo Sunday News Globe*, April 7, 1940.

McCarty, John L. *Maverick Town: The Story of Old Tascosa*. Enlarged ed. Norman: University of Oklahoma Press, 1988.

McClintock, Anne. *Imperial Leather: Race, Gender, and Sexuality in the Colonial Context*. New York: Routledge, 1995.

McClusky, Michael, and Luke Seaber, eds. *Aviation in Literature and Culture of Interwar Britain*. Studies in Mobilities, Literature, and Culture Series. London: Palgrave Macmillan, 2020.

McCombe, Leonard, and John Bryson. *The Cowboy: A Book of Pictures About His Life*. Garden City, NY: Garden City Books, 1951.

McGraw, Mike, and Steve Paul. "A Strange Saga: Texas Connections Keep Watercolors Shrouded in Mystery." *Kansas City Star*, January 14, 2001.

———. "Success, Disputes Mark Art Dealer's Business." *Kansas City Star*, January 14, 2001.

McHugh, Tom. *The Time of the Buffalo*. Lincoln, NE: Bison Books, 1979.

Meech-Pekarik, Julia. "Frank Lloyd Wright's Other Passion." In *The Nature of Frank Lloyd Wright*, edited by Carol R. Bolon, Robert S. Nelson, and Linda Seidel, 125–53. Chicago: University of Chicago Press, 1988.

Merleau-Ponty, Maurice. *Phenomenology of Perception*. Translated by Colin Smith. London: Routledge, 1981.

Miklovic, Sue. "The Surprisingly Interesting History of the Carport." *North Baltimore Express*, September 6, 2019. https://www.thenbxpress.com/the-surprisingl y-interesting-history-of-the-carport/.

Miner, Craig. "A Roar from the Sky: Air-Mindedness in Wichita, 1908–1950." *Journal of the West* 30 (January 1991): 37–44.

Molina, Eva Lorraine. "Ozymandias: A King, a Poem, and a Concrete Statue in a Cow Pasture." *Reporting Texas*, December 12, 2013. https://www.reportingtexas.com/ ozymandias-a-king-a-poem-and-a-chunk-of-cement-in-a-cow-pasture/.

Moyle, Terry. *Art Deco Airports: Dream Designs of the 1920s and 1930s*. London: New Holland, 2016.

Müller, Christian. *Ed Ruscha: Los Angeles Apartments*. Basel: Kunstmuseum Basel, 2013.

Murray, Joshua, and Michael Schwartz. *Wrecked: How the American Automobile Industry Destroyed Its Capacity to Compete*. New York: Russell Sage Foundation, 2019.

Newman, Brad. "Impressions by Caballero." *Amarillo Globe-News*, March 5, 2011.

Newton, Paula. "Artist Paints Over Amarillo's Mock Road Signs." *Glasstire*, July 8, 2013. https://glasstire.com/2013/07/08/artist-paints-over-amarillos-mock-road-signs/.

Nisbet, James. *Second Site*. Princeton, NJ: Princeton University Press, 2021.

Nolan, Frederick. *Tascosa: Its Life and Gaudy Times*. Lubbock: Texas Tech University Press, 2007.

O'Keeffe, Georgia. *Georgia O'Keeffe*. New York: Viking, 1976.

O'Rourke, Kathyrn E., and Ben Koush. *Home, Heat, Money, God: Texas and Modern Architecture*. Austin: University of Texas Press, 2024.

"Out of the Blue: Amarillo Turns Out to See Atlantis." *Amarillo Globe-News*, July 2, 2007.

OX5 Aviation Pioneers. Dallas, TX: private publisher, 1985.

"Parent Education Plans Home Tour." *Pampa Daily News*, April 14, 1957.

Paul, Steve. "Side by Side, Which Look Real?" *Kansas City Star*, January 14, 2001.

Paul, Steve, and Mike McGraw. "Art of the Deal: The Selling of the Canyon Suite." *Kansas City Star*, January 14, 2001.

Pfeiffer, Bruce Brooks. *Frank Lloyd Wright Drawings: Masterworks from the Frank Lloyd Wright Archives*. New York: Harry N. Abrams, 1990.

Pfeiffer, Bruce Brooks, and Yukio Futagawa. *Frank Lloyd Wright: Usonian Houses*. Global Architecture Traveler, no. 5. Tokyo: A.D.A., 2002.

Pietz, William. "Fetish." In *Critical Terms for Art History*. 2nd ed. Edited by Robert S. Nelson and Richard Shiff, 306–17. Chicago: University of Chicago Press, 2003.

Pollitzer, Anita. *A Woman on Paper: Georgia O'Keeffe*. New York: Simon and Schuster, 1988.

Price, Richard, and Sally Price. *Enigma Variations*. Cambridge, MA: Harvard University Press, 1997.

Radnóti, Sándor. *The Fake: Forgery and Its Place in Art*. Translated by Ervin Dunai. New York: Rowman & Littlefield, 1999.

Reins, Dusty. "Bob Lile: Cadilite Jewelry." *Dusty Reins Stories* (vlog), June 21, 2016. https://www.youtube.com/watch?v=5YUm9bkh4Yc.

"Restored Usonian House in Amarillo Once Again Shows Wrightian Touch." *Texas Architecture*, July–August 2009, 10, 14. https://issuu.com/taartdir/docs/ta09_07.08_web/12.

Revett, Jon, Ruth Pasquine, and Amy Von Lintel. *Southwest Abstractions of Emil Bisttram*. Canyon, TX: Panhandle-Plains Historical Museum, 2021.

Revett, Jon, and Amy Von Lintel. *Yellow City Art*. Plainview, TX: Contemporary Art Museum Plainview, 2018.

Reynolds, Gretchen. "If It's Not an O'Keeffe, Exactly What Is It?" *New York Times*, March 7, 2000. https://www.nytimes.com/2000/03/07/arts/arts-in-america-if-it-s-not-an-o-keeffe-exactly-what-is-it.html.

Rhys, John Llewelyn. *England Is My Village and the World Owes Me a Living*. Bath: Handheld Press, 2022.

Roach, Joyce Gibson. "Goodnight, Mary Ann Dyer [Molly]." *Handbook of Texas Online*. https://www.tshaonline.org/handbook/entries/goodnight-mary-ann-dyer-molly.

Robertson, Pauline Durrett, and R. L. Robertson. *Tascosa: Historic Site in the Texas Panhandle*. 2nd ed. Amarillo, TX: Paramount, 1995.

Robinson, Roxana. *Georgia O'Keeffe: A Life*. 2nd ed. Waltham, MA: Brandeis University Press, 2020.

Rod, Johannes. "Fake Fakes in the Forger's Oeuvre." *Elmyrstory* (blog), December 4, 2010. https://elmyrstory.wordpress.com/2010/12/04/fake-fakes-in-the-forger%E2%80%99s-oeuvre/.

Rosenzweig, Phyllis. "Sixteen (and Counting): Ed Ruscha's Books." In *Ed Ruscha*, Neal Benezra and Kerry Brougher, 178–88. Washington, DC: Hirschhorn Museum and Sculpture Garden, 2000.

"Ruby Marcelete Reid Dana." *Canyon News*, June 25, 2013.

Ruggles, Dan G. "The Perils of Ballooning." *Dallas Morning News*, September 14, 1930.

Rugoff, Ralph. "Heavenly Noise." In *Ed Ruscha: Fifty Years of Painting*, James Ellroy, et al., 10–27. London: Hayward, 2009.

Ruscha, Ed. *Twentysix Gasoline Stations.* Los Angeles: National Excelsior Press, 1963.

Scheer, Christopher M., Sarah Victoria Turner, and James G. Mansell. *Enchanted Modernities: Theosophy, the Arts, and the American West.* Somerset, UK: Fulgur, 2019.

Schivelbusch, Wolfgang. *The Railroad Journey: The Industrialization of Time and Space in the Nineteenth Century.* Berkeley: University of California Press, 1986.

Schjeldahl, Peter. "Early Success: Can It Be Lived Down?" *New York Times*, December 9, 1973.

Schwartz, A. Brad. *Broadcast Hysteria: Orson Welles's* War of the Worlds *and the Art of Fake News.* New York: Hill & Wang, 2015.

Schwartz, Alexandra. "A History Without Words." In *Ed Ruscha: Fifty Years of Painting*, James Ellroy, et al., 28–37. London: Hayward, 2009.

Schwartz, Vanessa R. *Jet Age Aesthetic: The Glamour of Media in Motion.* New Haven: Yale University Press, 2020.

———. *Spectacular Realities: Early Mass Culture in Fin-de-Siècle Paris.* Berkeley: University of California Press, 1999.

Schwartz, Vanessa R., and Jeannene Przyblyski, eds. *The Nineteenth-Century Visual Culture Reader.* New York: Routledge, 2004.

Scully, Vincent. Introduction to *The Nature of Frank Lloyd Wright*, edited by Carol R. Bolon, Robert S. Nelson, and Linda Seidel, xiii–xxii. Chicago: University of Chicago Press, 1988.

Searcy, Jerry. "Unorthodox Design Puts Emphasis on Lighting: Homes of Interest in the Area." *Amarillo Daily News*, January 27, 1964.

Secrest, Meryle. *Frank Lloyd Wright: A Biography.* Chicago: University of Chicago Press, 1992.

Self, Dana. *Intimate Landscapes: The Canyon Suite of Georgia O'Keeffe.* New York: Universe, in association with the Kemper Museum of Contemporary Art & Design, 1997.

Sergeant, John. *Frank Lloyd Wright's Usonian Houses: The Case for Organic Architecture.* New York: Watson-Guptill, 1984.

Siddons, Louise. *Centering Modernism: J. Jay McVicker and Postwar American Art.* Norman: University of Oklahoma Press, 2018.

Spiliakos, Alexandra. "Tragedy of the Commons: What It Is & 5 Examples." *Harvard Business School Online* (blog), February 6, 2019. https://online.hbs.edu/blog/post/tragedy-of-the-commons-impact-on-sustainability-issues.

Spinney, Laura. *Pale Rider: The Spanish Flu of 1918 and How It Changed the World.* New York: PublicAffairs, 2018.

Stockebrand, Marianne. *Chinati: The Vision of Donald Judd.* New Haven: Yale University

Press, 2010.

Sylvester, Julie, ed. *John Chamberlain: A Catalogue Raisonné of the Sculpture, 1954–1985*. New York: Hudson Hills Press and the Museum of Contemporary Art, Los Angeles, 1986.

"Tascosa, TX." *Handbook of Texas Online*. https://www.tshaonline.org/handbook/entries/tascosa-tx.

Taylor, A. J. "New Mexican Pastores and Priests in the Texas Panhandle, 1876–1915." *Panhandle-Plains Historical Review* 56 (1984): 65–79.

"Texas Ecoregions: High Plains." Trees of Texas, Texas A&M Forest Service. http://texas-treeid.tamu.edu/content/texasEcoRegions/HighPlains/.

"Tlaloc." *Encyclopedia Britannica*. https://www.britannica.com/topic/Tlaloc.

Townsend, Richard F., and Trent Barnes. "Tetzcotzingo." *Grove Art Online*. 2003. https://doi-org.databases.wtamu.edu/10.1093/gao/9781884446054.article.T084009.

"Trees for the Texas Panhandle." Randall County Master Gardener Society of the Texas A&M AgriLife Extension Service. https://txmg.org/randall/staying-connected/gardening-with-the-masters/gardening-tips-2/trees-for-the-texas-panhandle/.

Turner, David. *O'Keeffe Works on Paper*. Santa Fe: Museum of New Mexico; Albuquerque: University of New Mexico Press, 1985.

Twombly, Robert C. *Frank Lloyd Wright: An Interpretive Biography*. New York: Harper and Row, 1973.

Udall, Sharyn R. *O'Keeffe and Texas*. San Antonio: McNay Art Museum, 1998.

Van Vleck, Jenifer. *Empire of the Air: Aviation and the American Ascendancy*. Cambridge, MA: Harvard University Press, 2013.

Vicario, Gilbert, et al. *Agnes Pelton: Desert Transcendentalist*. Phoenix: Phoenix Art Museum and Hirmer, 2019.

Von Lintel, Amy. "Gassing Up in Amarillo." In *Yellow City Art*, edited by Kelly Alison. Plainview, TX: Contemporary Art Museum Plainview, 2018.

———. *Georgia O'Keeffe Watercolors, 1916–1918*. Santa Fe: Radius Books and Georgia O'Keeffe Museum, 2016.

———. *Georgia O'Keeffe's Wartime Texas Letters*. American Wests Series. College Station: Texas A&M University Press, 2020.

———. "Rodeos in the Skies." Caprock Chronicles. *Lubbock Avalanche-Journal*, June 11, 2023.

———. "West Texas Gets Taken by Art Fraud." Parts 1 and 2. Caprock Chronicles. *Lubbock Avalanche-Journal*, October 4 and October 26, 2018. https://www.lubbockon-line.com/story/news/state/2019/10/05/caprock-chronicles-west-texas-gets-taken-by-a rt-fraud-part-1/2607715007/.

Von Lintel, Amy, and Jon Revett. "Completing Smithson's Trilogy." In *Robert Smithson in Texas*, edited by Elyse Goldberg, 11–32. New York: Estate of Robert Smithson and James Cohan Gallery, 2015.

Von Lintel, Amy, and Bonnie Roos. "Abstract Expressionism in Amarillo, Texas: *The Women: Tops in Art* Exhibition in 1960." *Woman's Art Journal* 422 (Fall 2021): 12–21.

———. *Three Women Artists: Expanding Abstract Expressionism in the American West.*

American Wests Series. College Station: Texas A&M University Press, 2022.

Wade, Edwin L., ed. *The Arts of the North American Indian: Native Traditions in Evolution.* New York: Hudson Hills; Tulsa, OK: Philbrook Art Center, 1986.

Wallis, Michael. *Route 66: The Mother Road.* Revised ed. New York: St. Martin's Griffin, 2001.

Walsh, Judith. "Paper Study." In *Georgia O'Keeffe: Catalogue Raisonné.* 2 vols. Edited by Barbara Buhler Lynes. Washington, DC: National Gallery of Art, 1999.

Walsham, Alexandra. "Introduction: Relics and Remains." *Past & Present* 206 (2010): 9–36.

Warnick, Ron. "Arsonist Torches One of the Cars at *Cadillac Ranch*." *Route 66 News,* September 9, 2019. https://www.route66news.com/2019/09/09/arsonist-torche s-one-of-the-cars-at-cadillac-ranch/.

———. "Group Wants to Remove *Cadillac Ranch*." *Route 66 News,* October 31, 2015. https://www.route66news.com/2015/10/31/group-wants-to-remove-cadillac-ranch/.

Warren, Thomas. "Lile's Cadilite Brings Worldwide Attention to Amarillo." *Amarillo Pioneer* [blog], May 28, 2018. https://www.amarillopioneer.com/blog/2018/3/28/ liles-cadilite-brings-worldwide-attention-to-amarillo.

Weber, Bruce. "Stanley Marsh, Cadillac Rancher, Dies at 76, Shadowed by Charges." *New York Times,* June 23, 2014. https://www.nytimes.com/2014/06/23/arts/design/ stanley-marsh-patron-of-the-cadillac-ranch-dies-at-76.html.

Weems, Jason. *Barnstorming the Prairies: How Aerial Vision Shaped the Midwest.* Minneapolis: University of Minnesota Press, 2015.

Weintraub, Alan, and Alan Hess. *Frank Lloyd Wright: The Houses.* New York: Rizzoli, 2005.

Welch, Kevin, and Karen Smith Welch. "Daring or Devious?" *Amarillo Globe-News,* June 21, 2014.

Whiffen, Marcus, and Carla Breeze. *Pueblo Deco: The Art Deco Architecture of the Southwest.* Albuquerque: University of New Mexico Press, 1984.

Wicks, Robert. *European Aesthetics: A Critical Introduction from Kant to Derrida.* London: Oneworld, 2013.

Williams, Alena J., ed. *Nancy Holt: Sightlines.* Berkeley: University of California Press, 2011.

Wilmes, Ulrich. "Once Upon a Time in the Present." In *Ed Ruscha: Fifty Years of Painting,* James Ellroy, et al., 44–53. London: Hayward, 2009.

Wilson, Laurie. *Louise Nevelson: Light and Shadow.* New York: Thames and Hudson, 2016.

Wohl, Robert. *A Passion for Wings: Aviation and the Western Imagination, 1908–1918.* New Haven: Yale University Press, 1994.

Wright, Frank Lloyd. *An Autobiography.* New York: Duell, Sloan, and Pearce, 1943.

Wright, Gwendolyn. "Architectural Practice and Social Vision in Wright's Early Designs." In *The Nature of Frank Lloyd Wright,* edited by Carol R. Bolon, Robert S. Nelson, and Linda Seidel, 98–124. Chicago: University of Chicago Press, 1988.

Yeomans, P. A. *The Keyline Plan.* Sydney: self-published, 1954.

Ziff, Larzer. "The Prairie in Literary Culture and the Prairie Style of Frank Lloyd Wright." In *The Nature of Frank Lloyd Wright,* edited by Carol R. Bolon, Robert S. Nelson, and Linda Seidel, 173–86. Chicago: University of Chicago Press, 1988.

Zimmerman, John. "Abandoned Airfields: History in our Midst." *Air Facts*, January 31, 2013. https://airfactsjournal.com/2013/01/abandoned-airfields-history-in-our-midst/.

INDEX